Religion, Ethnicity,
and Politics

Owen S. Ireland

Religion, Ethnicity, and Politics

Ratifying the Constitution in Pennsylvania

*The Pennsylvania State University Press
University Park, Pennsylvania*

Library of Congress Cataloging-in-Publication Data

Ireland, Owen S.
    Religion, ethnicity, and politics :
Ratifying the Constitution in Pennsylvania /
Owen S. Ireland.
            p.   cm.
    Includes bibliographical references and index.
    ISBN 0-271-01433-4 (cloth : acid-free paper)
    ISBN 0-271-01434-2 (pbk. : acid-free paper)
    1. United States—Constitutional history. 2. Constitutional
conventions—Pennsylvania—History. 3. Pennsylvania—Politics and
government—1775–1865. 4. Pennsylvania—Economic conditions.
I. Title.
KF4512.P4I74   1995
342.73'029—dc20
[347.30229]   94-42605
                                                                      CIP

Copyright © 1995 The Pennsylvania State University
All rights reserved
Printed in the United States of America
Published by The Pennsylvania State University Press,
Barbara Building, Suite C, University Park, PA 16802-1003

It is the policy of The Pennsylvania State University Press to use acid-free paper for the first printing of all clothbound books. Publications on uncoated stock satisfy the minimum requirements of American National Standard for Information Sciences—Permanence of Paper for Printed Library Materials, ANSI Z39.48–1992.

Contents

List of Tables ... vii
Acknowledgments ... ix
Introduction ... xiii

Part I: The Contest

1 The Federalist Conspiracy, September 1787 ... 3
2 The Fall Campaign, October–November 1787 ... 35
3 The State Convention, November–December 1787 ... 71
4 The Antifederalist Counterattack, January–April 1788 ... 109

Part II: The Context

5 The Economy and the Constitution: The City ... 147
6 The Economy and the Constitution: The Backcountry ... 181
7 The Quiet Counterrevolution ... 217

Conclusion: The People's Triumph ... 255
Appendixes
  1 The Newspaper Debate ... 279
  2 The German Vote and the 1788 Congressional Election ... 283
Index ... 285

List of Tables

1.	Pennsylvania's revenue, 1785–1787	154
2.	Average vote by party, Philadelphia, 1784–1788	160
3.	Per capita unpaid back taxes as of November 1787	184
4.	Estimated cost (in shillings) of transporting one bushel of wheat to Philadelphia, 1760	185
5.	Rough estimate of percentage of Federalist support in seventeen of nineteen political subdivisions, 1787–1788	195
6.	Counties arrayed from most to least along two economic variables	197
7.	Land distribution; mills per capita	200
8.	Partisan complexion of county-wide delegations, Eleventh General Assembly (October 1786–September 1787) and State Convention (November 1787)	212
9.	Geographic distribution of partisan assembly seats, 1778 and 1786	219
10.	Increases in turnout and in Republican strength, Bucks County, 1783–1789	228
11.	Philadelphia County, partisan seats in Assembly, 1776–1788	239
12.	Probable voter turnout in Philadelphia County, 1764–1786	240

To Susan, whom I love more than life; and to those to whom our love gave life: Bridget, Timothy, Andrew, Sarah, and Louise, the family we created together.

Acknowledgments

I began work on this book in 1985, when the National Endowment for the Humanities collaborated with the State University of New York, College at Brockport to provide me with an uninterrupted year for research and writing. It builds on research that I started as a graduate student at the University of Pittsburgh in the early 1960s. The moral tragedy of the war in Vietnam distracted my family, my students, and me, and I put research on hold. Administrative responsibilities then absorbed much of my time during the 1970s and early 1980s. Since 1968, I have worked at SUNY–Brockport, where teaching and research complement each other and where I enjoy congenial colleagues who exemplify my ideal of an academic community.

In the thirty or so years I have devoted to the study of politics in late eighteenth-century Pennsylvania, I accumulated innumerable debts. Here I can do no more than acknowledge some of the more conspicuous of these. My sincere thanks to Emory Evans, who first cultivated my interest in early American history, introduced me to the study of the ratification controversy in Pennsylvania, and who, with his gracious wife, Winifred, has provided friendship and encouragement since we first met in Pittsburgh in 1961. Van Beck Hall stepped in at a crucial point in my research, gave generously of himself, and supervised the completion of my dissertation. John Kutolowski, Kempes Schnell, Arden Bucholz, and Bruce Leslie, my colleagues in the Department of History at SUNY–Brockport, over the years have read and criticized innumerable versions of the manuscript that eventually became this book. R. Scott Flieger, a former student, a current friend, and a vice-president at J. P.

Morgan Securities, read and commented critically on an earlier version of the manuscript. The National Endowment for the Humanities awarded me a Constitutional Fellowship. Presidents Albert W. Brown and John Van de Wetering of SUNY–Brockport, provided additional financial support over the years.

I also thank Thad Tate and Michael McGiffert, editors of the *William and Mary Quarterly*, who sensed something of value buried beneath the passive verbs, technical jargon, unintelligible charts, and elephantine sentences of my earlier essays. John McCusker, director of the Washington Area Seminar on Early American History at the University of Maryland; Richard Beeman and Richard Dunn at the Philadelphia Center for Early American Studies; and James Banner, director of the Washington Seminar on American History and Culture, all provided me with opportunities to share my work-in-progress with interested scholars and to benefit from their criticism. I thank John Frantz, of the Department of History at The Pennsylvania State University, whose friendship and support I have enjoyed for more than a decade, whose criticisms have saved me from innumerable errors, and whose invitation to deliver a paper at University Park provided me with an early opportunity to test some of the ideas central to the final study. Also, thanks to Marianne Wokeck, P. M. G. Harris, Joseph Foster, Michael Zuckerman, and John Murrin, whose graciousness and support enhanced my trips to Philadelphia; and George Rappaport of Wagner College, who read and commented on portions of the final manuscript and generously shared portions of his own work in manuscript with me.

Gratitude is owed to Merrill Jensen, John Kaminski, Gaspare Saladino, and the Center for the Study of the American Constitution, who continue to make available the documentary record of the ratification of the Constitution and the Bill of Rights; and the agencies that have supported their work over the years: the National Historical Publications and Records Commission, the National Endowment for the Humanities, and the University of Wisconsin. Together, they have made serious research on the nation's founding possible for scholars such as I, who teach full-time in locations that are relatively isolated from the major repositories. Robert Gilliam and the staff at the Interlibrary Loan Office in Drake Memorial Library at SUNY–Brockport, unfailingly, congenially, imaginatively, and persistently located and obtained for me the materials I needed.

I also thank John Alexander and William Pencak, who read the manuscript and provided valuable counsel, and Peter Potter, editor at Penn State Press, whose patience, support, and confidence have contributed substantially to the successful completion of this project. A host of students, both graduate and undergraduate, have knowingly and unknowingly contributed to my ongoing research over the years. James Warlick, Kathy Albrecht, and Karen Nowak have been particularly helpful in the past two years.

And special thanks to Susan Marie Pollard Ireland, with whom I have had the joy of sharing life's most important and satisfying work: creating and nurturing a family.

Introduction

Between September 1787 and April 1788, Pennsylvanians debated and ratified the proposed Federal Constitution—and then reconsidered. Since 1774 the Continental Congress had governed the emerging new nation, informally at first, and then under the Articles of Confederation. During those trying times, the Congress had accomplished much: it had declared independence from England, negotiated with foreign powers, won the war, and signed the Treaty of Paris (1783), in which the British formally recognized America's independence. By the mid-1780s, however, the Congress was under fire for its failure to solve a number of postwar problems.

In the spring of 1787 delegates from twelve states assembled in Philadelphia to consider ways to meet the "exigencies" of the union. In mid-September, after prolonged and often bitter debate, they proposed a substitute for the Articles of Confederation. By the summer of 1788 popularly elected conventions in the states had approved of the plan, and in the fall of that year Americans for the first time elected officials under the new Constitution for the United States of America.

In time, the Federal Constitution became for many the most sacred document of the founding of the nation, but in 1787–88 it generated much different feelings. Substantial numbers of voters—possibly a majority in many states—reacted passionately, even violently, to the proposal, and the controversy over ratification raged from the fall of 1787 well into the summer of 1788.

The dispute first erupted in Pennsylvania in late September 1787 and ended early in April 1788. In those six months, political leaders on each side of the issue vied for popular backing. In the end, the supporters of ratification—called Federalists—won; the opponents of the new system, the Antifederalists, lost. This study seeks to describe and explain that extended contest and the political behavior of the people of Pennsylvania.

On November 6, 1787, some seven weeks after publication of the proposed new Constitution, the voters of Pennsylvania elected delegates to a ratifying convention, and on December 12 that convention ratified the new plan by a large margin. Federalists, excited by their victory, claimed that the convention's decision demonstrated widespread popular support for the new frame of government. Antifederalists, however, thought otherwise. They denied the legitimacy of the convention and accused the Federalists of rushing the voters into an early and ill-considered decision. They claimed that only a fraction of the electorate had participated in the choice of delegates to the convention and that the majority of Pennsylvanians actually opposed the new Constitution, or would have opposed it if they had had time to understand it. Denying the legitimacy of the convention's decision, Antifederalists launched a three-month campaign to overturn it. In the end they failed, but throughout they claimed that they spoke for the people of Pennsylvania. The Federalists, in victory, made the same claim.

This difference of opinion between Federalists and Antifederalists about the true desires of the people foreshadowed a similar disagreement among later students of the controversy both in Pennsylvania and in the nation as a whole. Those who regard the Federalists as wise and virtuous leaders who devised popular and successful solutions to the problems the fledgling nation faced have preferred the Federalist view. This interpretation, probably dominant during most of the nineteenth century, has been a persistent but secondary historiographical strain in the twentieth century.[1]

---

1. See John P. Roche, "The Founding Fathers: A Reform Caucus in Action," *American Political Science Review* 60 (1961): 799–814; and, more recent, Leonard Levy, "Introduction: American Constitutional History, 1776–1789," in Leonard Levy and Dennis J. Mahoney, eds., *The Framing and Ratification of the Constitution* (New York: Macmillan, 1987), 16, 17; Roger Brown, *Redeeming the Republic: Federalists, Taxation, and the Origins of the Constitution* (Baltimore: Johns Hopkins University Press, 1993); Cathy Matson and Peter Onuf, *A Union of Interests: Political and Economic Thought in Revolutionary America* (Lawrence: University Press of Kansas, 1990); Bernard Bailyn, *The Ideological Origins of the American Revolution*, enl. ed. (Cambridge: Belknap Press of Harvard University Press, 1992), esp. "Postscript. Fulfillment: A Commentary on the Constitution," 321–79. For historiographic

Many modern historians of the founding of the nation have favored some variant of the Antifederalist interpretation. In one way or another, most view the Federalist victory as the triumph of the more cosmopolitan or modern few over the more parochial or traditional many, and explain the differences between the two sides largely in terms of ideology, class, or variations in degree of participation in a market economy.[2]

This study of the ratification controversy in Pennsylvania takes a different position. It argues three closely related points. First, a solid majority of the voters in Pennsylvania (the plebeians, or "the many," if you will) knowingly and enthusiastically favored ratification of the Federal Constitution. Second, the division into Federalist and Antifederalist camps in Pennsylvania largely reflected preexisting political attachments at both the leadership level and the electoral level; members of the Republican party supported it with near unanimity while Constitutionalists, with some exceptions, opposed it. Third, these partisan attachments were rooted in the ethnic-religious political confrontations of the previous decade.

---

essays, see James H. Hutson, "Country, Court, and Constitution: Antifederalism and the Historians," *William and Mary Quarterly* 38 (1981): 337–68; Peter Onuf, "Reflections on the Founding: Constitutional Historiography in Bicentennial Perspective," *William and Mary Quarterly* 46 (1989): 341–75; Alfred Young, "Introduction" and "Afterword" in Alfred Young, ed., *Beyond the American Revolution: Explanations in the History of American Radicalism* (DeKalb: Northern Illinois University Press, 1993), 3–26, 317–64, and esp. 10, 16–17, 336.

2. Jackson Turner Main's work has provided the conceptual framework and much of the evidence for this now common view. See Main, *The Anti-Federalists: Critics of the Constitution, 1781–1788* (Chapel Hill: University of North Carolina Press for IEAHC, 1961); and Main, *Political Parties Before the Constitution* (Chapel Hill: University of North Carolina Press for the Institute of Early American History and Culture, Williamsburg, Va., 1973). The most recent work is Gary J. Kornblith and John Murrin, "The Making and Unmaking of an American Ruling Class," in Young, ed., *Beyond the American Revolution*, 27–79, esp. 51, 54–58; and Allan Kulikoff, "The Revolution, Capitalism, and Formation of Yeomen Classes," in ibid., 80–119, esp. 100–103. For historiographic essays on ideology, see Hutson, "Country, Court, and Constitution"; and John Murrin, "The Great Inversion, or Court versus Country: A Comparison of the Revolutionary Settlements in England (1688–1721) and America (1776–1816)," in J. G. A. Pocock, ed., *Three British Revolutions: 1641, 1688, 1776* (Princeton: Princeton University Press, 1980), 368–453; on the market economy, see Allan Kulikoff, "The Transition to Capitalism in Rural America," *William and Mary Quarterly* 46 (1989): 120–45. For a view of the Antifederalists as the more modern, see Gordon Wood, "Interest and Disinterestedness in the Making of the Constitution," in Richard Beeman, Stephen Botein, and Edward C. Carter II, eds., *Beyond Confederation: Origins of the Constitution and American National Identity* (Chapel Hill: University of North Carolina Press, 1987), 69–109; and *The Radicalism of the American Revolution* (New York: Knopf, 1992), esp. 255–58.

This interpretation builds on conclusions I have advanced and defended elsewhere about the ethnic-religious dimension of partisan politics in revolutionary Pennsylvania. A summary of the main points of that earlier work may make it easier to follow the argument presented below.[3]

In 1778–79 two relatively modern political parties emerged in Pennsylvania: the Constitutionalists and the Republicans. Constitutionalists drew their leadership and their electoral support largely from Presbyterians, who were principally Scots-Irish, and from Germans of the Reformed faith. Republicans drew their leadership and electoral support from a more heterogeneous coalition. Led by Anglicans and by those who had migrated from their Quaker and Presbyterian origins into the Anglican community, they drew votes largely from Anglicans, Lutherans, Quakers, and the German Sectarians.

These two parties divided initially over three major issues. The Constitutionalists supported the Test Acts, which disenfranchised loyalists, neutrals, pacifists, and those who were unwilling to abjure former oaths of allegiance to the British Crown. They backed conversion of the Anglican-dominated College of Philadelphia into the Presbyterian-led University of Pennsylvania. And they defended the state constitution of 1776 with its all-powerful, unicameral legislature that had been the vehicle for their ascent to power. Republicans opposed Constitutionalists on these three issues, in part because of principle and in part as spokespersons for the Anglicans, the Quakers, the Lutherans, and the German Sectarians—loyalist, neutral, or pacifist groups that had suffered most at the hands of the predominant Constitutionalists.

Between 1778 and 1789 these three issues defined partisan politics in Pennsylvania. Bills dealing with such party questions as patronage, disputed elections, voter qualifications, and the creation or modification of electoral boundaries also produced near-perfect party alignments. In contrast, party discipline broke down on purely sectional questions, such as the distribution of tax quotas, the location of the capital, and

---

3. For details and defense, see Wayne Bockelman and Owen S. Ireland, "The Internal Revolution in Pennsylvania: An Ethnic-Religious Interpretation," *Pennsylvania History* 41 (April 1974): 125–59; Owen S. Ireland, "The Ethnic-Religious Dimension of Pennsylvania Politics, 1778–1779," *William and Mary Quarterly* 30 (1973): 423–48; Ireland, "The Crux of Politics: Religion and Party in Pennsylvania, 1778–1789," *William and Mary Quarterly* 42 (1985): 453–75; Ireland, "The People's Triumph: The Federalist Majority in Pennsylvania, 1787–1788," *Pennsylvania History* 56 (April 1989): 93–113.

the construction of transportation facilities, as well as on a range of economic issues, including legal-tender paper money, creation of a state land-bank, the price of land in the western part of the state, and debtor relief.

Within each county or region in Pennsylvania, the candidates of both parties came from the same upper ranks of society: they were the larger landholders, the professionals, and men of commerce. In Philadelphia, both parties recruited heavily from the merchant community. But whether in the city or in the backcountry, Constitutionalist candidates were mostly from the Scots-Irish Presbyterian or the German Reformed elite; Republicans attracted candidates from the elite of other religious groups—principally the Anglicans and to a lesser extent the Quakers, the Lutherans, and the German Sectarians.

To the degree that we can measure the behavior of the electorate, the voters of Pennsylvania in this period, 1778–88, divided along the same ethnic-religious lines. The two most detailed examples available to us are from Chester County, in the east, bordering on Philadelphia and from York County, on the western side of the Susquehanna River. District election returns for each of these counties indicate that areas with a higher concentration of Presbyterians voted for Presbyterian or Reformed candidates, who supported the Constitutionalist party when elected; areas with higher concentrations of Anglicans, Quakers, Lutherans, and German Sectarians voted for non-Presbyterian, non-Reformed candidates—who, when elected, joined the Republicans. Thus, among candidates and voters alike, Presbyterians (mostly Scots-Irish) and German Reformed from the west and east favored the Constitutionalists, while members of most other ethnic-religious groups from the west and the east favored the Republicans.

These two parties persisted throughout the 1780s with one party or the other in command of Pennsylvania's annually elected unicameral legislature. Initially the Constitutionalists dominated. Then, after a period of modest Republican majorities in the early 1780s, Constitutionalists regained an overwhelming majority of the seats in the Assembly in 1784 and continued their hold in 1785. In 1786 Republicans gained the edge, but the partisan history of the previous decade gave them little confidence in their ability to retain power. In 1787–88 this intense, volatile, and decade-long partisan contest set the stage for Pennsylvania's response to the proposed Federal Constitution, the subject of this book.

Although Pennsylvanians divided passionately, sometimes violently, over ratification of the Federal Constitution, they had long supported reform of the Articles of Confederation. America's central government lacked a reliable source of revenue: without money, it could not pay its debts, maintain its military and naval strength, protect America's borders, advance its economic interests abroad, suppress domestic violence, or deal effectively with disputes between states—or at least that is what most articulate Pennsylvanians were saying. So, like many concerned Americans in the winter of 1786–87, they favored augmenting the powers of the Congress.

In December 1786 the Pennsylvania legislature chose delegates to the interstate convention scheduled to meet in Philadelphia in May 1787 to consider changes in the Articles of Confederation. Before September 1787 the movement to strengthen the powers of the central government exhibited few partisan overtones, and the initial response to the proposed Federal Constitution in September gave few hints of the battle that would soon erupt in Pennsylvania. However, the events in September masked the fundamental political nature of the emerging contest. Although a variety of considerations helped shape individual reactions to the issue, past partisan behavior is the best predictor of response on both the elite level and the popular level. Republicans from Anglican, Quaker, Lutheran, and German-Sectarian backgrounds favored ratification, while Constitutionalists from Presbyterian and Reformed backgrounds opposed it.[4]

Other factors played subordinate roles. While economic concerns certainly contributed to these ethnic-religious–based popular alignments, they seldom altered. The fiscal condition of the state, the decline in the price of farm staples, the depression in the city, the physical insecurity and economic stagnation in the west, the problems with paper money, taxes, and debt—these and other economic difficulties

---

4. See especially Ireland, "Crux of Politics", esp. 457, and below. That essay, as well as the text to follow, refines the views I expressed in "Partisanship and the Constitution" to emphasize the long-term relationship between ethnic-religious party identification and alignment on the Federal Constitution. Although Constitutionalists in the legislature initially divided on the question, in time twenty-five of the twenty-eight Constitutionalists in the Eleventh General Assembly became opponents of the Federal Constitution. The voting record of the three who did not indicates that they were more peripheral members of the party. See Ireland, "Partisanship and the Constitution: Pennsylvania, 1787," *Pennsylvania History* 45 (1978): 321, 322, 328. Only in Philadelphia did Constitutionalists generally fail to unite in vigorous opposition to ratification.

predisposed most Pennsylvanians to support change. And in the ratification contest, concern about these kinds of problems generally strengthened the support of Republicans for ratification while sometimes mitigating Constitutionalist opposition, especially in Philadelphia.

Publicists on each side of the question generally operated within the bounds of a common political culture. Both Federalist and Antifederalists appealed to the autonomous individual, living in an egalitarian society, pursuing entrepreneurial interests within a moral framework, and enjoying broad government support, but largely free of public interference and distrustful of central authority.

Each side expected a close fight. The Republicans controlled the Pennsylvania legislature in 1787, but their tenure was short and precarious. Between 1784 and 1786, however, unbeknownst to both sides, a fundamental shift in relative electoral support had occurred. The Republicans became the majority party as increasing numbers of Quakers, Lutherans, and German Sectarians rejoined the political community and supported the party that had supported them. In 1787–88 this newfound Republican strength virtually ensured a Federalist victory and an Antifederalist defeat.

The protracted ratification controversy and the contingencies and ironies inherent in its outcome are closely related themes in this book. During the ratification campaign, talented and dedicated political leaders on each side of the issue competed for the votes of what was probably the broadest, most heterogeneous, and most sophisticated electorate in the new nation. It was one of America's earliest and most dramatic popular political engagements, involving complex legislative maneuvering, the production and distribution of masses of campaign literature, statewide voter mobilization efforts, rallies, speeches, demonstrations, verbal and physical attacks, intimidation, insults, ridicule, personal calumny, occasional violence, and repeated threats of bloodshed and civil war. These political leaders exhibited all the weaknesses of human beings. Motivated by fear, anger, ambition, idealism, and personal animosities, frustrated by their inability to control events, fatigued by the seemingly endless campaign, and confused by the swirl of events, they orchestrated an increasingly brutal, scabrous, and manipulative contest. In the end, however, their own myopia and miscalculations, combined with the complexity of the situation and human frailty, produced outcomes that neither side had fully anticipated, and for reasons neither side fully understood.

The "founding," at least as far as Pennsylvania was concerned, was neither a sanitized academic debate nor a bloodless confrontation of abstract historical forces. Rather, it was a highly personal, rough-and-tumble, no-holds-barred battle between two groups who knew each other well and had competed against each other for power for more than a decade. It was a very modern and very American political event.

Chapters 1 through 4 trace the contest from the September 1787 legislature call for a state ratification convention, through the fall election, the convention debates, and the effort of the Antifederalists in the spring of 1788 to nullify the convention's December ratification. These chapters provide the Pennsylvania storyline, or the specifics of what historian Peter Onuf has called the "founding narrative."[5] But these chapters also convey a sense of the human and idiosyncratic side of the struggle. And they rely heavily on analysis of the public debate to sketch out the boundaries of the popular political culture within which the campaign took place. My hope is that the grittiness, the pettiness, the complexity, and the ambiguities of this battle will help modern readers put the political contests of their own day in perspective.

In Chapters 5 and 6 I step back from the particular and the personal, and move away from the public rhetoric and the campaign strategies, to explore the economic pressures that influenced the political responses to the Federal Constitution in the city of Philadelphia, in the far western part of the state, and in the agricultural backcountry in between. Chapter 7 describes the ethnic-religious counterrevolution that preceded the ratification contest in Pennsylvania and largely determined its outcome. Chapter 8 explores some of the historiographical implications of this view of the founding in Pennsylvania, as well as some of the ironies inherent in the contest.

---

5. Peter Onuf, "Reflections on the Founding: Constitutional Historiography in Bicentennial Perspective," *William and Mary Quarterly* 46 (1989): 344.

PART ONE

The Contest

1

The Federalist Conspiracy

September 1787

On Tuesday, September 18, 1787, at eleven o'clock in the morning, the venerable Benjamin Franklin arrived in his chair at the State House in Philadelphia. Beset with a stone, crippled with gout, "a short, fat, truncated old man . . . [with a] bald pate, and short locks," this eighty-two-year-old philosopher-statesman had come to perform his last major public service. With seven of his fellow delegates from the Grand Convention, he brought to the Pennsylvania legislature the proposed new Constitution of the United States of America.[1]

The ceremony conveyed no hint of the long, vitriolic, even violent

---

1. Carl Van Doren, *Benjamin Franklin* (New York: Viking Press, 1938) 741, 742, 750, 751, 753, 759, 767, 779; *Pennsylvania Herald*, 9/20/87; *Pennsylvania Gazette*, 9/19/87; "Assembly Proceedings," 9/18/87 in Merrill Jensen, ed., *The Documentary History of the Ratification of the Constitution*, vol. 2, *Ratification of the Constitution by the States: Pennsylvania* (Madison, Wisc.: The State Historical Society of Wisconsin, 1976), 61; hereafter cited as Jensen 2.

contest soon to erupt. For now, all united in eager anticipation and awed reverence as the ritual unfolded. A special legislative committee introduced "the honorable" deputies and accompanied them to their seats. The public galleries, packed with dignitaries and the "most respectable" people of the city, maintained a strict silence. The legislators, usually voluble, sat mute.[2]

Franklin broke the silence. "Sir," he addressed the Speaker, Thomas Mifflin, "I have now the very great satisfaction of delivering to you, and to this Honorable House, the results of our deliberations in the late Convention. We hope and believe, that the measures recommended by that body will produce happy effects in this commonwealth, as well as to every other of the United States." Then, tired by the exertion, the old man presented the Constitution and its accompanying letter of transmittal from the honorable George Washington and sat down. Speaker Mifflin solemnly read both documents to the House.[3]

The close-packed crowd standing in the public galleries listened intently. The Grand Convention, made up of representatives from twelve of the thirteen states, had assembled in Philadelphia in May amid widespread expressions of concern. These United States, governed by Congress under the Articles of Confederation, faced serious fiscal, security, and commercial problems. Now, after working throughout the summer, the Convention was offering America a new frame of government.

The proposal would create a national government with an independent income, control over external commerce, the power to negotiate binding treaties with foreign nations, and the authority to suppress domestic insurrections. Equally important, the plan bypassed the impediment that had frustrated reform for years. The Articles could be amended only with unanimous approval. The new system would go into effect when ratified by nine states. In sum, the new Constitution promised a federal government capable of bringing peace, prosperity, respect abroad, and effective and efficient government at home. The Convention had done its work well.

Those who favored the new system had already organized themselves

---

2. Jensen 2:61; Hugh Henry Brackenridge, "Narrative of the Transactions in the late Session of Assembly," *Pittsburgh Gazette*, 10/27/87; Jensen 2: "Microform Supplement," item number [MFM] 167.

3. "Assembly Proceedings," 9/18/87, in Jensen 2:60; *Pennsylvania Herald*, 9/20/87, in Jensen 2:61.

to hurry Pennsylvanians toward an early ratification. Others, worried about the behavior of the proposal's champions, and increasingly convinced that the dangers inherent in the document outweighed its acknowledged benefits, mounted an opposition that ultimately accelerated into violence. But all of that was yet to come. For now, Pennsylvanians seemed united in praise of the Grand Convention's final product: the Constitution of the United States.

Franklin concluded the delegates' report by recommending that Pennsylvania create a special federal district for the new capital. With that he and his colleagues departed. "Silence was preserved until they had retired from the house; but then an universal acclamation was heard, and a current of joy ran through the city, and the bells rung." The *Pennsylvania Gazette* reported that the people "testified the highest pleasure in seeing that great work at last perfected, which promises, when adopted, to give security, stability, and dignity to the government of the United States."[4]

A Philadelphia businessman dashed off a letter: "This morning the new Constitution was read. . . . [W]e have been in high glee ever since; bells ringing and congratulations in every street." The *Pennsylvania Gazette* exclaimed: "The zeal of our citizens in favor of this excellent Constitution has never been equalled, but by their zeal for liberty in the year 1776." The new Constitution, the editors believed, "will abolish party and make us, once more, members of one great political family."[5]

By Thursday, September 20, most of the Philadelphia newspapers had printed the full text of the Constitution and observers reported widespread public enthusiasm. "The people," one resident wrote, "may be said to be violent in there [sic] desire to carry it into effect." Another reported that "There is little else talked of but the new foederal Government and the citizens are for it very generally indeed." Ezekiel Forman told Alexander Hamilton that in less than a week petitions

---

4. Brackenridge, "Narrative," in Jensen 2:MFM 167; *Pennsylvania Gazette*, 9/19/87, in Jensen 2:60–61.

5. Samuel Hodgdon to Timothy Pickering, Philadelphia, 9/17/87, in Jensen 2:131; *Pennsylvania Gazette*, 9/26/87, in Jensen 2:137–38. The phrase "abolish party" carried multiple meanings. To some it signified the desire to end divisions, and "make us . . . one great political family." For others, it implied the end of both the Republicans and the Constitutionalists through final triumph of the Republican. Hence, Republican-Federalists could use such an argument to appeal to both the nonaligned long upset by partisan bickering, and to their own partisan followers.

demanding an early state ratifying convention were "circulating in every ward of the City and thro' the Country." The *Pennsylvania Gazette* reported that the two state political parties (the Republicans and the Constitutionalists) as well as the Quakers and others, "have all united in signing this petition [for an early convention]."[6]

Few spoke openly against the Constitution during these early days of grace, and even those with major reservations testified to its popular support in the Philadelphia region. This widespread enthusiasm appalled David Redick. A member of the state Constitutionalist party, which later led the opposition to ratification, he lamented: "I cannot imagine why the people in this city are so anxious to have it adopted instantly before it can be digested or deliberately considered." He found support for it everywhere: "If you were only here to see and hear those people, . . . to hear the Tories declare they will draw their sword in its defense, . . . to see the [Quakers?] running about signing declarations and petitions in favor of it before the[y] have time to examine it, to see gentlemen running into the country and neighboring towns haranguing the rabble."[7]

James Pemberton, a leader of the Philadelphia Quaker community, acknowledged his denomination's support. Writing to his son in England, he explained that although disappointed with the Constitution's protection of slavery, he approved of the document: "the late Congress had become so very low in general estimation, a change with enlarged powers and a proper balance seemed to be absolutely necessary."[8]

Presbyterians also agreed, at least some of those in Philadelphia, much to the chagrin of the author of the essay "An Old Constitutionalist." He castigated his own people for their myopic behavior. He admitted that Congress lacked sufficient powers, that the central government needed the authority to regulate trade, tax imports, and collect a revenue, but he felt that the proposed changes went much too far. The Presbyterians, he worried, did not appreciate the dangers this change posed for them. "He thinks it strange," he said, "that a certain denomination

---

6. John P. Kaminski and Gaspare J. Saladino, eds., *The Documentary History of the Ratification of the Constitution*, vol. 13, *Commentaries on the Constitution, Public and Private* (Madison: The State Historical Society of Wisconsin, 1981), 21 February to 7 November 1787, p. 200; hereafter cited as Kaminski and Saladino 13. Forman to Alexander Hamilton 9/24/87, in Jensen 2:MFM 63; McConnell to Irvine, 9/25/87, in Jensen 2:MFM 65; *Pennsylvania Gazette*, 9/26/87, in Jensen 2:137–38.

7. David Redick to William Irvine, Philadelphia, 9/24/87, in Jensen 2:135.

8. James Pemberton to John Pemberton, Philadelphia, 9/20/87, in Jensen 2:133.

[Presbyterians] is so easily led astray in this matter, and so soon fall in with the multitude; when their overthrow seems almost unanimously to be determined upon by all the different religious, or other sects in this country."[9]

In the city, at least initially, Presbyterians and Quakers, merchants and mechanics, even Constitutionalists and Republicans all appeared to look favorably on the proposed Federal Constitution. And this near unanimity in September 1787 reflected hopes and expectations that Pennsylvanians had long expressed.

If past behavior and current press accounts give us any useful insight into public opinion, then most Pennsylvanians had for some time supported strengthening the central government. During and after the war the legislature, regardless of its partisan complexion, had regularly and reliably supported Congress. Partisans in Pennsylvania might disagree over particular Congressional proposals, but they agreed that Congress needed more real authority to accomplish its tasks. Well before the peace of 1783, state Constitutionalist party members (who supported the Pennsylvania Constitution of 1776) and state Republican party members (who opposed Pennsylvania's Constitution of 1776) had both recognized the need to grant Congress an independent income and control over international commerce.[10]

In the mid-to-late 1780s increasing concerns about an impending crisis strengthened demands for change. Times were bad under the Articles of Confederation and national political reform seemed to be the only solution. Accounts of backcountry violence in Massachusetts, commonly called "Shays's Rebellion," dominated the news in Philadelphia throughout the winter of 1786–87. By the end of February 1787, Shays's "army" had been defeated and the "rebels" disbursed but alarms persisted in the Pennsylvania press well into the spring. Then, as concern over Shays subsided, worry about insurrection in Pennsylvania grew. By late summer, rumors abounded of rebellious groups assembling at various points in the upper Susquehanna region from Tioga in the west, to Wilkes-Barre in the east. Civil peace remained elusive.[11]

    9. *Independent Gazetteer*, 10/26/87, in Jensen 2:MFM 162.
    10. Robert Brunhouse, *The Counter-Revolution in Pennsylvania, 1776–1790* (Harrisburg, Pa.: Pennsylvania Historical Commission, 1942), 84–87, 99, 100, 131–33, 172, 185–86. This work is impressive for its thoroughness and yet to be supplanted after fifty years.
    11. For a sample of stories about Shays, see *Pennsylvania Journal*, January 3, 6, 10, 24, 27, 31; February 3, 7, 17, 24; March 10, 14, 21; April 4, 7; May 12, 19, 23, 26; June 6, 20, 30, 1787, all of which tend to emphasize the danger. See ibid., 8/22/87, for more reassuring news.

From an international perspective, America's future looked grim. A letter from Kingston, Jamaica, on January 20, 1787, announced that "Every account pictures America as rapidly advancing toward political annihilation." Dr. Tucker, dean of Gloucester, concurred: "Thoughts of America being a rising empire under one head," he concluded, "are idle and visionary."[12]

What value was mere independence, some Pennsylvanians asked? Europe gives us "their fashions, [and] manners, and engrosses the profits of our industry," complained a correspondent to the *Journal*. Others added to the chorus: Congress possesses neither the power to demand nor the funds to purchase the release of Americans held in Algiers while the British monopolize our carrying trade and exclude us from the West Indies' trade. On September 5, 1787, the *Independent Gazetteer* reported sixteen ships with British "colours" at the docks of Philadelphia and "one solitary American loading lumber for the West Indies."[13]

Some saw calamity in the west; Spain claimed all lands south of the Ohio River; the Creeks prepared for war on Georgia and the Cumberland settlement with arms and ammunition from the Spanish; the British conspired with the Indians in northwest territories and had fitted out a twenty-gun ship, the "Maria," to cruise on Lake Champlain.[14]

Most also agreed that the domestic economy was a shambles. The government of Rhode Island had flooded the state with depreciating paper money and tried to force creditors to accept it at face value. Some saw in this a scheme to redistribute property and level all social distinctions. And Rhode Island was not alone. Other states also were experimenting with paper-money schemes. In addition, immigration had dried up, the shipbuilding industry had declined, Pennsylvania had imposed exorbitant land taxes, public revenues ran more than £230,000 in arrears, domestic manufacturing languished, mechanics lived on borrowed money, and Virginia placed duties on agricultural products from other states. Specie was scarce, loan money was tight, interest

---

For a discussion of press coverage of Shays and how news of Shays fit into the general press campaign for a convention, see John K. Alexander, *The Selling of the Constitutional Convention* (Madison, Wisc.: Madison House, 1990), esp. 54–55 and 142–45.

12. *Pennsylvania Journal*, 3/10/87 and 6/16/87.
13. *Pennsylvania Journal*, 3/24/87, 5/19/87, 2/24/87, 9/12/87; *Independent Gazetteer*, 9/5/87.
14. *Pennsylvania Journal*, 1/13/87, 6/9/87, 7/11/87.

rates were high, and the *Journal* reported on September 12 some ninety bankruptcy applications awaited court action.[15]

At the heart of the country's problems lay the ineffectual Congress of the United States whose very name signified "weakness, instability, . . . continental money . . . tender laws." The hopes of all Americans rested with the Grand Convention. "Calamities have at last opened . . . [Americans'] eyes and they again turn to a foederal government for safety and protection," the *Journal* reported in July. A month later it observed a "general determination among all classes of people to receive the government they are now forming [at the Convention]." Most believed that "even the political existence of the United States, perhaps, depends on the Convention meeting at Philadelphia."[16]

If all agreed that America faced a crisis, not all believed that changing the form of government would solve the problems. Some placed a loss of virtue at the heart of America's problems and prescribed moral reformation. "Whoever would be thought to consult the welfare of Pennsylvania, let them endeavour to stop the licentious manners of the times; the extravagance of youth and the venality of age," counseled one author. Another urged Americans to "confine our mode of living to what nature requires or even to the system that prevailed previous to the late revolution." "Frugality, disuse of foreign luxuries, industry and agriculture will help put us in the ranks of the rich and flourishing nations," explained a third. On September 1 a correspondent argued that it was "laughable" to assume that America's troubles could be fixed by tinkering with the political machine. He prescribed "A long course of frugality, disuse of foreign luxuries, encouragement of industry, application to agriculture, attention to home manufactures, and a spirit of union and national sobriety." But these minor contrapunctual strains only accented the mighty chorus calling for a stronger union to meet the current exigencies.[17]

15. *Pennsylvania Gazette*, 8/29/87; *Independent Gazetteer*, 8/23/87; *Pennsylvania Gazette*, 8/1/87; *Pennsylvania Packet*, 9/24/87; *Pennsylvania Journal*, 4/28/87, 6/30/87, 8/4/87; *Pennsylvania Gazette*, 10/3/87; *Pennsylvania Journal*, 2/17/87; and *Pennsylvania Journal*, 9/12/87. Also see *Pennsylvania Journal*, 3/3/87, 5/6/87, 6/20/87, 8/25/87, 6/23/87. For more on the paper-money controversy in Rhode Island, see Irwin H. Polishook, *Rhode Island and the Union, 1774–1795* (Evanston: Northwestern University Press, 1969), 131–33.

16. "Senex, Virginia," 8/28/87, in *Independent Gazetteer*, 9/10/87; *Pennsylvania Journal*, 7/21/87, 8/25/87, 4/14/87.

17. *Pennsylvania Journal*, 6/30/87, 8/4/87, 9/1/87, 8/29/87. For similar sentiments see *Freeman's Journal*, 9/5/87.

Even future Antifederalists testified to the near universal demands for revision of the Articles of Confederation. George Bryan, one of the leading opponents of ratification, later recalled that "previous to the appointment of the Convention there seemed to be in Pennsylvania a general Wish for a more efficient confederation" and "when the Federal Constitution was proposed to the people, the desire for increasing the powers of Congress were great, and this object had a mighty influence in its favor."[18]

Newspapers that later opposed ratification had originally shared in the general high hopes for the Grand Convention. The *Freeman's Journal*, with only minor exceptions, supported the Convention through August and most of September. On August 1, the editor opined that "it is hoped, . . . that the minds of the people throughout the United States are prepared to receive with respect, and to try with fortitude and perseverance, the plan which will be offered to them by men distinguished for their wisdom and patriotism." A week later he lamented the sorry state of Pennsylvania's merchants, shopkeepers, lawyers, doctors, and farmers and concluded that "an efficient federal government alone can relieve us from our oppressive . . . taxation, and realise all our hopes and wishes of national glory and prosperity."[19]

The *Independent Gazetteer*, which also later opposed ratification of the Federal Constitution, readily joined in the general praise of the Grand Convention until early October 1787. In the previous December the paper had called for a "vigorous and energetic continental government, which will crush and destroy faction, subdue insurrections, revive public and private credit, disappoint our transatlantic enemies and their lurking Emissaries among us, and finally . . . endure 'while the sun shines and the rivers flow.'" Between December 1786 and September 1787 few in Pennsylvania took issue with this view. And publication of the proposed new Federal Constitution initially elicited near unanimous praise in Philadelphia.[20]

On September 28, this apparent consensus in support of the new Constitution ended abruptly and dramatically. That morning, in the

18. George Bryan's postelection analysis misdated 1786. George Bryan "Papers," Historical Society of Pennsylvania.
19. *Freeman's Journal*, 8/1/87, 8/8/87.
20. *Independent Gazetteer*, 12/27/86. See Alexander, *The Selling of the Convention*, for analysis of consistent press support for the Convention.

Assembly, Republican legislator George Clymer introduced a resolution calling for the immediate election of a convention to consider the new Federal Constitution. This proposal precipitated two days of debate and desperate political maneuvering that sharply divided the House. The details of this two-day conflict reveal much about the nature of the emerging dispute over the Federal Constitution that would rage for more than six months in Pennsylvania.

On Friday, Clymer introduced his resolution into a thin House. Adjournment was set for Saturday. The members, facing reelection contests in eleven days and anxious to depart for home, expected only routine end-of-the-year business. Clymer's move, however, caught them by surprise and produced instant opposition. He had undoubtedly anticipated this.[21]

George Clymer and his Republican colleagues, like most Pennsylvanians, agreed that the country needed a stronger central government. Republicans, again like most Pennsylvanians, quickly saw that the proposed Federal Constitution would address this very need. However, Republicans also knew that the principles of the new Federal Constitution challenged those of the old state constitution. Acceptance of the new system implied rejection of the old. Thus ratification could bring them a decisive victory in their long battle against Pennsylvania's revolutionary frame of government and its staunch defenders, the state Constitutionalists.

Pennsylvania's state constitution of 1776, the sacred totem of the Constitutionalists, lodged all real power in an annually elected unicameral legislature. The courts remained subject to legislative influence and the executive body (composed of nineteen men in 1787) could neither initiate nor reject legislation. State Constitutionalists supported this system; Republicans condemned it; and this issue had defined partisanship in Pennsylvania for at least a decade.[22]

The proposed Federal Constitution took the Republican side of the

---

21. Assembly Proceedings, 9/28/87, in Jensen 2:65, 66; Assembly Debates, 9/28/87, in Jensen 2:84; Findley speech of the day. "An Assemblyman," in *Pittsburgh Gazette*, 10/27/87.

22. For details of the role of the state constitution of 1776 in producing the ethnic-religious partisan alignments among officeholders and within the electorate, see Owen S. Ireland, "The Ethnic-Religious Dimension of Pennsylvania Politics, 1778–1779," *William and Mary Quarterly* 30 (July 1973): 423–48; Ireland, "The Crux of Politics: Religion and Party in Pennsylvania, 1778–1789," *William and Mary Quarterly* 42 (October 1985): 453–75; Wayne Bockelman and Owen Ireland, "The Internal Revolution in Pennsylvania: An Ethnic-Religious Interpretation," *Pennsylvania History* 41 (April 1974): 125–59.

question. It provided for a bicameral legislature, a single executive with veto power over legislation, and an independent judiciary. As the *Pennsylvania Gazette* proclaimed on September 19: "The division of the powers of the United States into three branches gives the sincerest satisfaction to a great majority of our citizens, who have long suffered many inconveniences from being governed by a single legislature." In case anyone missed the point, the *Gazette* then translated its feelings about the state constitution into an eternal verity: "All single governments are tyrannies—whether they be lodged in one man—a few men—or a large body of the people."[23]

Approval of the Federal Constitution implied, if it did not require, rejection of the state constitution. "The nearer the American states can bring their constitutions to the form of the federal government," the editor of the *Gazette* pointed out a week after publication of the proposal, "the more harmony they will always have with Congress, and the more happily will they be governed." He did caution, however, "Where this is not the case, the comparisons will often be drawn to the disadvantages of the state government, which will lessen the principle of obligation and obedience in its citizens." Three weeks later the *Pennsylvania Herald* summarized what had become a consensus: "That the existing form of state government cannot survive the adoption of the projected confederation, is likewise an indisputable proposition."[24]

George Clymer and his fellow Republicans understood that ratification of the Federal Constitution promised a political revolution in Pennsylvania. Once the state Constitutionalists understood the provincial implications of the Federal Constitution, they would have little choice but to oppose it. Constitutionalists, despite their concern for the union, their historic support for Congress, and their agreement on the need to augment the powers of the general government, could not and

23. Kaminski and Saladino 13:217.
24. *Pennsylvania Gazette*, 9/26/87, in Kaminski and Saladino 13:253; *Pennsylvania Herald*, 10/20/87, in Jensen 2:MFM 150. Both Federalists and Antifederalists, east and west, agreed that ratification of the Federal Constitution constituted a repudiation of the principles of the state constitution of 1776. See, for example, the first Antifederalist pamphlet, dated Saturday, 9/29/87, "The Address of the Seceding Assemblymen," in Jensen 2:112–17; Matthew McConnell to Congressman William Irvine, 9/20/87, in Jensen 2:132; McConnell, 9/25/87, in Jensen 2:MFM 65; and the western *Carlisle Gazette* reporting that Thomas McKean, chief justice of Pennsylvania, and one of the few Constitutionalists publicly to favor ratification, had said, "it [the state constitution] must be altered so as to suit the Continental Government"; *Carlisle Gazette*, 10/3/87, in Jensen 2:MFM 94.

would not accept a proposal that put their power, their policies, and their principles at risk. Thus, Pennsylvania's Republicans had their work cut out for them.[25]

George Clymer brought to the Republican cause an impressive set of credentials. Born into an Anglican-Quaker family in 1739 and raised and trained in business by William Coleman, Clymer had carved out for himself an influential position in the Philadelphia mercantile community. His marriage to the daughter of Reese Meredith and his business ties to both her father and her brother linked him to a network of successful and influential Anglican-Quaker families in the Delaware valley. In the early 1770s he had plunged headlong into the agitation against Great Britain. He chaired the committee demanding the resignation of the tea agents for the East India Company, served on the Committee of Safety, ran as a pro-independence candidate for a seat in the legislature in May 1776, and, after Independence, represented Pennsylvania in Congress. During the discouraging and dangerous winter of 1776–77, while Congress took refuge in Baltimore, Clymer and two others remained in Philadelphia, conducting essential congressional business under the shadow of the advancing British army.[26]

From the beginning, Clymer had been a vocal opponent of Pennsylvania's constitution of 1776 and he later worked with like-minded men in the Republican party to force its modification. At least in part because of this, the Constitutionalist party, which dominated the state legislature in the late 1770s, forced him to retire from public life. In the 1780s, however, during one of the periods of Republican ascendancy, he returned to Congress and then won election to the General Assembly in his own right from the city of Philadelphia. In December 1786, the legislature chose him as one of Pennsylvania's delegates to the Federal Convention. A patriot, a successful businessman, a seasoned public official, a major figure in the Republican party, and now one of

---

25. The Constitution's anticipated impact on politics reinforced the Republicans' support for the document and largely shaped their campaign strategy. For the Constitutionalists, that realization converted them into opponents of a proposal they increasingly saw as threatening their principles, their policies, and their power.

26. Jerry Grundfest, *George Clymer: Philadelphia Revolutionary, 1739–1813* (New York, 1983; Arno reprint of Ph.D. diss., Columbia University, 1973); *Dictionary of American Biography*, 4:234–35; *Biographical Directory of the American Congress* (1961), 710; and *Pennsylvania Magazine of History and Biography* 1 (1877): 199; (1880): 200–201; (1886): 353–54.

the framers of the Federal Constitution, Clymer carried weight in Pennsylvania.

On September 28, 1787, Clymer and his Republican cohorts needed a quick victory. Republicans currently held a working majority in the Assembly. Speedy action before adjournment, they hoped, would lead to ratification in the fall. "In My mind to delay is to destroy," Republican Thomas FitzSimons explained.[27]

As early as August some observers, presumably Republicans, had worried that Constitutionalists were already organizing opposition to the Grand Convention. They probably erred. The evidence suggests that Constitutionalist leaders at that time had been suspicious but did not know what the Convention would propose and had not begun to plan resistance.[28] By now, however, Constitutionalists had had more than a week to study the document and had undoubtedly realized its partisan implications for Pennsylvania.

Delay for two days would postpone a decision until the newly elected Assembly convened in November. At best, such a delay would slow, if not destroy, the momentum. More important, the Constitutionalists, if given time, might well mobilize their supporters, and win back the majority that they had held as recently as 1785.[29] With renewed control of the legislature, Constitutionalists could derail the movement for ratification and end all immediate hopes for reform at either the national or the state level.

27. Thomas FitzSimons to Noah Webster, Philadelphia, 9/15/87, in Jensen 2:MFM 142.

28. For charges that Constitutionalists conspired against the Grand Convention while that body still sat, see "Federal Constitution," *Pennsylvania Gazette*, 10/10/87, in Kaminski and Saladino 13:362; "Item" and "Tar and Feathers," *Pennsylvania Gazette*, 8/8/87, 8/16/87. The Constitutionalist leadership, although suspicious, probably did not understand the partisan implications of the proposal until after its publication. Joseph Hart and Francis Murray, leading Constitutionalists in Bucks County and close political associates of George Bryan, remained ignorant of the partisan thrust of the document until well after its publication. See Joseph Hart to Bryan, 10/3/87, George Bryan, "Papers," H.S.P.; and Murray to John Nicholson, 11/1/87, in Jensen 2:207–8. The early expressions of concerns suggest fear of a Republican conspiracy but probably tell us more about the Republican anticipation than about Constitutionalist knowledge. For a different interpretation, see Steven Boyd, *The Policies of Opposition: Antifederalists and the Acceptance of the Constitution* (Millwood, N.Y.: KTO Press, 1979), 11, 12; and Roland Baumann, "The Democratic-Republicans of Philadelphia: The Origins, 1776–1797" (Ph.D. diss., Pennsylvania State University, 1970), 79.

29. Roland Baumann wrote that in the fall of 1787 "Many political observers acknowledged that . . . the balance of power between the opposing sides in the whole state still hung in the balance." Baumann, "The Democratic-Republicans of Philadelphia," 76–77. See also John Kaminski, "Paper Politics: The Northern State Loan-Offices During the Confederation, 1783–1790" (Ph.D. diss., University of Wisconsin, 1972), 85.

Gouverneur Morris's October 30 letter to George Washington probably best expressed Republican fears. Morris had represented Pennsylvania in the Grand Convention and the most often quoted portion of his letter reflects the Republican uncertainty about the behavior of the electorate. "I am far from being decided in my Opinion that they will consent," he wrote. "True it is that the City and its Neighbourhood are enthusiastic in the Cause; but I dread the cold and sower Temper of the back Counties." The remainder of Morris's comments, much less often quoted, suggests the reason for his fear: "[B]ut I dread . . . still more the wicked Industry of those who have long habituated themselves to live on the Public [i.e., Constitutionalist officeholders] and cannot bear the Idea of being removed from the Power and Profit of State Government, which has been, and still is the Means of supporting themselves their Families and Dependants; And . . . of depressing and humbling their political Adversaries [Republicans]."[30]

Pennsylvania's Republicans anticipated that ratification of the Federal Constitution would radically alter politics in Pennsylvania. How long they had seen revision of the Articles of Confederation as a vehicle for solving their state-level political problems remains unclear. Historian Jack Rakove has argued that before the winter of 1786–87 few if any of the future Federalists saw reformation of the national government as a means of affecting political change within the individual states.[31]

Be that as it may, the activities of the Republicans suggest a concerted and coordinated plan, if not a conspiracy. By the summer of 1787 a number of publications in the Philadelphia press hinted at a connection between reform of the Articles of Confederation and the Pennsylvania constitution of 1776. "A Letter from a Gentleman in Virginia" explicitly attacked the idea of a unicameral legislature. At about the same time, Richard Price's published letter to William Bingham tied this attack directly to Pennsylvania. Price, an English religious dissenter and an early supporter of the American cause, lamented that "the Constitution of your government in Pennsylvania is so imperfect" and

---

30. Morris to Washington, Philadelphia, 10/10/87, in Kaminski and Saladino 13:513.
31. Jack N. Rakove, *The Beginnings of National Politics: An Interpretative History of the Continental Congress* (Baltimore: Johns Hopkins University Press, 1979), 381, 382, 387, 389, 390, 392, 396. Antifederalists later charged that Republicans had long conspired to use the Grand Convention for provincial partisan purposes. I have, however, seen little evidence to suggest that before late spring of 1787 Republicans saw the Constitutional Convention as a vehicle for attacking the state constitution of 1776.

recommended "that the power of legislation ought to be lodged in more than one Assembly."³²

We may never know with certainty how early Republicans came to see the Federal Constitution as an indirect way of undermining a powerful political opponent they had failed to defeat in direct battle, or how early they had begun to "conspire" to hurry Pennsylvanians into a quick and uncritical approval. We do know, however, that before the Grand Convention ended in September, Republican Thomas FitzSimons had already arranged for Noah Webster to write on behalf of the expected Federal Constitution. Within two days of the Constitution's publication, articles supporting it began to appear in the press.³³

Meanwhile, supporters of the new plan held public meetings and organized a petition drive in the Philadelphia region. On Monday, September 24, just six days after Franklin had presented the Constitution to the Assembly, and before the legislature had authorized its printing and distribution, the first of these petitions reached the floor of the house. In the next three days petitions signed by nearly 4,000 people flooded in from the city of Philadelphia and its immediate surroundings.³⁴ Thus, in less than ten days, the supporters of ratification had persuaded approximately one out of every two taxables in the Philadelphia area to sign a petition favoring ratification, an extraordinary feat possible only through the effectively orchestrated efforts of dedicated and determined political workers.

While writing essays and mobilizing petitions, Republicans also closely monitored congressional action. Although Franklin had unofficially presented the proposed Federal Constitution to the legislature, the

---

32. "A Letter from a Gentleman in Virginia," *Independent Gazetteer*, 6/20/87, in Kaminski and Saladino 13:134. See also "Sidney," *Independent Gazetteer*, 6/6/87; "Huntington," *Pennsylvania Gazette*, 5/30/87, in Kaminski and Saladino 13:118, 119; and "Rustic," *Independent Gazetteer*, 5/31/87.

33. FitzSimons to Webster, Philadelphia, 9/15/87, in Jensen 2:MFM 142; "An American Citizen," *Independent Gazetteer*, 9/26/87, in Jensen 2:138ff.

34. The petitions came from Philadelphia city and county, and from Montgomery County. These three political units contained ten to twelve thousand taxables. Four thousand signatures thus represents at least one out of every three taxables. Since a significant portion of Montgomery County should be discounted because of distance, the actual rate was probably closer to one out of every two taxables. A commentator in the *Independent Gazetteer*, 10/10/87, arrived at approximately this ratio but by a different route. He identified "not above 3,000" signatures and then counted 5,000 taxables in Philadelphia city and 2000 in Southwark and the Northern Liberties for a total of 7,000 taxables in the Philadelphia area. "Assembly Proceedings," 9/26/87, 9/27/87, 9/28/87, in Jensen 2:64–65.

next step was up to Congress. The Grand Convention had met, at least nominally, under the auspices of Congress and had officially reported its recommendation to that body. America now waited for Congress to transmit the plan to the states.

What Republicans learned about the pace of congressional action was not encouraging. Congressman William Bingham, responding to FitzSimons's request for information, wrote on Friday, September 21, that the documents had reached New York City the day before, but that Congress had postponed consideration of the question until Wednesday, September 26. Even with quick action (a highly unlikely event in light of Congress's recent history), little chance remained that the Constitution would come to the state legislature with congressional endorsement before the Assembly adjourned on September 29.[35]

Bingham's letter arrived in Philadelphia on Monday, September 24, and within a short time Republican leaders must have understood its implications and begun to map out their final strategy: the timing, the arguments, and the attendance necessary for the legislature to call a convention without prior congressional approval.

On Tuesday, September 25, two articles appeared in the press that set the stage. The first, signed "A Freeman," vigorously rejected an earlier *Packet* prediction of a slow congressional response and a postponement of legislative action until after the October elections: "Confident of the hearty concurrence of Pennsylvania in the measures of the Convention, as we are hourly suffering in our interests and honor any unnecessary delay . . . is a deep injury to our country."[36]

The second, a satirical piece, cast aspersions on any who might resist. It advised the opponents of the Constitution "to put off the recommendation of a Convention, till the next session of your Assembly. This will give you time to look about you, and perhaps to throw a lock upon one of the wheels of the great continental waggon; for you may depend upon it [,] your wheelbarrow [the state constitution of 1776] and the new flying machine [the Federal Constitution], cannot long travel the same road together." It was signed: "With great regard, and sincere wishes for your success in every thing that tends to anarchy,

---

35. William Bingham to Thomas FitzSimons, NY 9/21/87, in Edmund C. Burnett, ed., *Letters of Members of the Continental Congress* (Washington, D.C.: The Carnegie Institute of Washington, 1921–36) 8:646.
36. *Packet*, 9/25/87.

distress, poverty, and tyranny, I am your friend and humble servant, DANIEL SHAYS."[37]

The authorship of these two essays remains unknown, but the timing of their publication is suggestive. Both pieces appeared the day after the Republicans learned of the probable congressional delay. The first essay made the case for an early convention; the second impugned the motives of any who would oppose such a call. Fortuitous or not, these essays, each reprinted a number of times in other organs throughout the week, set the stage for the bold and dramatic Republican venture on Friday 28.

George Clymer's resolution appeared reasonable enough. It called for a state convention elected at the same time and in the same manner as the next General Assembly, thus saving voters' time and taxpayers' money. Clymer defended his proposal on populist grounds: "whereas it is the sense of great numbers of the good people of this state, already signified in petitions and declarations to this House, that the earliest steps should be taken to assemble a convention within the state . . . Resolved That . . . the inhabitants of the state . . . choose suitable persons to serve as deputies to a state convention."[38]

Clymer's resolution, however, provoked an immediate response by the leading Constitutionalists in the house. Robert Whitehill, a Scots-Irish Presbyterian from Cumberland County, and a longtime champion of the Pennsylvania constitution of 1776, immediately objected. He needed time to consider this important matter, he said, and demanded a postponement.[39]

Republicans retorted that the people demanded action. Thomas FitzSimons, an Irish Catholic Republican from Philadelphia, insisted that no additional time was necessary. He reminded them that the House was voting not on the substance of the proposed Constitution, but simply on whether to call a convention to consider the document. In addition, he pointed out, "From the number of petitions on your table, it may be clearly inferred, that it is the wish and expectation of the

---

37. *Pennsylvania Gazette*, 9/26/87; *Independent Gazetteer*, 9/25/87, in Jensen 2:136–37.
38. Jensen 2:65–66.
39. Clymer's resolution should not have completely surprised the Constitutionalists. For a week, correspondents had been debating in the press whether the Assembly would call a convention before breaking up or leave the matter to the succeeding house. See *Pennsylvania Herald*, 9/22/87, in Jensen 2:MFM 59; *Packet* 9/25/87, in Jensen 2:MFM 67.

people, that this House should adopt speedy measures for calling a convention."[40]

FitzSimons was polite and restrained, but Daniel Clymer, cousin of the man who had introduced the resolutions and himself a Republican assemblyman from Berks County, changed the tone of the debate. He first cast aspersions on his opponents' motives. "I have heard, sir," he said, "that only four or five leading party men in this city are against it [the Federal Constitution]." He then condemned them and predicted that "they will be hereafter ashamed to show their faces among the good people, whose future prosperity they wish to blast in the bud." He ended with a threat: "let them be careful, lest they draw upon themselves the odium of that people."[41]

Hugh Henry Brackenridge, a Scots-born Princeton-educated New Light Presbyterian from Westmoreland, continued on this plane, charging that those who were not prepared to discuss and decide the issue were negligent. "This . . . has been on your table many days," he reminded them, and "must have been a subject of reflection to members, who wished to perform the duty they owed to their God, their conscience, and fellow citizens."[42]

Whitehill's response admitted what everyone already knew. He had not prepared himself to discuss the proposal, he explained, because he "did not expect any notice would be taken of it for Congress ought to send forward the plan before we do anything." Since Congress was not ready to act, and the House was about to adjourn he had felt no necessity to study the document in detail. With this Whitehill framed the central question of the remainder of the morning's debate: Could Pennsylvania act without a prior congressional recommendation?[43]

After the house voted against postponement, Brackenridge, in a rambling and patronizing oration made and remade one point: the Assembly need not wait for Congress. William Findley, a Scots-Irish Presbyterian from Westmoreland and one of the outstanding Constitutionalist party leaders, then entered the fray. He had had time to collect his thoughts and marshall his documents. He now demonstrated his political skills.

40. Jensen 2:69, Jensen 2:70.
41. Jensen 2:70.
42. Jensen 2:74.
43. Ibid.

Findley, who still spoke with a brogue, had migrated from Ireland in his early twenties and settled in a Scots-Irish community in southwestern Cumberland (later Franklin) County where he made a modest living as a teacher, a weaver, a tailor, and a farmer. During the Revolution he served on the Cumberland County Committee of Observation, enlisted in the local militia as a private, rose to the rank of captain, and then repeatedly won election to county office between 1776 and 1782. In the year the war ended he moved to Westmoreland and represented that new county in the Council of Censors. Although he later insisted that he had always disapproved of the state constitution of 1776, he joined its supporters in the Constitutionalist party in 1783, at least in part because it had become the party of the Scots-Irish Presbyterians. From 1784 until the end of the decade Findley served as a Constitutionalist in either the General Assembly or in the Supreme Executive Council (the multiple executive created by the constitution of 1776). He was one of the most respected and powerful of the Constitutional political chiefs, and that morning he demonstrated why.[44]

Findley argued that Pennsylvania still remained part of the union, still operated within the Confederation, and still functioned in a constitutional, or a "federal way." He quoted chapter and verse from an array of documents to demonstrate that until now Pennsylvania, the Continental Congress, and the Grand Convention had all acted in a "federal way": the state, in electing delegates to the Constitutional Convention in December 1786; Congress in sanctioning the meeting in the winter of 1787; and the Convention itself in forwarding its work to Congress just ten days ago. All of this had remained within the legitimate boundaries of the Articles of Confederation.

But now the danger arose. If Pennsylvania called a state convention without a previous congressional recommendation, Findley insisted, it would violate the Articles, act in an unfederal or antifederal way, breach the existing constitutional system of the nation, and dissolve the union. Findley admitted the defects of the Confederation, the wisdom of the authors of the Constitution, its apparent popularity in Pennsylvania, and the probability that Congress would soon forward the proposal to the states for consideration. He cautioned, however, that precipitous

---

44. For biographical details on William Findley, see *Biographical Directory of the American Congress* (1961), 887; *Dictionary of American Biography*, 15:385–86; *P.M.H.B.*, 5:440–50; 11:75, obituary, *Democratic Press* (Philadelphia), 4/11/1821.

action in advance of the congressional recommendation would dishonor the state. Furthermore, he said, this undue haste raised questions in his mind about the motives of its supporters.[45]

Findley stung the Republicans who responded with increasing vehemence. George Clymer stated the case rather simply: "The idea which he [Findley] has taken up may be traced undoubtedly in the original Confederation, but he will not find it at all attended to by the Convention."[46]

William Robinson, a Philadelphia lawyer probably of Quaker background, took the discussion a step further. He rejected Findley's history and then rested the Republican party position on the broad and solid ground of popular sovereignty. He believed that the Constitutional Convention and all that led up to it violated the Articles of Confederation. But the failure of the Articles necessitated such action. "America" he said, "has seen the Confederation totally inadequate to the purposes of an equal general government, incapable of affording security either within or without. . . . Hence resulted the necessity of having again recourse to the AUTHORITY OF THE PEOPLE. *Under this impression, sir, the* CONVENTION *originated.*"[47]

FitzSimons expanded on Robinson's appeal to popular authority. The Convention, he said, "found the Confederation without vigor and so decayed that it was impossible to graft a useful article upon it; . . . They knew . . . that the people only would be adequate to carry it into effect." And if Pennsylvania "neglect calling a convention, . . . the authority is with the people, and they will do it themselves."[48]

By this point, the Republicans had staked out a most radical position. Brackenridge, as was his wont, gave it a flamboyant expression: "We are not on federal ground but on the wild and extended field of nature, unrestrained by any former compact, bound by no peculiar tie, . . . It is on the principle of self-conservation that we act." But, he reassured his audience, we do after all act in a federal manner "inasmuch as it was sanctioned by the PEOPLE OF THE UNITED STATES."[49]

With that the Assembly voted 43 to 19 to call a convention and adjourned until 4:00 P.M. when it would establish the time, place, and

45. Jensen 2:81–85.
46. Jensen 2:86.
47. Jensen 2:87.
48. Jensen 2:89–90.
49. Jensen 2:93.

other specifics of the election and the convention. The majority included every Republican in the house plus seven Constitutionalists and six nonaligned assemblymen. The minority were, to a man, members of the state Constitutionalist party.[50]

The Republicans had started the day with a bold plan. By the end of the morning's session they could taste victory. Their solid majority on the first vote gave them confidence and that they would easily finish their business in the afternoon. They were wrong.

When the sergeant at arms called the roll at 4:00 P.M., the Republicans discovered their error. During the adjournment Findley, Whitehill, and other Constitutionalist assemblymen caucused at Major Boyd's boardinghouse with Constitutionalist leaders of the Supreme Executive Council. In all likelihood, Judge George Bryan himself, probably the most powerful and influential Constitutionalist officeholder in the state, also joined them. They soon had a plan. Faced with certain defeat, the Constitutionalist minority simply refused to attend the afternoon session. Because of the two-thirds quorum requirement in the Pennsylvania legislature, their absence would prevent the Assembly from establishing the specifics necessary to choose a Convention. Without this final step, no election could take place.[51]

The Republicans should have anticipated this old tactic. The Constitutionalists had used it three years before to prevent repeal of the Test Acts (wartime loyalty oaths); earlier, the Republicans themselves had done the same. A minority in November 1778, they had threatened to withdraw if the Constitutionalists did not accept a modification in the assemblymen's oaths to the state constitution. Still earlier, the radical minority in the old provincial legislature had brought that body to its knees in June 1776 with precisely the same tactic: the minority departed, broke the quorum and left the majority sitting in an important rage. On

---

50. The seven Constitutionalists who supported Clymer's resolution probably did so because of the overwhelming popularity of the Grand Convention, and the confusion generated by Clymer's surprise move. In time most of these seven either fell into line or were repudiated by their constituents. For more detailed analysis of this question, see Chapters 1 and 7. This view modifies the interpretation I offered earlier in "Partisanship and the Constitution, 1787," *Pennsylvania History* 14 (October 1978): 315–32.

51. Sixty-nine legislators sat in the Eleventh General Assembly; forty-six constituted a quorum, forty-five attended Friday afternoon. For details on Bryan, see esp. Chapters 2 and 4, and Joseph S. Foster, *In Pursuit of Equal Liberty: George Bryan and Revolution in Pennsylvania* (University Park: Pennsylvania State University Press, 1994).

Friday afternoon, September 28, 1787, the Constitutionalists did it to the Republicans again.

Frustrated and infuriated, the Republicans flailed about, seeking means to punish or bypass the minority. Gerardus Wynkoop, a Dutch Reformed representative from Bucks County and a recent convert to the Republican party, announced that he "would be glad to know, if there was no way to compel men, who deserted from the duty they owed their country, to a performance of it." Alexander Lowrey, an experienced Republican assemblyman from Lancaster, a farmer, a fur trader and himself an immigrant from Northern Ireland "believed that there was a law to compel the absent members to serve," but a frantic search of the statutes proved him wrong.[52]

William Robinson then urged a radical course of action. He proposed reconstituting the attending assemblymen as an extralegal committee, analogous to the committees that brought about the separation from Great Britain. Such a committee could then recommend what the Assembly could not legislate: the popular election of a state convention. Unwilling to move that far that fast the Republican leadership adjourned the legislature until nine-thirty the next morning, hoping against hope for some way around this impediment.[53]

Early Saturday morning, news from Congress promised to solve the Republicans' problem. William Bingham had dispatched a special overnight courier from New York to announce Congress's unanimous agreement to forward the Constitution to the states. By seven o'clock, Saturday morning, George Clymer had a copy of this congressional resolution and the Republican prospects looked considerably brighter.[54]

Samuel Hodgden, a Philadelphia businessman and political observer, anticipated the happy consequences. Drafting an early morning letter, he told his business partner, Timothy Pickering: "This [the express from New York] I suppose will bring the members to the House at the adjournment today, and finish the resolutions of yesterday for calling the convention." Hodgden, like at least some of the Republican leader-

---

52. Jensen 2:98. See *Pennsylvania Magazine of History & Biography* for a biographical sketch, 4:90–92. The act in question applied only to compelling attendance by members at the opening of a legislative session.
53. Jensen 2:98.
54. Samuel Hodgdon to Timothy Pickering, Philadelphia, 9/29/87, in Jensen 2:122; "Assembly Debates," 9/29/87, in Jensen 2:103; 2:102 n. 2. William Lewis to Thomas Shippen, Philadelphia, 10/11/87, in Jensen 2:MFM 125.

ship, had taken Findley's argument seriously, and believed that the issue of prior congressional recommendation was real. But Hodgden, like the Republican leadership, erred.[55]

Before the scheduled time of the meeting, Speaker Mifflin approached the nineteen seceders with the news that Congress had removed their principal concern. Much to his chagrin, they still refused to attend. The business, they said, was too important to be gone into so "precipitately." They now believed that "the succeeding house ought to take it up." With that, Findley completed his political education of the Republicans: the next move was up to them.[56]

In the short time between Mifflin's encounter with the absent members and the hour of the Assembly's meeting the Republicans concocted a desperate scheme, of dubious legality, but their only hope. When the Speaker called the roll at 9:30 the house lacked two for a quorum. It immediately sent the sergeant at arms and the assistant clerk to summon the absent members: the former to "require the members absenting themselves to attend"; the latter to convey to them the good news about the congressional resolution, and to record their responses.[57]

While the assemblymen waited in the State House, their official agents, accompanied by a considerable crowd under the informal leadership of Captain John Barry and Major William Jackson, went first to Major Alexander Boyd's boardinghouse on Sixth Street. The day before the sergeant had discovered most of the errant assemblymen caucusing there with the Constitutionalist party leadership. This morning he found only two: Jacob Miley and James McCalmont. Upon Miley and McCalmont's refusal to attend the legislature, the sergeant and the clerk departed in search of others.[58]

Then the mob took over. Miley and McCalmont hurried inside, slammed the doors, and hid. But the angry "citizens" smashed open the doors, caught the fleeing assemblymen, tore their clothes, and, while abusing them verbally, dragged them through the streets to the legislative chambers. There, in spite of repeated pleas, the Assembly and the mob forced the two assemblymen to remain.[59]

55. Hodgdon to Pickering, Philadelphia, 9/29/87, in Jensen 2:122–23.
56. Francis Johnston to Timothy Pickering, Philadelphia, 10/1/87, in Jensen 2:MFM 87.
57. Jensen 2:99, 103.
58. Jensen 2:110, 2:114 n. 1.
59. "Address of Seceding Assemblymen," Philadelphia, 10/2/87, in Jensen 2:114; Erkuries Beatly Diary, Philadelphia, 9/29/87, in Jensen 2:MFM 82; *N.Y. Morning Post*, 10/6/87. Phineas Bond to M. de Carmorthers, 9/29/87, in Jensen 2:MFM 83.

Meanwhile, the sergeant and the clerk pursued other missing assemblymen through the streets, up the alleys, and across the public square of downtown Philadelphia. They followed John Piper and a number of others from Boyd's to the corner of Arch and Sixth where they spied Findley. He saw them at about the same time and "hastened his pace," rounded a corner and disappeared "out of view." The *Pittsburgh Gazette* later reported that Findley had "run up into Robert Irwin's garrett, and lay there unperceived by the family a part of the afternoon" and later "escaped" to Colonel Coates's in the Northern Liberties.[60]

When the sergeant and the clerk reached Whitehill's lodgings the maid first said that Whitehill was in and went to fetch him. She then returned and denied that he was there and this set the pattern for the rest of the search. The sergeant and the clerk, in time, found most of the errant assemblymen but none would attend.[61]

Back in the legislature, the forced presence of Miley and McCalmont gave Republicans the quorum they needed. McCalmont, however, demanded his freedom. He had "been forcibly brought into the Assembly room, contrary to his wishes, this morning by a number of the citizens, whom he did not know," he said, and he "begged he might be dismissed." Republican Alexander Lowery insisted that McCalmont explain "why force was necessary to make him do his duty." FitzSimons shifted ground, and began to construct a defense of what the Republicans were about to do. He would "be glad to know" he said, "if any member of the House was guilty of forcing the gentlemen from the determination of absenting himself; if there was, he thought it necessary that the House mark such conduct with their disapprobation." Clearly, no member of the House had participated in the mob that carried McCalmont and Miley from their lodgings; but just as clearly, some members of the House had hoped, if not conspired, for just such an eventuality. This deceptively naive question, however, set the stage for the Republican self-justification. If no man in the House had forced McCalmont to attend, then, as Brackenridge made explicit, the House need not inquire into how McCalmont came to be in his seat. If he had been abused, if his rights had been infringed, if his dignity had been besmirched, then the Assembly would condemn such rude and unseemly

---

60. Hugh Henry Brackenridge, "Narrative of the Transactions of the late Session of Assembly," *Pittsburgh Gazette*, 10/27/87, in Jensen 2:MFM 167. H. H. Brackenridge, "Queries to the Assemblyman," *Pittsburgh Gazette*, 11/3/87, in Jensen 2:MFM 196.

61. Clerk's Report, Jensen 2:106.

action; but that was not the issue. The question the House must deal with was not how McCalmont came to be here, but whether to let him depart. FitzSimons answered the question unequivocably: since "the business of the state cannot be accomplished if anyone is suffered to withdraw, . . . it will be extremely improper for any member to leave this House until the laws and other unfinished business is completed."[62]

Most agreed, but Republican Robinson demurred. The House, he believed, could not keep a man against his will: "he cannot be detained as in prison. . . . Certainly you will not lock your doors." But FitzSimons was adamant: "yes, sir, if no other method could retain him." As he had already explained: "the member is now here, and we may determine that he shall stay, not only on constitutional ground, but from the law of nature that will not suffer any body to destroy its own existence prematurely."[63]

McCalmont tried a different tack. He demanded that the rules be read, offered to pay the five-shillings fine for unexcused absences, and pulled some coins from his pocket. The gallery laughed but the house was not amused. When McCalmont moved toward the door, the gallery, in great commotion, shouted "Stop him!" and blocked his way. McCalmont returned to his seat and the house then voted on the question: "Shall Mr. McCalmont have leave of absence?" which was determined, as Thomas Lloyd recorded it: "almost, if not quite, unanimously in the negative."[64]

With its quorum intact, the House proceeded to business. It scheduled the election of the state convention for the first Tuesday in November (the sixth), rejected McCalmont's motion that the convention meet in Lancaster instead of Philadelphia (by a vote of 15 to 30), and thanked the Speaker for his "able, upright, and faithful discharge of the important duties of his station." Then, in a simple move that speaks volumes about the all-pervasive reality of party among its members, the legislature gave each assemblyman a warrant for his pay, consigning to McCalmont "those intended for the members who had withdrawn themselves." With that the Eleventh Pennsylvania General Assembly adjourned sine die. The *Pennsylvania Gazette* reported that the "many hundred citizens" attendant at the session gave "three heartfelt cheers,"

62. Jensen 2:104.
63. Jensen 2:107, 108.
64. Jensen 2:109.

and "the bells of Christ [Episcopal] Church rang during the greatest part of Saturday."[65]

The Republicans had won a stunning victory. They followed it with a blistering public denunciation of the nineteen absentees. In an essay dated October 6, six Republican assemblymen charged the nineteen Constitutionalists with committing "a misdemeanor" "deserving of the highest" punishment. They had "violated the first condition of all political society, which obliges the few to give way to the many." Hugh Henry Brackenridge also condemned the nineteen, describing the crowd as a posse called out by the sergeant. In Brackenridge's opinion, only the Assembly's hurry to be done and on its way kept it from punishing the absent members for contempt.[66]

Others, less party to the original controversy, supported the Republican assault. The *Pennsylvania Herald*, later accused of being Antifederal, described the "wanton desertion of [the] nineteen" as a "scandal" and a "gross . . . violation of civil polity."[67] "Tar and Feathers," equating Antifederalists with Tories and disciples of Shays, proudly proclaimed "That we have frequently during the revolution terrified . . . [them] . . . into a moderate line of conduct . . . [and] . . . Should our country again demand our aid, we shall cheerfully obey the summons."[68]

Some, but not many, expressed a different opinion. A letter dated Philadelphia and published in the *New York Morning Post* called the Federalist crowd, "Canaille . . . [who] forceably broke into the lodgings of Miley and McCalmont whom they riotously carried to the House of Assembly." "Fair Play" braved the threats of "Tar and Feathers" to denounce "the *aristocratical* plan proposed by the late Convention" and then leveled a charge that would run throughout the fall campaign: "that must be a most *noble* form of government indeed which requires such infamous measures to support and establish it. That would be a *mob* government with a witness!"[69]

65. Jensen 2:110. *Pennsylvania Gazette*, 10/3/87, in Jensen 2:124.
66. "The Reply of Six Assemblymen," *Pennsylvania Packet*, 10/8/87, in Jensen 2:117–20. Brackenridge, "Narrative," *Pittsburgh Gazette*, 10/27/87, in Jensen 2:MFM 167.
67. *Pennsylvania Herald*, 9/29/87, in Jensen 2:123–24. For a discussion of the controversy over the "bias" of the reporting in the *Herald*, see Jensen 2:36–42.
68. "Tar & Feathers," *Independent Gazetteer*, 10/2/87, in Jensen 2:152–53.
69. "Extract of a letter from Philadelphia," 10/3/87, in *N.Y. Morning Post*, 10/6/87. Jensen 2:MFM 93; "Fair Play," *Independent Gazetteer*, 9/29/87, in Jensen 2:149.

The precipitous, even violent behavior of the Republicans had confirmed the growing Constitutionalist suspicion of a Republican conspiracy to foist the Federal Constitution on an unwary people. It also heightened their awareness that the principles of the Federal Constitution challenged those of the state constitution of 1776, which the Constitutionalists had long defended.

Before leaving town the dissident members defended their action in an "Address of the Subscribers Members of the late House of Representatives . . . to their Constituents." Everything about this broadside stamped it a Constitutionalist document. Constitutionalist leaders drafted the "Address" at a party caucus at Boyd's, the Constitutionalists' boardinghouse. In all likelihood, they worked under the guidance of Judge George Bryan, the titular head of the party.[70] Sixteen of the nineteen seceders signed it, including the leading and most conspicuous Constitutionalists in the legislature, and the document spoke directly to a Constitutionalist audience. Although its title proclaimed it an "Address . . . to their Constituents," its authors assumed that they spoke to those who "on every occasion manifested . . . attachment" to the state constitution of 1776.[71]

In the same vein the document's basic rhetorical strategy focused readers' attention on the Republican origins, the Republican implications, and the Republican support of the Federal Constitution. The first half of the "Address" branded the Federal Constitution a document drafted by "men who have been uniformly opposed to that constitution

---

70. The sergeant at arms reported that on Friday afternoon, September 28, he found Whitehill, Findley, and "several other members (being the whole of the minority upon the question of calling a convention, except Mr. Brown)" at the house of Alexander Boyd along with John Smilie and James McLean, leading Constitutionalists from the Supreme Executive Council. "Assembly Debates (Dallas), Friday 9/28/87," *Pennsylvania Herald*, 9/29/87, in Jensen 2:MFM 74. "Foederal Constitution" charged that "several of the persons whose names are subscribed to [the Address] left the city on Saturday, before there was time . . . to receive it from the *person* who is well known to have written it." The editors speculate that "the person" was perhaps George Bryan. *Pennsylvania Gazette*, 10/10/87, in Kaminski and Saladino 13:362, 366.

71. "The Address of the Seceding Assemblymen," Saturday, 9/29/87, Philadelphia, 10/2/87, in Jensen 2:112–17. Conflating constituents with partisans is consistent with the Constitutionalists' tendency to define "the people" narrowly and exclusively. The identity of the actual author(s) remains unknown. The Republicans charged that none of its signers had written it. *Pennsylvania Gazette*, 10/10/87, in Kaminski and Saladino 13:362. Findley later conceded that not all had participated in its drafting. "Assemblyman," *Pennsylvania Gazette*, 10/27/87, in Jensen 2:MFM 166. It seems likely that Judge George Bryan or his son, Samuel, supervised its creation.

[the state constitution of 1776]" and rushed through the legislature by the arbitrary Republican majority "with design to preclude you from having it in your power to deliberate on the subject."[72]

In a subordinate and complementary way, the broadside also sought to inflame rural resentment of the city, and to enkindle landed fears of the commercial interest. It pointed out that Pennsylvania had been represented at the convention by men "who were all citizens of Philadelphia, none of them calculated to represent the landed interests of Pennsylvania," and it gave much attention to the insults offered to the rural representatives and their home counties by the citizens of Philadelphia who had so abused McCalmont and Miley.[73]

The second half of the "Address" purported to examine the text of the proposed Federal Constitution but in fact devoted much of its attention to repeating the charges of a Republican conspiracy. Its authors admitted that they, too, felt the need for augmenting the power of Congress, but insisted that they expected the Grand Convention to recommend revisions or amendments to the Articles of Confederation, not to annihilate it. They quoted at length from the December 1786 Pennsylvania statute defining the purposes for which Pennsylvania sent delegates to the Grand Convention to show that the delegates had exceeded their power, and they twice listed the names of the delegates. Since most of those who had represented Pennsylvania at the Grand Convention were well-known Republicans, the lists indirectly but powerfully strengthened the charge of Republican conspiracy.

Late in its argument, the "Address" recited a short litany of particular criticisms against the proposed Federal Constitution. Even here, however, some of the particulars carried partisan overtones by highlighting the differences between the state's annually elected unicameral legislature and the Federal Constitution's proposal to create a "legislature consisting of three branches, neither of them chosen annually."[74]

The "Address" of the seceding Constitutionalists, in conjunction with the Republican tactics in the legislature, thus defined the immediate

---

72. Jensen 2:112, 113.
73. Jensen 2:112, 114.
74. Jensen 2:114–16. Pennsylvania's Antifederalists claimed that they would have accepted a proposal that simply augmented the external revenue, diplomatic, and commercial powers of Congress. See esp. Chapter 3, passim. Their earlier behavior was consistent with this claim. For example, a conspicuously Constitutionalist meeting in Bucks County in the summer of 1783 had demanded a "convention to amend the Confederation." *Pennsylvania Packet* 8/7/83, reporting in a political meeting at Bennett's Tavern on 7/29/83.

political framework within which the election of a convention would take place. It grounded opposition to the Federal Constitution in fear of a Republican conspiracy, in fear of unbridled central power with internal taxing powers, and in fear of threats to the state constitution that had, in the minds of its supporters, ably protected the rights and liberties of the people of Pennsylvania.[75]

Pennsylvania led the nation in calling a convention to consider the proposed Constitution, but the Republicans had taken a serious risk. With their approval, if not under their leadership, the "people" acting out-of-doors, in an extralegal manner, had imposed their will on members whose behavior threatened policies these people favored. This kind of crowd behavior, this violent handling and abuse of officers of civil government, had deep historic roots in the English-speaking world. It had played a major role in the coming of the American Revolution. The people had also used it to punish its perceived enemies. In 1779 the Philadelphia crowd had vented its anger at monopolizers and forestallers who inflated the price of bread, and at Tories, trimmers (those who trimmed their sails to the prevailing wind), the disaffected, and the "wives and children of those who had gone with the British." But, crowd action against a tyrant, against Tories, against the disaffected was one thing. Crowd action against popularly elected and legally constituted assemblymen in the independent commonwealth of Pennsylvania was quite another matter.[76]

Phineas Bond, the British consul in Philadelphia, writing to the British foreign secretary, worried about the unfortunate precedent this established: "The measure of force was, in this crisis of public affairs, deemed inevitable, but the expedient is a dangerous one, and may perhaps be retaliated upon some future occasion."[77]

Local political observers also anticipated trouble. Francis Johnson wrote to Pickering on October 1: "The public mi[nd] seems much

---

75. "The Gander," no. 2, on October 6, condemned both parties for turning the Federal Constitution into a partisan issue. *Pennsylvania Herald*, 10/6/87, in Jensen 2:MFM 111. On October 15 the *Connecticut Current* reported that "These proceedings . . . arise from a despicable party spirit," Jensen 2:MFM 131. By October 20 the *Pennsylvania Herald* summed the consensus: "party, so far from subsiding, seems to have collected additional vigor and virulence," Jensen 2:MFM 150.
76. See John K. Alexander, "The Fort Wilson Incident of 1779: A Case Study of the Revolutionary Crowd," *William and Mary Quarterly* 31 (October 1974): 589–612, esp. 600–602.
77. Phineas Bond to marquis of Carmarthen, Philadelphia, 9/29/87, in Jensen 2:MFM 83.

irritated at present and how this affair will end I really cannot pretend to say." The next day William Bradford, Jr., attorney general of Pennsylvania, predicted: "We shall have very serious disputes in Pennsylvania. . . . [T]here was an exhibition of folly on both sides."[78]

Republicans had used tactics that exemplified what they themselves had long said they most feared and distrusted about Pennsylvania politics: its volatile passions, its lack of restraint, and its violation of the rights and liberties of dissident minorities.

On a more immediate and practical level the Republicans, by resorting to violence and intimidation, had fueled Constitutionalist charges of conspiracy and tarnished the document that Republicans favored. Some observers believed that the Republicans had needlessly provoked a partisan response. Louis-Guillaume Otto, the French chargé d'affaires in New York reported home: "in forcing the minority to consent to the ratification [sic] of the new government without investigation, the legislature made use of a harshness and a precipitancy that should render this government very suspect." The French chargé credited the Republicans with the revival of a dormant partisan spirit and thereby the risk of ultimate popular rejection: "The public . . . seemed disposed to admire it [the Constitution] on the whole when the imprudence of the legislative Assembly . . . all at once revived the jealousy and the anxiety of the democratic party. . . . The alarm is sounded, the public is on its guard and they begin to examine strictly what they would have adopted almost blindly."[79]

James Madison arrived at a similar conclusion. "An unlucky ferment on the subject in their Assembly just before its late adjournment," he wrote to Thomas Jefferson, "has irritated both sides, particularly the opposition, and by redoubling the exertions of that party may render the event doubtful." Edward Carrington wrote to Jefferson at about the same time in less pessimistic terms: "Gentlemen well acquainted with the Country are of the opinion that their [the Seceders from the upper counties] opposition will have no extensive effect, as there is, in general, a Coalescence of the two parties . . . in support of the new Government." The difficulties that did emerge, however, Carrington attributed largely to the behavior of the Republicans. "The opposition" he wrote, "has

---

78. Francis Johnston to Timothy Pickering, Philadelphia, 10/8/87, in Jensen 2:MFM 87; William Bradford, 10/2/87, Jensen 2:MFM 88; Louis-Guillaume Otto to comte de Montmorin, New York, 10/10/87, in Jensen 2:124–26.
79. Otto, 10/10/87, in Jensen 2:125.

assumed a form somewhat more serious, but under circumstances which leave it doubtful whether it is founded in objection to the project or the intemperance of its more zealous friends." "[I]t is to be doubted" he concluded, "whether they [the Seceders] would have set themselves in opposition to it, had more moderation been used."[80]

Although the three commentators differed in their assessments of the magnitude of the opposition, they agreed that most of its intensity, and much of its size, was due to "the imprudence of the legislative Assembly," their "unlucky ferment," and "the intemperance of its more zealous friends"; in short, to the behavior of the Republicans and the response of the Constitutionalists.

To some degree Otto, Madison, and Carrington were correct. The precipitous action of the Republicans certainly alerted Constitutionalists to the provincial and partisan significance of the question. The Republican behavior may also have intensified, even possibly accelerated, the Constitutionalists' scrutiny of the document.

On the other hand, the nature of the Federal Constitution itself virtually guaranteed opposition by the state Constitutionalists. As all observers soon agreed, ratifying and implementing the proposal directly challenged the principles on which the state constitution rested. As the Seceding Assemblymen said in their "Address," they distrusted the proposal not because it attacked the obvious weaknesses of the union, but because it went far beyond what all agreed was necessary to solve those problems. In their minds, the Federal Constitution proposed to alter, fundamentally, both the relationship of the state to the national government, and the internal politics of the state itself.[81]

Twice before the Republicans had launched massive but ultimately unsuccessful frontal assaults on the state constitution. The Federal Constitution offered them a third and possibly a final opportunity.

80. James Madison to Thomas Jefferson, New York, 10/24/87, in Julian P. Boyd, ed., *The Papers of Thomas Jefferson* (Princeton: Princeton University Press, 1955), 12:281; Edward Carrington to Thomas Jefferson, New York, 10/23/87, J. Boyd, *Papers of Jefferson*, 12:253–54.

81. The Constitutionalists had long supported strengthening the powers of the "Continental Government"; they supported the calling of the Constitutional Convention; and they shared the general enthusiasm for the Convention throughout the summer and early fall of 1787. Late in the summer of 1787 the antics of some Republicans had made Constitutionalists uneasy, and apparently the core of the Constitutionalist leadership saw the partisan significance of the proposal almost immediately upon its publication. See David Redick to William Irvine, Philadelphia, 9/24/87, in Jensen 2:135–36; William Lewis to Thomas Lee Shippen, Philadelphia, 10/11/87, in Jensen 2:MFM 125.

Knowing that their opponents would resist mightily once the significance of the Constitution became clear, the Republicans had decided to strike hard and early.[82]

Hindsight suggests that the Republicans were both right and wrong: right in the sense that their swift action inhibited Antifederalist organization and opposition; and right also in that the Republicans ultimately won. They were wrong, however, in their initial estimate of the magnitude of the opposition they faced and hence wrong in their fear, their anxiety, and their perception of the need for haste. As the history of the contest demonstrates, Antifederalists, even with unlimited time and resources, had little chance of mobilizing an effective opposition to ratification.

In the fall of 1787, however, neither side could be sure of this, and by the end of September, the ratification fight had begun. Republicans, now the Federalists, defended the Federal Constitution with the language of popular sovereignty, contract theory, and the people's power to make and unmake governments. They remained unsure, however, of their ability to mobilize a popular majority in a protracted contest. The Constitutionalists, now Antifederalists, condemned the Federal Constitution as a Republican document that would not bear close scrutiny, and remained confident of their ability once again to rally the people to their cause. But they had been sobered (if not a little intimidated) by their rough treatment at the hands of the urban "rabble."[83] These partisan dimensions of the coming contest, revealed first in the late September fight over calling a convention, largely shaped the strategies developed by both Federalists and Antifederalists in the next phase of the ratification battle.

---

82. See Rakove, *Beginnings*, 381–92 and esp. 392, 396.
83. A news item on November 1, 1787, epitomizes the close identity between party and response to the Federal Constitution. The editor casually applied the two party labels of Republican and Constitutionalist to the respective Federalist and Antifederalist slates of candidates. *Independent Gazetteer*, 11/1/87.

2
The Fall Campaign
October–November 1787

The fate of the Federal Constitution in Pennsylvania now rested with the people. On November 6, 1787, they would elect delegates to a state convention that would, in turn, accept or reject the new frame of government. Both opponents and supporters of the proposal, anxious to shape the popular response, launched vigorous political campaigns. In the end, the Federalists won an overwhelming majority of the seats in the convention, assuring Pennsylvania's ratification.

Explaining that outcome is a difficult task. Most of the participants in the contest left us little written evidence about themselves and even less about their motives: a letter here; a diary there; signatures on a petition for a few; but for most, silence and anonymity. We must, therefore, approach them indirectly.

The public debates in the newspapers provide us with a starting point. Naturally, this campaign rhetoric must be used cautiously. Some authors may have been less than candid. Some may have misjudged their audience; others may have written with little thought about their intended readership. Further complicating the analysis, a welter of different, and sometimes conflicting, voices clamored for attention on each side of the issue.

Despite these limitations, however, the press debates can serve as a useful tool for probing the publicists' perception of the electorate. Surely, most of these penmen wrote to persuade. Hence the assumptions they made about the audience they addressed provide us with access to some of the best available contemporary understanding of the values and the interests of the voting public. The challenge is to identify the most frequent and persistent lines of argument on each side of the debate and then infer from these common patterns (1) the essential elements in the electoral strategy of the Federalists and the Antifederalists, and (2) the assumptions each made about the electorate.[1] This chapter considers each in turn.

The Antifederalists

Pennsylvania's Antifederalists faced an uphill struggle. They sought to persuade a majority of the voters to reject a document that came from the popular and prestigious "Grand Convention," which had promised the domestic tranquillity, economic revival, and international stature most Pennsylvanians sought, and which had had the support of authentic Revolutionary heroes such as George Washington and Benjamin Franklin. No easy task.[2] The Antifederalists' campaign literature suggests how they hoped to achieve their goal. An adequate appreciation of the implications of that body of evidence, however, requires a brief exploration of the recent political history of Pennsylvania, and especially the career of George Bryan, the titular head of the Constitutionalist

---

1. This analysis rests on a study of the entire body of extant literature but it is complemented by a quantitative analysis of a subset of some 550 Antifederalist and Federalist publications in four newspapers over a span of seven months. This systematic content analysis provides a useful baseline against which to evaluate impressions and insights derived from the total corpus of literature produced by these verbose and vigorous publicists. See Appendix 1.

2. Philadelphia newspapers had, with near unanimity, praised the Grand Convention lavishly for much of the previous six or seven months. See John K. Alexander, *The Selling of The Constitutional Convention: A History of News Coverage* (Madison, Wisc.: Madison House, 1990).

party and the one man most responsible for the initial definition of the Antifederalist position.

Born and raised a Presbyterian in a mercantile family in Ireland, Bryan had migrated to Philadelphia as a young man. Within a decade of his arrival, he had emerged as one of the most successful merchants in the city, as one of the most conspicuous lay leaders of the Presbyterians, and as one of the most active members of the Proprietary party (the loose political network surrounding the proprietary governor of the colony). When the conflict between Great Britain and her North American colonies erupted in the 1760s, Bryan, along with such Proprietary colleagues as John Dickinson, Robert Morris, James Wilson, William Allen, Joseph Hart, and Thomas McKean, led Pennsylvania's resistance.[3]

As Pennsylvania moved toward revolution, however, Bryan dropped from sight. Since his business failure in the early 1770s he had depended on public office under the proprietor. Agitation against British policy was one thing; the destruction of the government upon which he depended for his livelihood was quite another. In the summer and fall of 1776, while Pennsylvania declared independence, underwent a dramatic "internal revolution," and drafted a new state constitution, Bryan remained largely invisible.[4]

In the late winter of 1776–77 Bryan reemerged. He won election to a seat in the executive branch of the new government (the Supreme Executive Council), and then the vice presidency. A year later the death of the president made Bryan responsible for the day-to-day administration of the state.

---

3. This and the following paragraphs on Bryan's career and on Pennsylvania politics rely principally on Joseph Foster, *In Pursuit of Equal Liberty: George Bryan and the Revolution in Pennsylvania* (University Park: Pennsylvania State University Press, 1994); W. Bockelman and O. S. Ireland, "The Internal Revolution in Pennsylvania: An Ethnic-Religious Interpretation," *Pennsylvania History* 41 (1974): 125–59; and O. S. Ireland, "The Ethnic-Religious Dimension of Pennsylvania Politics, 1778–1779," *William and Mary Quarterly* 30 (1973): 423–48. For more on the Proprietary party, see James H. Hutson, *Pennsylvania Politics, 1746–1770* (Princeton: Princeton University Press, 1974) as well as Allen Tully, "Ethnicity, Religion and Politics in Early America," *Pennsylvania Magazine of History and Biography* [hereafter PMHB] 107 (October 1985); and Tully, *William Penn's Legacy: Politics and Social Structure in Provincial Pennsylvania, 1726–1755* (Baltimore: Johns Hopkins University Press, 1977).

4. Roland Baumann also describes Bryan as "a late convert to the Radicals' cause." Baumann, "The Democratic-Republicans of Philadelphia: The Origins, 1776–1797" (Ph.D. diss., Pennsylvania State University, 1970), 22.

By the spring of 1777, Pennsylvania's new government teetered on the brink of collapse. Many of the state's most prominent patriots argued that the state's constitution, by lodging all effective power in a unicameral legislature, threatened liberty. They demanded a two-house legislature and an independent executive. To strengthen their bargaining position, they refused to accept public offices until the constitution was revised. Bryan, with a vested interest in preserving the system that now employed him, campaigned for support. He wrote and published essays in defense of the state constitution, and urged his former Proprietary party colleagues to accept public office under it.[5]

Most of Bryan's former Anglican associates remained opposed, but he made substantial progress in recruiting those who shared his Presbyterian faith. In time, Thomas McKean became the state's chief justice; Joseph Reed its president; John Bayard the Speaker of the House; Jonathan B. Smith the prothonotary of Philadelphia; and John Ewing, pastor of Bryan's Presbyterian congregation, the provost of the new University of Pennsylvania.[6]

---

5. For a range of interpretations on the origins of the state constitution of 1776 and its role in dividing the patriots in 1776, see Brunhouse, *The Counter-Revolution in Pennsylvania, 1776–1790* (Harrisburg: Historical Commission, 1942); J. Paul Selsam, *The Pennsylvania Constitution of 1776. A Study in Revolutionary Democracy* (Philadelphia: University of Pennsylvania Press, 1935); Douglas Arnold "Political Ideology and the Internal Revolution In Pennsylvania, 1776–1790" (Ph.D. diss., Princeton University, 1976); now available, with a new introduction under the title *A Republican Revolution: Ideology and Politics in Pennsylvania, 1776–1790* (New York: Garland, 1989). David F. Hawke, *In the Midst of a Revolution* (Philadelphia: University of Pennsylvania Press, 1961); Eric Foner, *Thomas Paine and Revolutionary America* (New York: Oxford University Press, 1975); Steven Rosswurm, *Arms, Country, and Class: The Philadelphia Militia and the "Lower Sort" During the American Revolution, 1775–1783* (New Brunswick, N.J.: Rutgers University Press, 1987); and Ryerson, *The Revolution is Now Begun: The Radical Committees of Philadelphia, 1765–1776* (Philadelphia: University of Pennsylvania Press, 1978). Much work remains to be done on the nature and the meaning of the original controversy over the unicameral legislature. For our purposes, however, the relevant point is not the initial dispute in the fall of 1776 but how that question evolved over the next two years to produce, by 1778–79, two identifiable political configurations, each with a name, a well-defined stand on a range of policy issues, and a loyal, ethnoreligious electoral base.

6. For the Presbyterians' numerical domination of Pennsylvania's new government, and their increasing political self-consciousness, see Bockelman and Ireland, "The Internal Revolution," *Pennsylvania History* 41 (1974): 105–59. For a description of the office of prothonotary and its power and influence, see Francis S. Fox, "The Prothonotary: Linchpin of Provincial and State Government in Eighteenth-Century Pennsylvania," *Pennsylvania History* 59 (January 1992): 41–53. For more details on the "slow and subtle transformation of the Radical party" under Bryan and Jonathan B. Smith, see Baumann, "Democratic-Republicans," 22–23. Baumann adds William Moore, John Nicholson, Dr. James Hutchinson, and David Ritten-

These men then joined with the Presbyterian mercantile elite in the city and a core of Presbyterian leaders in the backcountry to led the new Constitutionalist party. With the support of a predominantly Presbyterian and Reformed electorate they soon dominated the state's all-powerful, unicameral legislature. Firmly in control by 1778, they defended the state constitution under which they had come to power, and then turned on their enemies, punishing Tories and traitors, disenfranchising pacifists and neutrals (especially Quakers and German Sectarians) and replacing the Anglican-controlled College of Philadelphia with the Presbyterian-dominated University of Pennsylvania.[7]

Attacks by the Constitutionalists drove Anglicans, Quakers, German Sectarians, and Lutherans into the emerging Republican coalition headed largely by Anglicans from the old Proprietary party. Then, from 1778 through 1787, Presbyterian-led Constitutionalists and the Anglican-led Republicans defined partisan politics in Pennsylvania. Throughout the decade the political leadership, the membership of the Assembly, and the electorate consistently divided along ethnic-religious lines: Scots-Irish Presbyterians and German and Dutch Reformed largely made up the Constitutionalist party while English Anglicans and their Quaker, Lutheran, and German Sectarian allies formed the basis for the Republican party. Party tickets and political patronage reflected these ethnic and religious divisions while institutions identified with one group or another rose and fell with the fortunes of their political patrons. It was to the long-standing supporters of the Constitutionalist party that George Bryan and his son Samuel appealed in the essay that inaugurated the Antifederalist campaign on October 5, 1787: the first of a series of eighteen essays signed "Centinel."[8]

---

house to this educated, middle-class, primarily Presbyterian and mostly Irish group of Bryanites.

7. Close analysis of 287 men who served in six annual legislatures (the Third, 1778–79; the Fifth, 1780–81; the Seventh, 1782–83; the Ninth, 1784–85; the Eleventh, 1786–87; and the Thirteenth, 1788–89) indicates that 239 (83 percent) voted consistently with either the Constitutionalists or the Republicans. Of those for whom religious data are available, 71 percent of the Calvinists voted with the Constitutionalists; 82 percent of the non-Calvinists voted with the Republicans. Presbyterian and Reformed assemblymen voted better than two to one with the Constitutionalists. Anglicans and Quakers voted a little more than ten to one with the Republicans. These patterns were independent of geographic, economic, and occupational differences. See Ireland, "The Crux of Politics: Religion and Party in Pennsylvania, 1778–1789," *William and Mary Quarterly* 42 (1985): 453–95, esp. 458, 461, 465, 466, 467.

8. For detailed analysis of the elected leadership, the policies, and the electoral base of both

Although published anonymously, most knowledgeable Pennsylvanians assumed, correctly, that this essay, as well as those that followed, emanated from the Bryan household and therefore carried the stamp of partisan approval.[9] Furthermore, the pseudonym "Centinel" carried strong reminders of earlier religious political struggles. In the 1760s George Bryan had joined with two others in publishing a series of "Centinel" essays attacking proposals to bring an Anglican bishop to America.[10] This earlier "Centinel" had denounced the "Arrogance and Superciliousness" of the "High Church Anglican clergy"; the "Maintenance" of bishops; compulsory tithes; episcopal courts; personal corruption; the monopoly of places of power and profit reserved for church members; and the "pride of supposed right opinion" that leads to "inquisitions, tortures and death."[11]

At the time, Bryan had been an active member of the Proprietary party in which Presbyterians had collaborated with such prominent Anglicans as Benjamin Chew, William Moore, Jacob Douché and the Reverend William Smith, provost of the College of Philadelphia. Presbyterians and Anglicans, however, reacted differently to the prospect of an Anglican bishop in America, and the anti-Anglican "Centinel" essays exacerbated these religious tensions.[12]

Twenty years later, in 1787, Bryan's choice of the pseudonym "Centinel" thus linked the earlier religious conflict to the current dispute over the Federal Constitution. It identified the Federalists with hierarchical, authoritarian English Anglicanism, and associated Antifederalists with that largely Presbyterian group that led the fight against an Anglican bishop. Antifederalism in Pennsylvania thus began with a strident anti-Anglican (now anti-Episcopalian) orientation.

---

the Constitutionalists and the Republicans from 1778 through 1789, see Ireland, "The Ethnic-Religious Dimension," *William and Mary Quarterly* 30 (1973): 423–48 and Ireland, "The Crux of Politics."

9. For more on the authorship of the "Centinel" essays, see John P. Kaminski and Gaspare J. Saladino, eds., *The Documentary History of the Ratification of the Constitution*, vol. 13, *The Commentaries on the Constitution* (Madison, Wisc.: State Historical Society of Wisconsin, 1981): 326–28.

10. Elizabeth I. Nybakken, ed. and intro., *The Centinel: Warnings of a Revolution* (Newark: University of Delaware Press, 1980), contains biographical sketches of two of the authors, Francis Alison and Bryan, and a narrative of the controversy over the establishment of an Anglican bishop in the 1760s, as well as the text of these original "Centinel" essays.

11. See Nybakken, *Centinel*.

12. See Hutson, *Pennsylvania Politics*, esp. 209–14 for tensions within the Proprietary Party and the emergence of a Presbyterian Party.

Pennsylvania's prevailing political mores added particular significance to Bryan's choice of this name. By common consent, political spokesmen seldom attacked identifiable religious groups. The religious scurrility surrounding the "March of the Paxton Boys" in the 1760s had made many Pennsylvanians uneasy, and the brief but intense flare-up between Deist and Trinitarian patriots in the dispute over the new state constitution in the fall of 1776 had worried gentlemen on both sides. Seldom thereafter did leaders of either party transgress that unwritten rule. As a result, popular political rhetoric seldom reflected the underlying ethnic-religious basis of party identification.[13]

The debates over ratification of the Federal Constitution in 1787–88 generally followed this pattern but one exception stands out. An essay signed "An Old Constitutionalist" criticized the initial Presbyterian enthusiasm for the proposed Federal Constitution, especially, he said, "when their '[the P—s] overthrow seems almost unanimously to be determined upon by all the different religions . . ." Deploring popular hostility against the Presbyterians and praising them for procuring the "liberty and independence of the United States" and for dominating the state constitutional convention of 1776, he thus explicitly linked Presbyterians, the Revolution, Constitutionalists, and Antifederalists. What the "Old Constitutionalist" did directly, the pseudonym "Centinel" did indirectly, repeatedly, and powerfully as it identified Antifederalism with those who, twenty years earlier, had led the fight against the Anglican bishop in Philadelphia.[14]

Thus, by its authorship as well as by its pseudonym, the first "Centinel" essay suggests the audience Pennsylvania's Antifederalists addressed: the religious dissenters in the Constitutionalist party who had long contended for control of the state against the Anglican-led Republicans. The main line of argument of the first "Centinel" essay

---

13. O. S. Ireland, "The Religious Dimensions of the First Debate on the Pennsylvania State Constitution, Fall 1776," unpublished paper. Historian Kenneth Keller also found that in Pennsylvania in the 1790s political leaders discussed ethnic and religious blocs in private, built balanced ethnic and religious tickets, and carefully allotted patronage to key ethnic and religious groups, but seldom if ever made explicit appeals to ethnic and religious groups. Keller concludes that although "it was considered especially unethical to depend upon what fashionable gentlemen called 'bigotry' in cultivating the electorate, . . . *it was an effective tactic*" (my emphasis). Kenneth Keller, "Divinity and Democracy: Ethnic Politics in Southeastern Pennsylvania, 1788–1799" (Ph.D. diss., Yale University, 1971), esp. 77–79, 82–83, 95, 108.

14. *Independent Gazetteer*, 10/26/87.

made explicit the link between support of the state constitution and opposition to the Federal Constitution.

The first sentence of the essay defined its central thrust: "Friends, Countrymen and Fellow Citizens: Permit one of yourselves to put you in mind of certain *liberties* and *privileges* secured to you by the constitution of this commonwealth . . . before you surrender [them] . . . up forever." Each of the next four sentences began with explicit reference to the state constitution:

> Your present frame of government secures to you a right to hold yourselves, houses, papers and possessions free from search and seizure . . .
>
> Your constitution further provides "that in controversies respecting property, and in suits between man and man, the parties have a right *to trial by jury* . . ."
>
> It also provides and declares, *"that the people have a right of FREEDOM OF SPEECH, and of WRITING and PUBLISHING their sentiments, . . ."*
>
> The constitution of Pennsylvania is *yet* in existence, *as yet* you have the right to *freedom of speech,* . . . and of *publishing your sentiments.*

This opening paragraph ended by reasserting the conclusion implicit in its first sentence: the Federal Constitution threatened the state constitution and thereby threatened the rights and the privileges of the people of Pennsylvania.[15]

After a substantial digression intended to neutralize the influence of George Washington and Benjamin Franklin, "Centinel" then plunged into its main argument: the principles of the state constitution versus those of the Federal Constitution; unicameral versus bicameral legislatures; simple, direct, responsible, and democratic government versus complex, balanced, and aristocratic government. He praised the former and ridiculed the latter.

The first major Antifederalist publication defined the emerging controversy principally in terms of ethnic-religious party loyalties. Its

---

15. *Independent Gazetteer*, 10/5/87, in Jensen 2:158–67.

presumed authorship, its use of the religiously salient name "Centinel," and its central line of argument all appealed to those who had long supported the Constitutionalists: Presbyterian and Reformed voters. This "Centinel" also contained a number of less prominent themes, and over time other Antifederalist publicists gave increased attention to some of these. Although the appeal to defenders of the state constitution was never far from the surface, the growing prominence of additional lines of argument suggests an effort to broaden the appeal and reach a more varied and heterogeneous audience. Take for instance, the question of a bill of rights.

The Federal Constitution did not explicitly protect freedom of the press, trial by jury, religious liberty, and the rights of conscientious objectors. This omission provided Pennsylvania's Antifederalists with a means to appeal beyond their traditional constituency. "Centinel" argued that the failure of the framers to guarantee free inquiry and jury trials revealed their despotic and aristocratic intentions. As the campaign evolved, later "Centinel" essays as well as other Antifederalist publications gave increased prominence to this concern for the protection of individual civil liberties. Trial by jury and freedom of press remained central, but liberty of conscience, which was an important issue in Pennsylvania, promised significant electoral rewards and hence drew frequent attention in the Antifederalist literature.

In broad terms, Pennsylvania's religious heterogeneity demanded practical toleration. Few denominations, aside from Quakers and possibly Baptists, supported the principle of separation of church and state. On a practical level, however, since no denomination could expect to dominate, the autonomy of each depended upon working toleration for all.

Antifederalists thus tilled potentially fertile soil when they emphasized the failure of the Federal Constitution to protect "liberty of conscience." The essay, "An Old Wig V," illustrates the approach. Published about a week before the November election, the piece began with the question of a bill of rights but quickly narrowed its focus to religion. The Constitution's failure to protect religious freedom, it argued, opened the door for a "zealot" to create a religious establishment, enforce religious orthodoxy, and use the taxing and military power of the central government to "invade the rights of conscience." With a special eye on the pacifist Quakers and German Sectarians, the essay threatened that those "conscientiously scrupulous of bearing arms" might be "dragged like a Prussian soldier to the camp."[16]

To heighten concern among these same groups, Antifederalists also linked liberty of conscience with the slavery issue. Suppose, "Philadelphiensis" said, that the slaves in a southern state, "prompted by the love of *sacred liberty*" rebelled. The government under the new Constitution could order the Pennsylvania militia to "march off to quell this insurrection." Since the Federal Constitution did not protect religious liberty, the government of the United States could also force those "conscientiously scrupulous against bearing arms" to fight to restore slavery.[17]

In theory, at least, this blending of concerns for religious liberty with apprehensions about military service and the perpetuation of slavery could have provided a persuasive argument for Quaker and Sectarian support of the Antifederalist cause. Unfortunately for them, the Antifederalists identification of themselves with the Constitutionalists frustrated this approach.

Too much had happened in the past to allow Quakers and Sectarians to join easily in a political coalition dominated by conspicuous Constitutionalists. Early in the Revolution, Presbyterians had harassed pacifist and neutral Quakers, sending many of their leading spokesmen into exile in the interior of Virginia where one died and the rest suffered. From 1778 on, Constitutionalist majorities in the legislature had used the Test Acts to coerce Quakers and Sectarians into support of the Revolution. The laws disenfranchised those refusing to take a loyalty oath, subjected them to double taxes, and interfered with the practice of their professions, the conduct of their schools, and the transfer of property to their heirs. After the war, Constitutionalists continued to resist Republican efforts to open the door to reconciliation. In 1787 at least some Quakers and pacifist Sectarians still suffered the political

---

16. "An Old Whig," 5, *Independent Gazetteer*, 11/1/87, in Kaminski and Saladino 13:534–43, esp. 540–41.

17. "Philadelphiensis" 2, *Freeman's Journal*, 11/28/87, in Kaminski and Saladino 14:253. In addition, slavery was, undoubtedly, an important personal issue for George Bryan himself. He had played a major role in building the coalition of Presbyterians, Anglicans, and Quakers to pass Pennsylvania's 1779 act for the gradual abolition of slavery. Here, at least for Bryan, principle and politics coincided. O. S. Ireland, "Germans Against Abolition: A Minority's View of Slavery in Revolutionary Pennsylvania," *Journal of Interdisciplinary History* 3 (1973): 685–706.

disabilities imposed upon then by earlier Constitutionalist-supported legislation.[18]

Antifederalists often claimed Quaker support but logic and the limited evidence we have suggests otherwise. For example, Quaker James Pemberton, chastised by Quaker leaders in other states for his people's early support of the ratification, admitted the truth of the charge. Many Quakers, he said, had indeed signed Federalist petitions in September 1787. He claimed, however, that Quaker leaders in Pennsylvania were seeking, with varying degrees of success, to prevent their people from publicly advocating ratification of the proposal.[19]

In the same vein, in Bucks County, an Antifederalist organizer gave up the struggle in the face of what he saw as solid Quaker support for ratification. In the city, one of the leading Antifederalists lamented that the Quakers, "the professed enemies of *negro* and every other species of *slavery*, should themselves join in the adoption of a constitution [the Federal Constitution] whose very basis is *despotism* and *slavery*."[20]

Antifederalists also utilized a third line of argument: the internal or domestic powers of the new government threatened local political autonomy. The first "Centinel" essay, and innumerable other Antifederalist pieces through the campaign, asserted again and again that the Federal Constitution would melt the states down into one large political unit whose size and diversity would preclude a popular government responsible to local needs and respectful of individual liberties.[21]

In response, Federalists insisted that the Constitution conferred on the general government only specifically delegated powers, and that it reserved all other powers to the states. Antifederalists rejected this explanation. "Centinel" reminded his readers that the Articles of Confederation specifically reserved powers to the states but there is, he insisted, "*no reservation* made in the whole of this plan [the Federal Constitution] *in favor of the rights of the separate states*."[22]

---

18. See below, Chapter 7, as well as Ireland, "The Ethnic-Religious Dimension" and "The Crux" for more on the history of this controversy.
19. For a discussion of the Quaker response to the Federal Constitution and a collection of relevant documents, see Kaminski and Saladino 14:503–30. Pemberton to Moses Brown, 11/16/87, in Kaminski and Saladino 14:524.
20. See Chapter 7 below and "Philadelphiensis" 2, *Freeman's Journal*, 11/28/87 in Kaminski and Saladino 14:254.
21. *Independent Gazetteer*, 10/5/87, 10/9/87, 10/15/87, 10/27/87, 12/15/87, 2/13/88, 4/22/88; *Freeman's Journal*, 4/23/88.
22. Wilson, "Speech in the State House Yard," Philadelphia, 10/6/87, in Jensen 2:167;

Rather, Antifederalists argued, the Federal Constitution conferred virtually unlimited powers on the general government. Look at its key words, they insisted. The preamble begins: "We the people of the United States." This is "the style of a compact between individuals entering into a state of society, and not that of a confederation of states." The body of the document declares that acts of Congress as well as treaties are *"the supreme law of the land, . . . anything in the constitutions or laws of any state to the contrary notwithstanding."* The necessary and proper clause extends this authority by granting the general government power "to make all laws which shall be necessary and proper for carrying into execution the foregoing powers and all other powers vested by this constitution in the government of the United States." Under the new system the powers of "Congress extend to the lives of every citizen."[23]

More specifically, Congress would have control over the state militia; the federal government could raise and maintain a standing army in peacetime; and the federal judiciary would have appellate jurisdiction, in some cases with respect to both fact and law. Most important, the proposed Federal Constitution would grant the general government the right to impose internal, domestic taxes. "It is an established maxim," Antifederalists pointed out, "that wherever the whole power of revenues . . . is vested, there virtually it is the whole effective, influential, sovereign power."[24] "It is a solecism in politics," "Centinel" insisted, "for two co-ordinate sovereignties to exist together, you must separate the sphere of their jurisdiction or . . . one would necessarily triumph over the other."[25]

Lodging the power of the purse and the power of the sword in the central government, and then conferring upon the federal judiciary the right to try the citizens of the states virtually ensured tyranny. The army

---

"Centinel V," *Independent Gazetteer*, 12/4/87. Herbert J. Storing, ed., and comm., *The Complete Anti-Federalist*, vol. 2, *Objections of the Non-Signers . . . and Major Series of Essays at the Outset* (Chicago: University of Chicago Press, 1981), doc. 7, para. 97. Hereafter cited as Storing 2.7.97.

23. *Packet*, 12/18/87; "Centinel V," *Independent Gazetteer*, 12/4/87; "Cincinnatus No. 5," *Independent Gazetteer*, 12/15/87; "An Honest American," *Independent Gazetteer*, 1/19/88; "Centinel V," *Independent Gazetteer*, 12/4/87; "An Old Constitutionalist," *Independent Gazetteer*, 10/26/87; "An Officer of the Late Continental Army," *Independent Gazetteer*, 11/6/87.

24. "Argus," *Independent Gazetteer*, 1/5/88, "A correspondent," *Independent Gazetteer*, 10/9/87; *Independent Gazetteer*, 1/30/88; "A Farmer," *Independent Gazetteer*, 4/22/88.

25. *Independent Gazetteer*, 12/4/87, in Storing 2.7.99.

could collect the taxes imposed for its maintenance, while the courts, with the backing of the army, could punish those who refused to pay. Antifederalists warned that rapacious and lascivious tax gatherers could abuse our property, our rights, and even our wives. "Suppose," wrote one, that "the excise or revenue officers . . . having a warrant to search for stolen goods, pulled down the clothes of a bed in which there was a woman, and searched under her shift . . . what satisfaction can we expect from a lordly court of justice, always ready to protect the officers of government against the weak and helpless citizen, and who will perhaps sit at the distance of many hundred miles from the place where the outrage was committed?"[26]

This line of reasoning sought to rouse some of the deepest fears of America's revolutionaries: apprehension about remote, unresponsive, and tyrannical central authority. As "Centinel" reminded his readers, John Dickinson in his 1767 "Letters from a Pennsylvania Farmer," had made the same point in opposition to centralized British power: "[I]f the British Parliament assumed the power of taxing the colonies, *internally*, as well as *externally*," Dickinson had written, "the several colonial legislatures would . . . before long fall into disuse.—'Nothing,' says he, [Dickinson], 'would be left for them to do, higher than to frame bye-laws for empounding of cattle or the yoking of hogs.' "[27]

The charge of "aristocracy" also pervaded the Antifederalist public rhetoric. Vague and amorphous yet dangerous, this all-purpose pejorative stirred a range of popular worries from fear of monarchy, to the loss of local self-government, and the rise of hierarchical religious

---

26. *Packet*, 10/10/87, in John B. McMaster and Frederick D. Stone, eds., *Pennsylvania and the Federal Constitution, 1787–1788* (Philadelphia: Historical Society of Pennsylvania, 1888), 150–54.

27. "Pennsylvania Minority," *Packet*, 2/18/87; "Centinel V," *Independent Gazetteer*, 12/4/87, in Storing 2.7.97. "Centinel II," *Freeman's Journal*, 10/24/87, in Storing 2.7.96. Also see "Philadelphiensis" for a similar expression, Storing 3.9.15; and "Fallacies of the Freeman," *Independent Gazetteer*, 4/18,22/88 in Storing 3.14.1–23. For an excellent exploration of the popular concern in America from the 1760s through the 1790s with the question of internal taxes imposed by central authority, see Thomas Slaughter, "The Tax Man Cometh: Ideological Opposition to Internal Taxes, 1760–1790," *William and Mary Quarterly* 41 (1984): 566–91; and Slaughter, *The Whiskey Rebellion: Frontier Epilogue to the American Revolution* (New York: Oxford University Press, 1986), esp. chap. 1, where he argues that resistance to internal taxation, rooted in economic, historical, and ideological soils, linked the Antifederalists of 1787–88 with opposition to the Stamp Act of 1765 (p. 26) and to a century of opposition in Great Britain particularly associated with Irish, Scots, Welsh, and remote rural residents of England (12, 16).

establishments. Some Antifederalists emphasized the "aristocratic" tendencies in the presidency. They charged that the Constitution created a *"President-general,* who is to be our king . . . vested with powers exceeding those of the most *despotic monarch* we know of in modern times." He will be "commander in chief of the army, navy and militia; with power of making treaties and of granting pardons." He will be surrounded by placemen, ride in a "gilded chariot, set with diamonds," and be drawn by "eight Arabian horses." He will "greatly resemble in his powers the might *Abdul Ahmed,* our august *Sultan."* "The Senate will be his *Divan";* the standing army his *"Janissaries";* and "bishop *Seabury* will [be his] *Musel."*[28]

Antifederalists also charged that a consolidated national government with internal domestic powers must, by definition, be an aristocracy. Conventional wisdom decreed that only a monarchy or an aristocracy could govern a diverse population spread over a large area. Elected officials in large republics lose touch with their constituents; the people in turn lose faith in their rulers; government then must use force to compel the obedience that citizens in a small republic give freely to laws made by spokesmen who understand their needs and their interests.[29]

The structure of the central government also pointed toward aristocratic rule. Small legislative bodies meant large electoral districts in which men with wealth, status, and wide connections had an advantage over their equally honest and deserving but less prominent neighbors. The small size of both the Senate and the House gave privilege to some in the competition for public office. As "Centinel" phrased it: "[the Senate] who I suppose will be composed of the *better sort, the well born."*[30]

Finally, the bicameral legislature proposed for the Federal government also fueled Antifederalist charges of aristocracy and it is this argument that most effectively blends the aristocratic theme with defense of the state constitution. In the minds of some Pennsylvanians, a second house meant an upper house peopled by a special order of men.

---

28. *Independent Gazetteer,* 10/9/87, 11/1/87; "Philadelphiensis," *Independent Gazetteer,* 11/7/87; "Old Whig," *Independent Gazetteer,* 11/24/87; *Independent Gazetteer,* 10/13/87; *Independent Gazetteer,* 1/31/88, 2/19/88, 3/14/88; "Hum-Strum," *Independent Gazetteer,* 1/10/88. "Philadelphiensis," in Storing 3.9.22.

29. "Centinel I," *Independent Gazetteer,* 10/5/87 in Storing 2.7.22–24.

30. "Centinel I," *Independent Gazetteer,* 10/5/87. See also Storing 3.11.35 for a similar statement.

Pennsylvanians had been debating this question since 1776 when their new state constitution provided for a single-house legislature. Many at the time, imbued with the principles of the British Constitution, and well versed in the writings of the radical and not-so-radical English Whigs, took issue with this unicameral system. In short order, however, these opponents of the state constitution discovered, as Bernard Bailyn and Gordon Wood have shown us, that they had stumbled headlong into one of the central constitutional dilemmas of the American revolutionary era: how to have a multiple-branched government without a multiple-ordered society.[31]

The problem was this. Both before and after the Revolution, many Americans revered the British constitution with its threefold distribution of power among king, lords, and commons. In Britain, however, each of these three branches represented a distinct order of society, a well-defined social group.

After independence, most Americans assumed that a two-house legislature was essential, but they faced semantic and substantive problems. One house could represent the people, the commons, the democracy that traditional British constitutional parlance designated the "lower house." But who did the second and upper house represent? Republican America had only one order of people and wanted to remain so.

The supporters of the Pennsylvania state constitution of 1776 solved the problem by denying the need for a two-house legislature and the necessity of a legislative check. They followed the logic of the social reality. Pennsylvania's one order of people annually elected one house that did the people's will while remaining subject to popular scrutiny and discipline.[32]

Pennsylvania's anti-Constitutionalists, later organized as the Republican Society, rejected this path. In time, their public rhetoric recognized the state's one order of people as right and good. They did not propose a titled aristocracy, an hereditary nobility, or a royal family. Unlike their opponents, however, they could not envision a stable and benevolent government without internal checks and balances. Their education,

---

31. Gordon Wood, *The Creation of the American Republic, 1776–1787* (Chapel Hill: University of North Carolina Press, for the Institute of Early American History and Culture, Williamsburg, Va., 1969), especially chap. 6, 197–255; Bernard Bailyn, *The Ideological Origins of the American Revolution* (Cambridge: Belknap Press of Harvard University Press, 1967), especially "The Democracy Unleashed," 272–301.

32. Wood, *Creation*, esp. 226–51.

training and fundamental assumptions about human nature, all supported the judgment that unchecked, unlimited, and unbalanced power would ultimately destroy liberty. Power anywhere was dangerous. Unbalanced power acting benignly over time was a chimera, a product of deluded minds. A government with a single all-powerful legislature must, sooner or later, degenerate into tyranny.[33]

In time, as Gordon Wood has suggested and as Douglas Arnold has demonstrated, Pennsylvania's Republicans worked out a solution that has long since become commonplace in American political culture. The two houses do not represent different orders of people, different ranks of citizens, different kinds of property, but rather different combinations or arrangements of the same people. In a republic composed of citizens all equal before the law, the two different houses of the legislature, as well as the chief executive, all represent the people configured in different ways, and all serve the people for varying lengths of time. This produces checks and balances, vigor and restraint, change and continuity, responsiveness and wisdom, without separate orders of men arranged in a hierarchical system of social gradations.[34]

In the partisan battles of the 1780s, Pennsylvania's Republicans built their campaign for revision of the state constitution on this nonaristocratic conception of a second legislative body. They remained, however, vulnerable to charges of favoring aristocracy. The popular mind, like many of the participants in the public debates, had difficulty in transcending the older political culture that had identified a second house with a privileged class of men: the aristocratic House of Lords. The Constitutionalists supported Pennsylvania's powerful unicameral legislature, and they had, for the better part of a decade, both expressed and nurtured this popular association of a second house with an aristocratic form of government.[35]

---

33. Ibid.

34. Wood, *Creation*, esp. 441, 444, 445; and Douglas Arnold, "Political Ideology." Arnold's work provides the most complete and persuasive treatment now available of the ideological dimension of politics in Pennsylvania between 1776 and 1790, as well as the relationship of that ideological dimension to the major issues separating the two parties.

35. See Arnold, "Political Ideology." Some men in Pennsylvania continued to conceive of a second house as an upper house peopled by "men deemed more qualified" and selected out by indirect election, property qualifications, or by defining electoral districts according to wealth rather than population. At least some Republicans shared this "traditional whig" ideology of representation based on social characteristics, as Joseph S. Foster makes clear in his recent

In the fall of 1787, Pennsylvania's Antifederalists turned this argument against the Federal Constitution, which proposed a government with two-house legislature. One, the House of Representatives, might represent the people. The other, the upper house, Antifederalists insisted, must represent the aristocracy. Hence the Federal Constitution promised to create an aristocratic government.

The "Address of the Seceding Assemblymen" had hinted at this argument; "Centinel" in his first essay developed it more fully. He first ridiculed the idea of a perfectly balanced government. No such government has ever existed; none ever will.[36] More important, he argued, that system of government might work in England where "they have a powerful hereditary nobility, and real distinctions of rank and interest." In America, however, such an arrangement would attract only the support of "the wealthy and ambitious, who in every community think they have a right to lord it over their fellow creatures." These men, "Centinel" said, were the same men who had opposed Pennsylvania's state government, that "aristocratic junto's [sic] of the *well-born few*, who had been zealously endeavoring . . . to humble that offensive *upstart, equal liberty* . . . the profligate and the needy office-hunters" who were known for their "strenuous and unremitted exertion . . . to destroy our admirable constitution."[37]

The charges of aristocracy blended well with concerns for civil liberties and the protection of state sovereignty. Taken together these themes created a powerful appeal that resonated well with America's image of itself as a fledgling republic in a monarchical world. They tapped into apprehensions about remote, unresponsive, and tyrannical central power that had first made colonials into rebels, then revolutionaries, and finally patriots. They tied opposition to the Federal Constitution

---

study of the voting alignments in the state's 1790 constitutional convention. As Foster also makes clear, however, the majority of this convention, including such prominent Republican-Federalists as James Wilson, rejected this view. See Foster, "The Politics of Ideology: The Pennsylvania Constitutional Convention of 1789–90," *Pennsylvania History* 59 (April 1992): 122–44; quotes from 124, 130.

36. *Independent Gazetteer*, 10/5/87.
37. "Centinel VII," *Independent Gazetteer*, 12/29/87, in Storing 2.7.7, 5, 65, 116, 127. Bernard Bailyn, *The Ideological Origins of the American Revolution*, enl. ed. (Cambridge: Belknap Press of Harvard University Press, 1992), especially "Postscript. Fulfillment: A Commentary on the Constitution," 321–80.

into the core beliefs that had shaped the patriot perception of their British heritage, of the conflict with the mother country, and of the republic they were creating.[38]

In the same vein, repeated reference to aristocratic upper houses, to the better sort, to the well-born, and to the aspiring aristocrats aroused Americans' republican concerns with equality. It also agitated the sensitivities of those in Pennsylvania who resented pretensions of social superiority and aspirations to political privilege; and it linked support for the Federal Constitution to those who in Pennsylvania had long sought to add a second and aristocratic upper house to the government of the state: the aristocratically inclined Anglicans who led the Republican party.

More important for our purposes, these themes suggest the voters whom these Antifederalist publicists thought they were addressing. First and foremost, they appealed to that largely Presbyterian and Reformed electorate that had brought the Constitutionalists to power in 1778, sustained them during the early 1780s, and then returned them to power in 1784 and 1785. Second, they sought to complement this essentially partisan strategy with appeal to Quakers and Sectarian pacifists, emphasizing the Constitution's compromise with slavery, its threats to liberty of conscience, and its failure to protect conscientious objectors. Finally, and throughout, they played on popular fears of remote and insensitive government and resentment of those who aspired to social and political privilege.

The Federalists

The Republicans inaugurated their fall campaign at a rally of the Friends of the Federal Constitution in the State House Yard on Saturday

---

38. For a sampling of some of the literature on the ideology of the American Revolution, see Arnold, "Political Ideology"; Gordon Wood, *Creation*, esp. part 1, "The Ideology of Revolution"; Bernard Bailyn, *Ideological Origins* (1967); Forrest McDonald, *Novus Ordo Seculorum: The Intellectual Origins of the Constitution* (Lawrence: University Press of Kansas, 1985); John Murrin, "The Great Inversion, or Court versus Country: A Comparison of the Revolution Settlements in England (1688–1721) and America (1776–1815)," in J. G. A. Pocock, ed., *Three British Revolutions, 1641, 1688, 1776* (Princeton: Princeton University Press, 1980), 368–453; Robert Shalhope, *The Roots of Democracy: American Thought and Culture, 1760–1800* (Boston: Twayne, 1990). For an interpretation of the American Revolu-

evening, October 6. The first order of business, and the ostensible reason for the gathering, was the nomination of Republican candidates for the upcoming Assembly elections, scheduled for Tuesday, October 9. The second and now more famous item on the evening's agenda was speeches on behalf of the Federal Constitution.[39]

Good advance work brought out a "great concourse of people" and the well-disciplined crowd quickly endorsed the five-man slate recommended by "a committee that had been previously appointed." The people shouted down a candidate nominated from the floor because, as a disgruntled participant later charged, "he had hitherto been esteemed an advocate of the constitution of Pennsylvania." After ratifying the nominations, the meeting voted that the "citizens of the respective wards" of the city would meet on Monday, October 8, the eve of the Assembly election, to "appoint proper persons for making out and circulating a sufficient number of tickets in favor of" the Republican slate.[40]

The Republicans had managed the event well: a large but tractable crowd; a predetermined slate of candidates nominated by acclamation; the quick and effective stifling of dissent; and the creation of ward-level teams to mobilize the voters. Their unquestioned control over this populous meeting in the heart of downtown Philadelphia testified to the Federalists' political sophistication, their organizational skills, and their mastery of popular, outdoor mass-based politics.

The five-man Republican slate represented a carefully crafted balance of cultural, occupational, and political groupings. It would solidify their own natural political base and reach out to nonaligned, and even to Constitutional voters. Both Irish Catholic Thomas FitzSimons and Anglican-Quaker George Clymer were merchants and longtime Republicans. Jacob Hiltzheimer, a German Reformed patriot who had married a woman from Quaker background, and William Lewis, a lawyer from an English Quaker family, were also Republicans but relatively new to elected public office. William Will headed the ticket. A German artisan, a maker of pewter, Will, a popular political figure with solid

---

tion as a dispute over the constitution of the British Empire, see Jack P. Greene, "Origins of the American Revolution: A Constitutional Interpretation," in Leonard Levy and Dennis Mahoney, eds., *The Framing and Ratification of the Constitution* (New York: Macmillan, 1987), 36–53.

39. *Packet*, 10/5/87.

40. *Pennsylvania Herald*, 10/9/87, in Jensen 2:174–75.

military credentials, was a longtime Constitutionalist who had recently exhibited a growing uneasiness with his party's continued support of the Test Acts (the wartime loyalty oaths). As an artisan, Will also undoubtedly shared his fellow mechanics' disillusionment with the failure of the Constitutionalists to protect them from foreign competition. Recently, Will had begun to vote with the Republicans on some key issues in the legislature.[41]

The Republican ticket thus contained a complicated balance: Englishmen and Germans; Anglicans, Quakers, and Reformed; lawyers, merchants, and mechanics; solid Republicans with varying degrees of public exposure, and at least one recognizable Constitutionalist, an artisan who had moved to a moderate, nonaligned position and enjoyed support in both camps.

Likewise, the choice of party label for the fall legislative campaign illustrates the same penchant for coalition building. Although knowledgeable voters would recognize this ticket as unmistakably Republican, the party ran its Assembly candidates as "The Friends of the Federal Constitution," and as "Friends of Equal Liberty." The first label linked Republicans and Federalists; the second reminded voters that the Republicans had resisted the oppressive Test Acts during the Revolution and had long championed restoration of full rights for those excluded from the political community during the revolutionary struggle.[42]

This linkage among Federalists, Republicans, and opponents of the Test Acts had considerable political significance. The Tests had borne heavily on Quakers, Mennonites, Schwenkfelders, and Moravians, as well as on some German Lutherans, English Anglicans, and others whose religious scruples had prevented them from abjuring the king of England. These people, a sizable portion of the population of the state, had endured unending harassments throughout much of the previous decade at the hands of the Presbyterian-led Constitutionalists. In 1785–86 the Republicans had achieved partial repeal of the Test Acts, but the Constitutionalists had vigorously resisted the full restoration of

41. See below, Chapter 5, for discussion of the artisans and their efforts to obtain tariff protection.
42. *Packet*, 10/5/87. For use of this party label in 1786, see Brunhouse, *Counter-Revolution*, 177, 191, n. 42 on p. 282; Baumann, "Democratic-Republicans," 73. For its continued use in the fall of 1787, see "The Friends of Equal Liberty" in the Pennsylvania *Packet*, 9/18/87. This is a notice of a political meeting in White March, Montgomery County, to prepare for the forthcoming fall Assembly election. Also, throughout the fall campaign Federalists and Antifederalists argued about whether the Federalists were in fact "friends to equal liberty."

citizenship to those who had not supported the glorious cause. In the fall of 1787, while Pennsylvanians debated the ratification of the Federal Constitution, the remnants of these wartime loyalty oaths continued to exclude some Pennsylvanians from the polls.

Republicans chose James Wilson and Dr. Benjamin Rush to inaugurate the Federalist rhetorical campaign. Wilson, a prominent Philadelphia lawyer and a leading Republican, had come to America almost a quarter of a century earlier as a poor Scots Presbyterian immigrant with a university degree, a sharp mind, and vaulting ambition. In Pennsylvania he studied law under Quaker John Dickinson and spent many of his leisure hours with Billy White, a young Anglican destined to be the first Episcopal bishop of Philadelphia. Wilson married into a prominent Berks County Anglican family, the Birds, associated closely with the Proprietary party leaders in Lancaster and Carlisle where he prospered as a lawyer, an entrepreneur, and as a speculator before and after the war. A conspicuous patriot by 1774 and one of the first in Pennsylvania to call for independence, he later drew the ire of some patriots for his loyal defense of Quakers accused of treason. In 1777–79 he helped found the Republican party and then pushed for reform of the state constitution throughout the 1780s. He represented Pennsylvania in the Grand Convention in 1787, and with his speech at the State House Yard he emerged as the leading Federalist spokesman in Pennsylvania.[43]

Rush had followed quite a different course. In sharp contrast to Wilson, Rush was the scion of one of the early settlers in Pennsylvania. His first American forebear, John, had fought under Cromwell, become a Quaker, and migrated to Pennsylvania with the first wave in the early 1680s. Benjamin Rush was born in Byberry, Philadelphia County, where his grandfather had first established the family home. Although Benjamin's father had been an Anglican, he was raised in his mother's Presbyterian faith, and educated at the Presbyterian College of New Jersey. After graduating in 1760 he studied medicine, first in America and then at Edinburgh. He returned home to Philadelphia in 1769 to set up his practice, and by most accounts did well. An early supporter of Thomas Paine and his advocacy of independence, Rush had been in the forefront of the revolutionary movement in Pennsylvania. In the fall of 1776 he had at first accepted the state constitution of 1776 but then

---

43. Page Smith, *James Wilson Founding Father, 1742–1798* (Chapel Hill: University of North Carolina Press, 1956), 30, 32, 42, 44–47.

turned against it, possibly under the tutelage of his friend John Adams, one of America's most eloquent and persistent opponents of the unicameral principle. An intensely religious man active in the Philadelphia Presbyterian community, Rush grew increasingly unhappy with those he saw as "newcomers" (probably the Scots-Irish) and in 1787 he formally shifted to the Philadelphia Episcopal (formerly Anglican) congregation.[44]

When Rush joined Wilson in speaking for ratification of the Federal Constitution at the rally at the State House Yard on October 6, the two men exemplified much about Pennsylvania's Federalists. Both were conspicuous patriots, leading Republicans, adamant opponents of the state constitution of 1776 and the wartime loyalty oaths. Equally important, each exhibited in himself, in his family, and in his close associates an ambiguous religious and ethnic identity: immigrant and native, Scots and English, Presbyterian, Quaker, and Anglican.

The Republican rhetorical strategy for the fall campaign, outlined first by Wilson and Rush in their State House speeches, and then expanded and reiterated by innumerable anonymous writers, developed naturally out of their management of the Saturday night rally. Seeking public support, Federalists made the "exigencies of the union" their first and most frequent argument. They decried the momentous and critical times. They deplored the "discord," "confusion and distresses which prevail in every part of our country"; they lamented the weaknesses of the government under the Articles of Confederation, *"now universally admitted to be inadequate to the preservation of liberty, property and the union,"* and they worried about the centrifugal tendencies of the states, each with "[a]n immoderate spirit of independency," tending to "dissolve the present weak federal union."[45]

---

44. David Freeman Hawke, *Benjamin Rush, Revolutionary Gadfly* (Indianapolis, Bobbs-Merrill, 1971), 433 and passim. Rush to John Adams, Philadelphia, 2/24/90, in L. H. Butterfield, ed., *Letters to Rush* (Princeton: Princeton University Press, 1951, 532–33.

45. *Independent Gazetteer*, 10/25/87; *Packet*, 11/27/87; *Pennsylvania Gazette*, 11/14/87; *Pennsylvania Journal*, 11/24/87, in Jensen 2:191, 139–40, *Independent Gazetteer*, 10/9/87. See Appendix 1 for a brief description of the technique used to analyze the press debate. Neither Wilson nor Rush opened up new or surprising lines of argument at this initial Federalist political rally. As John Alexander has well documented, the press had been trumpeting most of these themes for months. Wilson and Rush did, however, inaugurate the Federalist campaign and define the kinds of arguments Federalists in Philadelphia would emphasize. These decisions, in turn, suggest to us the Federalists' perception of the electorate and their strategy for aggregating a majority coalition. For details of the press support for and

Three related problems, Federalists argued, lay at the root of America's current difficulties: the lack of physical security, the disruption of the international trade, and the state of the domestic economy.

America was powerless. The British occupied her western posts; Indians slaughtered her families; and civil disorder threatened: Shays in Massachusetts, paper money in Rhode Island, and civil war on the upper reaches of the Susquehanna River. "By-Stander" feared the disintegration of the union. "A Gentleman in Favor of Promoting Federal Sentiments" painted a vivid picture of America's vulnerability: "[S]avages riot in blood and destruction, because the federal government cannot support a regiment of troops on the frontiers. The wail of the babe, who dies under the tomahawk on the mother's breast, the shrieks of the mother that fill the wilderness."[46]

Equally important, the Federalist argument continued, America's foreign trade had decayed. A divided America could obtain no commercial treaties, nor protect its shipping and sailors on the high seas. The Federalist maintained that the United States had virtually lost access to the West Indies, to the European markets, and to the Mississippi River valley: ships were "rotting in our harbours" while "[t]he trade of this state . . . [was] carried on in foreign bottoms."[47]

The decay of foreign commerce, Federalists insisted, produced widespread domestic suffering. Our "widows and orphans still dread the loss of the shattered remains of their dowries and portions"; "our artificers . . . droop their heads in despair of better times"; and "our farmers . . . [are] ground down under the weight of taxes which the impost of a well regulated commerce would alone be sufficient to pay."[48] "Flour, the staple commodity of the state, is become a drug . . . and the tiller of the earth is obliged frequently to sell . . . for less than the price of his labor." In the western country "the . . . crops . . . rot in the fields." America could not effectively encourage "manufactories" and the country was flooded with foreign imports. "[S]hoes, boots,

---

expectations of the Grand Convention, see John Alexander, *The Selling of the Constitutional Convention*.

46. *Packet*, 11/23/87; *Pennsylvania Gazette*, 11/7/87; *Independent Gazetteer*, 10/9/87; *Freeman's Journal*, 9/26/87.

47. *Independent Gazetteer*, 10/25/87; *Pennsylvania Gazette*, 10/17/87. *Independent Gazetteer*, 10/15/87; *Pennsylvania Gazette*, 10/17/87.

48. *Independent Gazetteer*, 10/19/87; *Pennsylvania Gazette*, 10/17/87, in Jensen 2:188.

made-up clothes, hats, nails, sheet iron, hinges, and all other utensils of iron are of British manufactory." America had become a nation of "bankrupt merchants, poor mechanics, and distressed farmers."[49]

All of this, the Federalists insisted, resulted from a bad system of government. The Articles of Confederation had been formed "in the confusions of a civil war." "The moment peace was established, and that sense of common danger was extinct, it [the confederation] was found inadequate to the government of this extensive country."[50] The Federal Constitution, Federalists predicted, would ensure "us an ample portion of liberty and security at home, and respect abroad." The new system would transform Americans into prospering merchants, mechanics, and farmers: "[O]ur ports will be crowded with our own ships, and we shall become the carriers of Europe." Duties on imports and bounties for exports would stimulate America's craftsmen and "[t]he manufactories of our country will flourish—our mechanics will lift up their heads, and rise to opulence and wealth." The world would pay decent prices for American flour and those who refuse could be "starve[d] . . . into a generous price."[51] Moreover, immigration from Europe would increase, western land values would rise, land taxes would drop, exports would double, the price of wheat would improve, the open navigation of the Mississippi would provide easy access to markets for western grain farmers, public securities would sell at par, and local disturbances, such as the rebellion in Tioga, would be snuffed out.[52]

The fundamental question, Federalists declared, was Shall we rise into one respectable nation, or sink into thirteen factions? "A mighty empire may be formed upon this basis" but action must be bold and quick. If not, Federalists warned, Shays's men would take over Massachusetts, tyranny would lead New Jersey to cry for reunion with England, ships' carpenters would migrate to Nova Scotia for work, wheat in Cumberland and the western counties would rot in its sacks for want of markets, high land taxes would stimulate mass migration to

---

49. *Pennsylvania Gazette*, 10/17/87, in Jensen 2:188. *Independent Gazetteer*, 10/25/87. *Pennsylvania Gazette*, 10/17/87, in Jensen 2:188; *Pennsylvania Gazette*, 10/17/87, in Jensen 2:187–88. *Independent Gazetteer*, 10/25/87, 10/15/87; *Pennsylvania Gazette*, 10/17/87, in Jensen 2:187.
50. *Independent Gazetteer*, 9/26/87. *Pennsylvania Gazette*, 10/17/87, in Jensen 2:187.
51. *Independent Gazetteer*, 11/1/87. *Pennsylvania Gazette*, 10/17/87, in Jensen 2:187–88.
52. *Packet*, 9/15/87.

Kentucky, mobs would burn to get paper money, while widows would starve for want of income from their securities. The proposed Constitution provided America's last chance.[53]

While detailing the great woes America faced, and the benefits, especially the economic ones, that the Federal Constitution would bring, Federalists seldom initiated a discussion of the document itself. Of all participants in the public debates, James Wilson was probably the best qualified to speak to the substance of the Constitution, but he chose not to do so. The editor of the *Pennsylvania Herald* described Wilson's address at the State House rally as "a long and eloquent speech upon the principles of the Federal Constitution," but it was no such thing. Long and eloquent it may have been; an exposition of the principles on which the Constitution rested, it was not.[54] Instead, Federalists, throughout the fall 1787 campaign, addressed the substance of the Federal Constitution largely in response to specific Antifederalist charges. Furthermore, even in these instances, they more often than not obfuscated what they could not evade.

The incessant Antifederalist attacks on the Constitution as an aristocratic document supported by aspiring aristocrats, however, forced Federalists to treat this issue with greater detail and candor. Federalists summarily dismissed the description of the president as a monarch. He achieves his position by election not by inheritance, they pointed out. He begins as one of the people, and "will always be *one of the people* at the end of four years." He can be removed from office for wrongdoing. His income will be far from princely, and he will enjoy no special privileges or exalted status. So unmonarchical is this office that the very person of its holder "*is not so much protected as that of a member of the House of Representatives; for he can be proceeded against like any other man in the ordinary course of law.*" No prerogative powers, no monarchical status, no hereditary perquisites accompanied the office. The charge was untenable.[55]

The Federalists had more difficulty with the accusation that the Constitution created an aristocratic system. In response, they empha-

---

53. *Independent Gazetteer*, 11/7/87. *Independent Gazetteer*, 10/19/87; *Packet*, 10/12/87. *Packet*, 9/15/87. *Independent Gazetteer*, 10/13/87. *Pennsylvania Gazette*, 10/17/87, in Jensen 2:187–88.

54. *Pennsylvania Herald*, 10/9/87, in Jensen 2:167.

55. Tench Coxe, "An American Citizen I," *Independent Gazetteer*, 9/26/87, in Jensen 2:140–42.

sized the popular character of the Constitution and the democratic government it would create. The Constitution guaranteed republican government to the states, they pointed out, and it imposed no religious tests or property qualifications for officeholding. It gave no special distinction to wealth and it left the determination of the qualifications of electors to the states. In contrast to the Articles of Confederation, the people would directly elect the House of Representatives and "the poor have equal voices in their election with the rich." Furthermore, the House had vast prerogatives. "Without their consent no monies can be obtained, no armies raised, no navies provided. They alone can originate bills for drawing forth the revenues of the Union, and they will have a negative upon every legislative act of the other house. So far, in short, as the sphere of federal jurisdiction extends, they will be controllable only by the people."[56]

Other Federalists argued that "the Senate . . . will be as much a democratic body as the House of Representatives." Senators were "elected out of the body of the people, without one qualification being necessary, but mere citizenship." Membership in the Senate neither required nor conferred special status, nor presupposed wealth requirements for election. Candidacy, as for the current Continental Congress, required no particular rank, wealth, education, or even intelligence. It was argued that "[m]any young men of genius and many characters of more matured abilities, without fortunes, have been honored with that trust [a seat in the Continental Congress]," but also that "[m]any instances of persons, not eminently endowed with mental qualities . . . have been sent thither from a reliance on their virtues, public and private."[57]

Once in office senators acquired no privileged status, Federalists continued. They were not appointed for life, possessed no titles, could not pass on their positions to their heirs. The state legislatures chose senators for a term of six years; at its end senators became indistinguishable from the people. State legislatures had been choosing representatives to the Continental Congress in this fashion for a decade without creating an aristocracy. No reason existed now to believe that these

---

56. *Independent Gazetteer*, 10/24/87. *Independent Gazetteer*, 10/10/87. *Packet*, 1/31/88. *Independent Gazetteer*, 10/19; 26/87. *Independent Gazetteer*, 9/29/87, in Jensen 2:145.

57. "A Democratic Federalist," *Independent Gazetteer*, 11/26/87, in Jensen 2:296–97. *Independent Gazetteer*, 9/28/87, in Jensen 2:142–43.

same state legislatures would suddenly establish a new aristocracy in the United States Senate.

But these responses did not directly address the Antifederalist argument that the Senate was aristocratic because it was an upper house, because its members remained less susceptible to popular scrutiny and control, and because its indirect elections limited candidacy to prominent men. When Antifederalist John Smilie charged that the Senate and the greater part of the House would be members of the natural aristocracy, he came close to the heart of the problem and thereby posed a serious challenge to the Federalists.[58]

Federalists in their more candid moments admitted that the Senate differed from the House, that it was intended to be so, and that they expected a somewhat different kind of men to people it. The Senate, Federalists anticipated, would bring to the constitutional balance the advantages of a hereditary aristocracy without being a hereditary body. Its indirect election, its longer term, its older age requirement, and its smaller size would buffer it from the momentary passions of the transient majority and render it "more independent of the people as to *the free exercise of their judgment and abilities* than the house of Representatives."[59]

Although candidacy for the Senate required no particular wealth, education, or intelligence, it demanded, in the minds of the Federalists, something equally rare: virtue, wisdom, talent, and the respect of the community. Wilson explained this briefly in his response to Smilie. Accusing Smilie of using the term "natural aristocracy" without defining it, Wilson sought to weaken Smilie's position by linking the Federalist argument to the Antifederalists' sacred document: the state constitution of 1776. A "natural aristocracy," Wilson explained, "means nothing more nor less than a government of the best men in the community, or those who are recommended by the words of the constitution of Pennsylvania where it is directed, that the representatives should consist of those most noted for wisdom and virtue." In short, men of character.[60]

Boosters of the Federal Constitution also envisioned a special role for the Senate. Tench Coxe in the "American Citizen" explained that

---

58. Jensen 2:465–66.
59. "An American Citizen II," *Independent Gazetteer*, 9/28/87.
60. Wilson, December 4, 1787, in Jensen 2:488, 489. "An American Citizen II," *Independent Gazetteer*, 9/18/87, in Jensen 2:143.

Senators would bring wisdom and virtue to the counsels of state. The House represents democracy, he said, but "it would be . . . dangerous to elect both houses in this manner." As Wilson put it, referring to the governor of Massachusetts, but expressing thoughts that could apply with equal validity to a U.S. Senator: "I apprehend it is of more consequence to be able to know the true interests of the people, than their faces, and of more consequence still, to have virtue enough to pursue the means of carrying that knowledge usefully into effect."[61]

On one level, then, the Federalists admitted the substance of the Antifederalists' charge. Special men would people the Senate and they would remain relatively free from public scrutiny and pressure. Their maturity, their experience, their greater insight and deeper wisdom would balance the House's sensitivity to popular demands, and give stability and ballast to the ship of state.

At another level, and with greater comfort, Federalists continued to insist on the democratic nature of the document they defended. James Wilson exemplified this approach. Summing up the Federalist position at the state convention in December, he explained again how the Federal Constitution solved the great conundrum of erecting a government of divided powers in a society that lacked the separate social orders on which such a division rested in Great Britain. "In its principle, it is purely democratical." The president, the Senate, and the House of Representatives, each with a different function, each with a different constituency, each with different powers, and each with its own unique contribution to make, all derived their authority from the same source: the people.[62] The relentless pounding of the Antifederalists had thus forced the Federalists to "explain and elucidate the principles and arrangements of the Constitution," but the Federalists had done so reluctantly.[63] The defense of a bicameral legislature and an independent executive as inherently democratic had not won them widespread electoral backing in Pennsylvania in the past.

The Federalists were more optimistic about attracting popular support on different grounds. Their emphasis on the "exigencies of the union" exemplified this approach. Their efforts to impugn the motives and hence the arguments of the Antifederalists represented another

---

61. "An American Citizen II," *Independent Gazetteer*, 9/28/87, in Jensen 2:143–44. Wilson, December 4, 1787, in Jensen 2:489.
62. Jensen 2:579. Wilson, in Jensen 2:587–89.
63. Wilson, in Jensen 2:167.

effort in the same direction. "Centinel," by identifying Antifederalism with defense of the state constitution (and thus with the Constitutionalists) had given the Federalists an opening. "It is neither extraordinary nor unexpected," Wilson said, "that every Person . . . who either enjoys or expects to enjoy a place of profit under the present establishment [i.e., the state constitution of 1776], will object to the proposed innovation; not, in truth, because it is injurious to the liberties of his country but because it affects his schemes of wealth and consequence."[64]

The theme Wilson established, others built on. The author of "Federal Constitution" traced the roots of the opposition back to the summer of 1787, when "[i]n the month of July last . . . it was agreed, 'that if the new constitution of Congress interfered in the least with the constitution of Pennsylvania, it ought to be opposed.'" He, like Wilson, concluded that "all the opposition to the new government, originate from the officers of government, who are afraid of losing their salaries or places."[65]

"An Independent Citizen" made the charge more specific and linked the extraordinary behavior of the "Seceding members of the late general assembly" on September 28–29 to a partisan conspiracy: at a

> meeting of the junto at a certain clergyman's house [Presbyterian minister Dr. John Ewing, provost of the university] in the neighbourhood of the University . . . not long since, when a Sunday's dinner was given by that clergyman to a chosen few . . . a scheme was laid . . . [that] they may save from deserved censure and disgrace those poor fools who [are] ready . . . to forward the sinister views and wicked designs of a wretched faction.[66]

A mock "Protest of the Minority" added nepotism to the indictment, and "Independent Citizen" named names. He asserted that fear of loss of jobs by incompetents lay at the heart of the Antifederalist movement, and joined this to Samuel, the son of George Bryan, whose "strut has long since announced his self-importance," and who, if the Federal Constitution is ratified, "shall no longer fill the offices for which he is totally unqualified."[67]

64. Jensen 2:171–72.
65. *Pennsylvania Gazette*, 10/10/87, in Kaminski and Saladino 13:362.
66. *Independent Gazetteer*, 10/9/87.
67. Jensen 2:156; *Independent Gazetteer*, 10/9/87.

"Agricola" heaped additional abuse on the Bryan family, and then did the same for the Ewings. "The *son of the red-nosed Vicar* [Provost Ewing] . . . has had modesty enough to solicit to be made Recorder of Deeds, and in order to induce those in whom the appointment lay to favor his application, generously offered to give a certain portion of his profits to an institution of which his father was president [the University of Pennsylvania]."[68]

"A Gaul" expanded the detailed list of interested officeholders to include Judge B——, Dr. E——g, C—— P——t (Charles Pettit, a Presbyterian financier in Philadelphia), J——n B. S——h (Jonathan Bayard Smith, brother-in-law of Judge George Bryan and prothonotary of Philadelphia), and Johnny S——y (John Smilie, Scots-Irish Presbyterian councilor from Fayette County).[69]

Other essays spewed venom on John Nicholson, the comptroller-general of the state, a heavy speculator in government certificates, and author of the Antifederalist "A View of the Proposed Constitution." "A Watchman," ridiculing Nicholson for confusing of *ante* with *anti*, suggested he "submit your Latin scraps to your brother-in-law for correction." He also impugned Nicholson's motives: "opposition to the *new government* comes with peculiar awkwardness from *placemen* under the *old*."[70]

"A Federalist" then condemned Nicholson's pamphlet as a "disgrace," "an insult" to the common sense of Pennsylvanians and concluded that the author

> appears to be but little removed from idiocy . . . how a booby of this blunted comprehension should have been betrayed into the lists of political controversy is truly astonishing. [It has] been conjectured, that he is some state clerk, the business of whose office having declined with the settlement of certificates by the *blessed funding law*, he is desirous, in this way, to make the public a return for the salary which he receives.[71]

Thus, beginning with Wilson and continuing throughout the fall campaign, Federalists identified a covey of Antifederalists with suspect

68. *Independent Gazetteer*, 11/1/76.
69. "A Gaul," *Independent Gazetteer*, 10/13/87. See "Reformation," *Independent Gazetteer*, 9/29/87, for additional names.
70. *Independent Gazetteer*, 10/20/87.
71. *Independent Gazetteer*, 10/23/87.

motives. These men, the core of the Antifederalist leadership, differed among themselves in numerous ways but they shared an impressive number of politically salient characteristics. All but one came from Presbyterian and especially Scots-Irish backgrounds; all held major public positions in the state and most had held these positions for a protracted period of time; all depended on continued Constitutionalist party success in Pennsylvania for public employment; and some, at least, had grown prosperous in public service. When "Plain Truth" charged that "[m]ost of the officers of government [in Pennsylvania] . . . have made fortunes out of the public," Constitutionalists lamely asserted that "prospering in public office is no crime if the [public's] business is done skillfully and honestly."[72]

Honest and skillful or not, some of these men earned princely sums. An item in the *Independent Gazetteer* in August charged that "Jonathan Bayard Smith [the prothonotary for the city and county of Philadelphia] . . . receives £2,000 from his office, and his brother-in-law George Bryan [Supreme Court justice] £600." Although the precise value of these offices remains unclear, Smith's income was sufficient to induce James Wilson to covet it; Bryan, his son Samuel, and Dr. Ewing's son all depended upon their salaries from public office, and John Nicholson used his position as comptroller to further a complex network of speculative schemes.[73]

The Federalists' charges may or may not have been just. The accusations were, however, sufficiently plausible to give them currency and thus to distract public attention from serious discussion of the Federal Constitution itself. Two other prominent themes in the Federalists' rhetoric also encouraged voters to make their decision on grounds other than the substance of the proposed changes: the revolutionary credentials of the framers and the growing popular support for ratification. Federalist literature during the fall campaign never tired of pointing out the exalted reputation, the disinterested motives, and the unquestioned revolutionary credentials of the drafters and the chief advocates of the new proposal, the members of the Grand Convention:

72. *Pennsylvania Herald*, "D" 10/6/86, in Jensen 2:MFM 110.
73. "Item," *Independent Gazetteer*, 8/8/87. George Turner to Winthrop Sargent, 11/6/87, in Jensen 2:209–10 and editor's note. "A Freeman," *Pennsylvania Gazette*, 11/7/87, in Jensen 2:285–86 and editor's note (also 11/7, 13, 15, 18/87). "Reformation" also estimated the annual income of the prothonotary of Philadelphia (city and county) at £2,000. *Independent Gazetteer*, 9/29/87.

"the most celebrated characters, the collected wisdom of America"; the "immortal WASHINGTON," the "venerable FRANKLIN," as well as William Livingston, James Madison, John Rutledge, and Rufus King. Could these patriots with impeccable revolutionary credentials, "a WASHINGTON and his colleagues, . . . tender a constitution . . . fraught with such evils" as are set forth by "these weak tools of party" who oppose ratification? To ask the question was to answer it.[74]

In addition, the Federalists' success in the October Assembly election, and their unquestionable popularity in and around the city, led their publicists into an increasing emphasis on the popular base of their support. With growing confidence they claimed to be the majority party, and to speak for the people. Antifederalists, they said, had started with few supporters and their support continued to decline with time. "It is with great pleasure we inform our customers," the *Pennsylvania Gazette* said on October 17, "that from the returns already come to hand . . . there is a large majority of persons strongly attached to the new Federal Constitution."[75]

Federalists complemented this with news of widespread popular support in Pennsylvania and elsewhere. Dispatches from Bethlehem, Germantown, and Carlisle all reported large meetings of respectable citizens championing ratification, as did news items from Boston and Northampton, Massachusetts; Richmond, George Town, Fairfax, and Petersburg, Virginia; Salem County, New Jersey; and Charleston, South Carolina. Whole states, Federalists reported, supported ratification. A man traveling through New Jersey wrote that out of hundreds of conversations there "he met with but *one* man who was opposed." "Accounts from Maryland leave little room for doubt that the Constitution will be adopted there," and in Massachusetts "at least nine tenths of [the people] . . . are willing to receive the new government." Portsmouth, New Hampshire, reported that "the new government meets with the greatest approbation here." Supposedly, God himself, who "permitted the sun to rise with all imaginable lustre" on Election Day, implicitly endorsed ratification. Even the dead apparently approved:

---

74. *Pennsylvania Gazette*, 10/17/87, in Jensen 2:181; *Pennsylvania Gazette*, 10/17/87, in Jensen 2:19; *Pennsylvania Gazette*, 10/17/87, in Jensen 2:178. For other references to Franklin and Washington, see *Independent Gazetteer*, 10/15, 25/87–11/9/87.

75. *Pennsylvania Gazette*, 10/17/87, in Jensen 2:178.

"[t]he soldier who has fought and bled . . . will rise in vengeance" against the opponents of the Constitution.[76]

In sum, the Federalists argued that the exigencies of the union demanded change; that patriots, both leaders and people, favored ratification; and that only self-interested state officeholders and selfish party leaders opposed. Some Federalists, particularly in the early stages of the campaign, argued the inherent superiority of a bicameral legislature and predicted that ratification of the Federal Constitution would repudiate the unicameral principle of the state constitution, and end the reign of the Constitutionalist party.

Most Federalists, however, avoided direct attacks on the state constitution and explicit comparisons of the state and the proposed Federal Constitution. A major Federalist publicist summed up this approach when he described one of his own pamphlets as "my attempt to *conciliate* our Constitutionalists."[77] Federalists more often approached the partisan question indirectly by reminding Quakers, Sectarians, and other nonjurors that the Antifederalists had harassed and abused them for the past decade, and by promising that ratification would put an end to party squabbles in Pennsylvania.

The Federalists' strategy sought to minimize or transcend partisan attachments. They respected the power their opponents had demonstrated in the past to mobilize majorities in defense of the state constitution. Federalist Tench Coxe's comment, early in the debate, exemplified their approach: "The question is not how far our state constitutions are good or otherwise—the object of our wishes is *to amend and supply the evident and allowed errors and defects of the federal government.*" Now, quite obviously, Coxe was misstating the case. In reality, a central question in Pennsylvania, for both the Constitutionalists and the Republicans, was precisely how far the state constitution was "good or otherwise." Antifederalists wanted to debate that question. Federalists, however, hesitated to risk ratification on their ability to win a popular majority on that issue. They had lost the battle over the state constitution repeatedly over the past decade or more. In 1787 they chose not to risk another contest on this issue.[78]

76. *Independent Gazetteer,* 10/26/87; *Mercury,* 10/19/87; *Pennsylvania Gazette,* 10/10/87; *Packet* 10/11/87, 10/29/87; *Pennsylvania Journal,* 11/3/87, 11/3/87; *Pennsylvania Gazette,* 10/10/87, 10/17/87, 11/7/8; *Pennsylvania Journal,* 10/13/87.
77. Tench Coxe to David S. Franks, Philadelphia, 11/26/87, in Jensen 2:298 n. 1.
78. "American Citizen I," in Jensen 2:139–40.

Instead, Federalists strove to shift the debate to more favorable ground. They emphasized the critical nature of the times, the exalted revolutionary reputations of those who favored ratification, the questionable motives of their opponents, and, in time, the apparent growing popularity of the Federal Constitution. In all of this, they sought to minimize the discussion of the domestic political implications of the change and thereby evade, or possibly transcend, partisanship.

Federalists worked to maintain their base among traditional Republican supporters, while reaching out to uncommitted neutrals, and to those Constitutionalist voters whose concern for their patriotism or their purses inclined them toward support of the new system. In this, Federalists acted like a minority seeking to win in a heterogeneous polity by nurturing their base and painstakingly aggregating the votes of diverse, possibly even hostile, elements, into a tenuous majority coalition. They identified themselves with the repeal of the Test Acts, built tickets that reflected the ethnic, religious, and occupational groupings of the voting public, minimized partisan identifications, promised that ratification would end parties in the state, and worked to build bridges to all of those who shared their apprehensions about the exigencies of the union. Thus, by their words and actions, Federalists sought to construct a majority out of the diversity that was the Pennsylvania electorate.

Federalist and Antifederalist spokesmen constructed quite different campaigns in the fall of 1787, but each side grounded its strategy on much the same set of assumptions about the electorate. Both believed that Pennsylvanians favored a more effective and energetic central government. Both, therefore, agreed that the Federal Constitution was addressing a legitimate problem. Federalists, however, attempted to focus the debate on the ineffective central government while Antifederalists stressed the dangers to liberty that they predicted would accompany the new system.

Both sides also assumed that the average voter in Pennsylvania did not wish to see state government subsumed under an all-powerful central government. Antifederalists played to popular distrust of distant and arbitrary central authority. Federalists, when they could not evade the issue, worked to convince voters that any changes would be minimal and relatively benign. Federalists seldom if ever defended the Federal Constitution as a device to discipline or control unruly state governments, but they did admit, on occasion, that a stronger central government would help deal with problems like that of Shays in Massachusetts or the irresponsible paper-money interests in Rhode Island. Antifederalists did not defend state issues of paper money or protest the specific limits the Federal Constitution placed on the states; rather, they argued that the Constitution would consolidate the states into a national union.

More important for our purposes, both Federalists and Antifederalists recognized the same political divisions within Pennsylvania. Furthermore, they understood the significance of these divisions for their respective campaigns. Both saw the Presbyterian-based Constitutionalists as the core of the opposition to ratification, and the Anglican-based Republicans as the core of the support. Antifederalists strove to mobilize their partisan followers and to identify Federalists as aspiring Anglican aristocrats committed to hierarchical religious establishments and political systems, and as men seeking personal privilege and status. Federalists sought to minimize the Antifederalist advantage by a hurried election, by discrediting the motives of the officeholding leaders of the Constitutionalist party, and by diverting and dividing the Constitutionalist electorate through appeals to patriotism and economic self-interest.

Both saw the Quakers and the Sectarians as swing groups. Antifederalists appealed to them on the basis of religious principles: slavery, pacifism, and toleration. Federalists reminded them of the economic crisis America faced and of the abuse the present Antifederalists had heaped upon Quakers and others in the past.

On November 6, 1787, the voters across the state elected an overwhelming majority of Federalist delegates to the state convention. This outcome pleased the Federalists and invigorated the Antifederalists, who almost immediately began to lay the groundwork for the future popular repudiation of the convention's inevitable ratification.

3
The State Convention
November–December 1787

The delegates to Pennsylvania's state convention, elected on November 6, 1787, achieved their quorum and organized themselves for business on November 21. They assembled at the State House in Philadelphia where the site added to the historic aura of the occasion. Here, eleven years earlier, the Continental Congress had declared America's independence. Here, again, during the long and hot summer of 1787, a cadre of America's revolutionary leaders had constructed a plan to direct the future course of the fledgling nation. Now, in the same building, representatives of the people of Pennsylvania were meeting to debate the merits of that plan.

The physical arrangement enhanced the drama of the event. Within the modest-sized room, the delegates seated themselves by persuasion, Federalists facing Antifederalists. The doors remained open and spectators crowded the room. Most observers had come to listen and applaud; some to heckle and intimidate; a few to record the proceedings for the broader audience outdoors. Delegates rising to address each other spoke to a crowded gallery almost within arm's reach, and, through the press, to an attentive public that extended up and down the Atlantic seaboard and across the state to the headwaters of the Ohio River.[1]

This chapter will look closely at these debates and at the political maneuverings both before the convention met and while it was in session. First, however, a few words about the political context within which this phase of the contest took place. On election night, November 6, Federalist mobs terrorized conspicuous Antifederalists in the city. At about midnight, plebeian supporters of the Federal Constitution attacked the Constitutionalist boardinghouse owned by Alexander Boyd on Sixth Street. They yelled, smashed windows, assaulted the door with large stones, and called the Constitutionalists "damned rascals," who "ought to be all hanged." William Findley and John Smilie, Antifederalist delegates to the state convention, were among those resident in Boyd's at the time, along with the hapless James McCalmont who had been dragged from this same house by a Federalist mob less than two months earlier.[2]

The same night, angry crowds also attacked the homes of other Constitutionalists who lived in the city. They hurled insults and missiles at the dwellings of Judge George Bryan of the Supreme Court, the Reverend John Ewing, provost of the university, John Nicholson, the comptroller general, and Dr. James Hutchinson.[3]

This violence frightened the Antifederalists and, for some, it shook their confidence in the future of popular government. Samuel Baird, writing from Montgomery County three days later, expressed his concern to Nicholson over "the insults offered to you." He firmly believed, Baird said, that "the moment a person is liable to insult for his sentiments on public affairs, that moment liberty is at an end." Rather

---

1. For a brief description of the physical features of the State House, see Edward Riley, *Starting America: The Story of Independence Hall* (Gettysburg, Pa.: Thomas Publications, 1954, 1990), esp. 8, 9, 20, 27. Alexander Dallas and Thomas Lloyd published reports of the debates at the convention. For a full discussion of the records of this convention, see "Notes on Sources," Jensen 2:36–44.

2. See depositions by John Beard [Biard] and Alexander Boyd, dated November 9, 1787, in "Assembly Debates," Jensen 2:241–243; and additional comments by James McCalmont and Colonel John Piper, ibid., 248. For a discussion of backcountry riots and popular traditions of "rough music," see Saul Cornell, "Aristocracy Assailed: The Ideology of Backcountry Antifederalism," *Journal of American History* 76 (March 1990): 1145–72, esp. 1151–53.

3. William Shippen, Jr., to Thomas Lee Shippen, Philadelphia, 11/7/87, in Jensen 2:235; and Samuel Biard to John Nicholson, Norristown (Montgomery County), 11/9/87, in Jensen 2:236.

than endure life under such circumstances, he would "with pleasure see another Caesar proclaim himself perpetual dictator."[4]

These Federalist rioters obviously intended to intimidate opponents of the Federal Constitution. At the time, neither side knew with certainty the final composition of the convention. From the Federalists' perspective, violence, or threats of violence might well push the undecided into the Federalist camp, and temper the behavior of the committed Antifederalists. More important for our purposes, these Federalist rioters assumed that the way to intimidate Antifederalists was to attack Constitutionalists.[5]

On November 10 Findley and his Constitutionalist colleagues in the legislature demanded that the Assembly condemn the rioters. The mob, they claimed, had insulted the dignity of the entire Assembly by abusing those of its members who lived at Boyd's.[6] The Republicans in the majority in the legislature and Federalists to a man, stalled. Richard Peters urged that the House go slowly. Thomas FitzSimons and George Clymer complained about the way the subject had been introduced. William Lewis inquired whether the House sought to punish a crime or a breach of its privilege. FitzSimons added that the House should not "offer a stigma upon the citizens [of the city] without hearing one word in their defense."[7]

Constitutionalist James McLene accused the Republicans of evading the issue, of trying to "give the go-by," as he phrased it, and of seeking to screen the rioters. Lewis responded sharply, denying a charge that most, by then, must have known to be true. The Republicans soon capitulated. Unable, as one observer phrased it, to "defend the traitors tho they loved the treason," they finally joined with the Constitutionalists to condemn the rioters for breach of the privilege of the Assembly.[8]

Meanwhile, news of the election results continued to arrive. Within a day or so most observers knew that the Federalists had won, but only in time did the magnitude of the Federalist victory become clear. By the

---

4. Baird to Nicholson, 11/9/87, in Jensen 2:236–37. William Shippen to Thomas Shippen, Philadelphia, 11/7,13,15,18/87, in Jensen 2:235–36. For a variety of documents detailing this Federalist violence against Antifederalists in the city, see Jensen 2:239–56.

5. Madison to Archibold Stuart, New York, 10/30/87, in Kaminski and Saladino 13:512. Shippen to Shippen, 11/7/87, in Jensen 2:235.

6. Supreme Executive Council Minutes, 11/9/87, in Jensen 2:237–38; Assembly Proceedings, 11/10/87, and "Assembly Debates," 11/10/87, in Jensen 2:238, 243, 144, 245.

7. Ibid.

8. Ibid., 245, 254; Shippen to Shippen, 11/4/87, in Jensen 2:236.

eve of the convention, however, the Philadelphia papers were predicting, quite accurately, a two-to-one Federalist majority.[9]

Moreover, despite the Antifederalists' hopes, the convention contained no undecided or swing votes. Some delegates, such as Chief Justice Thomas McKean and the entire Federalist delegation from Philadelphia, had pledged themselves in writing before the election. The rest of the elected representatives arrived in Philadelphia with their minds made up. The final alignment on December 12 replicated the initial division on procedural questions in the convention's first days. These sixty-nine men had come not to reason together: rather, forty-six had come to ratify the proposal; twenty-three to resist as best they could.[10]

Furthermore, the Federalists had demonstrated their popularity across the state. To no one's surprise they carried two staunch Republican bulwarks: the city of Philadelphia, and York County, on the far side of the Susquehanna River. They also did fairly well in the west, winning two of the four seats from Washington County in the far southwestern corner of the state, as well as the single seat from the new county of Huntingdon in the midst of the mountains, and two of the four seats from Franklin, just east of the mountains.[11]

Most disappointing from the Antifederalist perspective, the Federalists had won decisively in five eastern counties: Bucks, Chester, Montgomery, Lancaster, and Philadelphia County. These counties contained more than a third of the state's voters and sent twenty-five delegates to the convention, all but one a Federalist. Of greater import, these counties represented most of the original heartland of the Constitutionalists. Here, in the early years of independence, the Constitutionalists had emerged and developed their base; from here, they had drawn the electoral support that had made them majority party in the late 1770s and again in the mid-1780s. And here, on November 6, they had lost the election of delegates to the state convention.[12]

9. James Madison to Edmund Randolph, 11/18/87, in Jensen 2:224; *Pennsylvania Gazette*, 11/21/87, in Jensen 2:224, Jensen 2:MFM Pa.23. See Jensen 2:590–91 for the vote.

10. *Independent Gazetteer*, 11/6/87; *Pennsylvania Herald*, 11/7/87, in Jensen 2:227. Convention Proceedings, 11/21/87, 11/26/87, and 12/12/87, in Jensen 2:326–27, 364–65, 589–91.

11. For details on the geographic distribution of the Federalist and Antifederalist vote see maps in Chapter 6. Classifications of counties as Federalist or Antifederalist based on votes of delegates in the convention. See Convention Proceedings, 11/21/87, 11/26/87, and 12/12/87, in Jensen 2:326–27, 364–65, 589–91.

12. An even division here (13 Antifederalists and 12 Federalists) would have given the

Two powerful realities thus faced the Antifederalists as they approached the convention. First, the Federalists would hold an overwhelming majority of the seats. Unless the Antifederalists could think of something, the convention would quickly and easily ratify the Federal Constitution. Second, the Antifederalists had lost the election in those five eastern agricultural counties that had once provided them with the bulk of their electoral support. Their principal hope of frustrating the Federalists depended on building opposition to ratification among voters in that area.

Federalists faced a different challenge. Although their solid majority permitted them to ratify the Constitution at any moment, respect for public opinion demanded at least the semblance of an open debate. Federalists, therefore, needed to answer their opponents' questions and defend the proposal. In addition, they had to maintain discipline, avoid surprises, and ensure unconditional ratification *in toto*, with no crippling amendments or conditions.

Antifederalist Maneuverings

Antifederalists began their attack early. Within three days of the election they tried, through the legislature, to structure the convention's rules to their own advantage. On November 9, Constitutionalist James McLene moved that the Assembly establish a two-thirds quorum for the convention. On one level, the proposal appeared reasonable. The Assembly itself operated with a two-thirds quorum requirement. Both the Antifederalists and the Federalists, however, knew that more was involved. In the past, the legislative minority had often used the two-thirds quorum rule to break up the house. The nineteen seceding Constitutionalists had done just that on September 28 and 29 and their behavior exemplified an old pattern. Now, both parties knew that a two-thirds quorum requirement for the convention might once again allow a minority to frustrate the will of the majority.[13]

Antifederalists a 35 to 34 edge in the convention. For more on this early geographic distribution of party votes in Pennsylvania, see Chapter 7.

13. See Chapter 1. Jensen 2:268. J. Paul Selsam, *The Pennsylvania Constitution of 1776: A Study in Revolutionary Democracy* (Philadelphia: University of Pennsylvania Press, 1935), 134 n. 144. David Hawke, *In the Midst of a Revolution* (Philadelphia: University of Pennsylvania Press, 1961). See also Owen S. Ireland, "The Few and the Many," unpublished paper, for details of 1776.

McLene defended his proposal by suggesting a Federalist conspiracy. The gentlemen in the "near counties" he feared, might "get together and decide upon the business before the others can attend." William Findley supported McLene's resolution, arguing that it would "remove that ground of suspicion and jealousy."[14] The Federalists, however, accused the Antifederalists of seeking to frustrate the will of the people. Turning the earlier Antifederalists' rhetoric against them, George Logan declared that those who advance the power of a minority to dictate to the majority "are the advocates of an aristocracy indeed."[15]

The Federalists then gave this majoritarian argument a radical populist flavor. The Assembly, William Robinson argued, cannot determine the rules of the Convention because the Convention does not meet "under the authority of the House." Rather, he continued, it meets "under an authority superior to the authority of the legislature, under the authority of the people." William Lewis phrased the same sentiment more expansively. The convention would meet, he said, under "supreme original authority of the people at large." The Federalists then voted down McLene's motion, not, ostensibly, for partisan reasons, but because it would have infringed on the power of the sovereign people.[16]

The convention convened on November 22 and almost immediately Federalist Benjamin Rush threatened to disrupt the house. They should, he proposed, select a minister to "open the business with a prayer." A less auspicious beginning would be difficult to imagine. Few might object to prayer, but choosing an appropriate minister could exacerbate deep hostilities, and distract, if not immobilize, the convention. Rush, however, persisted, and then added partisan insult to denominational insensitivity. He recalled, he said, that the state constitutional convention of 1776 had not prefaced its business with prayer, and that, he asserted, "is probably the reason . . . that the state has ever since been distracted by their proceedings." Constitutionalist John Smilie "objected to the absurd superstition of that opinion, and moved a postponement." The Federalist majority, taking care to offend no one and anxious to move ahead, joined with the Antifederalists to smother this explosive suggestion from their earnest but impractical colleague.[17]

14. Jensen 2:268–71.
15. Jensen 2:272.
16. Jensen 2:267, 274, 276.
17. My discussion of the convention relies heavily on the documents printed in Merrill Jensen, ed., *The Documentary History of the Ratification of the Constitution*, vol. 2, *Ratifica-*

As the convention proceeded, Antifederalists took every opportunity to exploit both procedural matters and substantive issues with an eye to building popular support. On Friday, November 23, the Federalists moved to elect James Campbell as secretary. Antifederalists nominated the grandson of Benjamin Franklin, William Temple Franklin. Although they had little hope of electing him, the nomination might convey the message that the Franklin family "was opposed to the new plan of government."[18]

Saturday brought more procedural infighting. Federalist Thomas McKean moved the acceptance of the Constitution, not, he said, to force an immediate decision, but merely to open discussion. Smilie, however, was suspicious. McKean did not always say precisely what he meant. Earlier McKean had lectured his colleagues that they were to "minutely . . . investigate [the Federal Constitution] . . . before we . . . ratify or reject." McKean, however, had already pledged himself to vote for unconditional ratification, regardless of the debates.[19]

Assuming McKean meant to hurry the house into an early decision, Smilie delivered a "severe animadversion upon the motion." "No sir," he declared, "it is our duty to go coolly . . . into the consideration of this business, and . . . ask with firmness, 'Is such a sacrifice of civil liberty necessary to the national honor and happiness of America?' "[20] A nice touch by this wily old Irishman from Fayette County. In one rhetorical flurry he impugned the motives of his opponents and gave the question of ratification an Antifederalist's bias: Did America's plight demand the sacrifice of liberty?

Robert Whitehill then intervened, ostensibly to defuse the situation, but probably with quite a different end in mind. Suggesting that Smilie had misunderstood McKean's intention, Whitehill recommended that the convention accept McKean's motion and then suggested that they debate it in a committee of the whole.[21] Whitehill may well have been

---

tion of the Constitution by the States: Pennsylvania (Madison: State Historical Society of Wisconsin, 1976): 326–616. The exact sequence of exchanges between delegates remains speculative because, as the editors point out, "[t]he overall record of the debates is scattered and incomplete" and "the notes available make it difficult, if not impossible, to determine with precision, the order in which men spoke." Jensen 2:324–25. *Pennsylvania Herald*, 11/24/87; "Timothy Quandary," in Jensen 2:228, MFM 287.
18. *Independent Gazetteer*, 11/26/87, Jensen 2:332.
19. Jensen 2:334, 337.
20. Jensen 2:336–37.
21. Jensen 2:337.

innocent of ulterior motive, but his opponents thought otherwise. Debating the Constitution in the committee of the whole and then debating it again in the convention would provide the opponents of ratification with two opportunities to build their case with the public. In addition, and possibly of greater significance, the Federalists suspected that the Antifederalists planned to use the informality of the committee of the whole to modify or amend the document.[22] Soon, Whitehill admitted as much. The convention, he argued, was "not precluded from proposing amendments; ... [b]y proposing amendments we can hear what they say in other states, and then can accommodate." The Federalists, taking the position that "we must take the system in the whole, and, ... ratify or not," rejected Whitehill's request by a vote of 44 to 24.[23]

The Antifederalists then tried another stratagem. Whitehill requested that the convention, like the General Assembly, allow individual members to enter into the official record the reasons for their negative votes. The Federalists, suspecting a trap, resisted. Thomas Hartley, a staunch Episcopalian from York County, assumed that Whitehill aimed at delay. He, therefore, opposed the arrangement during the course of the debates but had no objection to it on the final vote. Other Federalists agreed. When Whitehill accepted this compromise, however, they changed their minds. Still uncertain about the Antifederalists' purposes, they denied the proposal. Dr. Rush, eschewing subtleties, put it bluntly: "We know, sir, of what nature the protests will be, and if they bear the complexion of the publications that have lately teemed from the press, I am sure they would not be honorable to this body." Wilson, usually more diplomatic, this time matched Rush's tone: "Look at the Journals of the legislature of Pennsylvania, and you will find altercations there which are adapted to the meridian of Billingsgate."[24]

Neither man fully discerned the Antifederalists' goal but Smilie soon explained it to them. If, Smilie argued, the Antifederalists could "produce a change in the minds of the people and incline them to new

22. For evidence that Federalists worried about Antifederalist use of the debate in the committee of the whole to propose amendments see *Pennsylvania Packet*, 11/27/87, in Jensen 2:367. On Monday, 11/26/87, the Federalists changed rule 10 in order to allow each man to "speak as often as he pleases" and thus weaken Whitehill's demand for debate in committee of the whole. "Convention Proceedings," 11/26/87, in Jensen 2:364, and newspaper report in *Packet*, 11/27/87, in Jensen 2:367.
23. Jensen 2:364–65.
24. Jensen 2:375, 373.

measures" then "the people . . . have a right to assemble another body [a second convention] . . . to abrogate this federal work." Using Wilson's own words, Smilie reminded them, "the people have at all times a power to alter and abolish government." Federalists, hoist on their own petard, but now aware of the Antifederalist goal, rejected Whitehill's request.[25]

Debates: More Strategic than Substantial

When the Federalists voted down Whitehill's proposal on Monday, November 26, the convention had been in session for a week, or approximately one third of its ultimate duration. The preliminaries over, the delegates now proceeded to the ostensible reason for their meeting: debate on the merits of the proposed Federal Constitution. By now, the Antifederalist strategy had become clear. They hoped first to amend and thus radically alter the central thrust of the document. That failing, they worked to build public support for a second convention to nullify the Federalist victory in this one. Or, as Antifederalist Smilie put it, their goal was "to refer all authority to the people."[26]

Much of what the Antifederalists said in the convention aimed at one or the other or both of these goals. Take for example, the issue of paper money. Few, if any leaders in Pennsylvania now advocated laws making paper money a legal tender equivalent in value to hard money (specie or gold and silver) in private business transactions. Furthermore, neither party in the past had consistently and uniformly pressed for such legislation, and most agreed in condemning Rhode Island's irresponsible behavior in this regard. Thus, in 1787 Federalists and Antifederalists could unite in applauding the Federal Constitution's ban on this kind of state paper money. The Antifederalists, however, went further. Attempting to revive and exploit the widespread memories of worthless paper

25. Jensen 2:376, 382.
26. 12/12/87, in Jensen 2:600. We have relatively complete transcripts of Antifederalist and Federalist speeches for only the first few days of the actual debate. For the remainder we have more or less verbatim accounts of many Federalist addresses but not those of their opponents. Our knowledge of much of the Antifederalist argument, therefore, must be inferred from bits and pieces of recorded speeches and from the summaries made by the Federalists. See Jensen 2:322–25.

money issued by the Continental Congress during the war, they condemned the Federal Constitution for not extending the ban on paper money to Congress.²⁷

Antifederalists also made good use of the Constitution's compromises with slavery and its lack of a bill of rights. Antifederalists needed to build popular support in the five crucial eastern counties that contained large concentrations of Quakers and Germans, especially German Sectarians. At the same time, they had to maintain their traditional support among the Scots-Irish Presbyterians and the German Reformed. Debates that focused on slavery and the bill of rights served this purpose well. The proposed Constitution accommodated itself to the continued existence of slavery in the new nation. Antifederalists had explored this issue in the fall campaign. Now they returned to it with vigor; in part from principle; moreso, one suspects, from practical politics.

Both Constitutionalists and Republicans deplored slavery. Their leaders had worked together in the past to end it in Pennsylvania. George Bryan looked back with great pride at Pennsylvania's 1780 law for the gradual abolition of slavery passed by a Constitutionalist-dominated legislature. "Our bill," he later wrote, "astonishes and pleases the Quakers. They looked for no such benevolent issue of our government, exercised by the Presbyterians." Bryan's party, however, had not fully united on the question and Republicans had cooperated in support of the bill.²⁸

Over the years the state legislature had acted often to tighten up the system, to plug loopholes, and to extend limited civil rights to those still enslaved in Pennsylvania. These measures generally received bipartisan support. Moreover, on an individual basis, Federalists probably had as strong an antislavery record as the Antifederalists. In the state legislature, Anglicans, Quakers, and Sectarian Assemblymen (principally Republican) had voted antislavery positions more consistently than had their Scots-Irish, Presbyterian, and Reformed colleagues (mostly, if not exclusively, Constitutionalists). Moreover, Pennsylvania's Society for

27. Owen S. Ireland, "Crux of Politics: Religion and Party in Pennsylvania, 1778–1789," *William and Mary Quarterly* 42 (October 1985): 457; Jensen 2:506.
28. Owen S. Ireland, "Germans Against Abolition," *Journal of Interdisciplinary History* 4 (1973): 687–89. Quote from Martha B. Clark, "Lancaster County's Relation to Slavery," Lancaster County (Pa.) Historical Society *Historical Papers and Addresses*, 15:50. Antifederalist leader Robert Whitehill and at least one other Antifederalist delegate at the convention owned slaves. See Forrest McDonald, *We the People* (Chicago: University of Chicago Press, 1958), 179, 180.

the Gradual Abolition of Slavery listed among its members a number of Republican-Federalists but no conspicuous Constitutionalist-Antifederalists.[29]

Both Federalists and Antifederalists also recognized that while the Federal Constitution accepted slavery it did not impose it on any state. Each state remained free to pursue its own course. Wilson, while deploring slavery, praised the Federal Constitution for "laying the foundation for banishing slavery out of this country" and for granting Congress the power (at least in his mind) to ensure that in the new states admitted to the union, "slaves will never be introduced amongst them."[30] Antifederalists undoubtedly raised the question of the Constitution's compromises with slavery because of their honest distaste for the institution. More important, however, this issue provided them with a means of exploiting the tensions within the Federalist coalition. Quakers, an essential element in the Federalist voting alliance, found the Constitution's compromises with slavery morally repugnant and a stumbling block in their support for ratification. Antifederalists struck a virtuous pose and encouraged this Quaker concern.

The exchanges over a bill of rights exhibited a similar pattern. In this instance, as in so many others, no principled difference emerged between the two sides. Antifederalists discovered a weakness and exploited it; Federalists hunkered down and waited for the storm to pass, hoping to contain the damage. The Grand Convention had failed to include a bill of rights in the Constitution; why remains puzzling. From a political perspective, the lack of a enumeration of basic civil liberties was a liability. Undoubtedly, Pennsylvania's Federalists would have gladly rectified that error, if they could have done so without endangering ratification itself. The lack of a bill of rights obviously embarrassed them. They had not anticipated an attack on this ground and, as the

---

29. Ireland, "Germans Against Abolition." See announcement and lists for the Society in *Packet*, 1/9/88.

30. Jensen 2:463. At the Grand Convention, both James Wilson and Gouverneur Morris had resisted the proposed compromises with slavery; Morris in particular anticipated one of the later Antifederalist arguments when he predicted that the Constitution's acceptance of slavery would force Northerners "to march their militia for the defense of the S. States . . . against the very slaves of whom they complain." See Paul Finkelman, "Slavery and the Constitutional Convention: Making a Covenant with Death," in Richard Beeman et al., eds., *Beyond Confederation: Origins of the Constitution and American National Identity* (Chapel Hill: University of North Carolina Press, for the Institute of Early American History and Culture, Williamsburg, Va., 1987), 188–225, esp. 197, 203–5, 212, 217–18. Quotation on 212.

tortured logic of their defense testifies, they had no ready answer to the Antifederalists' charges.

Yet, historically, Pennsylvania's Federalists stood on more solid ground than the Antifederalists in this area. True, during the fall 1787 campaign Federalists had countenanced mob violence against their opponents and had tried to limit Antifederalist access to the press. Still, they had established by far the stronger record over the previous decade on the local level.

Wilson, with impeccable patriot credentials, had served as legal counsel to accused "traitors," while Republicans in general had consistently acted to protect the rights of minorities. They had resisted popular demands for vengeance against suspected loyalists, trimmers, and collaborators in 1778–79; they had fought against the Constitutionalists' harassment of the Quakers and the pacifist Sectarians during the war; and they had led the drive to repeal the Test Acts once the war had ended. It was not they who had sent Quakers into exile in the wilds of western Virginia; hanged poor and possibly befuddled Philadelphians who had worked for the British during the occupation of the city; or silenced, disarmed, and then disfranchised those who had disagreed with them. Nor was it they who had invaded the consciences of those who opposed military service on religious grounds.[31]

Despite their previous record, however, Federalists now found themselves vulnerable and groping for a defense. At the state convention, Wilson initially argued that the democratic nature of the Constitution precluded the need for a bill of rights. "Supreme power resides in the people," he pointed out. The Constitution "is announced in their name, it receives its political existence from their authority. . . . Those who ordain and establish have the power, if they think proper, to repeal and annul . . . the people have a right to do what they please, with regard to the government."[32] John Smilie rejected this optimistic reliance on the will of the people: "The truth is that unless some criterion is established by which it could be easily and constitutionally ascertained how far our governors may proceed, and . . . when they transgressed their jurisdiction, this idea of altering and abolishing government is a mere sound without substance."[33]

---

31. Federalist Anthony Wayne pointed this out at the convention. Jensen 2:509, 511.
32. Jensen 2:383.
33. Jensen 2:385.

As a second line of defense, Wilson contended that a bill of rights was more appropriate in a monarchical system. In England, for example, the king had issued formal documents granting and enumerating specific liberties. In Magna Carta, "the king says, '*we* have *given* and *granted* to all . . . these liberties following, to be kept in our kingdom of England forever.'" In a similar vein, Wilson continued, the Petition of Right defined, expanded, and defended rights granted to the people by their sovereign. Now, however, with the new Constitution, Wilson concluded, the people are sovereign. They possess all their liberties as a matter of course, not as gifts. The government derives its powers from them. "What they have not expressly *granted* they have *retained*." Therefore a bill of rights is superfluous.[34]

Indeed, Wilson thought a bill of rights to be "highly imprudent." Federalist Thomas McKean argued that a bill of rights "though it can do no harm" was "an unnecessary instrument." Dr. Rush then embarrassed his friends and delighted his rivals by proclaiming: "I consider it as an honor to the late Convention that this system has not been disgraced with a bill of rights."[35]

After this brief diversion, Smilie challenged Wilson. The body of the document, he pointed out, expressly declared "that the writ of habeas corpus and trial by jury in criminal cases shall not be suspended or infringed." If the framers thought it necessary to list two rights, then all rights ought to be listed. Otherwise those not specified will be assumed to be abrogated.[36] Federalist Thomas Hartley then sought to put the Antifederalists on the defensive. A bill of rights might be desirable, he argued, but no group could agree on what to include: "while some are for this point, and others for that, it is now evidently impracticable to frame an instrument which will be satisfactory to the wishes of every man." McKean turned Hartley's taunt into a challenge: "I wish to see," he declared, "what kind of bill of rights these gentlemen would propose."[37]

In the heat of battle, McKean had misspoken. John Smilie seized the opportunity. "He was happy to hear [this]," he said, "for he had understood that the Convention [i.e., the Federalist majority] did not mean to admit either additions or amendments." If the Federalists

---
34. Jensen 2:383, 384.
35. 11/30/87, in Jensen 2:388, 434, 387–88.
36. Jensen 2:391–92.
37. Jensen 2:429–33; Jensen 2:441.

would agree to consider it, Smilie promised: "We will exhibit a bill of rights."[38] In short order, the Antifederalists hammered out a comprehensive list of fifteen amendments that Whitehill introduced dramatically on December 12. Hartley, with a second from Stephen Chambers, had just moved to ratify the Constitution and the end was in sight. The delegates waited quietly, if a bit impatiently, while Dr. Rush invited them to unanimity. Then Whitehill struck.

He introduced petitions from 750 inhabitants of Cumberland "praying . . . that the proposed Constitution should not be adopted without amendments, and particularly, without a bill of rights." McKean objected strenuously, reminding the convention that petitions were out of order and that it must vote on the document as a whole. Whitehill responded by demanding an indefinite adjournment and "offered as the ground of" such a motion, "the consideration of the following articles, which . . . might either be taken collectively as a bill of rights, or separately as amendments to the general form of government proposed."[39]

The logic of the situation exerted enormous pressure: many people wanted a bill of rights; Whitehill had a comprehensive compilation; let the people decide. Republican George Clymer had used similar logic in support of his September 28 call for a state convention. Whitehill had now turned this argument against the Federalists, and in case they missed the point, Smilie explained it to them: "If those gentlemen who have affected to refer all authority to the people, . . . are sincere, let them embrace this last opportunity to evince that sincerity."[40]

The personal liberties amendments presented by Whitehill were not, in themselves, particularly controversial. As Smilie pointed out, McKean himself had helped to construct such a list for the constitution of Delaware in 1776. The danger, from the Federalists' perspective, and hence the opportunity from the Antifederalists' point of view, was not that civil liberties amendments might be adopted. Rather, the addition of amendments at this point would produce a conditional ratification contingent upon the acceptance by other states of identical amendments. Years of experience with proposed modifications of the Articles of

---

38. *Pennsylvania Herald*, 12/1/87, in Jensen 2:444; Jensen 2:441.
39. Jensen 2:596; Jensen 2:597.
40. Jensen 2:600.

Confederation had demonstrated that such agreement was unlikely. Ratification tied to a specific set of changes probably meant no ratification at all.[41]

Of course, the Antifederalists were not being entirely candid. They had made the lack of a bill of rights one of their principal issues at the convention. They undoubtedly saw this as a major defect in the proposed system. They certainly deserve credit for their contribution to the later addition of the first ten amendments to the Constitution.[42] On the other hand, defense of individual rights was a relatively new stance for them. As an essay in the *Pennsylvania Gazette* pointed out, at least six of the Antifederalists in the convention, including Findley, Whitehill, and Smilie, had earlier approved of a legislative report attacking conscientious objectors. Moreover, Whitehill's proposal was not quite what it seemed. In addition to listing traditional civil liberties, it also contained at least six major alterations that would have gutted the framers' proposal and deprived the new general government of every species of domestic, internal power.[43]

Still, Whitehill's proposal posed a serious dilemma for the Federalists. If they accepted the motion, they would virtually preclude ratification in the foreseeable future. If they refused, they would reinforce the Antifederalist charges of a Federalist conspiracy, and of Federalists' aristocratic disdain for popular judgment. The Federalists, seeing no way out, rejected Whitehill's call for adjournment (23 to 46) and then, by exactly the same vote, ratified the Federal Constitution.[44] Whitehill made one last try. On Thursday, December 13, he protested that his amendments had not been properly inserted in the minutes of the Convention. Federalists saw that circulation of these Antifederalist propositions as part of the official proceedings of the convention would

---

41. Jensen 2:391. Robert Allen Rutland, *The Ordeal of the Constitution: The Antifederalists and the Ratification Struggle of 1787–1788* (Norman: University of Oklahoma Press, 1966), found major differences in the kinds of changes supported by Antifederalists in the various sections of the country. Jensen 2:589.

42. Both Federalists and Antifederalists agreed that the Antifederalists had focused their attacks on two broad issues: the lack of a bill of rights, and the consolidation of the annihilation of the states. See Jasper Yeates's notes in Jensen 2:434–35, Smilie's comments in Jensen 2:440, 441; and Wilson's speech on 12/4/87, in Jensen 2:469.

43. "A Citizen of Philadelphia," in *Pennsylvania Gazette*, 1/23/88, in Jensen 2:658. See particularly amendments 9, 10, 11, 13, 14, and 15, in Jensen 2:597–99.

44. Jensen 2:589–90.

both advertise the Antifederalist objections and, in a subtle way, lend them an aura of official recognition. On guard till the end, they summarily dismissed Whitehill's protest.[45]

Thus ended the convention's discussion of a bill of rights. Federalists, no less than Antifederalists, supported freedom of speech, freedom of the press, freedom of conscience, trial by jury, and the traditional British-American guarantees of personal freedom. Federalists, ironically, argued that these rights received adequate protection at the state level. The Antifederalists, with equal irony, disagreed and insisted on national-level protection. On this issue, as on the question of slavery, both sides may well have spoken from deep, principled concerns. For the Antifederalists, however, it hardly seems accidental that both of these issues touched directly on the sensitivities of Quakers and Sectarians living in key eastern counties.

Fundamental Issues

The issues of slavery and a bill of rights carried no obvious partisan overtones or messages. Thus, the Antifederalists at the convention, by focusing on these questions, moved away from earlier Antifederalist efforts to rouse ethnic-religious political loyalties. Their treatment of two other questions pointed in the same direction: the bicameral nature of the proposed Congress, and the relationship between the central government and the states.

The Federal Constitution called for a two-house legislature. Most observers in Pennsylvania saw approval of this new system as a challenge to the state's constitution and its most unique feature: the single-house legislature. Findley, Whitehill, and Smilie spoke for the state Constitutionalist party. They and their partisans had stood foursquare on the tenets of the state constitution of 1776 for more than a decade. In the fall contest for the state convention, "Centinel" had initially grounded the Antifederalist campaign on defense of that state constitution. On this question, if anywhere, one might expect a "great debate" over political principles.

At the convention, however, no such debate took place. Federalists,

---

45. Jensen 2:603–4.

continuing to minimize direct attacks on the Pennsylvania constitution, ignored the issue. Antifederalists, however, in a most astonishing reversal of positions, abandoned their commitment to unicameralism. Both Smilie and Findley accepted the principle of a divided legislature. Wilson, surprised to find "that the doctrine of a single legislature is not to be contended for," concluded that he need "say nothing on that point."[46]

The parallel concept of a multiple and relatively impotent executive died an even more obscure death. Antifederalists, long champions of legislative supremacy in Pennsylvania, now criticized the Federal Constitution for its failure to give sufficient independence and power to the office of the president. They feared, they said, that he would be a mere tool of the Senate. Furthermore, Pennsylvania's Antifederalists, now champions of separation of powers and internal checks and balances, discovered in the Federal Constitution a fateful blend of functions in such provisions as the negotiation of treaties, the appointment of judicial and administrative officers, and in impeachments. The Federalists conceded the case. They admitted the difficulty, said they wished it otherwise, but urged the convention to accept the Federal Constitution anyway. In their minds, it greatly improved upon the Articles of Confederation, which lodged all power in a unicameral Congress.[47]

Antifederalists at the convention thus quietly relinquished the central issue that had defined their political identity in Pennsylvania for a decade. Why remains unclear; most likely, they sought to build bridges. The more they focused public opinion on the state constitution of 1776, the more they would alienate those they needed, both in Pennsylvania and elsewhere. Smilie also said that he conceded the point because so many other states subscribed to the bicameral principle.[48] In addition, it seems possible that the Antifederalists' failure in the election of November 6 had shaken them. Both Findley and Smilie read the political winds well. They survived the demise of the Constitutionalist party in the late 1780s and were among the few who later acquired seats in Congress.

46. Jensen 2:459, 465, 466, 487, 504.
47. Jensen 2:491. The principle of a strong executive may not have consistently divided Constitutionalists from Republicans in Pennsylvania. In the summer of 1783 the Constitutionalists in Bucks County demanded protection and preservation of the state constitution while deploring the "feebleness of the executive." *Pennsylvania Packet*, 8/7/83, reporting on a meeting at Bennett's Tavern, 7/29/83.
48. Jensen 2:465.

This shift may also have reflected an emerging difference between the older and the newer members of the Constitutionalist party; a growing fissure between Findley and Smilie on the one hand, and the original supporters of the state constitution—the George Bryan group who lived in the city, held appointed offices, and had organized the Constitutionalist party in 1777–78.

Findley, a backcountry Scots-Irish Presbyterian, had entered state politics after the two parties had congealed in the Assembly along sharp ethnoreligious lines. He may have joined the Constitutionalists more because they were the party of the Scots-Irish Presbyterians than because of his commitment to the state constitution of 1776. Furthermore, Findley and Smilie had experienced the frustration facing the minority in a unicameral legislature. Both had also served in the relatively powerless Supreme Executive Council while their political opponents controlled the unicameral state legislature. In the fall of 1787, Findley had hinted at a growing disillusionment with simple majoritarian rule. He defended the minority's use of the two-thirds quorum rule to prevent hasty and imprudent legislation. Later, he claimed that he had never liked a unicameral legislature, and in 1790 he cooperated with James Wilson at the state's constitutional convention to give Pennsylvania a bicameral legislature.

Not all Antifederalists explicitly adopted this new position. Whitehill, who had been a member of the state convention that created the unicameral-based constitution in 1776, did not join Findley and Smilie in an explicit repudiation of unicameralism. Furthermore, "The Dissent of the Minority," the protest issued in the name of the Antifederalists after the convention, reintroduced the issue. Probably written by the same man who authored the "Centinel" essays, it reminded its readers that Republicans had dominated the state's delegation to the Federal Convention and it argued that the Federal Constitution would "alter and may annihilate the constitution of Pennsylvania." The "Dissent" clearly differed from the main line of argument developed by the Antifederalists at the convention.[49]

---

49. Whitehill's apparent ambivalence may reflect his unique position as one of the few elected backcountry Constitutionalists who had helped create the constitution in 1776. He had been among its earliest and most consistent supporters. On December 8 he argued that the oath to the Federal Constitution contradicted the one required by the state constitution and he worried that "the next thing will be to call conventions to alter the state government," Jensen 2:527. See "Dissent of the Minority," in Jensen 2:620, 621.

Be that as it may. The main point remains: Antifederalist spokesmen at the state Convention chose not to build their case on unicameralism. Instead, they emphasized what they referred to as "the annihilation" of the states, an issue with far greater appeal across partisan lines. In the course of these exchanges, the Antifederalists sharpened the focus of what appears to have been their principal fear: the internal, domestic powers of the new central government. In response, the Federalists, and especially James Wilson, redefined the concept of sovereignty and articulated a new way of thinking about the relationship between the states and the central government.

Robert Whitehill made the Antifederalist case against consolidation early, thoroughly and forcefully. This system, he argued, is "designed to abolish the independence and sovereignty of the states." Its preamble, "We the People of the United States," he said, "shows the old foundation of the Union is destroyed, the principle of confederation excluded." The body of the Constitution, he continued, details what the preamble announces. It authorizes Congress to make "all laws that are necessary to carry it [the Constitution] effectively into operation" and gives it control of "the place and manner of elections," and thus control of the results. It empowers the central government to impose internal taxes that will in time deprive "the several states of every means to support their governments"; and it makes treaties "the supreme law of the land." In short, "[t]hat government which possesses all the powers of raising and maintaining armies, of regulating and commanding the militia, and of laying imposts and taxes of every kind must be supreme and will (whether in twenty or in one year . . .) naturally absorb every subordinate jurisdiction."[50]

James Wilson again anticipated the Antifederalist attack. He, too, rejected a consolidated national government. Republicanism government, he conceded, worked best in small geographic areas with representatives close to the people, reflective of their diversity, responsive to their needs, and subject to their close scrutiny. On the other hand, no individual state could stand alone, and he himself opposed the division of the United States into two or three regional confederacies. The times and the circumstances demanded some degree and kind of national

---

50. Jensen 2:393, *Pennsylvania Herald*, 12/12/87. Jensen 2:395, 396, 398. Article I, sect. 8 of the U.S. Constitution provides that "Congress shall have power . . . to make all laws which shall be necessary and proper for carrying into Execution the foregoing Powers . . ."

unification. "Licentiousness was secretly undermining the rock on which she [America] stood." Internal anarchy, an excess of imports, an unreliable revenue for Congress, a lack of foreign markets, the decline of national credit, the inability of the United States to negotiate or enforce treaties—all of these threatened the existence of this new republic.[51]

America, in Wilson's mind, thus faced a cruel dilemma: on the one hand, a loose confederation of small republics assailed from within and from without by the forces of anarchy, economic depression, and tyranny; on the other, a consolidated union powerful enough to guarantee order and protect the national interest but dangerous to republican self-government. The proposed Federal Constitution, Wilson argued, solved this dilemma. It created a "confederate republic," an experiment without historic precedent, but one consistent with the needs and the aspirations of this republican people.[52]

Wilson explained a "confederate republic" with an analogy. Individuals in a state of nature come together and surrender some of their specific liberties in order to form a government and thus preserve their actual freedom. In the same way the states could come together, each sacrificing some autonomy in order to enhance the liberties of all. The states, like individuals in the compact, remained the essential building blocks of the society. Each retained most of its freedom of action. But their unity enhanced the actual freedom of each in much the same way that entering into the social compact enhanced the real freedoms of individual men.[53]

Such an arrangement, he argued, substituted limited but real liberty for the absolute but illusory freedom of the isolated and defenseless individual. "When a confederate republic is instituted," Wilson put it, "the communities, of which it is composed, surrender to it a part of their political independence, . . . [but] that part, and that part only, . . . which, placed in that government will produce more good to the whole than if it had remained in the several states."[54] The concept of the "confederate republic" cut the Gordian knot, at least for Wilson. America could be a collection of republics and one great nation at the same time.

Wilson complemented this grand vision with a simplistic and superfi-

51. Jensen 2:352, 357, 360.
52. Jensen 2:352.
53. Jensen 2:359.
54. Jensen 2:359–60.

cial argument, technically correct but too clever by half. The federal government cannot destroy the states, he explained, because federal elections presuppose the existence of the states. The Senate is chosen directly by the state legislature; the presidential electors are chosen in a manner prescribed by the state legislature; and the qualifications of the electors is the same as that of the most numerous branch of the state legislature. Hence, no state legislatures meant no U.S. House of Representatives, no Senate, and no presidential elections.[55]

Wilson then switched to haughty indignation and at best, half-truths. Assertions have been "hazarded on this floor," he continued, "that it was the business of [the framers] to destroy the state governments. . . . [Mr. Whitehill] may be better qualified to judge of their intentions than themselves. . . . Where did *he* obtain his information? Let the tree be judged by its fruit." He then concluded with what, in charity, we may call hyperbole: "The truth is, sir, that the framers of this system were particularly anxious . . . to preserve the state governments unimpaired—it was their favorite object."[56]

John Smilie, ignoring Wilson's imperious tone, responded with patient reasoning. That the organization and operation of the general government "naturally presuppose" the existence of the forms of the state government, he pointed out, was hardly the question. Forms may persist. It was power and not words that were at issue: the power to impose internal taxes, the power to maintain a standing army, the power to regulate and command the state militia, the power to "provide for the common defence and general welfare of the United States." "With such powers . . . what cannot the future governors accomplish?" This was not a "union of states which are sovereign and independent except in the specific objects of confederation." No, said Smilie, this was a consolidated government that would destroy the states.[57]

Not so, responded Federalist Thomas McKean. "The meaning which appears to be plain and well expressed is simply this, that Congress have the power of making laws upon any subject over which the proposed plan gives them a jurisdiction." The Constitution thus defined a restricted jurisdiction for the federal government. Not any laws, but only those laws passed by Congress upon subjects within that jurisdic-

---

55. Jensen 2:401.
56. Jensen 2:402, 405.
57. Jensen 2:407, 410, Jensen 2:407, 408.

tion were the supreme law of the land. Within its limited realm, the federal government was supreme. In all other matters the states remained supreme. Thus, each government was supreme in its own sphere.[58]

McKean here admitted one of the Antifederalists' central contentions: the Federal Constitution did indeed limit the sovereignty of the states. This, however, did not necessarily destroy the states, McKean argued. It was not a question of national *or* state supremacy, but rather, one of jurisdictions. Each government, the general and the state, remained autonomous within its own jurisdiction. The sovereignty of one did not infringe on the sovereignty of the other; the two coexisted in parallel but separate realms. Given this definition of the relationship between the two levels of government, the question then becomes not whether the general government will destroy the states, but whether this particular definition of the two spheres and this particular distribution of powers between the spheres is appropriate.

Whitehill would have none of this. In his mind sovereignty was absolute and indivisible. Either the states or the general government must be supreme and the Constitution favored the latter. He again detailed the specific grants of power to Congress and concluded that in this system the central government would "eventually annihilate the independent . . . sovereignty of the states." He, for one, was willing to follow Wilson's advice and judge the tree by its fruit. This tree bore the fruit of consolidation; the powerful central government would annihilate the states.[59]

Findley, however, continued to explore this new idea. Although he thundered against this "consolidated government," he implicitly accepted McKean's conception of sovereignty divided into spheres. However, he challenged the way the Constitution distributed powers between the two spheres. The Constitution was unacceptable, Findley said, because "the powers of the general government extended to state and internal purposes."[60]

This statement of the problem represented progress: not much, but some. Antifederalists had generally argued that any extension of federal powers beyond war, peace, and commercial regulation infringed upon

---

58. Jensen 2:416.
59. Jensen 2:440.
60. Ibid.

state sovereignty. Findley had not abandoned this position, but he had rephrased and possibly reconceptualized it. He had moved from a list of particular powers (war, peace, and commercial regulation) to general categories of powers: external and internal. He still thought of the states as sovereign entities and of the central government as their common agent for dealing with the rest of the world. Findley was thus no closer to Wilson and McKean than he had ever been, but the focus of the debate could now shift to the question of whether or not the central government should deal only with external (foreign) affairs and leave all internal (domestic) concerns to the individual states.

Federalist Jasper Yeates offered a parallel but quite different criterion for allocating powers between Congress and the states. Each state, he argued, should deal with those matters particular to itself while the central government focused its attention on those matters that "embrace[d] the general interests of the United States." To put it differently: the particular governments should deal with particular questions; the general government with general questions.[61]

Findley, however, continued to insist on a division between external and internal affairs. He accepted the need for central regulation of commerce, central handling of treaties, and an independent source of central revenue. He rejected internal taxing power, congressional control over elections, the extension of the federal judicial powers into the states, the dependence of the state officers on the general government (oaths of allegiance), and the payment of state congressional representatives out of the common treasury. More important, he could not conceive of two sovereign domestic powers. "There cannot be two sovereign powers," he argued. "A subordinate sovereignty is no sovereignty" and the powers granted to Congress, especially its internal taxing power, made it supreme.[62]

Findley, like Whitehill, conceived of sovereignty as absolute and indivisible. He also thought of sovereignty as the possession of a government: the king, the Congress, the states. Wilson now challenged these assumptions and thereby added a new dimension to the discussion. "The secret," he declared, "is now disclosed . . . a dread that the boasted states sovereignties will . . . be disrobed of part of their power." But this fear, he continued, rested on the erroneous principle that

61. Jensen 2:435, 438.
62. Jensen 2:445–46.

"sovereign power resides in the state governments." Nothing could be further from the truth. Sovereignty resides not in the states, and not in the nation, but in the people who "dispensed such portions of power as were conceived necessary for the public welfare." The people, in full possession of their sovereignty, Wilson continued, could "distribute one portion of power to the more contracted circle called state governments ... [and] ... also furnish another portion to the government of the United States."[63] In defining sovereignty in this way, Wilson provided a populist justification for McKean's delineation of the two spheres. The sovereign people bestowed some powers on one government and some on another, so as best to meet the needs and advance the interests of the total community. "Who," Wilson asked, "will undertake to say ... that the people may not give to the general government what powers, and for what purposes they please?"[64]

James Wilson, still imperious, still condescending, still infuriating; but also James Wilson the political thinker, the brilliant and imaginative legal mind, wrestling with one of the thorniest intellectual challenges in the political science of the late eighteenth-century English-speaking world: how to reconcile and integrate the local and the central, the particular and the general, the periphery and the center, the narrow community and the broader society. This problem had precipitated the imperial crises of the 1760s and early 1770s. The failure of statesmen in England and in America to solve it had torn the British Empire apart. Now, the same problem was causing crisis in the new nation. Wilson, in spite of his frailties, made a substantive contribution to the redefinition of this dilemma, and thus, possibly, to its ultimate solution.

Dr. Benjamin Rush, on the other hand, added only comic relief and consternation. His failure to understand in no way inhibited him. Threatening to set the debate back to its original starting ground, he accepted the Antifederalist conclusion that the Federal Constitution destroyed the states, and rejoiced. "A passion for state sovereignty," he asserted, "had dissolved the union of Greece. Britain—France—enjoyed more advantages *united* then *separate*. A plurality of sovereigns is political idolatry. The sovereignty of Pennsylvania is ceded to the United States. . . . I am a citizen of every state."[65] Rush's position was politically

---

63. Jensen 2:448, 449.
64. Ibid.
65. Jensen 2:457, 458.

imprudent. However reflective of the private opinions of his Federalist colleagues, few of them believed that the people would accept a dissolution of the states into one national political unit. Smilie moved quickly to exploit Rush's error. "It is admitted," he declared, "that state sovereignty is given up. . . . I never heard anything so ridiculous except a former [sentiment] of the same gentlemen."[66]

Smilie gladly redefined the issue in terms of incompatible sovereignties. Findley, however, did not. He seemed to be struggling toward Wilson's new formulation of the problem. He began with the obvious: "This [the Federal Constitution] is a government of individuals, and not a confederation of states." Hence, a consolidation. But he had listened to Wilson and thought about the new definition of sovereignty. Yes, he admitted, sovereignty did reside in the people, but it "is in the states and not in the people in its exercise." He was not sure quite where this left him, but he would listen. "I wish not to destroy this system" he said, "its outlines are well laid. By amendments it may answer our wishes."[67]

In time Findley accepted Wilson's position, or at least expressed sentiments almost identical to those of Wilson. When Wilson said that Findley believed "that the supreme power resides in the states, as governments" Findley corrected him. "Who denied that sovereignty was inalienable in the people?" he demanded. "Sovereignty essentially resides in the people, but they have *vested* certain parts of it in the state governments and other parts in the present Congress." Findley accepted that. The problem was that "[t]he states have already parted with a portion of their sovereignty. It is now proposed to give more. But the people did not mean that the whole should be given up to the general government." Wilson would certainly have rejected Findley's conclusion, but both men were now using much the same language to express their understanding of the problem.[68]

One could accept McKean's conception of two spheres and Wilson's descriptions of sovereign people conferring different powers on each sphere and still contest the particular distribution inherent in the proposed Federal Constitution, and this Findley did. While continuing to pay homage to the ultimately sovereign people and recognizing that

66. Jensen 2:459.
67. Ibid.
68. Jensen 2:473, 502, 503.

they could allocate and reallocate powers as they felt necessary, he worked to maintain his earlier distinction between internal and external powers. He believed that providing the general government with internal taxing powers tipped the balance irreversibly in the direction of central authority: "Internal powers in a federal government are *inadmissible*."[69]

Findley's colleagues continued to itemize these infringements on state sovereignty. The judicial power, Whitehill claimed, would be "blended with and will absorb the judicial powers of the several states. . . . Any kind of action may by contrivance, be brought into federal courts. . . . There is no line drawn, in the judicial department, between the general and the state governments."[70]

Smilie felt the same about the federal control over state militia: "militia officers will be obliged by oath to support the general government against that of their own state." He asked, "Will the states give up to Congress their last resource—the command of the militia?" If so, the "governor of each state will be only the drill sergeant of Congress."[71] At the session's end, Findley summed up the Antifederalist position: the proposed Constitution creates a consolidated government; "[i]n connection with this principle were all our arguments."[72]

Although Federalists and Antifederalists did not agree, did not like each other, and often showed mutual disrespect, they were coming to understand each other as Wilson illustrated in his valedictory address on Tuesday, December 11. On this, the last day before the final vote, Wilson regaled his audience with a four-hour-and-twenty-minute dissertation, mercifully halved by the midday adjournment. As a summary statement to the jury it was masterly. Slowly and carefully he isolated and attacked each of the Antifederalists' arguments. Then, changing pace and shifting focus, he painted an almost lyric word-picture of the future greatness awaiting this noble and blessed people once ratification had been achieved.

More to the point, he demonstrated that he too had come to better appreciate the nature of the problem and the differences that separated the Federalists and the Antifederalists. He succinctly defined the essence of the Antifederalists' position: "It has been alleged by honorable

69. Jensen 2:503.
70. Jensen 2:506, 513, 514.
71. Jensen 2:509, 508.
72. Jensen 2:547.

gentlemen, that this general government possesses powers, for *internal* purposes, and that the general government *cannot exercise* internal powers. The honorable member from Westmoreland [Findley] dilates on this subject and instances the opposition was [made] by the colonies against Great Britain, to prevent her imposing internal taxes or excises."

Wilson understood Findley's distinction, but argued that experience had demonstrated that such a division would not work. "Congress, under the present Articles of Confederation, possess no internal power, and we see the consequences." Some middle ground was needed, and "the great object now to be attended to, instead of disagreeing about who shall possess the supreme power, is to consider whether the present arrangement [i.e., the Federal Constitution] is well calculated to promote and secure the tranquility and happiness of our common country." He, for one, believed it was.[73]

By the end of the convention, the debate on sovereignty and on the relationship between the states and the central government had evolved, at least a bit. Antifederalists now agreed, at least some of the time, that the sovereign people could distribute "portions" of their sovereignty to discrete levels of government: some to the central government and some to the states. They disagreed with the Federalists over how to allocate specific powers between these discrete levels. Antifederalists still drew the line between the internal and external affairs. They argued that conferring domestic powers on the national government set the axe to the roots of state autonomy and would produce, sooner or later, a consolidated union.

Finally, the amendments proposed by Whitehill on December 12 suggest that on this distinction between internal and external powers, more than on most other questions, the Antifederalists disagreed fundamentally and in principle with the Federalists. Seven of Whitehill's proposals dealt with such traditional civil liberties as freedom of press and speech, trial by jury, the right to bear arms. One defended religious freedom and denied the federal government the authority to interfere with state protections of religious liberty. Another reiterated the need for strict separation of powers, called for judicial independence, and proposed the creation of a council to assist the president and thus further separate the operations of the president and the Senate in such areas as treaties and appointments.[74]

73. Jensen 2:557, 559.
74. Jensen 2:597–99.

Of the remaining six amendments, one articulated the principle underlying the others. Amendment 15 reserved to the states all powers not expressly delegated to the central government and, like the Articles of Confederation, firmly asserted the "sovereignty, freedom and independence of the several states." The remaining five attacked virtually every internal domestic power granted to the new central government: internal taxes, control of federal elections and of the state militia, federal judicial power within the states, and the power of treaties to abrogate federal law, state legislation, and state constitutions.[75]

What Whitehill left out is also suggestive. These amendments made no mention of slavery, the slave trade, paper money and tender laws, bicameral versus unicameral legislatures or a host of particular Antifederalist criticisms voiced both in the convention and in the public prints. All of these disappear in Whitehill's final distillation and we are left with one bold and indisputable thrust: the creation of a central government with virtually no authority to interfere in the sovereign internal affairs of states.

Whether these amendments reflect the central core of the Antifederalist beliefs or simply another rhetorical strategy is conjectural. The explicit denial of federal power to interfere with state constitutional protection of religious liberty, as well as the assertion of the need for greater separation of powers, may well have been included primarily for political effect. The remainder, however, appear to have defined the bedrock, authentic Antifederalist concern.[76]

Whatever the case, at the state convention Pennsylvania's Antifederalists had defined a position somewhat different from that with which "Centinel" had inaugurated the Antifederalist campaign back in early October. At least for now, the state constitution of 1776, unicameral legislatures, and partisan appeals were gone. The Antifederalists had rested their case on personal liberty and on state autonomy. This new stand transcended partisanship, and provided the Antifederalists with a potentially wider and more solid base for opposition both within Pennsylvania as well as in the neighboring states, a happy fusion of principle and partisan ploy.

75. Ibid.
76. Findley later wrote privately that "I do not object to the construction of the new system . . . but to the powers as they extend to internal objects." To William Irvine, 3/12/88, as quoted in Burnhouse, *The Counter-Revolution in Pennsylvania, 1776–1790* (Harrisburg: Pennsylvania Historical Commission, 1942), 213, 293.

Federalist Hubris

The exchanges on state sovereignty represent one aspect of the convention: rational, calculating, and cool. Parallel to this, and of equal significance, an increasingly acerbic and heated conflict raged, derived at least in part from the arrogance of the Federalists, and the frustration, the anger, and possibly the physical exhaustion of the Antifederalists. One protracted exchange illustrates the point and suggests both the tone and the temper of the convention's final week. Beginning on Saturday, December 8, and ending on Wednesday, December 12, the episode featured Findley, Smilie, Wilson, and McKean and reveals both the tension generated and the increasingly personal nature of the debate.

The flare-up began on Saturday morning with a long speech by Smilie on the questions of trial by jury in civil cases and on the appellate jurisdiction of the federal courts. Findley continued the argument, making the point that historically, those countries that had lost their right to a trial by jury had soon after lost their liberty. In Sweden, for example, he pointed out, "when the trial by jury, which was known [there] so late as the middle of the last century, fell into disuse, the commons of that nation lost their freedom and a tyrannical aristocracy prevailed."[77]

Wilson and McKean both leaped to correct Findley. These jurists prided themselves on their knowledge of history and of the law; one ranked among the most prominent lawyers in the state; the other was the chief justice of the province. Both "called warmly for his [Findley's] authority to prove that the trial by jury existed in Sweden, Mr. Wilson declaring that he had never met with such an idea in the course of his reading; and Mr. McKean asserting that the trial by jury was never known in any other country than England and the governments descended from that kingdom."[78]

Findley, surprised, said he "did not, at that moment, recollect his authority, but having formerly read histories of Sweden, he had received and retained the opinion which he now advanced." Smilie then reentered the fray. "The honorable gentleman had treated the opposition with contempt," he declared, "and with a *magisterial air* had condemned their arguments." Before he could continue, several members

77. Jensen 2:528.
78. Ibid.

protested. Stephen Chambers termed Smilie's language *"indecent"* and then, in words that may have inadvertently revealed much about the underlying Federalist thinking, "proceeded with great heat to reprobate" the Antifederalists. They had, he declared, *"abused* the *indulgence* which the other side of the house had *granted* to them in consenting to hear all their reasons"; he demanded to know "where had they been found in the day of danger" (i.e., during the Revolution); and he raised questions about the ability of recent immigrants to understand and judge the politics of Pennsylvania.[79] Smilie first took a defensive posture asking "whether he had used a single word which could be deemed *indecent.*" Then, shifting ground, he 'feelingly exclaimed that he was pleading for the interests of his country, and that no character should influence, and no violence overawe his proceeding."[80]

Findley rose to do battle: "[I] should take very little notice of the speech delivered by Mr. Chambers, as, indeed, [I have] never found occasion to take much notice of anything that dropt from that quarter [since] the characteristic of the conduct of the honorable members in public bodies was to discourse without reason and to talk without argument." Over cries of indignation, Findley continued that he had "always wished to avoid an investigation of characters, but at least he would take care never to engage on that subject but with a competent judge."[81] Chambers, infuriated by Findley, "retorted that he had a perfect contempt both for Mr. Findley's arguments and person." Findley, with what we might hope was a faint hint of a smile, replied "that he saw no reason for dispute since he and Mr. Chambers were in that respect so perfectly agreed."[82]

After Smilie, McKean, and McPherson had each added his mite, Findley appealed to the chair for a ruling. President Frederick Muhlenberg, loyal to his Federalist companions, admitted that no positive rule had been broken but said "he could not avoid considering Mr. Smilie's language highly improper." Before more could be said, a chorus of voices demanded adjournment, "which at last" the *Pennsylvania Herald* observed, "put a stop to the altercation."[83]

But only for a time. Findley returned triumphant on Monday. Over

79. Jensen 2:528–30.
80. Ibid.
81. Ibid.
82. Ibid.
83. Jensen 2:531.

the weekend he had found his sources: *The Modern Universal History* and the third volume of Blackstone's *Commentaries*. After sharing these with the house, he evened the score with Wilson and McKean: "That the account given in the *Universal History* should escape the recollection or observation of the best informed man is not extraordinary, but . . . if my son had been at the study of law for six months and was not acquainted with the passage in Blackstone, I should be justified in whipping him."[84] McKean knew he was beaten and offered no explicit rebuttal. Not so with Wilson. He acknowledged that Findley had been essentially correct but he could not bring himself to apologize and move on. First he whined: "I do not pretend to remember everything I read." He then pontificated: "It may therefore with propriety be said, by my honorable colleague [McKean] as it was formerly said by Sir John Maynard to a petulant student who reproached him with an ignorance of a trifling point: 'Young man, I have forgotten more law than ever you learned.'"[85]

Antifederalists inside and outside the convention enjoyed Findley's triumph. Although it could have little if any effect on the final outcome of the convention, it was a small and much appreciated victory. As William Shippen, Jr., wrote to his son: "Findley had gained great honor and proved himself vastly superior to Wilson and the whole Convention. . . . What a stroke to the pride of two men who think themselves the greatest in the United States!"[86] But the incident was not yet ended. McKean next began a three-hour summary statement of the Federalists' position. He slogged through a seemingly endless point-by-point refutation of the major Antifederalists' objections and then, near the end of his address, he took his revenge on Findley.

McKean apologized for not addressing every Antifederalist concern: "There have been some other small objections to, or rather criticisms of this work, which I rest assured the gentlemen who made them will, on reflection, excuse me in omitting to notice them." He also appeared to apologize for not responding to "some other things . . . said with acrimony." But, he continued, "they seemed to be personal; I heard the sound, but it was inarticulate. I can compare it to nothing better than the feeble noise occasioned by the working of small beer."[87] The gallery

84. Jensen 2:532.
85. Jensen 2:551.
86. Jensen 2:549.
87. Jensen 2:533, 542.

erupted with cheers and laughter. Sitting patiently for the better part of three hours, they had endured endless repetition of arguments they could almost recite by heart; they now had their reward. Findley's masterly thrusts and Smilie's accusations, all reduced to "the feeble noise occasioned by the working of small beer," not far removed from the grumbling of empty stomachs or the escape of flatulence from corpulent old men.

Smilie was infuriated. "Those who clap and laugh are not the people of Pennsylvania," he declared. "I have never found we had the worst of the argument until tonight. We have no people to laugh for us. . . . But, sir, let it be remembered that this is not the voice of the people of Pennsylvania . . . and were this Convention assembled at another place, the sound would be of a different nature." He ended on an ominous note: "In short, Mr. President, this is not the mode which will prevail on the citizens of Pennsylvania to adopt the proposed plan, let the decision here be what it may."[88]

The final exchange took place on Wednesday morning, December 12, the day of the ratification vote. McKean had monopolized Monday and Wilson Tuesday. On Wednesday morning Findley had his turn and "closed his arguments in opposition to the proposed federal system." He approached the subject seriously, citing Vattel, Locke, and Montesquieu, and delivering what the *Herald* called "an eloquent and argumentative speech." Throughout this performance, however, William Jackson, a leader of the mob that had carried Miley and McCalmont into the legislature on September 29, and a man noted for his impudence and "his contemptuous grin," sat in the gallery facing Findley, harassing him with grins, gestures, and laughs. He wore on Findley's patience until finally the tired Antifederalist lashed out: "Mr. President, . . . I have observed a person who has introduced himself among the members of this Convention, laughing for some time at everything I have said. This conduct does not, sir, proceed from a superiority of understanding, but from the want of a sense of decency and order. If he were a member I should certainly call him to order; but as it is, I shall be satisfied with despising him." As William Shippen, Jr., later described it to his son, "Even Jackson's impudence was not able to bear this merited stroke. He grew pale, laughed no more and did not appear in the afternoon."[89]

88. Jensen 2:547–48.
89. Jensen 2:586; William Shippen, Jr., to Thomas Shippen, Philadelphia, 12/18/87, in Jensen 2:588 n. 2.

The baseness of Jackson's behavior had embarrassed even this generally Federalist audience, and their sympathies were, at least for one brief moment, with Findley. "A crowded house were delighted and thought Findley should have moved his expulsion," William Shippen reported. A small victory for the outnumbered Antifederalists.[90]

The four-day exchange had been a moral victory for the Antifederalists. As James Winthrop, a leading Massachusetts Antifederalist described it: "Wilson and M'Kean, two Scottish names, were repeatedly worsted in the argument. To make amends for their own incapacity, the gallery was filled with rabble, who shouted their applause, and these heroes of aristocracy were not ashamed . . . to vindicate such a violation of decency."[91] But moral victories did not help much, and Findley, the most cautious of men, was finally driven to desperate lengths. By midday on Wednesday, he was saying things that some might consider seditious, that "he did not conceive under all the circumstances of the case, the minority of the state could be bound by the proceedings at this day, but would still have a right, . . . to object to the ratification of the proposed Constitution, and, if they pleased, to associate under another form of government."[92] Findley thus appeared to conclude his morning remarks with threats to dismember the polity. Smilie started the afternoon session with hints of civil war: "If this constitution is adopted, I look upon the liberties of America as gone, until they shall be recovered by arms."[93]

Tempers were short, tensions high, and the Federalists were about to exert their power and crush their opponents. At that point Dr. Benjamin Rush, a Presbyterian from Quaker stock who had recently joined the Anglican Church, rose and made a bizarre plea for unity. "Nothing will satisfy me perfectly but a unanimous vote," he declared and then proposed that they "bury the hatchet of civil discord and smoke the calumet of peace together." Should that happen, he promised, "I shall feel myself strongly disposed to run across the room, and take every member of the opposition in my arms. I should think it, sir, the beginning of a year of jubilee in Pennsylvania."[94]

A hug from Benjamin Rush may not have been much comfort to

90. Ibid.
91. "Agrippa," *Massachusetts Gazette*, 1/8/88, in Jensen 2:548 n. 6.
92. Jensen 2:587.
93. Jensen 2:592.
94. Jensen 2:595–96.

tough old Antifederalists like Findley, Smilie, and Whitehill, but it was one of Rush's better offerings in his long and circuitous harangue. Before reaching that final exhortation, he had cast aspersions on their religion, insulted their intelligence, and questioned their morals, their principles, and their good works, and their personal integrity. Although not unusual for Rush, this style of persuasion invites our closer scrutiny; on occasion, the comments of this passionate, naive, and candid Federalist may suggest more about the social reality undergirding politics than the carefully crafted and sophisticated reasonings of his more calculating colleagues.

The good doctor introduced his pleas for unanimity and peace "by recapitulating the many harsh epithets that have been given to the new government by the opposition," and then dismissing them as phantoms conjured up by the unduly suspicious minds. "[T]he misery and the evil Mr. Findley had discovered in the new Constitution," Rush hoped, "was in the minds of the members who opposed it, and not in the Constitution itself."[95] The evils of contemporary society, on the other hand, Rush felt were quite real. They also resulted from the "want of justice and fidelity in government," a government created by the state constitution of 1776 and one in which "there is more weakness in *form*, and more *corruption* in the *administration* . . . than in any of the states in the Union." He then proceeded to lay at the doorstep of those responsible for that government (i.e., the Presbyterian and Reformed Constitutionalists) an extraordinary diversity of social ills, including the "difficulty of borrowing and the danger of lending money . . . the deficiency in parishes to pay their ministers . . . [and] the numerous instances of conjugal infelicity and divorces." Oppression, fraud, delinquency, and scarcity of money and a surfeit of "conjugal infelicity"—these, indeed, constituted a heavy burden of sin and responsibility, even for Calvinists to bear.[96]

Rush had dismissed his opponents' religion; ridiculed their fears; laid a host of fiscal, financial, religious, and sexual evils at their door; and converted the state's benevolence into evidence of widespread moral failure. Not yet convinced that he had fully persuaded them, he tried another tack. After rhapsodizing on "the general approbation of the Constitution by all classes of people," he concluded that "the adoption

---

95. Jensen 2:594, 595.
96. Ibid.

of the government was agreeable to the will of Heaven, for VOX-POPULI—VOX DEI." "The same voice that thundered on Mount Sinai, 'thou shalt not steal' now proclaimed in our ears, . . . 'thou shalt not reject the new federal government.' "[97] In spite of his best efforts, Rush failed; Antifederalists stood firm. Federalist Stephen Chambers "remarked upon the doctor's wish of conciliation and unanimity, that *it was an event which he neither expected nor wished for.*" The inveterate Antifederalist Robert Whitehill commented that he "regretted that so imperfect a work should have been ascribed to God."[98]

What had been said, and how it had been said in these heated, personal exchanges in the final week of the convention reveal much about both the individuals involved and about the nature of the contest. The Federalists were increasingly confident, condescending, and superior, reflecting their self-assigned status, and possibly their uncontrollable excitement as their long-sought but ever uncertain victory loomed closer. The crowd was mocking, disrespectful, insulting in a good-humored sort of way, reflecting the Federalism of the city and its amused disdain for its country cousins. The Antifederalists were hostile, resentful, a bit insecure, frustrated, showing the effects of the strain, but defiant, threatening and angry; put down by eastern snobs and put upon by urban boors; and now well positioned to mount a vigorous counterattack within Pennsylvania, and to reach out to Antifederalists in neighboring states, especially in New York and Virginia.

When the state convention adjourned on Saturday, December 15, the Federalists had won an overwhelming victory. They had evaded most of the Antifederalists' snares. They had also maintained their basic coalition-building approach, seldom attacking either the state constitution of 1776 and its supporters, or any ethnic or religious group—Dr. Rush, always excepted. They made few obvious partisan appeals; they reiterated their concern about the slave trade; and they continued to insist that they had no desire to end or "annihilate" the states. Furthermore, they had strengthened their populist credentials by arguing that the democratic nature of the government negated the need for a bill of rights; by insisting that the Antifederalist minority should acquiesce in the popular will; by defining a convention of the people as superior to

97. Jensen 2:595.
98. Jensen 2:596.

established governments; and by rooting their understanding of a federal republic in a conception of a sovereign people freely distributing powers between two distinct spheres of government.

Although unable to silence the guileless Dr. Rush, other Federalists had rarely supported his condemnation of the state constitution of 1776, or its Presbyterian and Reformed supporters, and they had taken some pains to distance themselves from his hope that the Federal Constitution would annihilate the states. Precisely how the Federalist leadership felt about the views of this candid but impolitic physician remain unknown. His explicit comments differed markedly from the expressed views of his colleagues but his comments are nevertheless valuable for the way they contradict and thus highlight the central thrust of the Federalist rhetorical strategy: building and nurturing a complex coalition of Pennsylvania's diverse electorate.

On the other hand, the Federalists' behavior toward their vanquished foes, especially in the final week of the convention, did them no credit. Nor did it auger well for the future of their cause. Dr. Rush's diatribe would win no converts among Presbyterians or Reformed Constitutionalists. At the same time, Federalist arrogance and condescension might well increase the Antifederalist strength among the yeoman farmers who constituted the vast bulk of the electorate. Federalists had also bought considerable trouble for themselves and for Federalists in other states by provoking the Antifederalists into the production of a systematic body of proposed amendments.

The Antifederalists, although they failed to disrupt the convention, to attach amendments to the proposal, or to produce a conditional ratification, did not leave the convention empty-handed. Findley and Smilie had scored enough verbal victories to gratify the pride of their partisan allies. They may also have embarrassed the Federalists on the questions of slavery, paper money, and a bill of rights. More important, they had turned the Federalists' defense of popular sovereignty to their own ends. If one popular-based convention could change the government, Antifederalists reasoned, then a second could do the same.

In addition, Antifederalists had rested their case essentially on defense of individual and state rights. They, too, seemed to be trying to build a coalition. They had quietly abandoned their party's commitment to the state constitution of 1776 and its unicameral principle. They explicitly accepted bicameralism and a complex separation of powers, and then criticized the Federal Constitution for its failure to fully match this ideal. Instead of continuing the partisan-based rhetoric of the early days of the fall campaign, they emphasized the Constitution's compromise with slavery, its lack of a bill of rights, and its threats to the states: the federal government's domestic taxing, military, and judicial powers, its control over federal elections, and the power of its treaties to supersede state constitutions and state and federal law.

Antifederalists thus defined a potentially powerful position that transcended partisanship and antagonized no identifiable ethnic or religious group. It also appealed to the widespread popular concerns that had contributed so much to the earlier controversy with Great Britain. Furthermore, it spoke with equal or greater force to audiences outside of the state and therefore provided the basis for constructing a common front with Antifederalists beyond the bounds of Pennsylvania. In short, the Antifederalist rhetoric at the convention had created a broad and solid foundation from which to launch a campaign for popular repudiation of the Federalists' initial victory.

4
The Antifederalist Counterattack

January–April 1788

In late December 1787 Pennsylvania's Antifederalists launched a two-pronged campaign to reverse their state's ratification. First, they unleashed a massive publicity barrage to build public support for repudiation of the convention's work. Second, they worked to channel public indignation into concrete political action, most conspicuously, a petition drive for legislative nullification of the decision of December 12. Federalists, caught napping, quickly regrouped. Early in January they met at Epple's Tavern in Philadelphia to raise money and to coordinate their response. With that, the final phase of the ratification struggle reached full throttle.[1]

Antifederalists set the pace. Between mid-December 1787 and early

---

1. William Shippen, Jr., to Thomas Shippen, Philadelphia, 1/3/88, in Jensen 2:MFM 271; "Tom Peep," *Independent Gazetteer*, 1/10/88; "Peep, Jr." *Independent Gazetteer*, 1/14/88; "A Freeman," *Independent Gazetteer*, 1/15/88.

April 1788, they flooded Pennsylvania's newspapers with hundreds of polemical pieces, ranging from short squibs to long and ponderous dissertations. Their rate of publication began to climb in late December, accelerated throughout January, slowed in February, surged again in March, and petered out in early April. Two comparisons suggest the magnitude of their productivity: in January alone, the number of Antifederalist essays published approximated the total number printed during the entire fall 1787 campaign. In the end, January's effort represented about a third of all Antifederalist essays published in the entire ratification contest.[2] In this last stage of the campaign neither side significantly altered its basic strategy, but each shifted its emphasis and revealed dimensions of the struggle only dimly visible before. This chapter will bring those facets into sharper focus, and then describe in some detail the ultimately futile efforts of the Antifederalists to nullify Pennsylvania's ratification.

Aristocracies and Personalities

Much of the new Antifederalist literature continued to focus on the issues raised earlier: the annihilation of the states, the domestic powers of the central government, and the lack of protection of basic civil liberties. This was bedrock; an unshakable foundation on which to build. It appealed across partisan lines; it revived revolutionary fears of unresponsive and arbitrary authority; it exercised deep-seated concerns about individual rights, personal freedoms, and liberty of conscience.[3]

Antifederalists also talked incessantly about "aristocracy," and "aris-

2. Historians have generally neglected this phase of the ratification conflict in Pennsylvania. For important exceptions, see Roland Baumann, "The Democratic-Republicans of Philadelphia: The Origins, 1776–1797" (Ph.D. diss., Pennsylvania State University, 1970), esp. 114–20; and Saul Cornell, "Aristocracy Assailed: The Ideology of Backcountry Anti-Federalism," *Journal of American History* 76 (March 1990): 1148–73. The above figures are projections based on actual counts in four Philadelphia newspapers. See Appendix 1 for further details.

3. This Antifederalist literature lacked the sharply defined focus of the convention debates. Its diverse and sometimes incompatible themes preclude easy generalization and illustrate the point made first by John Kaminski and then by Saul Cornell, that historians who assume a simple uniformity among Antifederalists probably err. John Kaminski, "Antifederalism and the Perils of Homogenized History: A Review Essay," *Rhode Island History* 42 (1983): 30–37. Cornell, "Aristocracy Assailed," *Journal of American History* 76 (March 1990): 1148–73.

tocratic" conspiracies. Not all Antifederalists, however, used these terms in the same way. A few Antifederalists employed aristocracy to describe one of three traditional forms of government: monarchy, aristocracy, and democracy. As the Federalists pointed out, and as Antifederalists themselves generally recognized, the Federal Constitution created no legally privileged class of people. In this sense, the proposal did not create an aristocracy or an aristocratic government.[4]

Other Antifederalists emphasized ways in which the structure of the new system fostered aristocracy, seen as rule by a limited number of men isolated from popular control. In this sense, the small size of the Senate, the power of its members, and their relative freedom from popular supervision made that body inherently aristocratic. Most also agreed that a large consolidated union could be governed only on monarchical or aristocratic principles.[5]

Many Antifederalists worried more about the social characteristics of those who would control this new government. A bicameral legislature implied an upper house and a superior order of men. "Centinel," for example, repeatedly predicted that the Senate would be peopled by "the better sort," the "well-born." The large electoral constituencies for the House of Representatives also gave men of wealth and social standing a competitive advantage in electoral contests.[6] Some Antifederalists defined these social distinctions in terms of already existing, sharply defined class differences. "Philadelphiensis," a recent immigrant from Ireland, gave some of this old-world shading to his writing. He referred to himself and to other Antifederalists as "mean fellows," "base wreteches" "plebeians"; and he praised "the back counties of Pennsylvania, where the *well-born* have no influence." The author who signed himself "Aristocrotis," a new arrival from Scotland, conveyed a similar image of society sharply divided into the privileged and the poor, the lettered and ignorant, the patricians and the plebeians.[7]

---

4. "Fallacies," *Freeman's Journal*, 4/16, 23/88, in Storing 3.14.3; "William Penn," *Independent Gazetteer*, 1/3/88; Herbert Storing, ed., commentary, *The Complete Antifederalist* (Chicago: University of Chicago Press, 1981), vol. 3, document 12, paragraph 11. For a fuller discussion of the structural aspects of the Antifederalist use of aristocracy, see Chapter 2.
5. *Independent Gazetteer*, 11/6/87.
6. Storing 2.7.22.
7. "Philadelphiensis," in Storing 3.9.6; 3.9.69; "Aristocrotis," in Storing 3.16.passim, 3:196–213. "John Humble" and "Montezuma," presumably residents of longer duration, used similar language. *Independent Gazetteer*, 10/29/90, in Storing 3.7.1; *Independent Gazetteer*, 10/17/87, in Storing 3.4.1.

A few Antifederalists also associated aristocracy with the new sophisticated Deism popular in some gentlemanly circles. "James de Caledonia" linked Deism and social pretensions. He complained that the lack of religious tests for office under the Federal Constitution meant "that a pagan, deist or any other gentleman can hold any office under it." "Aristocrotis," speaking as a mock-Federalist, also linked the Federal Constitution, Deism, and social hierarchies. "The religion of nature [Deism?]," he said, "admits of proper degrees and distinctions amongst mankind" in ways impossible under Christianity with its "commands to call no man upon earth master or lord."[8]

Most Antifederalist writers, however, seem to have thought of aristocrats and aristocracy at least as much in terms of attitude and aspiration. They used the term to depict men who thought of themselves as superior to the rest of mankind; who aspired to set themselves above their fellows; who claimed a degree of deference not allotted to all: the "aspiring aristocrats," those who would "lord it over their fellow citizens."[9] And, in this postconvention stage of the campaign, Antifederalists increasingly linked these attitudes to specific and identifiable men.

The first hint of this tendency came in an isolated personal attack on James Wilson early in the fall. Signed "An Officer of the late Continental Army," it condemned Wilson for his "lofty carriage," his contempt for "the inferior order of the people," his ambition for "the pomp and pageantry of courts," and his conception of himself and his friends as "born a different race from the rest of the sons of men."[10] In the winter and spring of 1788, as tempers flared and men began to speak their minds, an increasing number of Antifederalist essays took this tack. Wilson, in particular, drew venomous attacks. Antifederalists ridiculed his pretensions; they gloated when his personal notes were protested (i.e., his checks bounced); they howled with glee at his prospective bankruptcy. Something about Wilson, his posture, his public and private attitudes, his apparent arrogance and condescension drove Antifederalists into a fury.

Robert Morris also attracted specific and brutal attention. "Centinel," in particular, singled out Morris for personal vilification. In his early essays, "Centinel" had generalized and thus impersonalized his concerns

---

8. "James de Caledonia," *Independent Gazetteer*, 3/4/88; "Aristocrotis," in Storing 3.16.15.
9. See, for example, "Philadelphiensis," in Storing 3.9.36.
10. *Independent Gazetteer*, 11/6/87, in Storing 3.8.5.

about "the wealthy and ambitious who . . . think they have a right to lord it over their fellow creatures." By late December, however, he had become more specific. He attacked the selfish and myopic merchants who, "immersed in schemes of wealth, . . . do not consider that commerce is the hand-maid of liberty, a plant of free growth that withers under the hand of despotism." These men in power, he predicted will "institute injurious monopolies, and shackle commerce" and threaten each man's property.[11] In time, "Centinel" narrowed his attack directly to Morris. "See him," "Centinel" declared, "converting a bank, instituted for common benefit, to his own and [his] creatures['] emolument." View him, this "Robert, the cofferer," mixing his private and his public business to his own advantage, building his current affluence on his misuse of the public's trust. Consider "his bankrupt situation at the commencement of the late war, and the immense wealth he has dazzled the world with since." View, also, "the vassalage of our merchants, the thraldom of the city of Philadelphia, and the extinction of that spirit of independency in most of its citizens," that has resulted from Morris's machinations.[12] Remember also, "Centinel" continued, Morris's many dependents, particularly the bankrupt Wilson, "whose superlative arrogance, ambition, and rapacity, would need the spoils of thousands to gratify." And, finally, "recollect the strenuous and unremitted exertion of these men, for years past, to destroy our admirable constitution, whose object is to secure equal liberty and advantages to all."[13]

Here we may well have the core, the central elements, the irreducible essence of what aristocracy meant for "Centinel." For him, aristocrats were men like Morris and Wilson, who thought of themselves as superior to the common herd and had sought for more than a decade to institutionalize that assumption in the fundamental law of the state. Moreover, this concern would appear to have deep personal roots in the parallel business and political careers of George Bryan, father of the author of the "Centinel" essays, and Robert Morris himself.

George Bryan was the godfather of the state constitution of 1776,

---

11. "Centinel," 10/5/87, in Storing 2.7.5; "Centinel," 11/5/87, in Storing 2.7.65, 2.7.66. Storing 2.7.126.
12. Storing 2.7.127, 2.7.171, 2.7.136. For some insight into how Robert Morris mixed his commercial interests and his public responsibilities, see E. James Ferguson, *The Power of the Purse* (Chapel Hill: University of North Carolina Press, 1961), esp. 78–80.
13. Storing 2.7.127.

and "patron saint" of the Constitutionalist party. Robert Morris formed part of the inner core of the Republican opposition. Both men had arrived in Philadelphia at about the same time, Bryan from Dublin, Ireland; Morris from London. Both had came from business families; both had prospered as merchants. In the 1760s both also participated in the Anglican-Presbyterian Proprietary party; and both had played honorable roles in the resistance to Great Britain.[14] Before the Revolution, however, Bryan and Morris had differed in two principal respects. First, Bryan surpassed Morris in business success and in political prominence. He had staked out for himself an important place among the mercantile community, represented Pennsylvania at the Stamp Act congress, won a seat in the provincial legislature, and complemented his business activities with patronage appointments from the Proprietary party.[15]

Second, the two men differed significantly in religious orientation. Bryan was a serious and dedicated Presbyterian living in what his most recent biographer has called the hard-working, "clannish" Presbyterian community of Philadelphia. He married the daughter of a prominent Presbyterian merchant, focused his social life on his church, and over time, expressed fears about the Anglican Church, which insulated itself "from reform or redress under the presumption of Divine Right." Morris was an Anglican. He married the sister of the future Episcopalian (American Anglican) bishop of Philadelphia, and associated largely in business and social life with Anglicans. He appeared, moreover, to wear his religion more lightly than did Bryan.[16]

In the 1770s the two men moved in quite different economic and political directions. Bryan, bankrupt by the early 1770s, depended for the rest of his life on income from public office. This meant patronage: first from the Proprietary party and then from the revolutionary government of Pennsylvania. Morris, on the other hand, became one of the richest merchants in Philadelphia, holding major appointed and elected

---

14. This, and most of the material about Bryan and Morris in the following paragraphs is based on Joseph Foster, "George Bryan and the Politics of Revolution" (Ph.D. diss., Temple University, 1989), passim; and *Dictionary of American Biography*, 3:189–90, 13:219–23.

15. Bryan and Morris were neighbors in Philadelphia's Dock Ward where in 1769 Bryan's tax obligation exceeded Morris's by a factor of five. *Pennsylvania Archives, Series Three*, 14:152, 168, 189.

16. Foster, "George Bryan," esp. 3, 116.

offices in the state and national governments, while continuing his extensive mercantile affairs.[17]

The two men also followed quite different political paths. Both remained relatively invisible in state politics during the crucial summer and fall of 1776 as Pennsylvania underwent its own peculiar and unique internal revolution. By the spring of 1777 Bryan had emerged as the focal point, if not the essential organizing genius, of the emerging Constitutionalist party. Two years later Morris helped organize the opposition party: the Republican Society. For the next decade these two men played conspicuous roles in the partisan conflicts of the state. Thus, in 1787 and 1788, "Centinel," the Presbyterian son of the Presbyterian judge who had fathered the Constitutionalist party, personalized his attacks on the Federalists by focusing his attention increasingly on Robert Morris and his associates, principally Anglicans, who, in "Centinel's" mind, looked down on lesser men, and had long sought to add to the state legislature an aristocratic upper house in which they could sit.

It is important here to note that "Centinel" attacked not wealth, not industry, not commerce, not learning or education, not banking and finance. Rather, he concentrated on those men who sought social and political privilege. He castigated not men who had succeeded economically by dint of labor, industry, intelligence, or education, but those who acted in a superior way and who expected deference from lesser men.

For "Centinel" and for those who spoke with a similar voice, "aristocrats" were not necessarily the rich, but those who acted as though they were superior. The category included "avaricious office hunters," public defaulters, and other plunderers of the public treasury; men without credit whose notes have been rejected; those who thought they deserved to be rich and privileged; the aspiring aristocracy who composed the "junto" conspiring to "enslave the rest of their fellow citizens."[18]

These Antifederalists saw Federalists as aristocrats less because of the kinds or quantities of property Federalists possessed than because of

---

17. In 1774, Bryan, no longer listed as a merchant, paid £31.6.0 in taxes in the city's Dock Ward; Morris paid £115.16.8. In 1779 Morris's tax in the Dock Ward exceeded Bryan's by a factor of ten and Bryan was apparently occupying rental property. *Pennsylvania Archives, Third Series,* 14:237, 238, 483, 484, 759.

18. "Fallacies," *Independent Gazetteer,* 4/22/88; *Independent Gazetteer,* 1/19/88; *Freeman's Journal,* 2/27/88; *Freeman's Journal,* 4/2/88; Wilson, *Freeman's Journal,* 3/12/88.

how Federalists thought, how they treated their fellow Pennsylvanians, and how they had behaved over the previous ten to twelve years. These Antifederalists resented the mental habits, the social attitudes, "the dictatorial air," "the magisterial voice," "the imperious tone," "the haughty countenance," "the lofty look," "the magestic mien" of those who considered "themselves as Gods, and all the rest of mankind as two legged brutes."[19]

In "Centinel's" mind, the state constitution of 1776 had frustrated the desire of such men to set themselves apart and rule. That document, for "Centinel," had made Pennsylvania unique. "The few," he argued, "generally prevail over the many," but here "the *well-born* have been baffled in all their efforts to prostrate the altar of liberty for the purpose of substituting their own insolent sway." Having failed on the state level, he charged, these aspiring aristocrats now sought to achieve their ends through the Federal Constitution.[20]

Minor Chords: Rural and Religious Resentments

The Antifederalist charge of aristocracy, in most of its forms, cast a broad net. It appealed to many; it antagonized few. It spoke, presumedly, to deep-seated resentments of pretension and condescension.[21] Other strains of thought in this late-winter Antifederalist rhetoric suggest the presence of more divisive impulses. By early spring 1788 at least some Antifederalists were venting anti-urban, anti-Anglican and anti-Deist sentiments. Antifederalists also returned to explicit party appeals temporarily abandoned at the state Convention. Let us begin with the evolving Antifederalist treatment of the people of Philadelphia.

---

19. "Aristocrotis," in Storing 3.16.3; 37.16.198. Within any given political unit (i.e., the City of Philadelphia or any one of the state's counties) Republicans (hence Federalists) and Constitutionalists (hence Antifederalists) drew their leadership largely from the same socioeconomic elite. See Ireland, "The Crux of Politics," *William and Mary Quarterly* 42 (October 1985): esp. 460–65.

20. Storing 2.7.129.

21. At the same time it did not demand of its readers that they accept all other people as their equals. It encouraged readers to resent those who aspired to be above them, but it did not require them to accept those they themselves looked down on or disliked: the poor, the weak, the idle, the lazy, the failed, bankrupts, pimps, drunks, foreigners, slaves, and those from different ethnic backgrounds or those with different religious traditions.

Antifederalists devoted much attention to the City and its persistent Federalism. At first they expected to inform and convert these good but confused people. In time, they expressed growing frustration as Philadelphians refused to see the light. Finally, Antifederalists rejected and condemned the ignorant and pliable urban masses who did the bidding of powerful Federalist forces.

The City was important to Antifederalists. Although it contained a minuscule proportion of the total population of the state, the psychological value of its support far outweighed its numerical significance. In the decade before the ratification contest, the Constitutionalists, who now led the Antifederalists, had never ceased to contest the annual legislative elections in the City. Occasionally they had won. Furthermore, some of the most powerful, prestigious, and senior leaders of the Constitutionalist party were Philadelphians. George Bryan, Jonathan Bayard Smith, John Nicholson, Charles Pettit, Adam Kuhl, Jonathan Dickinson Sergeant, and the Reverend Ewing all lived and worked in Philadelphia, thought of it as their bailiwick, and refused to concede it to their opponents.

On a broader plane, the undeniable success of the Federalists in the City contradicted the Antifederalist self-proclaimed image as the voice of the people. The Antifederalists asserted, as they undoubtedly believed, that they voiced the desires and aspirations of the common people, the honest laborers, the industrious workmen, or as "John Humble" said with mock-humility, "our *low-born* brethren [who] . . . have had the horrid audacity to think for themselves." Yet, here in America's largest urban area, the honest and industrious workmen, the humble people, had not only voted against the Antifederalists, but had also insulted, mocked, intimidated, abused, and physically attacked them.[22]

Despite the City's obvious hostility, Antifederalists at first worked hard to gain its favor. Some simply denied reality and asserted that the majority of the City actually opposed the Federal Constitution. Others claimed that the people of Philadelphia were coming to their senses, losing their infatuation with the new system and seeing its dangers. Still others sought the support of the City's sizable Quaker and Sectarian populations by emphasizing the problems of slavery and pacifism.[23]

22. Storing 3.7.1.
23. "John Humble," *Independent Gazetteer*, 10/29/87; William Shippen, Jr., to Thomas

Another group, however, wrote off the Quaker and Sectarian voters. They sought to revive the City's wartime hostility toward loyalists and neutrals. "Poplcola," for example, implied that the new government could use its treaty-making power to entitle traitors to the rights of citizenship, to restore their confiscated estates, and even to allow men like Arnold to return and claim back pay.[24]

In time, most Antifederalist writers reluctantly accepted the City's strong commitment to the Federalist cause. Some attributed it to the influence of the Bank of North America, others, to the economic coercion of the merchants, or to the machinations of Robert Morris, James Wilson, and their ilk. One concluded that the artisans followed the merchants who "would consent to go to the devil, if they thought they could again sell as many British goods as they formerly did." A few continued to hope that "although the tide seems to run so high at present in favor of the new constitution, there is no doubt but the people will soon change their minds."[25]

A different and more hostile attitude toward the City had run through the Antifederalist writings from early on. After the convention it grew in intensity and directness. "The Address to the Minority," for example, signed by thirty men from Carlisle, called Philadelphians a "senseless, ignorant rabble." A local observer attributed urban backing for the Constitution to the inherent moral weakness of city. Anyone with money for drinks, he asserted, could assemble a Federalist crowd in minutes. "Hum-Strum" called Philadelphians the "mob-ocratical boys." Others condemned the urban population as ignorant riffraff. "Argarius" dismissed the Federalist voters in Philadelphia County as "illiterates," more ignorant, if possible, than "the illiterate, . . . rustic, . . . mongrell Quaker[s]" who ran the county.[26]

By spring 1788 the Antifederalists had generally abandoned Philadelphia. Mr. Bailey's paper continued to hope, and "Philadelphiensis" retained his concern for trade and commerce and by implication, the

---

Lee Shippen, Philadelphia, 12/12/87, in Jensen 2:601; "Hampden," *Pittsburgh Gazette*, 2/16/88, in Jensen 2:665; "Address of Thanks," *Independent Gazetteer*, 2/14/88.

24. See Chapters 2 and 3 for details of Antifederalist appeal to Quakers and Sectarians. "Poplcola," *Independent Gazetteer*, 10/31/87.

25. *Independent Gazetteer*, 2/27/88. See also a number of essays in the *Freeman's Journal*, the paper that probably most often expressed this antimerchant feeling. *Independent Gazetteer*, 10/6/87.

26. "Address of Thanks," *Independent Gazetteer*, 2/14/88; "Gouvero," *Independent Gazetteer*, 1/10/88, "Argarius," *Independent Gazetteer*, 2/29/88; *Independent Gazetteer*, 1/10/88.

ship-building trades. However, for all intents and purposes, Antifederalism in Pennsylvania had taken on a decided anti-urban cast. In this late winter exchange, Antifederalist publications also began to hint at the ethnic-religious dimension of the contest. The initial stages of the public debates offered little explicit evidence of this underlying basis of partisanship in Pennsylvania. True, Federalists and Antifederalists competed for the Quaker and pacifist Sectarian vote. In addition, publicists on both sides sometimes claimed the support of specific ethnic or religious groups: the Germans, the Dutch, the Baptists. Also, the Antifederalists occasionally used ethnic or religious names as pejoratives, but these accusations were relatively safe, almost symbolic: the Scots, Jews, Jesuits, Turks. Only the pseudonym "Centinel" and the implicit links between the hierarchical Anglican Church and the charges of "aristocracy" hinted at the continued relevance of ethnic-religious considerations in the ratification contest during most of the fall of 1787.[27]

Overall, however, and from the beginning, Antifederalist essays tended to differ from Federalist pieces in what might be called their religious tone. Federalists consistently projected an image of religious neutrality, possibly indifference. They generally avoided references to religious or ethnic groups, and seldom relied on religious imagery, scriptural citations, or familiar biblical words or phrases. (Here, Dr. Benjamin Rush stands out as a major exception.) Such an approach comported well with local political mores and with the Federalist need to build a heterogeneous coalition.

Antifederalists exhibited a more open, possibly more unself-conscious, religiosity in their writings. Like the Federalists, most Antifederalist essays made largely secular and political arguments. On occasion, however, and much more casually, Antifederalists buttressed their positions and sprinkled their essays with scriptural citations, and with words and phrases with a biblical and a Nonconformist (dissenters from the established Anglican Church) flavor. "Centinel," for example, often cited Scripture; "Philadelphiensis" used scriptural passages to begin, to end, or to strengthen his text in five of his first six essays; and the "Address of the Seceders" closed with the invocation: "may He who alone has dominion over the passions and understandings of men enlighten and direct you aright, that posterity may bless God for the wisdom of their ancestors."[28]

27. *Freeman's Journal*, 3/19/88; *Independent Gazetteer*, 3/3/88.
28. Jensen 2:116–17.

After ratification, as tempers rose and the level of the discourse declined, some Antifederalist publications took on a more visibly religious hue. In February, William Findley signed his Antifederalist essay "Hampden," in reference to John Hampden, who, in England in the 1630s, had led the parliamentary resistance to King Charles and his chief Anglican prelate, Archbishop Laud. The pseudonym thus recalled the origins of the English Civil War and the historic fight against royal and ecclesiastical abuses. It undoubtedly reminded its readers of the days when John Hampden, Oliver Cromwell, and the English Puritans, Presbyterians, and dissenters warred against kingly authority, priestly power, and the authoritative church.[29]

Another Antifederalist signed himself "Algernon Sidney," a name that recalled the religious and political conflicts of later seventeenth-century England: the Restoration, and the Exclusion Crisis and the Glorious Revolution of 1688. He used phrases reminiscent of those religious Nonconformists who had resisted the established Anglican Church. He reminded his readers that the original Algernon Sidney had died for the "good old cause," and he instructed them that "under the dispensation of the gospel . . . every man is to search within himself for a monitor to direct him, 'for the law is nigh thee, even in thy heart.' " Like the "Address of the Seceders," "Algernon Sidney" also closed with an invocation: "Bless thy people, and save them. Defend thy own cause, and defend those that defend it. Stir up such as are faint; direct those that are willing; confirm those that waver."[30]

The pen names "Hampden" and "Algernon Sidney" carried a rich and complex symbolism. Both recalled popular resistance to royal tyranny. Both may also have brought to mind the religious challenge to Anglican bishops, to the tax-supported Anglican Church, and to the centralized and hierarchical Anglican systems. We cannot know with certainty that Antifederalists used these names to stir a religious-based response from an anti-Anglican, dissenter, or Nonconformist electorate.

29. "Hampden," *Pittsburgh Gazette*, 2/16/88, in Jensen 2:663–69. For identification of Findley as "Hampden" see editor's note, ibid., 669. John Hampden, an English lawyer, landowner, and member of Parliament with strong puritan leanings and associations had led parliamentary opposition to King Charles's imposition of forced loans and a special tax called ship-money in the 1620s and 1630s. He also urged reform of ecclesiastical abuses. During the English Civil War he was among the best known of the "puritan party." He died from wounds he received in battle. His name became a watchword among English religious dissenters for resistance to unjust taxation and to the structure and power of the Anglican church.

30. "Algernon Sidney," *Independent Gazetteer*, 2/13/88; *Freeman's Journal*, 2/20/88.

Still, religious imagery and allusions, especially those with a Nonconformist, dissenter, or anti-Anglican flavor, came more easily and frequently to and from Antifederalist pens. Certainly, the Anglican-oriented leadership of the Federalists would not have associated themselves with these seventeenth-century English religious and political rebels.

Few Antifederalists explicitly identified themselves with a particular denomination but those who did all agreed. The author of the "Old Constitutionalist" had appealed to Presbyterians, and had referred to them (and himself) as a harried and despised minority. A number of casual references, scattered throughout the Antifederalist literature in the spring of 1788 point in the same direction. Three examples illustrate variations on the theme. A mock-Federalist essay condemning a Maryland delegate to the Constitutional Convention for revealing its secrets, called him a scoundrel, a rogue, a villain, and a Presbyterian.[31] Another mock-Federalist essay, "James de Caledonia," discussed Dr. Benjamin Rush's mixed contribution to the Federalist cause: "This man has been of some service to us," the purported Federalists said, "by sowing dissentions among the Presbyterians, whose garb he wore for that purpose many years." At about the same time, a letter responding to criticism of the Antifederalist violence in Carlisle, referred positively to the western Antifederalists as "the sons of Paxton and Tuscorura," names made infamous twenty-five years earlier when frontiersmen, usually depicted as Presbyterians, had massacred unarmed Indians and then marched east threatening to do the same for Philadelphia's Quakers.[32]

This occasional but consistent Antifederalist orientation complements the anti-Anglican and anti-Deist sentiments that Antifederalists expressed with increasing frankness. On occasion, Antifederalists had projected an anti-Anglican image. Bryan's choice of "Centinel" as a pseudonym symbolized this stance and the sobriquets "Hampden" and "Algernon Sidney" may have conveyed the same message. More directly, "Philadelphiensis," in his second number, charged that the framers had intended to establish a religion for the nation, "to compel the whole continent to conform to their own [presumably Anglican or Episcopal]." "The Turk" equated Samuel Seabury, the recently conse-

---

31. *Independent Gazetteer*, 3/26/88.
32. *Independent Gazetteer*, 3/4/88, 1/21/88.

crated Anglican bishop of Connecticut and the soon-to-be first bishop of the American Protestant Episcopal Church, with the eastern Musel.[33]

More explicit references to the Anglican Church came after ratification. In January 1788 "Hum-Strum" renamed James Wilson, "Jamey Wolsey," linking Wilson and the Federalists to the great sixteenth-century English cardinal who had played high-stakes politics under Henry VIII. "Hum-Strum" also wondered why "the bells that rung . . . [to celebrate the Constitution] in the steeple of the new *mitred-church* [Anglican], were not bemuffled a little toward the end of the tune, to give us a few doleful cling-clangs at the expulsion of liberty and the triumph of the despocratics for a season."[34]

The "miter," a tall, pointed hat worn by Anglican bishops, symbolized hierarchical and authoritarian religious establishments. "Hum-Strum's" explicit and irreverent use of the term elicited a Federalist attack. An Antifederalist, defending "Hum-Strum," complained that while Federalists offered "insults to Judge B—— and Dr. E——g and thus to a considerable [Presbyterian] congregation in this city," "Hum-Strum's" religious references had produced "growling and grumbling." As if, the author concluded, "Episcopacy were unmitered [i.e., had no bishops], and the cassocks of our Right Rev. Fathers [robes of the Anglican priests] [had been] conjured into Scotch-bonnets, for Presbyterians."[35]

Shortly after the "Hum-Strum" essay, "A Baptist" asserted that he himself had heard a conversation between two gentlemen about a "deep laid scheme to make the Episcopal Church the only established and lawful one in the United States." A Federalist retorted that, in fact, most Baptists supported ratification. "A Baptist" then responded that his critic had evaded the central point: Federalists conspired to establish the Episcopal religion with its bishops and its compulsory tithes.[36] The mock-Federalist essay signed "James de Caledonia" also sought to depict the Federalists as Anglicans seeking to impose their orthodoxy on dissidents. It purported to show James Wilson as believing it was "high time . . . to get rid of such a mungrel breed of imposters and sectaries from the *real* church."[37]

33. *Independent Gazetteer*, 11/28/87, 10/12/87.
34. *Independent Gazetteer*, 1/10/88.
35. *Independent Gazetteer*, 3/17/88.
36. "A Baptist," *Freeman's Journal*, 1/23/88; "Real Baptist," *Freeman's Journal*, 1/30/88; *Freeman's Journal*, 2/6/88.
37. *Independent Gazetteer*, 3/4/88.

If Anglicans threatened from one direction, Deists, Unitarians, and heathens (all of whom denied the divinity of Christ) threatened from the other and this concern Antifederalists expressed rather more openly. "Philadelphiensis" delineated both evils. "From the proceedings of the convention, respecting liberty of *conscience*," he wrote, one might conclude that they were "either men of *no* religion, or all of *one* religion; either . . . indifferent about religion, or determined to compel the whole continent to conform to their own."[38]

A mock-Federalist essay signed "Unitarian" linked "Yellow Whigs," Loyalists, office-seekers, and Federalists with those who denied the divinity of Christ (i.e., Unitarians). Another Antifederalist essay explicitly attacked Deists. Pretending to be a Federalist, the author lamented the embarrassing outbursts of an unruly Federalist colleague (probably Dr. Rush). It called him a "*quack* politician," a "perfect *idiot*" with his babbling about the "divine origin of our scheme." This supposed Federalist then bragged that under the Constitution "a pagan, deist or any other gentleman, can hold any offices . . . , and that there is not the least security for the Christian religion."[39]

A more extensive criticism of the perceived anti-Christian (probably Deist) orientation of the Federalists and the Constitution appeared in the pamphlet "The Government of Nature Delineated, or An Exact Picture of the New Federal Constitution" by "Aristocrotis," published in Carlisle, Pennsylvania, in the spring of 1788. The pseudonym "Aristocrotis" suggests an attack on the "aristocratic" nature of the Federal Constitution and the "aristocratic" aspirations of its advocate. The title "The Government of Nature . . ." implies the more complex argument: that amoral, elitist, aristocratic secularists (possibly Deists, certainly non-Christians) created and supported a godless scheme designed to exalt themselves while suppressing popular freedom.[40]

At least two features of this essay deserve close attention: the intensity of its class-based rhetoric, and its explicit discussion of religion. First, its class-based language. "Aristocrotis" was far from unique in his railings against aristocratic conspiracies and in his list of particular criticisms of the Constitution. He distinguished himself, however, by his determination to attribute each and every flaw to the contempt the well-

---

38. Storing 3.9.13.
39. *Independent Gazetteer*, 12/21/87, 3/4/88.
40. "Aristocrotis," Storing 3:196.

born felt for the base-born, the superior for the inferior, the "noble" for the "ignoble," the "virtuous" for the "vicious," the "precious" for the "vile," the "few" for the "vulgar" "rabble."[41]

Take, for instance, the question of trial by jury, a staple item in virtually every extended Antifederalist criticism of the Federal Constitution. "Aristocrotis," speaking as a Federalist and thus imputing motives to those who favor ratification, praises the Federal Constitution for properly ending the jury system. Trial by jury, he asserts, is "the most absurd" power "which the people have wrested from government." It is a "gross violation of common sense" to believe that "twelve ignorant plebians [sic]" should judge the law created by "a learned legislature," "explained and commented" on by "learned writers," "twisted, turned and new modeled" by "learned lawyers," and "opened up and explained" by a "learned judge." Furthermore, an "ignorant stupid jury, cannot discern the merit of persons—it is the merits of the cause they examine."[42]

The elimination of the trial by jury, as well as the creation of an aristocratic Senate, a standing army, internal taxes, the supremacy of treaties, and other particular advances of the Federal Constitution, "Aristocrotis" argued, all contribute to the kind of government "founded upon nature." Nature, in the sense that "nature hath placed proper degrees and subordinations amongst mankind, and ordained a few to rule, and many to obey." Nature, also in that a "government founded agreeable to nature must be intirely independent; that is, it must be beyond the reach of annoyance or controul from every power on earth." And nature, finally, in the sense that it conforms to the precept of "the religion of nature."[43]

With this, we come to the second distinguishing feature of this essay: its explicit depiction of the Federalists as enemy of Christianity, indeed, of all inspired religions, and as advocates of "natural religion." "Aristocrotis" posited a fundamental incompatibility between "nature" and Christianity, and praised the framers for preferring "nature." He commended the Convention for expunging religion from government, and especially for separating it from "the christian religion, which . . . is of all others the most unfavourable to a government founded upon na-

---

41. "Aristocrotis," Storing 3:16 passim, esp. 3.16.4–14, 17, 13, pp. 199–205, 209–11, and 204–5.
42. Storing 3.16.12–13, pp. 204–5.
43. Storing 3.16.3, 5, 15; pp. 198, 201, 207.

ture." The difficulty with Christianity, and hence the need to "expunge" it, says this mock Federalist, is that "it pretends to be of . . . divine origin" and its moral precepts make it impossible for any "gentleman of fashion or good breeding to comply" and still enjoy his "genteel amusement and fashionable accomplishment."[44]

"Aristocrotis," still speaking as a Federalist, also praised the new government for disdaining such traditional Christian beliefs as the existence of "a Deity, the immortality of the soul, or the resurrection of the body, a day of judgment, or a future state of rewards and punishments." Finally he praised the Constitution for resting its foundation on the religion of nature, for "if some religion must be had, the religion of nature will certainly be preferred by a government founded upon the law of nature." He concluded: "One great argument in favour of this religion [of nature]" is that "most of the members of the grand convention are great admirers of it; and they certainly are the best models to form our religious, as well as our civil belief on."[45]

The essay "The Government of Nature Delineated" was unusual. The bulk of the Antifederalist writings, like most of the Federalist publications, emphasized secular themes. Yet, "Aristocrotis's" assault on gentlemen "Deists" or heathens, combined with the hostility other Antifederalists expressed toward Anglicans and the few favorable references to Presbyterians all point in the same direction. Taken together, they imply that these opponents of the Federal Constitution saw themselves and the audience they addressed as essentially Trinitarian (anti-Deist), dissenting (anti-Episcopalian), Protestant Christian patriots from the middling ranks of rural society. They also saw themselves and the voters to whom they spoke as supporters of the state constitution and the party that had long defended it.

"Centinel," the most powerful, prolific, and authoritative voice of Antifederalism in Pennsylvania, repeatedly returned to this partisan argument. He defended the state constitution as the "great palladium of equal liberty, and the property of the people." He identified the Federalists as "the ambitious and profligate" who "have been united in a constant conspiracy to destroy it [the state constitution]." Federalists, he said, were a faction that had "for ten years past . . . kept the people in continual alarm over their liberties." "Centinel" seldom failed to

44. Storing 3.16.14.
45. Storing 3.16.15.

remind his readers that conspirators against the constitution of 1776, led by "James, the Caledonian, lieutenant general of the myrmidons of power, under Robert, the cofferer [Morris]" constituted his principal opposition.[46]

And "Centinel" was certainly not unique. William Findley, who had acted the political apostate at the convention, redeemed himself in the spring. Writing as "Hampden," he castigated the Federalist assemblymen who, having "sworn to preserve the [state] constitution . . . were using the utmost violence to destroy it." An Antifederalist petition from Franklin County in January accused the Federal Constitution of "subverting the state constitution"; another from the same county in March, signed by 156 men, said that the new system was "injurious" to the old. As most recognized, and as Francis Hutchinson wrote to Jefferson in April: "George Bryan and his party (formerly called the Constitutional Party) have been moving heaven and Earth against the Establishment of a federal Government."[47]

Vicious Words and Violent Acts

During this final phase of the ratification contest in Pennsylvania, the public discourse took on an increasingly personal and acerbic flavor. This bare-knuckles, back-alley kind of politics lowered the level of discourse and raised tempers to a white heat. It accompanied sporadic outbursts of violence in the backcountry, and it may have reflected and exacerbated long-standing personal animosities.

Francis Hopkinson's "New Roof" essay inaugurated this new trend, probably more by chance than by design. The piece mocked a fallen foe, heaping clever and witty abuse on these lesser men. Published soon after the convention, Hopkinson undoubtedly intended it as a parting shot of the victorious force in a war they had just won. Inadvertently, it turned out to be the opening gun in a renewed battle.

46. "Centinel," 9:1/5/88, in Storing 2.7.129 (2:80), 2.7.129 (2:179–80); "Centinel," 10, in Storing 2.7.136 (2:183).

47. "Hampden," *Pittsburgh Gazette*, 2/16/88, in Jensen 2:663–69; *Carlisle Gazette*, 1/30/88, 3/22/88; Francis Hutchinson to Thomas Jefferson, Philadelphia, 4/6/88, in *Documentary History of the Constitution of the United States of America, 1786–1870* (Washington, D.C.: Department of State), 1:562–64.

The "New Roof" is an allegory in which an old woman, Margery (Judge George Bryan) organizes opposition to the architects (the framers) trying to erect a new roof (the Constitution) to save the building (the Union). Margery opposes the improvements in part because she is "of an intriguing spirit, of a restless and inveterate temper, fond of tattle, and a general mischief maker." More important, she sees in the new construction a direct threat to her status and to her physical well-being. The "New Roof" will considerably lessen the size of her apartment, deprive her of the old shingles she burns to boil her pot, and take away that portion of the great cornice she has used as a mantle piece. To preserve the size of her current room and to continue to profit from the deterioration of the old structure, Margery "instigated" three of the tenants "to oppose the plan": "William [Findley], Jack [John Smilie] and Robert [Whitehill]." She also has employed a "half crazy fellow ["Philadelphiensis"], who was suffered to go at large because he was a harmless lunatic," to promote opposition. She "exasperated this poor fellow against the architects" by filling "him with the most terrible apprehensions from the new roof; making him believe that the architects had provided a dark hole in the garret, where he was to be chained for life."[48]

"Hum-Strum" responded for the Antifederalists. Calling Hopkinson "Little Franciani, the exquisite fiddler" or "Frankie" for short, "Hum-Strum" suggested that Hopkinson, the state admiralty court judge, wrote in hopes of earning an equally lucrative post under the new government. The author asked the local sailors what they thought of the large current salary the judge now earned (£500 per year) while the fleet was out of commission.

"Hum-Strum" also suggested selfish personal motives for James Wilson, "the Scotch architect, [who] has sketched out a snug *dining room for himself.*" If that be so, "Hum-Strum" instructed Franky, then you "may sing to your fiddler, Jamey's farewell to poverty, and his dependence on bankers forever." "Study the bag-pipes, Franciani," "Hum-Strum" admonished Hopkinson, "set to the tune of the Battle of the Kegs, the swan's song of the mob-ocratical boys in the gallery, . . . who . . . damned, hissed . . . poor Findley, Whitehill, and Smilie."[49]

The Federalists answered with a string of "Margery" letters, accusing

---

48. *Packet,* 12/29/87.
49. "Hum-Strum," *Independent Gazetteer,* 1/10/88.

George Bryan of lying, of demagoguery, of failing in business, and of consorting with deserters, with Shays, and with Arnold.[50] They also disparaged Benjamin Workman, author of the "Philadelphiensis" series, as "this tutor . . . in our university," three years in America from Ireland, and "without a foot of land, in our country, or property of any kind."[51]

The Federalist organ, the *Mercury*, charged that the Antifederalists resorted to scurrility because their arguments had failed to persuade. The *Mercury* itself, however, stood second to none in multiplying insults against its opponents. At one time or another between January and April 1778 it cast aspersions on both the Antifederalist spokesmen and on most of their following. "Centinel," and thus by implication George Bryan, was the *Mercury's* favorite target. It described him as "*un pauvre* superannuated judge" who had failed in business. It called one Antifederalist writer "a crazy old crony" of Bryan's, and charged that the British and Hessians precipitated the Antifederalist riots in Carlisle. In Philadelphia, it charged, only lunatics, drunks, and criminals opposed ratification.[52]

Antifederalists gave as good as they got. They ridiculed the Grand Convention, or as they called it, the "immaculate convention." They categorized the framers as "nine of the principal public *defaulters* . . . 25 . . . hackneyed lawyers, . . . and one . . . whose conduct . . . favored more of the *Jesuit* than the rest." They labeled Federalists "loyalists," "avaricious office hunter[s]" with poor war records, and "*British deserters . . . traitors, tories, ingrates*, [and] cowardly *jack-ass*[es]." They also called them "low quibbling lawyer[s]," "ignorant," "*liars* and *dunces*," hirelings who wrote for money, and "whore[s]." They depicted Morris, Mifflin, and William Bingham as war profiteers who owed the government millions of dollars and who needed the Constitution's prohibition of ex post facto laws to protect themselves from future collection by the new government. Wilson they characterized as a penniless sycophant, a bankrupt, and a Scotsman unfit for republican government because of

50. *Mercury*, 2/21/88, 2/23/88, 3/11/88, 3/20/88. *Independent Gazetteer*, 3/1/88, 3/8/88.
51. "AB," in *Independent Gazetteer*, 3/11/88. "Centinel," 17, defended Mr. Workman of the university, the supposed author of "Philadelphiensis," as originally "a professor in an eminent academy in Dublin" (incidentally, George Bryan's earlier home) who had been in Philadelphia for four years, longer than Thomas Paine had been when he wrote *Common Sense*. *Independent Gazetteer*, 3/24/88.
52. *Mercury*, 3/15/88, 1/31/88, 3/11/88, 3/20/88, 3/15/88, 2/18/88, 1/15/88, 1/17/88, 1/29/88, 2/9/88, 2/12/88, 3/8/88, 3/11/88.

his longing for Stuart despotism. Hopkinson they dismissed: "You were from your infancy *known* to be little, and little folks *will always be dirty*. . . . You are a 'pimp,' —or at least you have used 'pimping methods.' " "You are a 'pettyfogger and insignificant.' "[53]

Why the public debate took this direction remains unclear. It may have resulted from the initial Federalist exuberance at their victory over a tough foe and an Antifederalist response in kind, exacerbated by increasing frustration and anger. Federalist Thomas FitzSimons, apparently without irony, lamented the "vindictive and virulent" conduct of the Antifederalists. Rufus King, a Federalist from Massachusetts, was appalled at what he saw as the unmatched level of personal abuse in Pennsylvania. He wrote to Tench Coxe: "I dont see so much virulence, and illiberal party zeal . . . from all the other States together."[54] On the other hand, the "New Roof," as well as the "Margery" series, also involved a certain element of mean-spirited, clever, elite condescension: the talented and witty authors amusing their literary friends by mocking a once-powerful but wounded and staggering opponent.

Whatever its source, this explosion of personal invective accompanied and exacerbated Antifederalist threats of violence and predictions of civil war. William Findley, in the closing days of the convention, had hinted at some kind of resistance. As the press reported, Findley "concluded . . . that he did not conceive . . . the minority of the state could be bound by the proceedings at this day." "Philadelphiensis," writing immediately after the convention, declared that the convention's refusal to receive Antifederalist petitions left the people with only the *"ultima ratio regum"* to secure their rights.[55]

In January Antifederalists warned of civil war "with all its dreadful train of evils." "An Address of Thanks to the Minority," from Carlisle came close to calling for blood: *"little* less than the lives of their

---

53. *Independent Gazetteer*, 3/3/88, 3/15/88, 4/22/88, 3/15/88, 3/14/88, 3/22/88, 2/14/88, 3/17/88, and 1/31/88. "To Hopkinson from Scordato," *Pennsylvania Mercury*, 4/5/88.

54. King to Tench Coxe, 3/18/88, in John P. Kaminski and Gaspare J. Saladino, eds., *The Documentary History of the Ratification of the Constitution* (Madison: State Historical Society of Wisconsin, 1976–86), 16:408.

55. *Independent Gazetteer*, 12/21/87. What precisely Findley had in mind remains unclear. Findley represented Westmoreland County, west of the mountains, and some Federalists worried that Pennsylvania's western counties might dismember the state and "cast in their lot" with the "settlements in Ohio." See Benjamin Rush to Hugh Williamson, 2/16/88, as quoted in Paul Leicester Ford, *The Origin, Purpose and Result of the Harrisburg Convention of 1788: A Study of Popular Government* (Brooklyn, N.Y., 1890), 12.

betrayers, will satiate their [the people's] revenge." A correspondent in the *Independent Gazetteer* linked Antifederalism to the patriot of 1775 who had taught the British that "to pass a bill for shutting up the port of Boston was one thing, but to carry it into effect was another." Rumors that the state was disarming the militia led "An Old Militia Officer" to urge the people to arm themselves at their own expense in order to "convince the enemies of liberty, that the people . . . are prepared for the worst."[56]

Federalists first dismissed the danger and then, in turn, threatened the Antifederalists. "A Citizen of Philadelphia" ridiculed the military prowess and the Revolutionary War record of "Centinel" (Bryan). It asked "whether he will risk himself, at the head of a company of his Carlisle *white* boys." It also warned them. Remember, it told them, "the wealth . . . numbers, virtue, courage and military skill are all on the federal side of the question" and if necessary, the Federalist militia of New Jersey and Delaware would intervene. By the end of the month the Federalist press had begun to charge the Antifederalists with sedition.[57]

Antifederalists accompanied their threats with efforts to revitalize the revolutionary instruments of popular opposition. In mid-January, "GR" urged the people to create local committees, and "a gentleman of character" from Montgomery County reported that "communities are forming in every county . . . to prevent its [i.e., the Constitution] taking place." Later in the month "Centinel" called for the institution of "societies" in every county, and a system of communication between them. Early in the spring, Washington County reported that it waited only for the snow to melt to begin its meetings.[58]

Actual violence did, indeed, break out in several backcountry locations. In Carlisle, for example, a midwinter Federalist celebration sparked a series of violent encounters that continued until spring. At dusk on December 26, Carlisle Federalists assembled in the public square to light a bonfire and to discharge a cannon in honor of Pennsylvania's ratification. Antifederalists, "armed with bludgeons" marched into the midst of the festivities and ordered the celebrants to desist.

56. *Freeman's Journal*, 1/23/88; *Independent Gazetteer*, 2/14/88, 1/22/88, 1/9/88, 1/16/88, 1/18/88.
57. *Pennsylvania Gazette*, 1/23/88, in Jensen 2:658–60; Coxe to Barry, 1/26/88, in Jensen 2:475–76; *Mercury*, 2/21/88, 2/28/88.
58. *New York Journal*, 1/24/88, Kaminski and Saladino 15:12; *Independent Gazetteer*, 1/16/88. "Centinel," 13, 1/30/88, in Storing 2.7.160 (2:192); *Freeman's Journal*, 3/19/88.

Hot words led to blows. Federalists later said that they had politely invited those opposing the celebration to leave. Antifederalists claimed that the Federalists had threatened to "blow them into the air" with their cannon. Whatever the provocation, Antifederalists initiated the violence. They "threw barrels and staves" at Major James Wilson, the man in charge of the cannon. Wilson struck back and then six or seven Antifederalists knocked him to the ground and "continued beating him after he fell." Wilson died early in March, presumedly from this beating.[59]

The Antifederalists then spiked the cannon and burned it and its sledge. The Federalists, prudent men, ran away because, as they later said, they lacked arms. Antifederalists explained it differently; Federalists, they said, lacked not arms but "spirit and courage."[60]

The next day, Federalists reassembled at noon. Now, definitely armed, and more stouthearted in broad daylight, they completed their celebration. Exactly how is a matter of dispute. They themselves claimed that, surrounded by a taunting and armed Antifederalist mob, they bravely demonstrated their mettle for two hours by reading the state's ratification, by numerous acclamations, by repeated volleys of muskets and by firing of cannons. The Antifederalists told a different story. The Federalists, they said, had met, quickly fired their cannon three instead of the planned thirteen times, and then "immediately left."[61] That afternoon the Antifederalists marched to the court house, where they burned effigies of Judge Thomas McKean and "James Wilson, the Caledonian" (the Scotsman). In the evening the Federalists, now in-doors and feeling more secure, enjoyed "an elegant supper" at Mr. Joseph Postlethwait's tavern.[62]

These dramatic confrontations stimulated a war of printed words whose volume and viciousness threatened to overwhelm the editor of the *Carlisle Gazette*. On January 23, he announced that "necessity and

---

59. "One of the People," *Carlisle Gazette*, 1/9/88, in Jensen 2:675; "An Old Man," *Carlisle Gazette*, 1/2/88, in Jensen 2:671.

60. Jensen 2:671; "One of the People," *Carlisle Gazette*, 1/9/88, in Jensen 2:676.

61. Jensen 2:676. Compare the Federalist celebration in Lancaster, December 20, where the inhabitants "fired a morning gun, and at twelve o'clock thirteen rounds were fired. . . . From that time until night all the bells in town were ringing." *Pennsylvania Packet*, 1/5/88. And at Chambersburg: "The people . . . demonstrated their joy on the arrival of the news with thirteen discharges of cannon, and the madeira flowed plentifully." John Clark to Jasper Yeates, York, Pa., 12/28/87, in Jensen 2:651.

62. "An Old Man," *Carlisle Gazette*, 1/2/88, in Jensen 2:672.

decency" obliged him "to discontinue publishing any more upon that subject."[63] On the same day the Supreme Court ordered the county sheriff, Charles Leeper, to arrest the known Antifederalist rioters. On February 25 most of these men appeared and posted bond. Seven, however, refused to give bond and went to jail in protest.[64] Within days hundreds, possibly thousands, of Antifederalist militia from at least three counties had assembled in support of the jailed protesters. After protracted discussion, and, presumably, some informal counting of heads, Sheriff Leeper, on March 1 released the seven imprisoned Antifederalists. On March 20 the Supreme Executive Council ordered all charges against them dropped.

The prudence (or the timidity) of the Federalists in Carlisle prevented a bloodbath. As a sympathetic observer wrote at the time: "for want of a sufficient number to repel . . . [the Antifederalists] the gentlemen of the town, . . . though it most proper to let them alone." "Not that they were afraid," he said, "for if they could but have raised two or three hundred men, well armed," they would have acted with courage.[65]

Sporadic violence also erupted in other backcountry areas. In Huntingdon County officials tried to jail Antifederalists who had paraded effigies of leading Federalists but "the county took alarm, assembled, and liberated the sons of liberty." Reports from Washington County claimed that eight men had died "in a battle between advocates and opponents of the Constitution."[66] In the backcountry through the winter and spring of 1788, as in the city during the previous fall, the heated rhetoric, the personal provocations, and probably, the conjunction of this dispute with already existing animosities, kept tempers hot, friction frequent, and local mayhem an ever-present possibility. For most Antifederalist publicists, however, one senses that predictions of violence were rhetorical ploys. They wanted to bargain not fight. Even the most ardent Antifederalists talked of civil war only in contingent terms. The die was not yet cast. Another convention, called to "form a

---

63. *Carlisle Gazette*, 1/23/88.

64. "Editorial note," Jensen 2:670, and Pennsylvania Supreme Court to Sheriff Charles Leeper, 1/23/88, in Jensen 2:684; "Release of the Prisoners," *Carlisle Gazette*, 3/5/88, in Jensen 2:699–701.

65. John Shippen to Joseph Shippen, Carlisle, 3/3/88, in Jensen 2:707. For an essay that emphasizes the ideological and the socioeconomic differences between the Carlisle Federalists and Antifederalists, see Cornell, "Aristocracy Assailed."

66. *Freeman's Journal*, 3/19/88; Thomas Rodney's report, 5/10/88, in Jensen 2:MFM 676.

new constitution on the principles of the revolution" could avoid bloodshed, "preventing these evils [of anarchy or worse]."[67]

The Final Failure

Calling for the rejection of the Convention's decision was one thing; convincing the voters that they could do so was quite another matter. Regardless of the dangers inherent in the new system, or the nefarious motives of its creators and supporters, the people of the state had apparently given their approval. Popular belief in the legitimacy of that process stood in the way of overturning its outcome. The challenge here, as James R. Reid explained to Tench Coxe, was to "offer a legal and constitutional proof that the people of Pennsylvania were not represented in the last convention." Such proof aimed to undermine popular confidence in both the Grand Convention of the summer of 1787 and the state convention of November–December 1787.[68]

To this end, Antifederalists argued that the state had sent delegates to the Constitutional Convention without the explicit endorsement of the people, and that those delegates had assumed powers far beyond any imagined by their constituents. The framers, this "highflying body" of men, led by the "soaring Catalin" Wilson, had practiced their artful inequities, and produced a document whose "affected brevity" was intended to deceive, "to be a *fraud upon the people*." The members of the Constitutional Convention, looked to by the people of America to solve the exigencies of the union, had betrayed the people's trust, like "the villain who protects virgin innocence only with a view that he may himself become the ravisher."[69] And, the Antifederalist argument continued, the state legislature had acted with no more honor or honesty in calling for an early state convention. During the truncated campaign for delegates to the convention, they pointed out, threats of physical

67. *Independent Gazetteer*, 1/19/88.
68. Reid to Coxe, New York, 1/15/88, Kaminski and Saladino, eds., *Documentary History*, 15:373–74. "The Dissent of the Minority" emphasizes this line of argument. See Jensen 2:618–40, esp. 618–22.
69. "Fallacies of the Farmer," *Independent Gazetteer*, 4/22/88; "Secrets," *Freeman's Journal*, 1/16/88; "A Citizen," *Independent Gazetteer*, 3/3/88; "Cicero," *Independent Gazetteer*, 1/30/88; "Philadelphiensis," *Independent Gazetteer*, 12/19/87.

violence had inhibited free discussion. In addition, Federalist control of some vehicles of communication had prevented a careful examination of the document. Distance and ignorance had kept people from the polls.[70]

Not one sixth of the electorate of the state had given countenance to this convention, the Antifederalists charged, although the artful Federalists had used numerous ruses to create an illusion of popular support. In rural communities they assembled together the "well-born" of the area, praising the Constitution, and declaring their decision to be the voice of the people. "Gouvero" prescribed a parallel process for exploiting the ignorant and the immoral in the towns such as Pittsburgh, Carlisle, and Easton. Start with a set of resolves and a five-dollar note, he explained. Then "get the townsmen . . . into a Tavern," lay out the five dollars in grog and beer, "place a *hero* in the chair," read a set of resolves, have all approve by raising their hands, and then "separate as soon as may be, as the farmers may hear of the meeting and give you interruption."[71]

Even some elected representatives acted contrary to the wishes of their electors, or so an Antifederalist from Bucks County claimed. "We send them down to your town," he said, "but they [let] themselves under the city faction and become their representatives." The urban junto wines and dines them and the elected representatives "in return are always sure to give their votes to carry the lowest party purposes."[72]

Furthermore, Antifederalists contended, the majority at the state convention represented only a minority of the electorate. In some counties large numbers of Antifederalists had not voted; in others the Federalists had won by narrow margins; and in still others the Antifederalists had overwhelmed their opponents. By combining the undelivered Antifederalist votes in some counties, with the large Antifederalist minorities in others, and the overwhelming Antifederalist majorities in the remainder, Antifederalist election analysts demonstrated, at least to their own satisfaction, that Antifederalists at the convention represented more Pennsylvanians than did the Federalists.[73]

---

70. George Bryan writing in March 1788 recalled that "Here [in the city] in October, we were forced to hold our tongues, lest well dressed ruffians should fall upon us. At this day, the case is otherwise. Yet many are still silent." Bryan, in Jensen 16:487. *Freeman's Journal,* 10/31/87.
71. *Freeman's Journal,* 10/31/87; "A Correspondent," *Independent Gazetteer,* 12/5/87; "Gouvero," *Independent Gazetteer,* 1/10/88.
72. "One of the People," *Independent Gazetteer,* 2/26/88.
73. "A correspondent," *Independent Gazetteer,* 12/5/87. "The Dissent of the Minority" makes the same point with different numbers. It claims a potential electorate of 70,000; a turnout of 13,000; and a Federalist vote of 6,800. Jensen 2:622.

The state convention had also acted improperly. The majority had refused to allow the minority to enter the reasons for their dissent on the minutes; it had encouraged the gallery to insult and abuse the minority; it had refused to hear and respond to petitions from foes of ratification; and it had not allowed amendments. Equally damning, in the Antifederalists' eyes, the convention violated the state constitution of 1776 by altering Pennsylvania's government, which only the Council of Censors (an amending body elected once every seven years) could legitimately do.[74]

Finally, Antifederalists argued, the majority of the people had opposed ratification in November and a larger number did so now, in the spring of 1788. "Investigator" reported on March 19, 1788, that the Federalists could count on only minuscule support: 38 people in Dauphin, 53 in Berks; one sixth of the people in Northampton, one fourth in Montgomery, and possibly a third in Chester, Bucks, and Lancaster. "*Most* of those counted as friends" to the Constitution, he claimed are "doubtful or wavering." They see "great defects, and say that they will not interfere on either side." They are, he said, "chiefly composed of that respectable denomination of people called Quaker."[75]

Had the election been held in January instead of November, another Antifederalist claimed, Antifederalists would have had a majority of "[a]t last four to one." Both the Constitutionalist party and a number of that "respectable class of citizens called Quakers" oppose it, he claimed. Berks is "almost to a man . . . determined enemies to the new constitution." So too was the greater part of Northampton, for these "honest Germans have no idea of giving their *hard earnings* to the Nabobs" in the new government.[76]

"The Real Federalist," writing late in March 1788, pulled all these threads together and thereby summarized the Antifederalist case against the legitimacy of Pennsylvania's ratification. "[T]he evil genius of darkness presided at it's [sic] birth"; it "came forth under the veil of mystery . . . , its true features being carefully concealed, and every deceptive art has been and is practising to have the spurious brat received as the genuine offspring of heaven-born Liberty." Its advocates stifled criticism, hurried "on its adoption with the greatest precipitancy," intimi-

---

74. "Columbian Patriot," *Freeman's Journal*, 3/26/88; "Item," in *Independent Gazetteer*, 3/22/88; "Fallacies of the Freeman," *Independent Gazetteer*, 4/22/88; "Philadelphiensis No. 5," *Independent Gazetteer*, 12/19/87.
75. "Investigator," *Freeman's Journal*, 3/19/88.
76. "Correspondent," *Independent Gazetteer*, 1/11/88.

dated all opposition, "procured a packed Convention," abridged the discussion and attempted to corrupt their opponents by proffering "lucrative offices to those . . . who should give up their opposition." The conclusion hardly needed to be stated: the December vote of the state convention did not represent the will of the people and therefore deserved to be overthrown.[77]

But how to overturn the state's ratification was the question. Certainly Findley, Smilie, and Whitehill had used the ratifying convention to develop both the rhetoric and the logic for popular repudiation of the convention's expected conclusion. The postconvention press barrage sought the same end. The limited evidence we have, however, suggests that the Antifederalists were not of one mind on how to proceed. At least two different plans competed against each other.

The first, probably supported by the established leadership of the Constitutionalist party, looked to locally elected revolutionary committees. In the early 1770s such committees, emerging on the county level, had allowed a dedicated minority to seize control of the provincial government, declare Pennsylvania independent, and then draft and promulgate a new constitution. Smilie implied this approach at the convention when he declared that "after this Convention . . . the people . . . still have a right to assemble another body . . . to abrogate this federal work so ratified." Findley's speech in the closing days of the convention, as well as an essay published on December 22, point toward a second, popularly elected state convention sometime "before the new Constitution shall become the SUPREME LAW OF THE LAND."[78]

To this apparent end, "Centinel," in late January, urged the people to establish county committees of correspondence. The next month, George Bryan explained to Governor George Clinton of New York that "as soon as the season permit we plan to hold . . . a meeting of delegates who shall decide how far the majority of the people of this state are to abide by the decision of the violent and tyrannous minority." In mid-March, a report from west of the mountains indicated that they anticipated sending delegates to a meeting in Reading "as early in April as possible."[79]

---

77. *Freeman's Journal*, 3/26/88.
78. *Pennsylvania Herald*, 11/27/87, 12/5/87, in Jensen 2:376. Findley's speech, 12/12/87, *Pennsylvania Herald*, 12/19/87, in Jensen 2:587; "A Few Queries," *Independent Gazetteer*, 12/22/87.
79. Bryan to Clinton, 2/9/88, in Jensen 2:714. *Freeman's Journal*, 3/19/88.

At the same time, other opponents of ratification moved off in another direction. Comptroller John Nicholson, in particular, mounted a statewide petition effort to induce the legislature, scheduled to meet again in mid-February, to nullify the convention's ratification. The extant evidence gives us a fuller picture of this more conspicuous and ultimately disastrous strategy. In late December 1787 Nicholson printed and circulated a petition demanding "that it [the Federal Constitution] may not be confirmed by the legislature of this state, nor adopted in the said United States, and that the delegates of Congress from this state be instructed for that purpose." By January 14, copies were in Lancaster; by February 1 in Franklin, York, and Bedford, west of the Susquehanna; and by February 2 in Washington County, across the mountains in the far southwestern corner of the state.[80]

The Antifederalist press commented favorably on the project, and some, at least, blended the petition drive with the movement for a second convention. The *Freeman's Journal*, for example, observed that "from the general temper of the farmers and the complexion of the assembly, it is almost certain that we will have another convention in a legal constitutional manner . . . we may expect a power of petitions will be laid before the assembly . . . for this purpose."[81]

Reports from the field were initially optimistic. Richard Bard, a Nicholson Antifederalist organizer, wrote to his mentor on February 1 that he was circulating a petition in his township (Mercersberg) and believed that "There will be at [least] ten persons that will sighn [sic] the petition for one that will refuse to do it." His brother, he added, was meeting with good response in Bedford, and that people beyond the Allegheny Mountains "are enraged at it [the Constitution], and even in york county where all the members in the late Convention voted for sd[?] constitution there are great numbers of the people much dissatisfyd."[82]

Federalists reported much the same thing. Thomas Hartley of York worried in January that "[i]n this idle and inclement Season" the Antifederalists were making great efforts "to inflame the Minds and imbark the Passions of the People . . . against the New Constitution." John Black from Marsh Creek warned Federalist Benjamin Rush in

---

80. Jensen 2:711; Richard Bard to Nicholson 2/1/88, in Jensen 2:712; and James Marshall to John Nicholson, Washington County, February 2, 1788, in Jensen 2:713.
81. *Freeman's Journal*, 1/2/88.
82. Richard Bard to John Nicholson, Mercerberg, 2/1/88, in Jensen 2:712.

early February that "[s]ome of the people of Franklin County . . . are preparing a petition to the Assembly to interpose their authority that the new Constitution may not be adopted."[83]

In mid-March, the petitions cascaded into the legislature. On March 17, Peter Trexler of Northampton introduced appeals signed by about 230 people. By the end of that week the numbers had grown to nearly 4,000 as Dauphin, Bedford, Franklin, and Cumberland joined. The next week brought another 2000 or so from Cumberland and Westmoreland, and by March 29 the legislature had before it pleas from more than 6,000 people demanding nullification of the state's ratification of the Federal Constitution.[84] Massive petitioning was an old and effective political technique in Pennsylvania. A similar petition campaign in the winter of 1778–79 had pressured legislators into reversing their call for a referendum on the state constitution. Antifederalists obviously hoped for much the same result now, but they hoped in vain. The legislature tabled the petitions and adjourned.[85]

At least three factors account for the Assembly's indifference to the Antifederalist petitions. First, most of these legislators had taken a public stand on the Federal Constitution when they had stood for election to the Assembly earlier in October 1787. Their constituents, knowing where they stood, had chosen them. This alone should have strengthened the confidence of the sitting legislators.

Equally important, 6,000 was not a particularly large number of signatures. Almost a decade earlier, in the winter of 1779, petitions from rural Pennsylvania bearing some 13,000 signatures had come to Assembly supporting the state constitution of 1776; almost 4,000 of these from one county: Lancaster. Recall, also, that in a few days in September 1787 Federalists in Philadelphia had gathered some 4,000 signatures in favor of an early state convention. More recently, in February and March 1788, upward of 2,000 Quakers had petitioned the Assembly to strengthen the state's laws against slavery while some eighteen petitions with hundreds (probably thousands) of signatures

---

83. Thomas Hartley to Tench Coxe, 1/11/88, Tench Coxe Papers, ser. 2, Correspondence and General Papers, Historical Society of Pennsylvania, quoted in Kaminski and Saladino, 15:12. John Black to Benjamin Rush, Marsh Creek, 2/13/88, in Jensen 2:660–61.

84. "Summary of Petitions Against the Adoption of the New Constitution Presented to the Assembly, March, 1788," in "Assembly Proceedings," 3/29/88, in Jensen 2:720–21.

85. Robert Brunhouse, *The Counter-Revolution in Pennsylvania 1776–1790* (Harrisburg: Pennsylvania Historical Commission, 1942), 58–60, 248 n. 26.

from across the state prayed for relief from taxes, debts, and land payments. Six thousand signatures on Antifederalist petitions did not overawe these legislators.[86]

Finally, most of these men had spent the winter recess (January and February) at home, among their constituents, after the convention had ratified the Federal Constitution. They thus knew what a close analysis of the geographic origins of the petitions reveals: the shrill cries for nullification of the state's ratification came not from a broad cross-section of the electorate, but from a highly concentrated minority of voters in a small number of Antifederalist counties. Three counties alone, Cumberland, Dauphin, and Franklin, accounted for more than eighty percent of the total signatures. The bulk of the remainder came from Berks and Westmoreland, all well-established and commonly recognized Antifederalist centers. This petition campaign posed no threat to the Federalist majority in the house. They could safely ignore it, and they did.[87]

The failure of the petition drive in the winter and early spring of 1788 ended organized opposition to ratification in Pennsylvania. "Centinel" attempted to put the best face on the disaster. The opposition drive had done quite well, he argued, considering that it had been undertaken by an individual (Nicholson?) "unadvisedly and without concert, and contrary to the system of conduct generally agreed upon." If time had permitted, "Centinel" continued, it "would have been subscribed by five-sixth of the freemen of this state."[88]

"Valerius," writing on April 4, underscored the point but with

---

86. *Journal of the House of Representatives of the Commonwealth of Pennsylvania*, 2/18/79, 2/27/79, Philadelphia, 1781, in Clifford K. Shipton, ed., *Early American Imprints. Reproduction on Readex Microprint of the Works Listed in Charles Evans, American Bibliography* (Worcester: American Antiquarian Society, 1955–69): Evans number 7658. *Pennsylvania Packet*, 2/27/88, 2/29/88, 3/15/88, 3/31/88; Thomas Lloyd, *Proceedings and Debates of the General Assembly*, 2/25/88, 2/26/88, 3/5/88, 3/7/88, 3/12/88, 3/20/88, 3/25/88, 3/27/88, Philadelphia (vol. 3), 1788. Two of these eighteen petitions contained between them some 689 names.

87. News in late February that Massachusetts had ratified the Constitution certainly reinforced the Assembly's determination to ignore the Antifederalists' petitions. Earlier in the month George Bryan had suggested that the decision in other states would influence Pennsylvania's behavior. Bryan to Clinton, 2/9/88, in Jensen 2:714. See also the comments by Federalist Thomas FitzSimons to William Irvine on February 22, and by former Antifederalist James Marshall to Nicholson, February 2. FitzSimons to Irvine, Philadelphia, 2/22/88, in Jensen 2:716; Marshall to Nicholson, Washington County, 2/2/88, in Jensen 2:713.

88. "Centinel," in Storing 2.7.184.

different particulars. "It is well known," he said, "this measure [the petitions] was started by an individual in *Franklin County*, who took this step notwithstanding he was desired to desist by the party who oppose the new Constitution." "Centinel" and "Valerius" struggled to turn an embarrassment into a victory and "Valerius," at least, remained optimistic: "other measures much more *solid* are on the carpet, and which, I make no doubt, will procure the desired amendments."[89]

The weight of the evidence, however, is against the conclusion that more time or better coordination would have produced a more effective petition campaign. Possibly with prior consultation Bryan, and the legislative leaders Findley and Smilie would have joined Nicholson in the petition drive. Probably not. They apparently had a different, more cautious plan in mind, one better adapted to the needs of a committed minority. They also had extensive and reliable political contacts in virtually every corner of the state and may have suspected in January what the petitions revealed in March: Antifederalists in Pennsylvania were a decided minority.

More sophisticated political operators than Nicholson might well have realized sooner that the scheme was in trouble. Some of Nicholson's correspondents brought back good news, but some reported mixed results, and others, failure. Samuel Turbett informed Nicholson in January that he had received the petition but probably would not circulate it in his home county of Lancaster. After consulting with "some warm friends," he reported, "it was adjudged best not to attempt anything at this place, as there are a large majority on the other side of the question."[90]

James Marshall also reported pessimistic news from Washington County, west of the mountains. "The new Federal Constitution is seldom mentioned in this county," he wrote. "The people's minds are so well prepared for a change that even those who opposed it with considerable warmth appear to be in suspense whether it is not our true interest to receive it. . . . Nor do I believe that a petition would be very generally signed for calling another convention." In addition, Marshall, who, at the state convention, had opposed ratification, now admitted to uncertainty. "I freely confess," he wrote to Nicholson, "that I'm not able to determine with precision what is our true interest as a people in

---

89. *Independent Gazetteer*, 4/4/88, in Jensen 2:724.
90. Turbett to Nicholson, Lancaster, 1/14/88, 1/28/88, in Jensen 2:711–12.

the present crisis for I neither think the proposed government so diabolical as some in the opposition seem to hold forth nor so good as its advocates represent."[91]

The polite but noncommittal response to Nicholson from John Craighead on February 9 also pointed toward trouble for the petition effort. Craighead, the minister to the Rocky Springs Presbyterian Church in Franklin County, acknowledged Nicholson's many earlier favors and thanked him for transacting "the business I troubled you with relative to my Nephew's land." He then got down to particulars. Nicholson apparently had chided Craighead for speaking favorably of the Federal Constitution from the pulpit. Craighead responded cautiously but a bit tartly that he could not "see how my being in favour of, or opposed to, the proposed constitution should affect my character." More to the point, he said, "You have been wrong informed." He asserted that he had "never been strenuous on either side," and that he was "more undecided, than in any other [question] since the revolution."[92]

Why Nicholson moved off on his own (if, indeed, he did so) and how other Antifederalists felt about it remain unclear. Robert Whitehill, from Cumberland, probably cooperated with Nicholson. He was the most powerful Antifederalist in the central part of the state, and the preponderance of signatures from Cumberland and its two Antifederalist neighbors (Franklin to the west and Dauphin to the east) suggests his support.

Be that as it may, the results are unequivocal. The failed petition campaign killed organized opposition to ratification in Pennsylvania. While the issue remained undecided in such other crucial states as Virginia and New York, the press debate in Pennsylvania largely ended by mid-April. The Harrisburg Antifederalist convention in September 1788 acknowledged the legitimacy of the new system, urged the people of Pennsylvania to accept it, nominated candidates for the fall congressional elections, and suggested amendments.[93]

---

91. James Marshall to John Nicholson, Washington, Pennsylvania, 2/2/88, in Jensen 2:713.
92. John Craighead to John Nicholson, Rocky Springs, Pennsylvania, 2/9/88, in Kaminski and Saladino 16:94–95.
93. For details of the Antifederalist Harrisburg Convention, see Brunhouse, *Counter-Revolution*, 214–15; John B. McMaster and Frederick D. Stone, eds., *Pennsylvania and the Federal Constitution, 1787–1788* (Philadelphia: Historical Society of Pennsylvania, 1888), 533–37; Paul Leicester Ford, *Origin, Purpose*; Roland Baumann, "The Democratic-Republicans of Philadelphia: The Origins 1776–1797" (Ph.D. diss., Pennsylvania State University, 1970), 127–32. Merrill Jensen and Robert Becker, eds., *The Documentary History of the First Federal Elections, 1788–1790* (Madison: University of Wisconsin Press, 1976) 1:258–82.

The fall Assembly election (October 1788) illustrates the magnitude of the Antifederalists' defeat. The voters reelected seventy percent of the incumbents and the returns evince no popular anger at those who had ignored the Antifederalist petitions and stood firm in their support of the proposed Federal Constitution. The changes that did take place favored the Republicans. Half of the new men represented the same party as those they replaced (eight Republicans and two Constitutionalists). In nine of the remaining ten instances, the Constitutionalists lost, giving up six seats to the Republicans and three to men who voted with neither bloc. When the dust settled the Constitutionalists had lost nearly thirty percent of the twenty-eight seats they had held in the previous legislature.[94]

By any measure, this was a devastating blow. A year earlier the Constitutionalists had been a viable political force with a long history of electoral success; a sizable minority within striking distance of future control of the state. Now, they had atrophied into an impotent and powerless faction, with little hope of recovery. The once powerful and popular Constitutionalist party, rebuffed by the majority of the voters, was on its way to oblivion. For all intents and purposes, this defeat ended an era in Pennsylvania history.[95]

Of greater immediate significance, the fall Assembly election of 1788 demonstrates the extent of popular commitment to the new Federal Constitution. The Constitutionalists had provided both the leadership and the bulk of the electoral support for the opposition to ratification. In Pennsylvania by the winter of 1787–88, Constitutionalists and Antifederalists were one; and in October 1788, the voters repudiated both. Opposition to the Federal Constitution was dead in Pennsylvania, killed by those for whom the Antifederalists had purported to speak: the people of Pennsylvania.

During the course of their late winter effort, Antifederalists built an apparently powerful case against the Federal Constitution. The bulk of

---

94. For a fuller discussion of the magnitude of the Federalist electoral majority, see Chapter 6 and O. S. Ireland, "The People's Triumph: The Federalist Majority in Pennsylvania, 1787–1788," *Pennsylvania History* 56 (April 1989): 93–113.

95. At a state constitutional convention of 1789–90, Federalist James Wilson and Antifederalist William Findley cooperated in writing a state constitution that provided for a bicameral legislature, a single executive with substantial power, and an independent judiciary. See Joseph Foster, "The Politics of Ideology: The Pennsylvania Constitutional Convention of 1789–90," *Pennsylvania History* 59 (1992): 122–44.

their literature focused on concerns first articulated during the fall: attachments to local autonomy; fears of internal taxes, standing armies and established churches; concern for jury trials, freedom of the press, liberty of conscience; worry about the danger to traditional English civil liberties; and apprehensions about remote, insensitive, unresponsive, and tyrannical central authority. These themes in themselves constituted a extraordinarily powerful vehicle for mobilizing widespread electoral support.

The newer elements complemented this basic approach, and, at the same time, offered glimpses of the social reality hidden behind the earlier, more polite abstractions. The Antifederalist expanded and particularized the protean pejorative "aristocracy," while attacking hierarchical Anglicans, urbane Deists, the rabble of the city, and the aspirations and the posturing of Robert Morris and James Wilson. This array of enemies, in turn, suggests the principal electorate to whom and for whom the Antifederalists thought they spoke: backcountry, Trinitarian Christian, dissenting Protestants of middle rank, intolerant of artificial distinctions and social pretensions, vehemently opposed to claims of superiority and privilege, and longtime supporters of the state constitution of 1776.

In some ways, these elements in the Antifederalist publications narrowed their appeal and constricted their potential audience. Deprecating Philadelphians; abusing Anglicans, heathens, and Deists; spewing invectives at Francis Hopkinson, James Wilson, and Robert Morris; threatening, inciting, and sanctioning rural tumult—each and all of these would certainly antagonize particular individuals and groups in Pennsylvania. On the other hand, those attacked by the Antifederalists constituted a small proportion of the state's total population. Abusing city people, Anglican, Deists, and aspiring aristocrats cost little and might pay rich dividends. If effective, such a strategy could well strengthen Antifederalist support among those rural, Trinitarian Christian dissenters and Protestants of modest property who made up the great majority of the electorate.

In much the same vein, the Antifederalists' muted defense of the state constitution promised to gain more voters than it lost. In the past, more often than not, this issue, and the ethnic-religious partisan responses that it had elicited, had served to gain and regain control of the state for the Constitutionalist party. Federalist behavior should also have advanced the Antifederalists' cause. The system the Federalists supported would, indeed, reduce the relative power and autonomy of the states, grant the new central government many of the same military, judicial, and internal domestic taxing powers that Americans had fought a revolution to deny to the British, and offer little protection for traditional civil liberties.

Furthermore, Pennsylvania's supporters of the Federal Constitution had acted secretly, like men with something to hide. They had hurried the ratification process along at breakneck speed, relied on mob violence at crucial points, and avoided discussion of the proposed changes whenever possible. In addition, and of no small consequence, Wilson, the Federalists' chief spokesman, conveyed a secular, urbane, aloof, condescending and "aristocratic" image, while Robert Morris, possibly the most disliked and distrusted Republican in the state, had left a confused and suspicious trail of personal financial manipulations. Finally, in this phase of the campaign, Federalists revealed an increasingly patronizing attitude as they followed their convention victory with ridicule of their fallen foes.

And, yet, the Antifederalists lost, decisively, repeatedly, and by increasingly large margins. The question remains: Why?

PART TWO

The Context

5
The Economy and The Constitution

The City

In April 1788 the contest over ratification in Pennsylvania ended. The Antifederalists had lost. Their appeals to hatred of social pretension, to fear of remote government, to apprehension about conspiring aristocrats, and to hostility felt by Christian dissenters for hierarchical Anglicanism and anti-Christian Deism had failed. The problems besetting the union, and especially its economic difficulties, played a complex part in this outcome.

Perceptions of the Economy

In 1787 America faced critical times, nearly every publicist agreed. In December 1786, the Pennsylvania legislature had readily elected delegates to an interstate convention for rendering "the federal constitution fully adequate to the exigencies of the Union." For two years or more the newspapers had teemed with accounts of the nation's impotency, vulnerability, and stagnation. America, the press argued, had not fulfilled the promises of the Revolution.[1]

In the campaign for ratification, Federalists made the exigencies of the union their first and most frequent argument.[2] More important, Antifederalists generally accepted the basic Federalist contention. They recognized that Congress could not effectively negotiate international agreements, protect American ships and sailors on the high seas, pay the national debt, maintain the national credit, or nurture America's international trade. They had, they readily conceded, supported calling the Grand Convention and had eagerly anticipated its recommendations. As the "Seceding Assemblymen" said in their early October "Address": "The Confederation no doubt is defective and requires amendment and revision." Congress, they conceded, needed the power to "regulate commerce, equalize the impost, collect it throughout the United States, and have the entire jurisdiction over maritime affairs." Had the Grand Convention granted these powers to the national government and left "the exercise of internal taxation to the separate states," these opponents of ratification would have had "no objection to the plan of government."[3]

Three months later, at the end of the state convention in December, the Antifederalist "Dissent" said much the same thing: "It was not until after the termination of the late glorious contest . . . that the powers vested in Congress were found to be inadequate to the procuring of the benefits that should result from the union." These leading Antifederalists again enumerated America's problems: "our national character was sinking in the opinion of foreign nations. . . . Congress could make treaties of commerce, but could not enforce the observance of them. We were suffering from the restrictions of foreign nations, who had shackled our commerce, while we were unable to retaliate."[4]

---

1. For a detailed account of this newspaper coverage of America's mounting difficulties, see John Alexander, *The Selling of the Constitutional Convention* (Madison, Wisc.: Madison House, 1990). Alexander suggests that newspaper editors' favorable disposition toward the convention influenced their coverage. See also Merrill Jensen, *The Documentary History of the Ratification of the Constitution* (Madison: State Historical Society of Wisconsin, 1976), 2:34.
2. *Freeman's Journal*, 10/10/87. See Chapter 2 for details of the Federalist argument.
3. Jensen 2:116.
4. Jensen 2:618–19.

Not all Antifederalists agreed as to the severity of the crisis or the role of congressional weakness in causing it. "Centinel" admitted that America faced "distresses and difficulties" but doubted that these could be "ascribed to the impotency of the present confederation." Remember, he reminded his readers, Congress had failed to impose taxes in 1780–81, at least in part, because "the country . . . was very much impoverished and exhausted; commerce had been suspended for near six years; the husbandman, for want of a market, limited his crops to his own subsistence." He asserted that "any government . . . in similar circumstances" would have experienced the same fate.[5]

"Centinel" admitted the need for changes, but he deplored the popular infatuation with false hopes, with this "*golden phantom*," as he called it, that promised "the halcyon days, consequent on the establishment of the new constitution." "Centinel" favored a modest augmentation of the powers of the general government as a step toward opening the world's markets to America's farmers.[6]

The Antifederalist who signed himself "Philadelphiensis" developed a different line of argument. For him, the problem was the vulnerability of America's ships and men on the high seas. He admitted "that the present distresses of America are in consequence of the want of the states delegating sufficient powers to congress," but criticized that body for poorly managing the powers it already possessed. Congress, he said, "never attempted to build a navy; but, . . . to . . . our disgrace, sold the only ship of war we had." "If America is to be a commercial neutral power," he continued, "she ought to have some naval strength to intitle her to the appellation." Without a navy, "Her trade may be destroyed with impunity; her seamen taken to man the fleets of her enemies, . . . and her government insulted and her cities laid in ashes by her enemies ships riding triumphant in her rivers and harbours."[7]

Other Antifederalists, especially those published in Francis Bailey's *Freeman's Journal*, denied the need to protect America's sailors, commerce, or honor on the high seas. They argued that international trade was not America's boon but her bane, and that an end to foreign trade

---

5. "Centinel," in Cecelia M. Kenyon, *The Antifederalists* (Indianapolis, Ind.: Bobbs-Merrill, 1966), 2–14; *Independent Gazetteer*, 10/5/87; Herbert Storing, ed. and commentary, *The Complete Anti-federalist* (Chicago: University of Chicago Press, 1981), vol. 2, document 7, paragraph 79 (hereafter Storing 2.7.79).
6. Storing 2.7.102.
7. "Philadelphiensis," in Storing 3.9.48, 3.9.44.

would solve America's ills. Bailey admitted that he had "felt and lamented the effects of the wretched system under which we are suffering." In late October 1787, however, he concluded that "a gradual decay of trade would rather suit the interests of this country, as it must greatly increase our own manufacturers."[8]

A few Antifederalists declared that moral not constitutional weakness caused America's difficulties. Our problems derive, one insisted, not from the "political machine" but from the people themselves. The proper remedy is to reform the people, not tinker with their constitution. We need, he declared, "a long course of frugality, disuse of foreign luxuries, encouragement of industry, application to agriculture, attending to home manufactures, and a spirit of union and national sobriety." Sacrifice, sobriety, frugality, and discipline might, indeed, have solved America's problems in the late 1780s, but not many advocated such draconian measures.[9]

In sum, not all Antifederalists shared the same vision of America's future. Some, like "Centinel," anticipated a nation of farmers producing agricultural staples for the world market; others, like "Philadelphiensis," dreamed of America as a "commercial neutral," proudly sailing the world's seas, tolerating insults from none while providing jobs and prosperity for those domestic craftsmen linked to the maritime trades. Still others, such as Francis Bailey and many of the essays he chose to publish, aspired to a self-sufficient America in which farmers and craftsmen prospered by supplying each other's needs.

Despite these differences, however, the bulk of the Antifederalist publicists assumed that America's prosperity depended upon trade and commerce, be it among American artisans and farmers, or between America and the world. Few argued that America's future depended upon frugality, sobriety, and moral reform and only an occasional Antifederalist preached a return to the simple Spartan life of self-denial, moral rectitude, and humble Christian self-sufficiency.

Antifederalist and Federalist spokesmen thus agreed that America had a problem; that deficiencies in the Confederation contributed to that problem; and that an augmentation of the external powers of the central government over trade, commerce, imposts (or "oceanic" powers, to use historian John Murrin's apt phrase) would help solve

8. *Freeman's Journal*, 10/10/87, 10/24/87.
9. *Freeman's Journal*, 8/29/87.

this problem. They disagreed about the political, not the economic consequences of ratification; they disagreed about the new government's internal or domestic, not its external or "oceanic" powers.[10] Antifederalists argued that the Federal Constitution granted the central government more power than was necessary to deal with the current crisis. As John Smilie phrased it at the convention: "Is such a sacrifice of civil liberty necessary to the national honor and happiness of America?"[11]

If Federalists and Antifederalists in Pennsylvania agreed on the broad outlines of the economic problems faced by people of Pennsylvania, historians have not. The scarcity of reliable data contributes to the difficulty in reaching agreement. The current status of our understanding thus promises, at best, some plausible but tentative conclusions about the nature of the economy and its relationship to the electoral behavior of the people of Pennsylvania.[12]

The Fiscal Status of the State Government

At least one public official claimed that the state government itself was in good financial shape. John Nicholson, comptroller general of Pennsylvania, repeatedly presented optimistic reports to the Ways and

10. John Murrin, "The British and Colonial Background to American Constitutionalism," in Leonard Levy and Dennis Mahoney, eds., *The Framing and Ratification of the Constitution* (New York: Macmillan, 1987), 19–36.
11. "Convention Debates," Saturday, 11/24/87, in Jensen 2:336–37.
12. Alexander, *Selling of the Constitutional Convention*, suggests that the press painted a one-sided picture. Twentieth-century historians have reached no consensus on the question of the American economy in the late 1780s and its impact on the ratification contest. For examples of those who minimize it, see Merrill Jensen, *The New Nation: A History of the United States During the Confederation, 1781–1789* (New York: Vintage Books, 1950); Gordon Wood, *The Creation of the American Republic, 1776–1787* (Chapel Hill: University of North Carolina Press, for the Institute of Early American History and Culture, Williamsburg, Va., 1969). For a different view, see Drew McCoy, *The Last of the Fathers* (New York: Cambridge University Press, 1989), 179; and Curtis Nettels, *The Emergence of a National Economy, 1775–1815* (New York: Holt, Rinehart and Winston, 1962), 90–94. Contemporaries, apparently, also disagreed. For example, Charles Thomson, secretary to the Continental Congress, wrote to Thomas Jefferson on April 6, 1786: "there is not upon the face of the earth a body of people more happy or rising into consequence with more rapid strides than the inhabitants of the United States of America." Quoted in Kaminski, "Paper Politics," 83, from *The Charles Thomson Papers: Collections, 1878* (New York: New-York Historical Society, 1879), 205–6.

Means Committee of the state legislature. Late in 1786 he predicted a year-end surplus. The legislators, excited by the good news, abandoned plans to cut their own salaries.[13] Looked at in one light, Nicholson's facts and figures supported his conclusions. The basic costs of government remained modest. User fees covered such normal operational expenses as the prothonotaries' office and the maintenance of the port facilities at Philadelphia. Anticipated taxes, already imposed, would easily cover the state's current £100,000 a year obligations: the interest on the state's own funded debt, its various pension obligations, the salaries and other minor costs of government, as well as the annual payment to the Proprietors for lands confiscated during the war.

Furthermore, in Nicholson's frame of analysis, the state's two newest obligations promised to return more than they cost. The first was the state's new issue of paper money. In 1785 Pennsylvania printed £150,000 worth of paper certificates. Although this paper money had no specie backing (i.e., its value did not rest on gold or silver) the state pledged a variety of its assets to redeem it and promised to retire it from circulation at the rate of £20,000 per year. It used £100,000 of this money to meet current obligations and loaned the rest at interest to real property holders. The paper money served as a legal-tender equivalent to specie for payment of taxes and in purchases of public lands but not in private transactions.

This £150,000 looked like a new debt, and so it was. But paying it off at £20,000 a year posed no serious difficulties. Much of that amount would come into the state treasury in payment for state lands or taxes and could then simply be destroyed. The rest could be redeemed out of other revenues. In the meanwhile, the state would earn approximately £3,000 a year on the £50,000 it had loaned out at 6 percent interest. Moreover, the increased quantity of money in circulation would provide

---

13. The following analysis of Pennsylvania's fiscal condition rests principally on my reading of three documents produced by Nicholson in 1786–88: (1) *A View of the Debts and Expenses of the Commonwealth of Pennsylvania, December 1786* (Philadelphia, 1786), Clifford K. Shipton, ed., *Early American Imprints. Reproduction on Readex Microprint of the Works Listed in Charles Evans, American Bibliography* (Worcester: American Antiquarian Society, 1955–69): Evans number 19904 (also "A Report to . . . the Committee on Ways and Means, 12/6/86); (2) *A State of the Finances of the Commonwealth of Pennsylvania* (Philadelphia, 11/7/87: Evans 45137); and (3) "Report to the Pennsylvania General Assembly," *Minutes of . . . the General Assembly of the Commonwealth of Pennsylvania* (Philadelphia: Francis Bailey, 1784–90), 3/29/88, pp. 184–95 (hereafter cited as MPGA).

much-needed credit to agricultural entrepreneurs, and stimulate internal commerce.[14]

Nicholson also viewed optimistically the state's 1786 assumption of an even larger financial obligation: responsibility for paying the interest and the principal of debt owed by the United States to the citizens of Pennsylvania. The state did this by exchanging its own interest-bearing securities for the securities of the United States held by Pennsylvanians. Former creditors of the United States became creditors of the state, and the state became a creditor of the United States.

At first sight, this new financial responsibility seemed to place a staggering burden on Pennsylvania. The state became responsible for over £2,000,000 of federal debt, for an annual interest payment of about £120,000, and for accrued back interest of approximately £150,000. The annual interest alone exceeded all other ongoing state responsibilities.

Nevertheless, Nicholson argued, this system would produce long-term profit for Pennsylvania. The state could easily pay the interest out of current tax revenues and the new tax on property that the legislature had imposed. Over time, the state would gradually reduce the principal of this debt by allowing individuals to use these securities to pay for lands purchased from Pennsylvania. As the securities came into the land office the state would destroy them. Eventually, Pennsylvania might well retire the entire debt in this fashion.

Moreover, in giving state securities to its citizens in exchange for the Federal securities, Pennsylvania acquired an asset that in time would bring it handsome profits. When Congress finally reassumed responsibility for its own debt, Pennsylvania as a major holder of Federal securities, would receive literally millions of pounds in payment from the national government.

---

14. The most thorough and balanced treatment of Pennsylvania's paper-money issue of 1785 is John Paul Kaminski, "Paper Politics: The Northern State Loan-Offices During the Confederation, 1783–1790" (Ph.D. diss., University of Wisconsin, 1972), 76 n. 78, pp. 52, 74, 79, 83. Kaminski points out that this issue of paper money held up well during its first two years, depreciating only moderately until the recharter of the Bank of North America in the spring of 1787. The bank's avowed opposition to the paper-money issue, and the Federal Constitution's implicit condemnation of all state issues of paper money, Kaminski argues, undermined public confidence in Pennsylvania's paper money, which depreciated rapidly in the fall and winter of 1787–88. (79, esp. note 85). For the estimated interest income of £3,000, see Kaminski, 90 n. 57.

Despite Nicholson's happy predictions, two additional considerations suggest quite a different picture. First, Congress had little money and even less hope of obtaining more in the future. Without fundamental constitutional change, Congress would never meet its obligations and the securities of the United States now possessed by Pennsylvania would never generate the income Nicholson anticipated. Equally important, Nicholson's estimates of the state's tax revenues bore little relationship to reality. Pennsylvania had four principal sources of tax income: the impost on imports; the tax on property; the excise on spiritous liquors; and the tax on pleasure carriages. Nicholson estimated that these four would produce about £187,045 per year.

This prediction was simply absurd. The impost annually produced about one third of Nicholson's estimate; the annual property tax ran about 50 percent in arrears; the excise, the most reliable source of income in the state, also fell below Nicholson's estimates, while the tax on pleasure carriages remained largely uncollected. At best these four sources of revenue might generate about £80,000 a year, or less than half of the £187,000 Nicholson projected (see Table 1).

Since actual income never approximated actual expenditures, Pennsylvania could neither meet its current obligations nor whittle away at its accumulation of past debts. By November 1787 it had fallen behind at least £350,000 in meeting its ongoing responsibilities. By the spring of 1788 Pennsylvanians owed more than six hundred thousand pounds in back taxes or about ten pounds per head of household.[15]

Table 1. Pennsylvania's Revenue, 1785–1787

Tax	Anticipated Revenue (£)	Actual Revenue[a] (£)
Impost	90,000	36,574
Property	76,945	30,600
Excise	17,500	13,894
Carriages	2,600	—
Totals	187,045	81,068

[a]Three-year averages reported by Nicholson to the Pennsylvania General Assembly on March 29, 1788.

15. Estimating the precise quantity of tax arrearages in Pennsylvania is risky business. Nicholson's categories change and his details vary over time. I derived the sum of £661,658 by adding together the figures in a number of apparently different categories. The final sum is

The basic data we have thus suggest that the state of Pennsylvania faced a fiscal problem of mounting proportions: 1786 had been bad; 1787 had been worse; 1788 promised to be a disaster. Year after year income fell short of obligations and debt accumulated. Ratification of the Federal Constitution promised a solution. A national government with independent revenues could reassume responsibility for its own debts and thereby cut Pennsylvania's annual tax obligations by half or more. In addition, a stronger central government might, in turn, strengthen the state's will to collect its own taxes.[16]

The Working People of Philadelphia

The general economic situation of the city, and particularly the plight of its middle and lower orders, contributed to the city's Federalism.[17] A number of historians, building mostly on the earlier work of Gary Nash, generally agree that in the 1780s the always precarious existence of the city's workers deteriorated. Sharon Salinger has argued that by the late eighteenth century most master craftsmen had shifted from bound to

---

only an approximation but other observations confirm its general magnitude. In March 1785, opponents of the state assumption argued that "there remains due to the State, between four and five hundred thousand pounds (arrearages on taxes) exclusive of duties arising from the impost, equal to one hundred thousand pounds per annum" (*MPGA*, 3/16/85). In the same vein, the Ways and Means Committee reported to the legislature three years later that some £527,542 in back taxes remained unpaid (*MPGA*, 3/29/88).

16. Roger Brown has recently argued that the desire for a central government strong enough to collect internal, domestic taxes lay at the heart of support for the Federal Constitution in 1787–88. See Brown, *Redeeming the Republic: Federalists, Taxation, and The Origins of the Constitution* (Baltimore, Md.: Johns Hopkins University Press, 1993). Peter S. Onuf has also argued persuasively that a stronger union would also enhance each state's authority within its own territory by providing a powerful, external, and collective guarantee of disputed boundaries, of public order, and of political legitimacy; see Onuf, *The Origins of the Federal Republic: Jurisdictional Controversies in the United States, 1775–1787* (Philadelphia: University of Pennsylvania Press, 1983); and most recently, "Anarchy and the Crisis of the Union," in Ronald Hoffman et al., eds., *To Form A More Perfect Union: The Critical Ideas of the Constitution* (Charlottesville; University Press of Virginia, for the U.S. Capitol Historical Society, 1992), 272–302.

17. See above for descriptions of the city's Federalism and especially for details of the election-day violence against Antifederalists. Roland Baumann's dissertation is the most thorough and useful analysis we have of the politics of ratification in the city of Philadelphia. "The Democratic-Republicans of Philadelphia: The Origins, 1776–1797" (Ph.D. diss., Pennsylvania State University, 1970).

free labor and operated under a capitalist mode of production: paying wages, hiring journeymen in good times, dismissing them in bad. The city's general economic slowdown in the 1780s, she believes, placed great pressures on journeymen and many suffered.[18]

John Alexander, in his study of relief in late eighteenth-century Philadelphia, identifies a number of indicators of protracted hard times for working people. Popular concern about the "increase of vagabonds and social disorder in the streets" and widespread perception of a dramatic increase in crime both suggest growing unemployment and poverty. As late as the winter of 1790–91 observers found many willing to work but "destitute and starving for want of employ." In 1787 at least two newspapers printed versions of the story of "Dennis K——y," the Irish immigrant who, after a six-week search for employment, learned that the city punished thieves with hard labor but fed, clothed, and housed them well. "That was all I wanted" K——y wrote. He "had no objection to working," so he robbed and was arrested. From jail he wrote to his brother in Ireland to join him. Historian George Geib indicates that the numbers of men, women, and children in the city's almshouses as well as those receiving public assistance continued to increase each year during the 1780s. The number in 1786–87 exceeded those in 1783–84 by close to a factor of three.[19]

Professor Billy Smith has also described the deteriorating conditions of the city's working orders. He studied the material lives of shoemakers, tailors, common laborers, and mariners. These people together constituted "at least one-third and probably one-half of the free male workers" in the city. Smith's complex and painstaking calculations indicate that for all four groups real wages remained low throughout the late 1780s and into the early 1790s. "For the city's laboring people," he concluded, "the Confederation era was a period of adversity that ended for many, although not all, only by the mid-1790s."[20]

---

18. Gary Nash, *The Urban Crucible: Social Change, Political Consciousness and the Origins of the American Revolution* (Cambridge: Harvard University Press, 1979). Sharon V. Salinger, "Artisans, Journeymen, and the Transformation of Labor in Late Eighteenth-Century Philadelphia," *William and Mary Quarterly* 40 (January 1983): 62–84, esp. 73, 83.

19. John K. Alexander, *Render Them Submissive: Responses to Poverty in Philadelphia, 1760–1800* (Amherst: University of Massachusetts Press, 1980), 81, 76, 14, 17, and 17 n. 24. *Independent Gazetteer*, 7/10/87; and *Pennsylvania Evening Herald*, 9/18/87. George Geib, "A History of Philadelphia, 1776–1789" (Ph.D. diss., University of Wisconsin, 1969), 203.

20. Billy G. Smith, "The Material Lives of Laboring Philadelphians, 1750–1800," *William*

Philadelphia's artisans, those self-employed master craftsmen who produced durable products for sale on the local market, also faced hard times. They made up about a third of the propertied heads of households in the city and they constituted one of the most politically conscious and effective economic interest groups in the state.[21] Indeed, economic woes beset these urban entrepreneurs on every side. Shipbuilding, for example, was one of the city's major industries; but, after a momentary burst of prosperity at the close of the war, it had fallen onto hard times. In 1784 Philadelphia produced forty-four vessels, in 1786, thirteen, the lowest peacetime level since 1745. The disaster in the shipyards idled scores of craftsmen and sent shockwaves throughout the city's entire economy.[22]

In addition, massive quantities of British manufactured goods imported in 1783 and 1784 glutted the market and drove down prices of locally produced products. Contemporary observers described staggering quantities of goods flooding into the city, and the wholesale price index for industrial goods in Philadelphia declined every year between 1785 and 1788.[23]

Artisans faced further difficulties. The wholesale prices for agricultural products and for raw materials also fell but at slower rates. This discrepancy widened the gap between the market value of what artisans sold and the market value of what they bought. In addition, the general economic hard times suffered by the merchants (see below, this chapter) intensified the problems of the artisans by constricting local demand for

---

and Mary Quarterly 38 (April 1981): 166, 167, 202. See also Billy G. Smith, *The "Lower Sort": Philadelphia's Laboring People, 1750–1800* (Ithaca: Cornell University Press, 1990).

21. Charles Olton, *Artisans for Independence: Philadelphia Mechanics and the American Revolution* (Syracuse: Syracuse University Press, 1975), 115, 3, 7–8; Ronald D. Schultz, "Thoughts Among the People: Popular Thought, Radical Politics and the Making of Philadelphia's Working Class, 1765–1828" (Ph.D. diss., University of California at Los Angeles, 1985), 7–8; revised and published as *The Republic of Labor: Philadelphia Artisans and the Politics of Class, 1720–1830* (New York: Oxford University Press, 1993).

22. Thomas Doerflinger, *A Vigorous Spirit of Enterprise: Merchants and Economic Development in Revolutionary Pennsylvania* (Chapel Hill: University of North Carolina Press, for the Institute of Early American History and Culture, Williamsburg, Va., 1986), 265–66; Schultz, "Thoughts Among the People," 150.

23. The most recent scholar to address this question tentatively concluded that "the total influx of dry goods in 1783 and 1784 was roughly twice as great as the largest importations for two consecutive years before the Revolution (1771 and 1772)." Doerflinger, *Vigorous Spirit*, 244.

their products. As a result, in 1785 and 1786 Philadelphia's craftsmen arguably suffered economic dislocation as great as any other occupational group in the state.[24]

Between 1784 and 1787 artisans sought political solutions to their economic problems, first on the state and then on the national level. They wanted protection from foreign competition, and in the fall 1784 election Constitutionalists promised them a state tariff. With the apparent support of substantial numbers of artisans, Constitutionalists won control of the city's legislative delegation. That victory, in conjunction with an increase in Lancaster and elsewhere, gave them a strong majority of the seats in the Assembly. Throughout the winter of 1784–85, however, the legislature procrastinated, reflecting, as one observer explained, "a well known fact, that perhaps three-fourths of the members consist of farmers and country gentlemen, who never had any opportunity or desire to inform themselves of the fundamental principles of trade and commerce."[25]

Pennsylvania's evolving economic policy further alienated the artisans. Between 1784 and 1786 the Assembly authorized a new issue of paper money, created a land bank, opened a state land office, assumed responsibility for servicing that portion of the national debt owed to the citizens of Pennsylvania, attacked the charter of the Bank of North America, and, as an afterthought, enacted a state tariff. With the exception of the tariff, none of this promised to benefit the artisans, and in operation, even the tariff proved disastrous. Rather than protecting domestic manufacturing in Pennsylvania, the law simply moved the point of entry for foreign manufacturers from Philadelphia to New

---

24. Olton, *Artisans*, 101. It is also unclear at this time as to the degree to which Pennsylvanians in general and artisans in particular saw the state's economy as dependent upon international trade rather than domestic consumption. The artisan demand for tariff protection, and the essays in Bailey's paper extolling the mutual interdependence of farmers and mechanics suggests one view, but Steven Rosswurm has reminded us of the "role that merchant capital played in" the lives of Philadelphia's petty producers and wage-earners, and the degree to which their livelihood depended on the general level of commercial activity, through wages, or the sale of maritime-related commodities, or trade-generated money. He has also pointed out the general dearth of scholarly attention to "the ties that bound artisans and shopkeepers to their customers and suppliers." Steven Rosswurm, *Arms, Country, and Class: The Philadelphia Militia and the "Lower Sort" During the American Revolution, 1775–1783* (New Brunswick: Rutgers University Press, 1987), 21, 27.

25. Olton, *Artisans*, 103 n. 48; *Pennsylvania Gazette*, 7/27/85. Bill transcribed in Assembly, 3/22/85. See *Pennsylvania Packet*, 5/13/85; Schultz, "Thoughts Among the People," 186–88.

Castle and Wilmington, Delaware, recently made "free ports" to compete with Philadelphia.[26]

An essay in Oswald's *Independent Gazetteer* revealed the depth of the chasm separating farmers from urban artisans: "We are sincerely sorry for the manufacturing Americans," a rural "Constitutionalist" reassured his city cousins, but see their plight as "a partial misfortune to those who are bro't up mechanics, instead of farmers, the pride and support of the land." But, he continued, "we hope the evil will cure itself, and that the necessary number of mechanics amongst us will, like water, find their level."[27] Republicans sought to capitalize on the artisan discontent. They advocated a national tariff, called for congressional control of United States commerce, and then organized the Philadelphia Society for the Encouragement of Manufacturers and Useful Arts. Although merchants predominated in the Society, mechanics also played leadership roles.[28]

In the Assembly elections of 1785 and 1786 significant numbers of artisans deserted the Constitutionalists. Philadelphia elected a solid Republican delegation to the state legislature in the fall of 1785 but Constitutionalists remained in control of the state government. By the summer of 1786 the city's other artisan-oriented editor, Eleazer Oswald, was hurling thunderbolts against paper money and its friends.[29] In the fall of 1786 Philadelphia voters turned out in record numbers. Nearly two thirds cast their ballots for Republicans, thereby giving that party its highest level of support in the city, to date. The magnitude of the turnout suggests that a sizable number of artisans voted for the Republican candidates (see Table 2).

All the evidence we have considered so far suggests a number of

---

26. Olton, *Artisans*, 100–104. For a more extensive discussion of this policy, see below. The attack on the bank threatened at least some artisans. Doerflinger, *Vigorous Spirit*, 304–5, indicates that artisans and shopkeepers constituted a substantial proportion of the bank's customers. The *Pennsylvania Gazette* reported on April 27, 1785, that "[t]he attack upon the Bank, by stopping the circulation of cash, has involved thousands in difficulties. Several mechanical businesses have been suspended, and the tradesmen, who have large sums of money due to them, suffer from the want of market money" (4/27/85). See *Packet*, 3/6/86, for the announcement of the opening of Wilmington and New Castle.

27. "A Constitutionalist," *Independent Gazetteer*, 1/15/85; Olton, *Artisans*, 102.

28. Olton, *Artisans*, 100, 101, 106. Schultz points out that the mechanics most closely associated with the merchants in organizing the petitioning in 1785 were only slightly less wealthy than their merchant peers. Schultz, "Thoughts Among the People," 188–89.

29. Olton, *Artisans*, 101.

Table 2. Average Vote by Party, Philadelphia, 1784–88

Year	Estimated Turnout	Average Party Vote	
		Republican	Constitutionalist
1784	1,777	763	1,014
1785	2,348	1,231	1,117
1786	2,564	1,565	999
1787 (Oct.)		1,496	
1787 (Nov.)	1,358	1,198	160
1788 (Oct.)		1,976	
1788 (Nov.)	2,051	1,729[a]	322

SOURCE: Based on calculations from data in Robert Brunhouse, *The Counter-Revolution in Pennsylvania* (Harrisburg: Pennsylvania Historical Commission, 1942), 338–39, 343–44. For a discussion of the impact of the German vote on the election returns for November 1788, see Appendix 2.

[a] These averages are for the 6 out of the 8 candidates on each slate who received the party vote unskewed by the confusion and cross-voting caused by the conspicuous German vote on two candidates.

conclusions about the economic condition and the political behavior of the working people of Philadelphia. Master craftsmen, journeymen, apprentices, laborers, and mariners all faced severe economic hardship in the late 1780s. The more articulate and the better organized segments of this population blamed the weakness of the Congress under the Articles of Confederation for their troubles and looked to a stronger national government for economic relief. Those who expressed themselves on Election Day, either by voting or by public crowd action, favored ratification. In addition, the logic of the situation suggest that support for the Constitution by Philadelphia's working people in 1787–88 reflected economically rational thinking. The new system clearly promised much needed relief from bad economic times. Two other pieces of evidence, however, suggest the need for caution: the behavior of two editors closely associated with the artisans, and the actual vote on ratification in the city. The city's two widely recognized artisan-oriented newspapers became Antifederalist organs. Francis Bailey, editor of the *Freeman's Journal*, and Eleazer Oswald, editor of the *Independent Gazetteer*, had long urged constitutional change on the national level. Yet both came to oppose the proposed Federal Constitution in the fall of 1787.

Oswald's change of heart probably reveals little more than personal idiosyncrasy. A prickly and a volatile character, he punctuated his career with personal conflicts of great intensity and notoriety. Although a longtime opponent of the state Constitutionalists, in 1787–88 Oswald reacted vigorously to what he saw as the Federalist efforts to coerce him into publishing only Federalist pieces. He appears to have moved toward the Antifederalists in large part to demonstrate his independence.[30]

Bailey's conversion, however, appears to reflect the tensions within the artisan community between political loyalty and economic need. He, like many in his intended artisan audience, had long championed the state constitution of 1776 and the party that defended it. He disliked and distrusted Republicans and urged a union of farmers and craftsmen against merchants, whom he condemned as those who prefer their "own present interest to that of the community." He praised the confluence of the "interests of the land-holder, . . . of the mechanics, and of the manufacturer . . . [which] form the great general interest of the state [and] on which its solid riches and strength must depend."[31]

Throughout the spring and summer of 1787, Bailey's paper had participated in the general demand for stronger national government. By mid-August, however, Bailey had begun to suspect the Republicans of manipulating the Grand Convention for partisan purposes. His paper praised the state constitution, and warned of a conspiracy by a wealthy and powerful junto "inspired with principles inimical to the rights of freemen" and "in command of all the money in the state."[32]

During September, Bailey maintained a supportive but cautious posture on the proposed Federalist Constitution, and in early October he denied that he opposed ratification. He admitted that he worried about some specific provisions and he denounced those who sought to "silence him and deprive him of his citizen's right to publish his opinions," but he remained, he said, a "friend to an efficient federal government." By the middle of October, however, Bailey had completed his conversion to outright opposition, and his newspaper became one of the principal outlets for Antifederalist publications.[33]

Bailey's agonizing odyssey may well have exemplified the path followed by many others in Philadelphia with close ties to both the artisan

30. G. S. Rowe, *Thomas McKean: The Shaping of an American Republicanism* (Boulder: Colorado Associated University Press, 1978), 184, 253–54; John Clyde Oswald, *Printing in the Americas* (New York: Gregg Publishing Company, 1937), 1:160, 197; William Steirer, Jr., "Philadelphia Newspapers: Years of Revolution and Transition, 1764–1794" (Ph.D. diss., University of Pennsylvania, 1972), 83–84, 142, 150–52.
31. Olton, *Artisans*, 99; *Freeman's Journal*, 4/13/85.
32. *Freeman's Journal*, 8/15/87, 8/22/87.
33. *Freeman's Journal* 10/10/87.

community and the Constitutionalist party. These people faced a serious dilemma. Like Bailey, they wanted a stronger central government, especially one capable of imposing a uniform national tariff. The proposed Federal Constitution promised them that. In addition, however, it also promised to undermine their cherished state constitution and enhance the power of their longtime political rivals. Thus, if they supported ratification, they would advance their economic interests at the expense of their political attachments and principles.[34]

Few followed Bailey into active Antifederalism but the election returns suggest that many sat out the November election of delegates to the state convention. The Constitutionalist candidates running on an Antifederalist ticket drew only 10 to 15 percent of the support they had enjoyed in the Assembly elections of 1784, 1785, and 1786. At the same time, however, Republican candidates running as Federalists did no better than might have been expected on the basis of their votes in the previous four years (see Table 2). Presumably, a substantial number of artisans, cross-pressured by their desire for a tariff, their dislike of Republicans, and their attachment to the Constitutionalists, chose not to vote.[35]

At least two major considerations shaped the electoral behavior of the city's laboring classes: their perceived economic need for a stronger central government (especially for protection from foreign competition), and their partisan loyalties. Those allied with the Republican party found their economic and their political interests pointing in the same direction. They enthusiastically accepted the Federal Constitution as an appropriate vehicle to advance both ends. Those deeply attached to the state Constitutionalist party hesitated. Some did not vote and others joined Bailey and the minuscule minority who supported Antifederalist candidates. A similar pattern emerged among the merchants.[36]

---

34. Schultz explains the division among working-class Philadelphia in part on occupational grounds (those most dependent upon the maritime trades were most ardent Federalists), and in part on the growing ability of the Antifederalists to make working-class men aware of the Federal Constitution's threat to liberty. Schultz, *The Republic of Labor*, 83.

35. Or, possibly the uncertainty and ambiguity among the city-based Constitutionalist leadership deprived the rank and file of the direction they needed to participate.

36. In 1786 in Philadelphia, Constitutionalist merchant candidates for the state legislature polled about 1,000 votes out of a total of about 2,600, or approximately 38 percent (see Table 2). Thomas Purvis estimates that the city's population was about 28 percent Irish and Scots-Irish, or 37 percent Gaelic if we include the Scots; about 34 percent German; and about 25 percent English and Welsh. Few of the German were Reformed and few of the English or Welsh were Presbyterian. If we assume that most of the Gaelic were Calvinists and that most

Divisions Among the City's Merchants

The bulk of Philadelphia's merchants, those five hundred to six hundred men engaged in international trade and commerce, probably supported the Federal Constitution. A small number of merchants from Philadelphia played a conspicuous role in drafting and ratifying that document. Robert Morris, George Clymer, Thomas FitzSimons, Jared Ingersoll, all merchants, sat in the Grand Convention. Clymer and FitzSimons then won election to the state convention where they helped argue the Federalists' cause. In the November 6 election, most merchants undoubtedly voted Federalist.[37]

Explaining the response of these Federalist merchants, however, requires great care. The conspicuous role of a small number of wealthy merchants among the Federalist leaders, combined with the Antifederalists' incessant depiction of the Federalists as aspiring aristocrats, can be deceiving. Two points here deserve emphasis. First, the bulk of the merchants, in supporting ratification, acted more as an occupational group than as the city's elite, or as a self-conscious social class. Equally important, for some of the city's merchants, partisan political concerns dampened, if they did not smother, support for the new system.

Much about their work and the context within which they operated divided Philadelphia's merchants. Individual enterprise and competition characterized the training, the dispositions, and the day-to-day activities of these men. Ambitious, acquisitive, and inclined to be distrustful, these tough, grasping, risk-oriented entrepreneurs strove for fortunes and status in a contest of all against all and the devil take the hindmost.

---

of the English, Germans, and Welsh were non-Calvinist, then the Calvinist/non-Calvinist proportion of the city's population approximates its partisan proportions: 30–40 percent Calvinist and 30–40 percent Constitutionalist. Obviously, we need to approach these parallels with some caution. The numbers are soft to begin with, and the ethnicity and religion of the active electorate may not have reflected the ethnicity and the religion of the city's total population. At the least, the apparent ethnoreligious composition of the city is consistent with the presumed ethnic-religious basis of the partisan voting in the city. See Thomas Purvis, "Patterns of Ethnic Settlement in Late Eighteenth Century Pennsylvania," *Western Pennsylvania Historical Magazine* 70 (April 1987): 107–22, especially 115, table 2. George Geib, "A History of Philadelphia," 14–15, estimates that the city's population was more than half Anglican and Lutheran and about 20 percent Calvinist.

37. The four unequivocal Antifederalist candidates from Philadelphia polled between 132 and 150 votes, averaging 142. The fifth, B. Franklin, polled 235. Robert Brunhouse, *The Counter-Revolution in Pennsylvania, 1776–1790* (Harrisburg: Pennsylvania Historical Commission, 1942), 338.

Success was precarious; failure was never far away: "One man's opportunity was another man's brutal competition"; and nerve-racking, demanding uncertainty defined the typical merchant's work environment.[38]

The uncertainties of the revolutionary era intensified the challenges and the opportunities. Some rose but many fell. Of the 109 merchants present in the city in 1774 and traceable to 1791, 25 percent had become gentlemen or esquires. On the other hand, at least 108 of the traders active between 1750 and 1791 went bankrupt or near bankrupt. In the same vein, 45 of 266 merchants present in Philadelphia between 1785 and 1791 moved into lower-status occupations and at least 68 declared bankruptcy. Before the end of the century the Philadelphia economic landscape was littered with the remains of prominent merchants who had failed, including such great figures as Robert Morris, Abel James, John Scott, John Ross, and Thomas FitzSimons.[39] Transience increased instability. The city directory of 1785 listed 514 merchants; that of 1791 listed 440. Approximately seventy percent of the men listed in 1791 were not listed in 1785.[40]

Furthermore, Philadelphia's merchants did not, in themselves, constitute the city's elite, nor did they form a single status group. Degrees of wealth divided them. A small number, such as Robert Morris, William Bingham, Thomas Willing, Blair McClenanchan, and possibly Charles Pettit, possessed enormous wealth and approximated the life-style of the lesser gentry in England: elegant three-story townhouses, country estates, lavish entertainment during the winter season, and, in one or two instances, formal coaches (the most conspicuous symbol of wealth in Philadelphia).

These "great oaks," however, made up no more than 10 to 15 percent of all those engaged in international trade. The lesser merchants spread out below these "great oaks" in an array that ended among the middle level. Lowest-echelon merchants ranked below the upper levels of the more successful artisans. Merchants at the lower and broader reaches of the occupation remained virtually indistinguishable from the great run of families who formed the respectable middle ranks of the city's population. They lived in modest houses, employed a servant or two,

---

38. Doerflinger, *Vigorous Spirit*, 62, 15–16, 157, 135.
39. Ibid., 57, 58, 247, 141.
40. Ibid., 249, 386. My calculations are based on Doerflinger's data.

ventured most of their limited capital and much of their personal reputation on sharply focused trading ventures.[41]

This dispersal of the merchants up and down the city's economic hierarchy made for sharp social distinctions and, on occasion, merchant princes failed to conceal their disdain for the lesser men in their field. William Pollard, a successful but middle-rank merchant, described an unpleasant encounter in 1789 with one of the richest merchants in the city. William Bingham, he reported, "has treated me with greater hauteur than I ever was treated by my Master during my youthful apprenticeship."[42]

If all merchants did not belong to a single social stratum, neither did the richest among them, by themselves, constitute the dominant elite in the city. The fifty or sixty most successful traders joined with an approximately equal number of wealthy nonmerchants to form the top of the city's socioeconomic hierarchy. Most of the nonmerchants in this category were professional men or wealthy gentlemen living on investment income: Bishop William White; Drs. William Shippen, Benjamin Rush, and James Hutchinson; lawyers Benjamin Chew and Thomas McKean; public officials such as state treasurer David Rittenhouse and state attorney general Jonathan D. Sergeant, as well as the scions of such old families as the Cadwalader and the Pembertons.[43]

Moreover, both the elite, and the merchants who were part of that elite, further divided along ethnic-religious lines. Quakers, for example, did not easily or frequently associate with non-Quakers, whether in business, in civic organizations, or in their private and personal lives. Regardless of wealth, occupation, or status, Quakers associated primar-

---

41. Ibid., 20–24, 30–37.
42. To Nicholson, in Nicholson papers, Pennsylvania Historical and Museum Commission (Harrisburg, Pa) cited in Doerflinger, *Vigorous Spirit*, 36, 36 n. 22. Bingham's wealth was estimated in the early 1790s as at least £600,000. Ibid., 134.
43. Robert Alberts, *The Golden Voyage: The Life and Times of William Bingham, 1752–1804* (Boston: Houghton Mifflin, 1969), passim. Thomas Slaughter, *The Whiskey Rebellion* (New York: Oxford University Press, 1986), 257 n. 1. Jerry Grundfest, *George Clymer: Philadelphia Revolutionary* (New York: Dissertations in American Biography, Arno Press, 1982) passim, but especially 271, 89–90, and quotes from 141, 145. It should also be noted that those who lived on rents from real property may have had interests different from those who lived on the profits of mercantile enterprise. Gordon Wood, "Interests and Disinterestedness in the Making of the Constitution," in Richard Beeman, Stephen Botein, and Edward Carter II, eds., *Beyond Confederation: Origins of the Constitution and American National Identity* (Chapel Hill: University of North Carolina Press for the Institute of Early American History and Culture, Williamsburg, Va., 1987): 69–109.

ily with other Quakers. Quaker merchants had Quaker partners; Quaker children married Quaker children across socioeconomic lines; Quaker families participated in Quaker civic organizations; the Philadelphia Hospital and the Library Company in the 1780s, or the Philadelphia Contributionship and the Friendly Association before the war.[44]

The non-Quaker elite, including the non-Quaker merchants, further split into two well-defined, sharply differentiated and mutually exclusive subsets: a minority that was largely Presbyterian in religion, Constitutionalist in politics, and somewhat less wealthy; and a majority that was largely Episcopalian in religion, Republican in politics, and somewhat more wealthy.[45] Presbyterian Charles Pettit was the most active and conspicuous merchant in the smaller of these two configurations. Merchant Blair McClenachan shared Pettit's religious preferences and his partisan identification. Germans Frederick Kuhl, a baker and a merchant, as well as John Steinmetz, a merchant, were also part of this group, along with Charles Biddle, Dr. James Hutchinson, and Calvinist officeholders Thomas McKean, the chief justice of the state, Joseph Reed, president of the Supreme Executive Council, David Rittenhouse, treasurer, and Jonathan D. Sergeant, attorney-general and son-in-law of Constitutionalist leader George Bryan.[46]

The larger group consisted of distinct but overlapping Anglican-oriented religious groups: Episcopalians such as Robert Morris, Thomas Willing, John Nixon, and William Bingham; disowned Quakers such as

---

44. Doerflinger, *Vigorous Spirit*, 59–60; and Stephen Brobeck, "Changes in the Composition and Structure of Philadelphia Elite Groups, 1756–1790" (Ph.D. diss., University of Pennsylvania, 1972), 197–238, 310. Brobeck estimates that in the 1770s about 54 percent of the Quaker elite were merchants (135–36), and that about 25 percent of Philadelphians were Quakers (77).

45. Brobeck estimates that more than 90 percent of non-Quaker elite were merchants, doctors, lawyers, and ministers (99). Gough's study indicates that the rich Philadelphians who supported independence later split about eleven to four in favor of Republicans over Constitutionalists. Robert James Gough, "Toward a Theory of Class and Social Conflict: A Social History of Wealthy Philadelphians, 1775 and 1800" (Ph.D. diss., University of Pennsylvania, 1977), 507–8.

46. Brobeck, "Changes in Elite," 353–64; Howard Miller, "The Grammar of Liberty: Presbyterians and the First American Constitution," *Journal of Presbyterian History* 54 (1976): 142–64, esp. 151; Jensen 2:234 n. 3; Gough, "Toward a Theory," 519; supplemented by biographical information from a variety of sources including *Pennsylvania Evening Post*, 9/23/78; *Pennsylvania Journal*, 8/6/77; William B. Reed, *Life and Correspondence of President Joseph Reed* (Philadelphia: Lindsay and Blakiston, 1847), 2:128; Benjamin Rush, *Letters of Benjamin Rush*, ed. Lyman Butterfield (Princeton: Princeton University Press, 1951): 36, 98, 103.

Thomas Mifflin; and Episcopalians who had been raised in Quaker homes, such as George Clymer and Henry Hill. Nonmerchants such as James Wilson and Benjamin Rush (both former Presbyterians) associated socially, politically, and financially, with this collection of non-Quaker merchants.[47]

The partisan affiliation of the Philadelphia merchants elected to the legislature illustrate this ethnic-religious political division. In 1778 six men represented Philadelphia in the legislature and five came from mercantile backgrounds. Between 1779 and 1783 Philadelphia elected only three merchants to the legislature; two Republicans and one Constitutionalist. Throughout the remainder of the era (1785–88) both parties ran merchants who differed from each other principally in their religious backgrounds. Constitutionalist merchant candidates came largely from dissenter backgrounds, primarily Presbyterian; Republican merchant candidates came mostly from English Anglican or Quaker roots.[48] In sum, Philadelphia's merchants ranged up and down the economic scale from the very wealthy to the modest and the middle-level. The richest among them formed a part of the city's elite, but that elite, as well as the merchants who were part of it, divided along ethnic-religious and political lines. Thus, Philadelphia's merchants formed neither a single status group, nor a cohesive society connected by marriage, blood, religion, common membership in voluntary associations and intimate social linkages, nor a unified political force.

Merchants: Occupational Interests and Politics

That Philadelphia's merchants were not a single status or a cohesive social group does not mean that they had no common interests. Their jobs united them, made them a community, molded them into a fraternity. They shared a code of conduct, a set of work-related values that

---

47. Brobeck, "Changes in Elite, 353; Brobeck found that more than 20 percent of Philadelphia's non-Quaker elite men had been raised in Quaker households (156).
48. Of the sixteen men who ran, we know the occupation of eleven: five of the six Constitutionalists were merchants; four of the five Republicans were merchants. Biographical information from Brobeck, "Changes in Elite," 353–64, supplemented by additional biographical information from a variety of sources.

established and defined the range of acceptable behavior. They lived in a small city. They interacted regularly on a face-to-face basis. They congregated in public houses, such as the London Coffee House, to read the papers, to gossip, to assess each other, and to negotiate. This incessant socialization defined the boundaries of the group, facilitated communication among them, and articulated and enforced the rules of the game they all played. Although they competed in what many undoubtedly assumed was a zero-sum game, all recognized their common interest in preserving the game. To this end they cooperated to punish flagrant violators of the rules, and to protect the boundaries of the game from outside invasion. Threats to individuals, or to small groups, or even to major sectors of the population might elicit little sympathy and less help. After all, one man's disaster might well be another's boon. Threats to the game itself, however, were a different matter. Challenges to particular rules, or major systematic changes that jeopardized the entire process could elicit quick, vigorous, and powerful group responses.

The general conditions in America in the late 1780s presented a number of equivocal but potentially serious threats to merchants, as an occupational group. On the broadest level, they shared with most other Pennsylvanians a sense that things were not going well. Congress needed a regular revenue and exclusive control over commerce. Discrimination and violence abroad limited America's participation in the Atlantic trading community, while dissension and division at home precluded full exploitation of the extraordinary potential inherent in a domestic market. More particularly, Philadelphia merchants tended to specialize. Those in the export trade encountered problems quite different from those in the import business, but both suffered. Exporters faced stagnation and disappointment rather than economic disaster. Average exports from the city fell from a high of £3,724,527 in 1784 to a low of £2,058,601 in 1786, a decline of 44.7 percent in two years. Compared to 1784, 1787 was dismal, but 1784 had been an exceptional year: the first full year of peace after eight years of war, and nine years of disrupted commerce. Pent-up trade virtually exploded and the total value of exports in 1784 exceeded 1773, the last full year of peacetime trade, by more than 80 percent. After the initial effluence in 1784, exports fell off sharply in the next two years, but the total never dropped below that of 1773. In fact, 1785 exceeded 1773 by 22 percent, while 1786, the low point in the export cycle, also exceeded 1773 if only marginally.⁴⁹

The mix of exports in 1786 also differed substantially from that of 1773. The quantity and value of flour had declined (from 27 to 18 percent) while the value of tobacco, rice, indigo, and naval stores exported from the city had increased (from virtually nothing to over 20 percent). Merchants involved in handling the new southern staples probably did better than those in the declining flour trade but both had hoped for more.⁵⁰ Export merchants could blame these difficulties on the Confederation government. Flour, among the most depressed of the export commodities, illustrates the point. Export merchants could blame external forces for the disruption of two of Philadelphia's prime flour markets: southern Europe and the West Indies. In the first, the Barbary pirates practically closed the Mediterranean to American shipping. In the second, the British government worked actively to exclude Americans.

In reality, a stronger national government could probably do little to help. Europeans had substantially increased their own grain production and only extraordinary circumstances, such as war or drought, would have increased their demand for American wheat. In the West Indies, illegal trade to the British islands and legal trade with the others may have compensated for the loss due to British governmental intervention.⁵¹ Philadelphia's export merchants, however, thought otherwise, or so at least the press suggested. The Philadelphia newspapers, and especially those like the *Packet*, which aimed at the merchant readership, continued to define the problems in terms of the need for a vigorous central government powerful enough to open the markets of the world and protect American interests on the high seas. No known merchant opposed this diagnosis of the disease or this prescription for its cure.

If the business of the export merchants stagnated, importers faced wholesale disaster. British exports to America jumped in 1784 to over £3,670,000 pounds sterling and then crashed to £1,603,000 in 1786: a 56 percent falloff in two years.⁵² Philadelphia's experience was more

49. Doerflinger, *Vigorous Spirit*, 263–65.
50. Gordon Bjork, *Stagnation and Growth in the American Economy, 1784–1792* (New York: Garland, 1985), 52, 53, 54, 55.
51. Bjork, *Stagnation and Growth*, 28, 114–16, 133, 166–69.
52. Ibid., 107.

severe. In 1784 British exports to this city exceeded any prewar year save 1774 and were almost 20 percent ahead of the average for the period 1771 to 1774. In 1785, this plummeted 46.6 percent and then dropped another 23 percent the next year for a total decline of almost 70 percent in two years. At the same time prices fell dramatically. The wholesale index of all imports dropped from 104.8 in 1784 to 76.3 in 1789, a total decline of some 28.5 points (or 27 percent) in a five-year period. Bankruptcies abounded and by 1787 Philadelphia's import merchants were in the midst of an economic crisis that promised only to grow worse.[53]

No simple or direct political-constitutional change, however, offered much hope of relief. The import merchants' problems grew directly out of the operation of the free market. British mercantile houses supplied most of the goods, the shipping, and the credit. Ambitious Americans of slender capital but solid character (or well-established family) found British firms willing to ship them products on generous credit terms. In good times, this practice rapidly expanded the number of men and the quantity of goods. Gluts then depressed prices and left both retailers and wholesalers with uncollectable debts and inventories whose cost often exceeded current market price. This cyclical nature of the business remained largely beyond the ability of any American government to remedy. Although many import merchants may have known this, understanding is small comfort in the midst of disaster, and Philadelphia's importers faced an unequivocal disaster in 1786 and 1787.[54]

Furthermore, the state's misguided tariff policy intensified their problems. Intended to protect domestic manufacturers, it simply shifted the point of entry for British manufactured goods to New Castle, Wilmington, and possibly Baltimore. Philadelphia's importers would have preferred no tariff, but a national tariff would hurt them less than the one they had. It would place all ports on an equal plane and gave competitive advantage to none. In sum, export and import merchants suffered from a massive failure of great expectations. More specifically, exporters lacked adequate foreign markets and importers faced a glut on the

---

53. Jacob Price, "New Time Series for Scotland's and Britain's Trade with the Thirteen Colonies and States," *William and Mary Quarterly* 32 (April 1975): 325. Doerflinger, *Vigorous Spirit*, 262–65. "Wholesale Price Indexes," U.S. Census Bureau, *Historical Statistics of the United States, Colonial Times to 1970* (Washington, D.C.: U.S. Department of Commerce, Bureau of the Census, 1975), series 99, p. 205.

54. Doerflinger, *Vigorous Spirit*, 68–69, 91–96, 127–28.

domestic market exacerbated by a disastrous state tariff policy. Both seemed to believe that a stronger central government would help.

Two additional and closely related factors pressed merchants as an occupational group toward increased central control: Daniel Shays and the growing burden of state taxes, on one hand; and the economic policy adopted by the state legislature, on the other. Daniel Shays posed a vague, incalculable but disquieting threat throughout the winter and spring of 1787. No one could say with certainty whether the farmer-based violence in western Massachusetts represented an isolated disturbance or more general uprising. These questions disturbed many in Pennsylvania and none more than the merchants. Charles Pettit, merchant, Constitutionalist, future Antifederalist, illustrates the case. As one of Pennsylvania's representatives in Congress, he wrote in near hysteria to President Benjamin Franklin in October 1786 about the horrors implicit in the Shays uprising: "A total Abolition of all Debt . . . a general Distribution of Property . . . [they will] reliquidate the public Debts and then pay them off in a Paper Money."[55]

Philadelphia merchants differed with Pennsylvania's farmers on issues parallel to those in Massachusetts. Farmers preferred a tax on commerce, such as the impost; merchants wanted a tax on real property such as land and livestock. In addition, Philadelphians paid their taxes with some degree of regularity, but the farming areas did not. Justice, merchants might believe, demanded strict enforcement of the tax code. Prudence, however, suggested caution. Shays illustrated the explosive potential in a countryside pushed too far. Collecting £200,000 a year in current taxes would enable Pennsylvania to meet most of its present obligations; collecting the £600,000 due in back taxes would pay off much of the state's debt. But seriously attempting to collect either of these amounts in the late 1780s might have precipitated political problems far more serious than an unbalanced budget. Paying back taxes in one lump sum could consume a major proportion of the total income of the typical farm family in one of the richest and most productive grain-growing regions in the new United States.[56]

55. "Charles Pettit to the President of Pennsylvania (Benjamin Franklin), 10/18/86," in Edmund C. Burnett, ed., *Letters of Members of the Continental Congress* (Washington, D.C., Carnegie Institution of Washington, 1921–36), 8:487.

56. With wheat prices ranging between five and seven shillings a bushel, a farmer marketing 100 bushels of wheat (an exceptional quantity) would thus earn between £25 and £35 gross income before expenses, or possibly £20 to £25 net. George Franz, "Paxton: A Study of Community Structure and Mobility" (Ph.D. diss., Rutgers University, 1974), 171,289. Duane

Most Federalists and Antifederalists in Pennsylvania saw a stronger central government as the solution to their problems. This broad consensus, however, masked the presence of at least two competing ideas about the kinds of powers that should be assigned to the national government, and how such changes should relate to the state's economic policy. The first, implicit in Comptroller Nicholson's annual reports to the state legislature, supported modest augmentation of the powers of Congress and heavy reliance on state. It would grant Congress a regular income from the impost and exclusive control over external or oceanic matters, while relying on the state to solve the internal or domestic economic problems through paper money, a land bank, tax relief, and liquidation of the public debt through land sales. This approach would favor landholders, farmers producing for market, and land speculator-developers. It resonated well with the worldview and the life experiences of most Pennsylvanians.[57]

The second approach was advocated by men whom historian E. James Ferguson has labeled the "nationalists" of 1783. It drew its backers primarily from the Philadelphia merchant community and especially, but not exclusively, from those men who looked to Robert Morris as their leader and spokesmen. It was essentially nationalist, financial, and commercial in its origins and in its consequences. Its supporters wanted a vigorous central authority with extensive revenues, a funded debt, a national bank, and the power to limit the economic powers of the states.[58]

Robert Morris and the financial-commercial nationalists had long worked to strengthen the power of Congress, to establish national credit, and to lay the foundations of a great and developing commercial empire. They envisioned America as an expanding nation with a rapidly

---

E. Ball, "Process of Settlement in Chester County, Pennsylvania" (Ph.D. diss., University of Pennsylvania, 1973), 145–50, estimates that farms in Chester averaged 107 bushels of wheat a year but kept a portion for their own use.

57. For a brief exploration of the commercial thinking of what she calls "antinationalists" or the Antifederalists' commercial political economy see Janet A. Riesman, "Money, Credit, and Federalist Political Economy," in Beeman et al., eds., *Beyond Confederation* (1987), esp. 156–60. Riesman cites Constitutionalist-Antifederalist William Findley defending state paper money in 1786 as conducive to "prosperous days," "the backbone of commerce," and the base for "confidence in the future of trade" (158).

58. E. James Ferguson, "The Nationalists of 1781–1783 and the Economic Interpretation of the Constitution," *Journal of American History* 56 (September 1969), 241. For a recent treatment of two general approaches to these questions in late eighteenth-century America, see Riesman, "Money, Credit," in Beeman et al., eds., *Beyond Confederation*, 128–61.

developing economy and untold wealth and prestige. Some of them saw riches as a vehicle for national power; others saw national strength as a means of acquiring and defending wealth. For both, the practical consequences were the same. Their dream depended upon three essential ingredients: a central government with sufficient revenues to fund its own debt (i.e., guarantee regular payment of the debt's interest); a sound national currency; and a viable and secure national bank.[59]

These three elements formed a single integrated engine for transforming America. Funding the national debt would improve the credit rating of the new nation and allow the government to borrow additional funds in times of necessity. More important, regular interest payments on the national securities would raise the market value of the securities now circulating at depreciated rates, and thus create vast new quantities of investment capital, almost out of whole cloth.

These newly appreciated securities could themselves serve as a national medium of exchange, as money. Their large denominations, however, limited this to major transactions. Invested in bank stock, on the other hand, these securities could support a bank-issued national currency and, at the same time, further increase the amount of credit available for business and investment.[60] Putting in place the necessary pieces in this grand scheme, however, depended on political action. Morris, while superintendent of finance for the Continental Congress in the early 1780s had made substantial progress on this front. He had presided over the repudiation of continental currency (the national paper-money monster); he had acquired a congressional and a Pennsylvania charter for the Bank of North America; he had accumulated sufficient bullion to put the bank into operation; he had built widespread public support for a grant of regular revenues to Congress (the 5

---

59. This and the following discussion of Morris's plan and of "currency finance" is based largely on the work of E. James Ferguson, especially "State Assumption of the Federal Debt During the Confederation," *Mississippi Valley Historical Review* 38 (December 1951): 403–24; *The Power of the Purse* (Chapel Hill: University of North Carolina Press, 1961), esp. 120–24, 220–29; 289–90, 331–41; Stuart Bruchey, "The Forces Behind the Constitution: A Critical Review of the Framework of E. James Ferguson's *The Power of the Purse* with a Rebuttal by E. James Ferguson," *William and Mary Quarterly* 19 (July 1962): 429–36; "The Nationalists of 1781–1783 and the Economic Interpretation of the Constitution," *Journal of American History* 56 (September 1969): 241–61; "Political Economy, Public Liberty, and the Formation of the Constitution," *William and Mary Quarterly* 40 (July 1983): 389–412.

60. Little in this scheme was new. Ferguson most fully develops the linkage among Morris, Hamilton, and Wilson in eighteenth-century America with the financial revolution in late seventeenth-century Great Britain in his "Political Economy."

percent impost); and he had systematized the debt for which Congress was responsible.

Unfortunately for Morris and for his like-minded fellows, the political foundations of this system disintegrated during the middle years of the decade. The movement for a national impost foundered on the vote of first one state and then another. Then, as hard times intensified, the states began to deal with the mounting economic difficulties in ways that promised to take America in a different direction. Pennsylvania was no exception. In 1785 and 1786 the state legislature assumed responsibility for paying that portion of the national debt held by Pennsylvanians. This measure, generally referred to as the "assumption" act, benefited many in Pennsylvania. Security holders could count on regular interest payments while speculators who had purchased certificates on the open market for as little as one third to one fourth of face value, reaped large profits. Moreover, the increase in market value of these securities augmented the quantity of investment capital available. At the same time, Pennsylvania's land policy promised relatively painless extinction of that debt burden. The state land office, accepting these securities at face value, equal to specie, retired approximately $1,800,000 of this debt between 1785 and 1790.[61]

As part of the "assumption" legislation, Pennsylvania also issued £150,000 in paper money: £100,000 to meet current obligations, and £50,000 for a land bank. Both represented time-tested techniques for dealing with the chronic shortages of currency and credit in an agricultural economy. The first was a form of tax-anticipation borrowing. The second loaned paper money against mortgages on land, thereby increasing the money supply while providing long-term, low-interest loans to farmers and bringing revenue into the treasury from the interest on the loans.[62]

Victory on the "assumption" and the paper-money issues set the stage

---

61. Norman B. Wilkinson, *Land Policy and Speculation in Pennsylvania, 1779–1800: A Test of the New Democracy* (New York: Arno Press, 1979; revision of Ph.D. diss., University of Pennsylvania, 1958), 65.

62. Kaminski, "Paper Politics," esp. 50–96. See above for more details on this paper money. Although the Constitutionalist party dominated the state legislature at the time, "assumption" and paper money did not represent strict partisan measures. The political maneuvering behind this reorientation of state economic policy has not been fully explored. Public creditors, many of whom who were Republicans, joined with old-line agrarian leaders in the Constitutionalist party to push "assumption." They may also have supported a new issue of paper money in return for help from agricultural interests on the assumption issue.

for an assault on the Bank of North America, the third ingredient in the program of the "nationalists" of 1783. The bank stirred strong emotions. Its opponents ranged from those who feared and hated all commercial banks to those who themselves wanted to share the profits of commercial banking. Until 1785 the bank had successfully fought off or absorbed its challengers but in September of that year the Constitutionalist-dominated Assembly repealed the bank's Pennsylvania charter.[63] In the legislature, the agrarian wing of the Constitutionalist party led the fight. Longtime foes of Robert Morris successfully mobilized deep-seated popular prejudice against banks. The bank's implacable opposition to the paper-money issue of March 1785 also multiplied its enemies, particularly among farmers already upset over high interest rates and scarce agricultural credit.

The successful attack on the Bank of North America completed the reorientation of the political economy of the state in a direction largely consistent with the assumptions and the aspirations of men like John Nicholson and Pennsylvania's landholders. This new policy defined major economic problems from the point of view of farmers and land speculator-developers. It looked primarily to the state, rather than the central government, for solutions. It met most of the legitimate demands of national public creditors who lived in Pennsylvania. It supplied the credit needs of farmers enmeshed in a complex market economy and in need of liquidating a portion of their real estate. It provided a medium of exchange, relieved the pressure to collect taxes, and tided the state over a difficult time. It promised to pay off much of the war debt through the sale of state land. Moderately augmenting the powers of Congress by granting it a tax on imports and exclusive control of foreign trade and diplomacy would complement and complete this approach.

It is important to emphasize that the political conflicts represented here, especially but not exclusively in the question of state paper money, reflect occupational more than class differences. The struggle over paper money in Pennsylvania was complex. For our purposes, however, two points are essential. First, Philadelphia's merchants reacted vigorously and emotionally against Pennsylvania's new note issue in the spring of 1785. Paper money frightened them. They remembered the runaway

---

63. Brunhouse, *Counter-Revolution*, 173–75; George Rappaport's study of the Bank of North America is the best treatment of this complicated matter; see "The Sources and Development of the Hostility to Banks in Early America" (Ph.D. diss., New York University, 1970).

inflation of the continental currency of the late 1770s, the popular attempts in the city to fix prices, and the violence in Philadelphia in 1779 against those the urban populace saw as seeking to monopolize scarce goods and benefit from the necessity of others. Opponents of paper money stigmatized its supporters as "debtors" and that pejorative subtly shaped the history of the issue.

Second, and of equal importance, the new paper money did not succor the poor, reward the profligate, or allow debtors to cheat creditors. It was not a legal tender equal to specie for private transactions. In addition, and probably of greater importance for our understanding of the issue involved, only substantial property holders could borrow this paper money. The state land bank made no loans less than £25 and required a mortgage against land worth at least three times the amount borrowed.[64] Thus, the paper-money contest did not pit the rich against the poor; or large wealthy merchants against small yeoman farmers. Rather, it represented a conflict between two relatively well-to-do occupational groups. At its simplest level, propertied agricultural entrepreneurs wanted relatively low interest, long-term (measured in years) credit backed with mortgages on real property. During the colonial era, provincial land banks had provided this kind of credit. Landed men producing for market may also have expected to benefit from a modest currency expansion, and an upward pressure on prices.[65]

Merchants had quite different credit needs. They used short-term (measured in days), relatively high interest loans usually backed by commercial paper. In the 1780s, the Bank of North America provided this kind of credit. The annulment of the bank's charter and the new issue of paper money thus represented the triumph of the landed interest over the merchants. These two victories, in turn, were part and parcel of a state economic policy that also encouraged land speculators such as Antifederalist John Nicholson, at the expense of rentiers, such as Federalist George Clymer.[66]

64. Kaminski points out these requirements meant that many farmers, and especially the poorer ones ("perhaps over fifty percent in some towns and counties") could not make use of this state land bank. See "Paper Politics," 76 n. 78.

65. Mary M. Schweitzer, *Custom and Contract: Household, Government, and the Economy in Colonial Pennsylvania* (New York: Columbia University Press, 1987), esp. chaps. 4 and 5, explains how the colonial land bank worked and describes the typical mortgagor in the 1740s as a yeoman farmer with clear title to 167 acres of land, and at least in Chester County "among the upper one-fifth of the wealth holders" (160–61).

66. Some evidence suggests that artisans in Philadelphia also benefited from and relied on the kinds of credit issued by the Bank of North America. See above, note 26.

The economic policy adopted by Pennsylvania in 1785 and 1786 thus added another compelling reason for merchants to support the Federal Constitution. Although that document itself did not commit the new nation to funded debts, commercial banking, and rapid development, it placed obstacles in the path of those who wanted to take the country in the direction of an agrarian-oriented and locally determined political economy. It forbade states to issue legal-tender paper money and it restricted their ability to interfere with contracts, a provision that might have prevented Pennsylvania from rescinding the charter of the Bank of North America.[67] Not all merchants, however, enthusiastically favored ratification. Charles Pettit, Frederick Kuhl, Blair McClenanchan and John Steinmetz were time-honored spokesmen for the business wing of the Constitutionalist party. They and other urban-commercial Constitutionalists may well have shared their fellow merchants' fears and aspirations, as well as Morris's vision of America's future.

Their political considerations, however, clashed with their economic interests. They were out of sympathy with the agrarian commercial orientation their party had taken on since 1785. They were also aware of the public and private benefits that ratification would confer on themselves and on their mercantile associates. Yet, they remained ambivalent. These Presbyterian Constitutionalist merchants found it difficult to publicly support constitutional changes that promised to repudiate their political principles and destroy their political organization. Their political loyalties, their political commitments, possibly even their calculation of political self-interest warred with their mercantile needs. Pettit, and apparently others, solved the dilemma by standing for office as Antifederalist while doing little to mobilize the usual Constitutionalist constituency. By running as an Antifederalist, he met his political obligations. By losing, he minimized the threat to his economic interests.

Both Federalist and Antifederalist publicists generally agreed that Pennsylvanians faced serious economic difficulties. The state's fiscal problems both reflected and exacerbated these difficulties. Strengthening the powers of the central government, especially its "oceanic" powers, could do much to restore prosperity. Federalists and Antifederalists disagreed,

---

67. "No State shall . . . pass any . . . Law impairing the obligation of contracts"; U.S. Constitution, Article I, sect. 10.

however, as to whether the Federal Constitution was the appropriate vehicle to that end.

"Centinel" and a host of Antifederalist publicists had sought to mobilize the people of Pennsylvania against ratification by rousing popular resentment of the pretensions, the aspirations, the lavish lifestyle, the wealth, and the war-related profits of such towering mercantile figures as Robert Morris, William Bingham, and Thomas FitzSimons. The people of Philadelphia, however, did not care, or at least did not care enough to reject constitutional changes that promised to alleviate the fiscal problems of the state, the employment problems of the laborers, the marketing problems of the artisans, and the commercial and political problems of the merchants.

To the degree that the ratification issue divided the people of Philadelphia, it did not align them along class lines: the elites against the masses, patricians against plebeians, upper against lower classes. However real and powerful such divisions were, they did not play the decisive role in determining the city's response to the Federal Constitution. Working-class people as well as most of the elite favored the new system. When the elite did divide, it was largely along ethnic-religious and party lines. English Anglican merchants, as well as English Anglican-Quaker merchants who supported the Republican party became Federalists. Presbyterian and Reformed merchants who supported the Constitutionalist party became Antifederalists, however reluctantly.

Federalists had hoped that economic imperatives would overcome, or at least neutralize, partisan attachments as well as popular fears of remote and unresponsive governments. In large part, the two specific groups we know the most about in Philadelphia behaved largely as the Federalists hoped. Both artisans and merchants faced major economic problems that the proposed Federal Constitution promised to alleviate. For those artisans and merchants who, as Republicans, were also anxious to undermine the power of the Constitutionalists and the legitimacy of the state constitution, ratification of the new system held out both economic and political promise.

Those artisans and merchants with partisan attachments to the Constitutionalists, however, found themselves in much less happy circumstances. Aware of the economic potential inherent in the proposed changes, but unhappy with the political implications of the new system, they faced a serious dilemma. Most appear to have remained inactive, neither supporting nor opposing ratification; and the Federalists won a lopsided victory in the city.

But Philadelphia was not Pennsylvania. The ultimate decision on ratification lay with the voters in the backcountry, and it is to their economic situation and their political behavior that we must next turn our attention.

6
The Economy and the Constitution

The Backcountry

Backcountry voters decided the fate of the Federal Constitution in Pennsylvania. The majority favored it from the beginning while a stubborn and vehement minority resisted. Assessing the ways in which the economy shaped this backcountry response requires an examination of the general conditions of the farm economy in 1787–88 and an analysis of how Federalist voters differed from Antifederalist voters in their relationship to that economy. Here, as with the city of Philadelphia, the available data do not offer definitive answers but we can tease some tentative and suggestive conclusions from the extant evidence.[1]

---

1. Measuring precisely the relationship between political behavior and the economic status of voters in particular geographical areas in late eighteenth-century Pennsylvania is virtually impossible now. We lack the theoretically defined, precise, and reliable measures of relative development and relative prosperity. Moreover, the raw data to construct such indexes remains to be collected. Of equal importance, the extant electoral data are usually aggregated at the county level and late eighteenth-century Pennsylvania's counties were relatively large and internally varied. Thus, the best we can hope for at present is a tentative assessment in broad

The Backcountry and the Economy

In the fall and winter of 1787–88 backcountry Pennsylvanians faced two major problems: back taxes and declining prices. Together, these two threatened the prosperity, the livelihood, and possibly even the property of substantial numbers of yeoman farm families. We need to look at each of these in some detail.

First, taxes. On the eve of the ratification controversy, Pennsylvanians faced a state tax burden of historic proportions. In the immediate postwar years, the state appropriated approximately £100,000 a year and had difficulty in raising sufficient tax revenues to meet these commitments. In 1786 Pennsylvania increased its financial obligations dramatically. The legislature, under Constitutionalist control, assumed responsibility for paying the interest and the principal on that portion of the national debt owed to its citizens. This doubled Pennsylvania's annual obligations to well over £200,000. To finance this new expenditure, the Constitutionalists had imposed a direct annual tax of £76,945 on property. Such an assessment, if collected, would cost each household about one pound per year, or approximately the expenses of providing grain for an additional nonproductive adult.[2]

In the late 1780s popular resistance limited the collection of this, as well as most other taxes in Pennsylvania. Thomas FitzSimons complained in September 1787 of a "ruinous deficiency in the collection of the public revenues." "[T]he city and county of Philadelphia," he continued, "have only paid into the treasury the insignificant sum of £1250 . . . [and] . . . some counties have not paid anything."[3]

Comptroller John Nicholson explained that the state lacked the will and the way to collect these monies. "In many cases," he reported, "it is dangerous to entrust constables with so many warrants as are

---

terms of the probability of a link between the gross economic status of a county and its political complexion.

2. Robert Brunhouse, *The Counter-Revolution in Pennsylvania, 1776–1790* (Harrisburg: Pennsylvania Historical Commission, 1942), 170–73. See above for details of the state budget and "assumption." Max George Schumacher, *The Northern Farmer and His Market During the Late Colonial Period* (New York: Arno Press, 1975; revision of his Ph.D. diss., University of California, 1948), 44. The U.S. Census of 1790 counted 73,332 heads of household in Pennsylvania. See Thomas Purvis, "Patterns of Ethnic Settlement in Late Eighteenth-Century Pennsylvania," *Western Pennsylvania Historical Magazine* 70 (April 1987): 111.

3. "General Assembly Minutes," 9/20/1787, p. 230, *Packet*, 9/24/87. [U.S. Census], *Return of the Whole Number of Inhabitants Within Several Districts of the United States* (Philadelphia, 1791), 45.

necessary to be issued" and often the "cost for issuing and serving warrants . . . amounts to as much as the tax." Events in York County during the winter of 1786–87 document Nicholson's analysis. In November 1786 some 100 men armed with guns and clubs marched to York Town to recover farm property seized for taxes. They failed, but two months later, in January 1787 an armed group of about 120 successfully "rescued" cattle about to be sold for back taxes. In the process these rural protestors insulted "divers justices of the peace," and assaulted and struck the sheriff.[4]

Nicholson's November 1787 report detailed the problem of back taxes by county (see Table 3). Collecting back taxes of this magnitude could threaten the economic base of farm families across the state. For example, in Lancaster, one of the richest and most productive wheat-growing areas in late eighteenth-century America, payment of back taxes could cost the equivalent of half of the average annual profits from the grain production of a moderate-sized farm.[5]

A rapid decline in farm prices intensified the economic plight of backcountry Pennsylvanians. Until late summer, 1787, the wholesale prices of agricultural staples had held up fairly well. Wheat was eighteenth-century Pennsylvania's most important cash crop. Its price on the Philadelphia market had peaked at 8.75 shillings a bushel in December 1784 and then slowly and fitfully declined for the next thirty months (8.75 shillings = 8 shillings and 9 pence). In June 1787 it had spiked to 8.25 shillings a bushel, but in July it was at 7.25, approximately its average for the first eight months in the year.[6]

In the next few months, the bottom fell out of the market. In August

---

4. John Nicholson, *State of the Finances of the Commonwealth of Pennsylvania*, Philadelphia, 11/1787, in Clifford K. Shipton, ed., *Early American Imprints. Reproduction on Readex Microprint of the Works Listed in Charles Evans, American Bibliography* (Worcester: American Antiquarian Society, 1955–69): Evans number 45137. For details of these York County "public tumults," see *Pennsylvania Mercury*, 6/8/87.

5. Lancaster's 6,000 households owed £51,951 in back taxes, or about 8.7 pounds each, on average. Schumacher, *Northern Farmer*, 41, estimates 40 to 100 bushels average surplus per farm. Duane Ball estimates that between 1775 and 1790 Chester County soils averaged 7.5 bushels of wheat per acre and Chester farmers averaged 14.25 acres of wheat per year for a total harvest of 107 bushels. See Ball, "The Process of Settlement in 18th Century Chester County, Pennsylvania: A Social and Economic History" (Ph.D. diss., University of Pennsylvania, 1973), 145–50.

6. Schumacher, *Northern Farmer*, 38. Anne Bezanson, *Prices and Inflation During the American Revolution, 1770–1790* (Philadelphia: University of Pennsylvania Press, 1951), 339, 340–41.

Table 3. Per Capita Unpaid Back Taxes as of November 1787

Political Unit	Unpaid Taxes due in Specie or Bills of 3/85 (£)	Adult White Males, 16 or older	Unpaid tax per Adult White Male (£)
City, County of Philadelphia	53,086	14,486	[a]3.660
Bucks	9,201	6,575	1.399
Chester	26,555	10,024	2.649
Lancaster	51,951	9,713	5.349
York	36,481	9,213	3.960
Cumberland (& Mifflin)	50,069	6,775	7.390
Berks	33,991	7,714	4.406
Northampton	8,752	6,008	1.457
Bedford (& Huntingdon)	14,766	4,759	3.103
Northumberland	25,369	4,191	6.053
Westmoreland	15,433	6,648	2.321
Washington	9,986	5,334	1.872
Fayette	389	3,425	0.114
Franklin	5,569	4,022	1.385
Montgomery	8,366	6,008	1.392
Dauphin	4,687	4,657	1.006
Totals	354,651	109,552[b]	mean = 3.237

SOURCE: Unpaid taxes from Nicholson, John Nicholson, *State of the Finances of the Commonwealth of Pennsylvania*, Philadelphia, November 1787. Evans 45137; United States Bureau of the Census, *Heads of Families at the First Census of the United States taken in the Year 1790* (Washington, D.C.: Government Printing Office, 1907–8), 45.

[a]Amount given in decimal form, i.e., £3.66 = 3⅔ pounds. Two-thirds of a pound was about 7 shillings at 20 shillings per pound.

[b]The Census lists this total as 110,788.

the price dropped to 6.50 shillings a bushel. In September it dropped again to 5.75, and remained there until December when it slipped further, finally bottoming out at 5.25 shillings a bushel, 23 percent below its price in January 1787, and more than 40 percent below its 1784 high. Wholesale prices of flour, ship bread, and beef followed similar downward patterns, each losing 20 to 25 percent of its January 1787 value by December 1787.[7]

Wheat prices most directly affected those who lived within what historian John Walzer has labeled "the Philadelphia trading area"—that is, in counties from which they could ship wheat to the city for costs well under the current wholesale price. In 1787 this included practically

7. Bezanson, *Prices and Inflation*, 339, 340–41.

every county east of Bedford, astride the mountains some 150 to 200 miles from Philadelphia. When wheat sold for seven or eight shillings a bushel, farmers in remote regions such as the Juniata River area north of Carlisle, about 150 miles from Philadelphia, or in the Shippensburg area, a day or so west of Carlisle by wagon, could profitably ship grain to market.[8]

If wholesale prices dropped below seven shillings a bushel, however, the profit margin narrowed significantly. At five shillings a bushel, farmers close to the city could still profitably market wheat but those living on the periphery of the trading region could not cover their costs of production and transportation. For many living in counties such as Cumberland, with extraordinarily high levels of uncollected back taxes, and relatively high transportation costs (see Table 4), wheat at five shillings a bushel threatened imminent disaster.[9]

Farm families thus faced serious economic problems as the price of wheat declined and back taxes accumulated. As the winter of 1787–88 approached, a chorus of voices demanded help from the state. In December 1787, "A Farmer" urged the state convention to truncate its discussions and thereby save the hard-pressed taxpayer the costs of continued meetings. "[T]he times are now too hard, and the country cannot bear it," he wrote. "Wheat is falling to nothing, for want of trade, and taxes very heavy."[10]

In the spring of 1788, petitions poured into the legislature begging

Table 4. Estimated Cost (in shillings) of Transporting One Bushel of Wheat to Philadelphia, 1760

Area	Estimated Cost
Cumberland & Franklin	2.5 to 3.0
York & Dauphin	1.5 to 2.5
Lancaster & Berks	1.0 to 2.0
Areas east of Lancaster & south of Berks	< 1.0

SOURCE: John F. Walzer, "Transportation in the Philadelphia Trading Area, 1740–1775" (Ph.D. diss., University of Wisconsin, 1968), 309.

8. John Walzer, "Transportation in the Philadelphia Trading Area" (Ph.D. diss., University of Wisconsin, 1968), 40–45, 307.
9. In the quarter-century between then and the ratification controversy, the construction of roads and the expansion of settlement undoubtedly reduced transportation costs, but I used the 1760 estimates, in Table 4, to define the least extensive boundaries of the Philadelphia marketing area at the time of the divisions over ratification, rather than the most extensive.
10. *Packet*, 12/7/87.

for relief. Farmers in Bucks County beseeched the legislature for relief from high taxes and debt, as did "a number of the inhabitants of the county of Montgomery" and some 579 inhabitants of Chester. These petitioners complained of low prices, of scarcity of a circulating medium, and of creditors' need for payment and of forced land sales. The loan office of 1785 and the infusion of currency had helped, they said, but now much of that paper had been redeemed and borrowers faced the prospect of repaying the loans in specie. Sheriff's sales to pay debts or taxes particularly concerned them, they said, because hurried disposal of real estate in a depressed market deprived owners of the true value of their property.[11] Petitioners sought help in meeting the demands of their creditors. Some asked for the creation of special juries to establish the true market value of farm property and to force creditors to accept the property at that price. Others, fewer in number, demanded stay laws to postpone payment of principal until the times improved.[12]

Reform of the national government would also help to relieve the tax burden and to stimulate price recovery. Because Congress could not pay its debts, Pennsylvania landholders faced an extraordinary tax on their real property. At the same time, because the government of the United States could not effectively negotiate foreign trade agreements, American farmers found their products excluded from traditional markets. Thus, by the winter of 1787–88 farmers living within the Philadelphia trading region had ample economic reasons for supporting a political-constitutional change that promised to allow the central government to pay its own debts and to open foreign markets for Pennsylvania's staple crops.

West of the mountains additional frustrations compounded the difficulties faced by those involved in the faltering agricultural economy. In the late 1780s some 60,000 to 75,000 people lived in Pennsylvania beyond the mountains and Pittsburgh was a growing urban area with a score of stores, a weekly newspaper, a printing press, and an academy. Although the rich farmland and the good water transportation promised

---

11. "Assembly Minutes," 3/27/88, 3/25/88, pp. 169, 161–62; *Packet*, 3/31/88; *Packet*, 3/29/88; and 3/15/88. The extent of the public perception of the economic dislocations is suggested by a comment in the spring of 1788: "General complaints were, indeed, heard about the present hard times, the great scarcity of money, and consequent severe suffering" (*Minutes and Letters* Coetus of the German Reformed Congregations, 418–19).

12. Petition to Assembly on March 12, 1788, in *Packet* 3/15/88, Petition to Assembly on March 27, 1788, in *Packet*, 3/31/88, Petition from Chester (579 signatures) to Assembly March 25, 1788, in *Packet*, 3/29/88. Stay law request in *Packet* 3/20/88.

future abundance, the region remained physically insecure and economically stunted. As Ephraim Douglass wrote in 1784 describing the area near Uniontown, Fayette County: "I can say little of the country, but that it is very poor in everything but its soil, which is excellent. . . . But money we have not nor any practicable way of making it."[13]

High taxes, scarce specie, and sluggish trade produced widespread uncertainty and unrest. In addition, the state was demanding late payments in specie on lands patented before December 1776. A petition to the Assembly in October 1786 emphasized the accelerating economic problems of farmers who lacked specie to pay for land purchases, surveys, back taxes, and the excise tax on spiritous liquors.[14]

Some believed that the British "retention of the frontier posts" lay at the root of the troubles. Congress could neither remove the pretext for the continued British presence (the complaints of British creditors against the various state courts), nor finance military expeditions to subdue the Indians and force out the British.[15] Others in the West linked economic difficulties to moral imperfections and prescribed discipline, hard work, and the avoidance of such luxuries as sugar, coffee, tea, and rum. In sharp contrast, at least one looked to a strong central government to preserve liberty, virtue, equality, and democracy. An anonymous author writing in support of the Federal Convention in the summer of 1787 advocated entrusting Congress "with sufficient powers to regulate commerce, to . . . enforce an effective revenue system, to enforce sumptuary regulations." He also favored "laws to level, as it were, the inequalities, by the duties laid upon the rich."[16]

Most westerners, however, analyzed the problem differently. As one said: "trade down the River is virtually vanished." Western Pennsylva-

---

13. "Political Centinel II," *Pittsburgh Gazette*, 6/30/87; Russell J. Ferguson, *Early Western Pennsylvania Politics* (Pittsburgh: University of Pittsburgh Press, 1938), 7, 13, 14; U.S. Census, 1790; Douglass to General James Irving, Uniontown, 1784, published in *Pennsylvania Magazine of History and Biography* 1 (1877): 50–51. See also Robert Eugene Harper, "The Class Structure of Western Pennsylvania in the Late Eighteenth Century" (Ph.D. diss., University of Pittsburgh, 1969); Dorothy Fennell, "From Rebelliousness to Insurrection: A Social History of the Whiskey Rebellion, 1765–1802" (Ph.D. diss., University of Pittsburgh, 1981); Thomas Slaughter, *Whiskey Rebellion: Frontier Epilogue to the American Revolution* (New York: Oxford University Press, 1986), esp. 30–37, 57–71.

14. Ferguson, *Early Western Pennsylvania*, 62–63; *Pittsburgh Gazette*, 10/28/86, 12/9/86; Brunhouse, *Counter-Revolution*, agrees (172).

15. *Packet*, 3/4/86; 6/5/86; quotation is from 3/4/86.

16. *Pittsburgh Gazette*, 11/18/86; "The Political Centinel I and II," *Pittsburgh Gazette*, June 23 and 30, 1787.

nia produced wheat, corn, rye, oats, barley, buckwheat, flax, and hemp. The Mississippi River provided critical access to processing and re-export facilities and the Spanish threatened this lifeline. Westerners could survive without foreign trade but few could prosper.[17] Political observers in the east appreciated the explosive potential involved in the question of free navigation of the Mississippi. As early as 1784 Congressman David Jackson had warned Constitutionalist leader George Bryan that America must secure free navigation of the river or "otherwise our territory in that quarter would be of little consequence."[18]

By 1786 no satisfactory solution had emerged. Rumor had it, that downriver, the Spanish would soon garrison Natchez with 300 regulars. Of greater concern to many, Congress itself was seeking to betray Pennsylvania's westerners. On August 29, 1786, it had voted seven to five to pursue a treaty with Spain in which the United States would forbear navigation on the Mississippi River in return for trading opportunities in the Spanish empire. The Pennsylvania delegation, including Constitutionalists Charles Pettit and John Bayard, supported this action.[19]

Outraged westerners elected Republican Hugh Henry Brackenridge to the state legislature in October 1786 on a platform calling for immediate opening of the Mississippi. Brackenridge brought with him to Philadelphia a petition warning that "no people can long continue in mutual police where their interests become separate."[20]

If, throughout the backcountry an economic case could be made for ratification, equally important considerations urged caution. In the far west, distrust of the east, and especially a powerful eastern-dominated

17. *Pittsburgh Gazette*, 12/9/86; Slaughter, *Whiskey Rebellion*, 27.
18. Jackson to Bryan, June 4, 1784, Bryan Papers, Historical Society of Pennsylvania.
19. *Packet*, 4/27/86, *Packet* 7/7/87; Samuel Flagg Bemis, *A Diplomatic History of the United States*, 5th edition (New York: Holt, Rinehart and Winston, 1965), 75–80; Brunhouse, *Counter-Revolution*, 188–89; Allan Nevins, *The American States During and After the Revolution* (New York: Macmillan, 1924), 567; Ferguson, *Early Western Pennsylvania*, 63. Slaughter, *Whiskey Rebellion*, describes the growing western exasperation with Congress (30–31) and distrust of eastern motives as John Jay appeared to negotiate away America's interests in the Mississippi (55, 60).
20. Second reading, 12/30/86, sent to committee of Clymer, Findley, and Wright. *Journals of Assembly*, 12/29/86, pp. 105ff. *Packet*, 1/5/88. Note: Some westerners contemplated violence against the Spanish; see *Packet* 7/7/87. For fuller treatment of the shifting moods of westerners in the 1780s see Slaughter, *Whiskey Rebellion*, esp. part 3: "Consequences," 175–222.

Congress, weighed heavy on the minds of Pennsylvanians. On a more general level, the state economic policy had generally favored the landed interest, and a modest increase in the powers of Congress promised to alleviate most immediate problems. Moreover, the proposed central government would have the power to impose direct property and excise taxes. Efforts by a distant and unresponsive government to impose similar taxes had had much to do with the outbreak of the American Revolution.[21]

In sum, backcountry Pennsylvanians faced conflicting pressures. On the one hand, the Federal Constitution promised solutions to some of their most pressing problems, especially declining prices and rising taxes. On the other hand, it also posed threats. The problems were immediate and direct; the dangers, more long-range and indirect. The evidence we now have makes it difficult to know just how most backcountry Pennsylvanians would see the balance between benefits and threats. That, in turn, makes economic explanations of their political behavior risky. The actual distribution of Federalist and Antifederalist electoral support confirms this caution.

The Backcountry: Voting Alignments

In the far west, the bulk of the voters favored the Antifederalists, strongly in Westmoreland and Fayette, less so in Washington. East of the mountains, in the Philadelphia trading region, however, voters split sharply and consistently. In this area both Federalist and Antifederalist voters took firm positions early in October 1787, and then, over the next eight months, changed very little.

In October 1787, when they first voted on the question, few farmers east of the mountains faced a serious and unequivocal economic crisis. Wheat prices had plummeted in August and September, but no one yet knew whether this decline represented a long-term trend or a momentary fluctuation. Four months earlier, wheat prices had approached historic highs (8.25 shillings a bushel), only slightly less than the giddy

---

21. See Slaughter, *Whiskey Rebellion*, especially chap. 1, "The Tax Man Commeth" for an impressive and succinct exploration of the power of this concern and for its historic roots, particularly among backcountry Britons (i.e., those in Wales, Scotland, and Ireland).

levels reached in the immediate postwar boom of 1784. Furthermore, the state had, apparently, abandoned systematic efforts to recover back taxes on farm property. Thus, when the majority of the rural voters living in the Philadelphia market area first committed themselves to ratification, no conspicuous economic crisis compelled their assent. On the other hand, in the following six months, the deteriorating farm economy would certainly have reinforced their initial decision.

Antifederalist voters, however, appear to have increasingly acted against their economic interests. They opposed the Federal Constitution in October and persisted in this opposition as the economic depression worsened. Possibly the best example of this apparent economic irrationality occurred when thousands of residents of Cumberland County signed petitions in February and March 1788 demanding nullification of the state's ratification. At the time they signed, the agricultural depression was in its eighth month, the wholesale price of wheat scarcely (if at all) covered production and transportation costs; and the Cumberland County sheriff was regularly advertising his intention to seize lands for unpaid taxes.[22] In October 1787, when Cumberland voters first committed themselves to the Antifederalist cause, they might not have fully appreciated the nature of the economic crisis they would soon face. By March 1788, however, few could have remained in doubt. And yet, to the best of our knowledge, they persisted in their opposition.

In the backcountry, Federalist voters committed themselves before they could have fully appreciated the intensity of the emerging economic crisis. The Antifederalists persisted in their opposition in the face of accumulating economic difficulties. The behavior of these backcountry farmers argues against a simple economic interpretation—unless Federalist voters were significantly more sensitive to subtle economic shifts, and Antifederalist voters too isolated to feel the effects, understand the causes, or worry about the decline in agricultural prices.[23]

22. *Carlisle Gazette*, 1/23/88, 2/4/88, 2/27/88, 3/5/88.
23. The interpretations offered by politician George Bryan in the eighteenth century and by historian Jackson Turner Main in the twentieth century, imply such a situation. A number of recent studies suggest the existence of a premarket, precapitalist mentalité among many eighteenth-century northern farmers. Such a mentalité would be consistent with Main's understanding of backcountry Antifederalism. See Saul Cornell, "Notes and Documents: Reflections on 'The Late Remarkable Revolution in Government': Aedanus Burke and Samuel Bryan's Unpublished History of the Ratification of the Federal Constitution," *Pennsylvania Magazine of History and Biography* 112 (January 1988): 103–30; Jackson T. Main, *The Antifederalists: Critics of the Constitution, 1781–1788* (Chapel Hill: University of North

The geographical distribution of the Federalist and Antifederalist vote within the Philadelphia trading area does not make such an explanation likely. Two sets of election returns provide the basis for mapping the electoral support enjoyed by each side. The November 6, 1787, election of delegates to the state convention gave Antifederalists control of two quite distinct clusters of counties. The first, west of the mountains at the headwaters of the Ohio, included Westmoreland, Fayette, and half of Washington. Delegates from these counties made up about 22 percent of the total statewide Antifederalist support at the convention. The second, east of the mountains, included Cumberland and half of Franklin on the west side of the Susquehanna River, and Berks and Dauphin to the east of that river. Federalist strength began in Franklin on the western periphery of the Philadelphia trading area and stretched east in an unbroken line along the southern and eastern boundaries of the state. It included York, Lancaster, Chester, Philadelphia, Montgomery, and Bucks. In addition, all the northern frontier and part of the western frontier elected Federalist (see Map 1).

The results of the popular vote in the congressional elections in November 1788 allow us to refine and sharpen the definition of the geographic support of each party. Pennsylvania was to elect eight men to the new House of Representatives. The Republicans knew that if they divided the state into eight separate congressional districts, Constitutionalists would win in strong Constitutionalist districts. The legislature, under Republican control, therefore provided for an at-large election in which all candidates competed against each other; those with the highest statewide total winning.

The Antifederalists, meeting in Harrisburg, and the Federalists, meeting in Lancaster, each nominated a slate of candidates and some 14,500 voters participated in the November 26 election. The Federalists won, this time by approximately 56 to 44 percent.[24]

Carolina Press for the Institute of Early American History and Culture, Williamsburg, Va., 1961), and Main, *Political Parties Before the Constitution* (Chapel Hill: University of North Carolina Press for the Institute of Early American History and Culture, Williamsburg, Va., 1973). For a systematic analysis of the geographical distribution of Federalist and Antifederalist support in Massachusetts, see Van Beck Hall, *Politics without Parties: Massachusetts, 1780–1791* (Pittsburgh: University of Pittsburgh Press, 1972).

24. The Antifederalist Harrisburg Convention of September 1788 asked the people of Pennsylvania to accept peacefully the new frame of government and then went on to nominate candidates for the fall elections and to propose amendments to the Federal Constitution. See Roland Baumann, "The Democratic-Republicans of Philadelphia," 127–30; and Roland

Few counties, however, cast a unanimous vote for either ticket and the distribution of the Antifederalist vote in Federalist counties is particularly revealing. In this 1788 congressional race, the Antifederalist slate drew substantial popular backing (30 to 43 percent) in six Federalist counties. Five of these were east of the Susquehanna River: Montgomery, Bucks, Lancaster, Northampton, and Philadelphia County (see Map 2).[25] Thus, of the counties casting a majority Federalist vote in November 1787 and again in 1788, only three lacked significant numbers of Antifederalist voters: York, on the far side of the Susquehanna River, Chester on the Delaware, and the City of Philadelphia.

Combining the results of the two elections indicates that the Antifederalist cluster in the Philadelphia trading area began in Franklin (possibly eastern Bedford); reached overwhelming proportions in Cumberland, Dauphin, and Berks; included major elements of Northampton and Montgomery; and shaded off in two counties contiguous to the City: Bucks and Philadelphia County (see Table 5 and Map 3).[26] The distribution of Federalist and Antifederalist electoral support[27] does not correlate with either of the two broad measures of economic distress:

Baumann, "The Harrisburg Convention" in Robert G. Crist, ed., *Pennsylvania and The Bill of Rights* (University Park, Pa: Pennsylvania Historical Association, 1990), 41–52. See Merrill Jensen and Robert Becker, eds., *The Documentary History of the First Federal Elections, 1788–1790* (Madison: University of Wisconsin Press, 1976), 1:259–64 for details of the Harrisburg Antifederalist convention and its proposed amendments. For a discussion of the assumptions underlying the analysis of these election returns, see Appendix 2.

25. Huntingdon, recently subdivided from Bedford in the mountains, also cast a sizable Antifederalist vote; and Northumberland, on the northwest frontier reversed itself once again and voted Antifederalist.

26. One caution: These votes provide only a rough approximation of the extent of Antifederalist support. The Harrisburg slate was labeled the Antifederalist ticket, but its leading men were also conspicuous Constitutionalists. Some voters who supported this slate may have intended to vote for Constitutionalists, not Antifederalists. On the other hand, in the minds of most Pennsylvanians, Antifederalist and Constitutionalist had become synonymous terms by the fall of 1788 and we can probably safely consider the two as equivalents.

27. The partisan identification of the successful candidates in the first three elections (October and November 1787, and October 1788) allowed the initial categorization of each county as Federalist or Antifederalist. The actual voting returns for the election of November 1788 provide the data for the rough rank ordering of the counties according to their degree of Federalist support, based on a comparison of the vote for two prominent Federalists (Clymer and FitzSimons) and that for two prominent Antifederalists (Findley and Pettit). The complication caused by the "German vote" precluded a simple calculation of average vote for the Lancaster ticket and the Harrisburg ticket (see Appendix 2). It should be noted that the assigned percentages in Table 5 reflect an estimate, not a precise calculation, of relative magnitude.

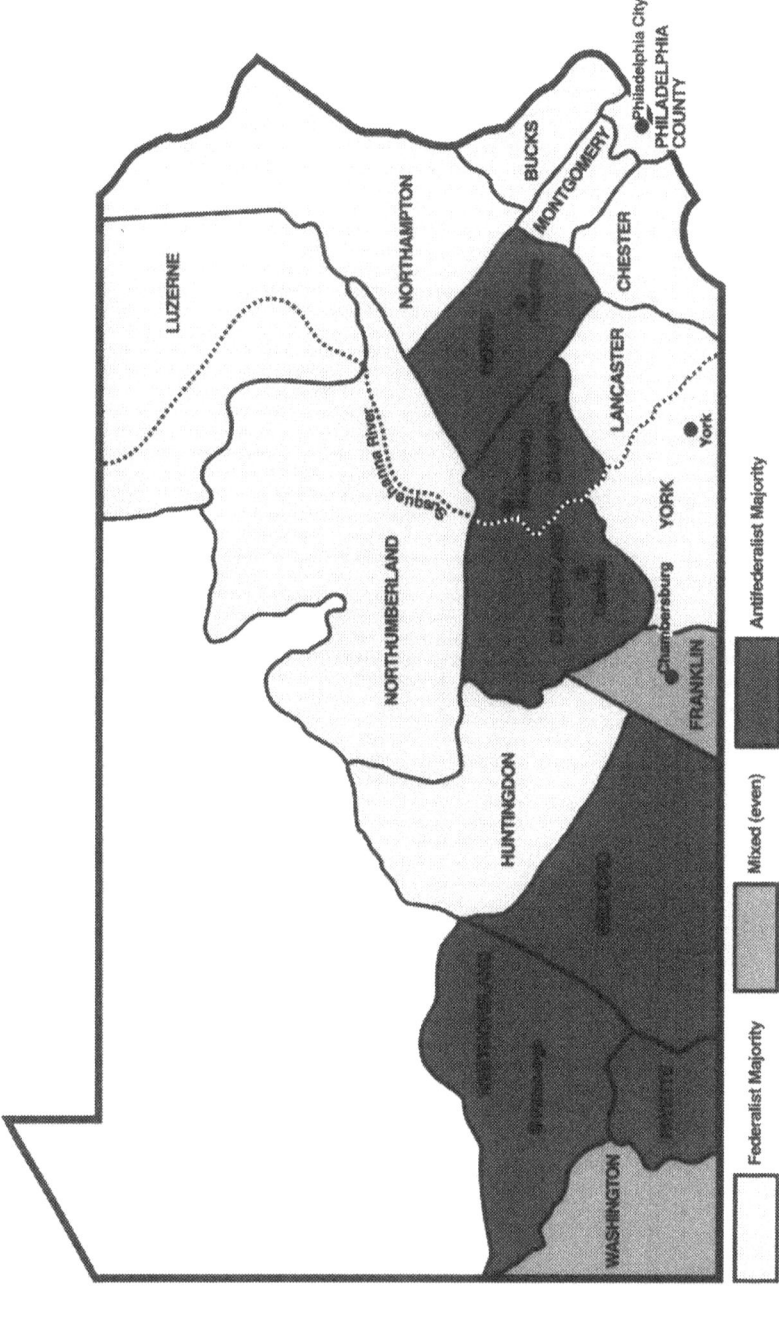

Counties Classified According to Delegates Elected to the State Convention, November 1787

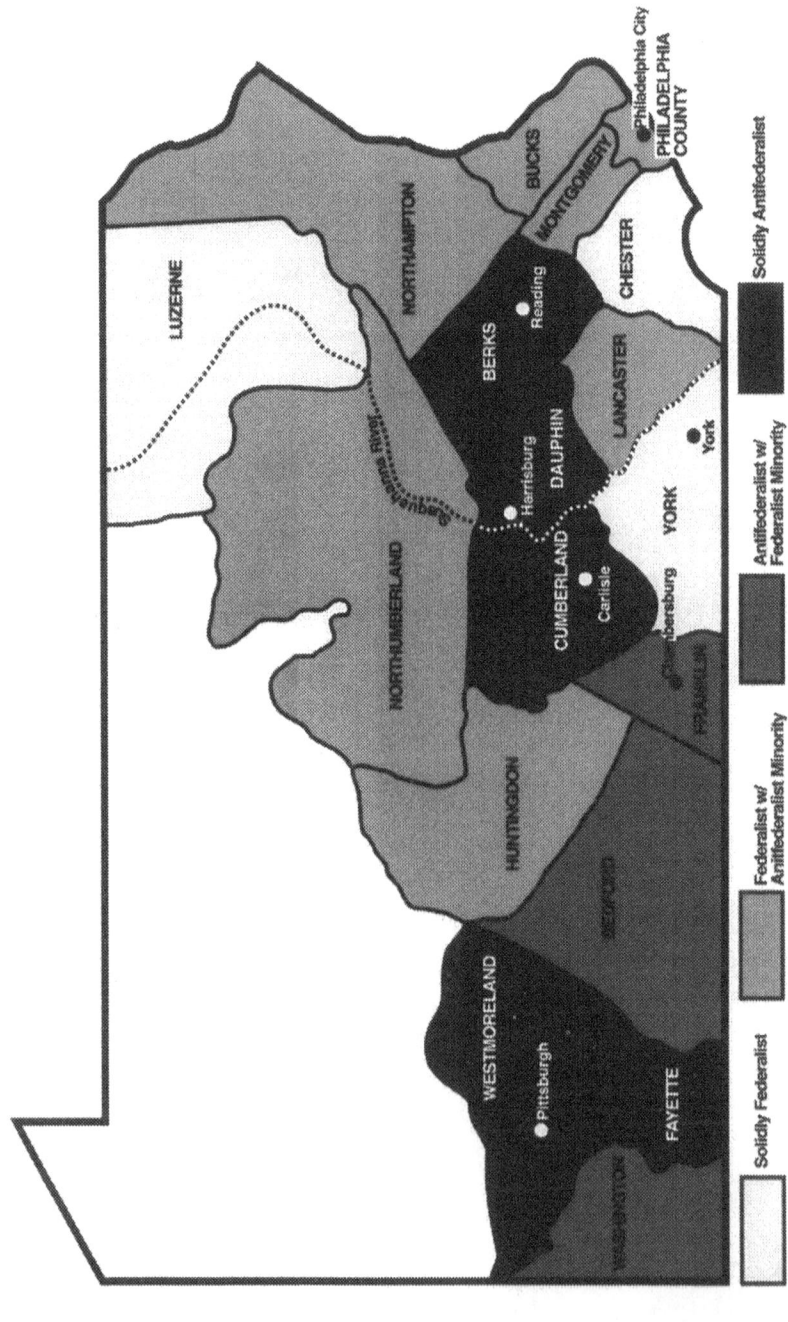

Counties Classified According to Votes Cast in the Congressional Election, November 1788

Table 5. Rough Estimate of Percentage of Federalist Support in Seventeen of Nineteen Political Subdivisions, 1787–1788

Solidly Federalist		Federalist with Antifederalist Minority		Antifederalist with Federalist Minority		Solidly Antifederalist	
Philadelphia	90	Lancaster	65	Franklin	40	Westmoreland	20
York	88	Huntingdon	65	Washington	40	Dauphin	15
Chester	82	Northampton	60	Bedford	36	Cumberland	15
Bucks	70	Montgomery	57			Berks	05
Luzerne[a]		Northumberland	50[?]			Fayette[a]	
Philadelphia County	70						

NOTE: See also note 27 for this chapter.

[a]Returns for these counties do not encourage calculations of percentages.

the distance from the Philadelphia market; or the per capita accumulation of unpaid back taxes (see Table 6). Furthermore, this distribution corresponded in no discernible way to obvious variations in access to transportation, information, or the market. Among the Antifederalist counties, the variation in distance to the Philadelphia market represented much the same range one could find throughout the entire Philadelphia trading region. Montgomery, approximately 43 percent Antifederalist, was a former part of Philadelphia County, and within easy distance of the metropolis. Berks, in excess of 90 percent Antifederalist, had its county seat at Reading and was also close to the city (about fifty miles). Cumberland, about 85 percent Antifederalist, was west of the Susquehanna River, on the outer rim of the city's trading area (Philadelphia to Carlisle, about 110 miles), and Franklin, about 60 percent Antifederalist was centered on Chambersburg, further west. Differences in costs for transporting a bushel of wheat from these Antifederalist areas to Philadelphia tell the story: Montgomery to Philadelphia, .25 to .75 shillings; Reading to Philadelphia, 1.0 to 1.5 shillings; Carlisle and Chambersburg to Philadelphia, 2.5 to 3.0 shillings.

Furthermore, the Antifederalist counties differed significantly from each other in their economic relationship to the city. Montgomery County neighbored on Philadelphia. Berks was connected to the city by the Schuylkill River, poorly and spasmodically, but nonetheless usefully. Reading, its county seat, was a major inland commercial town. It

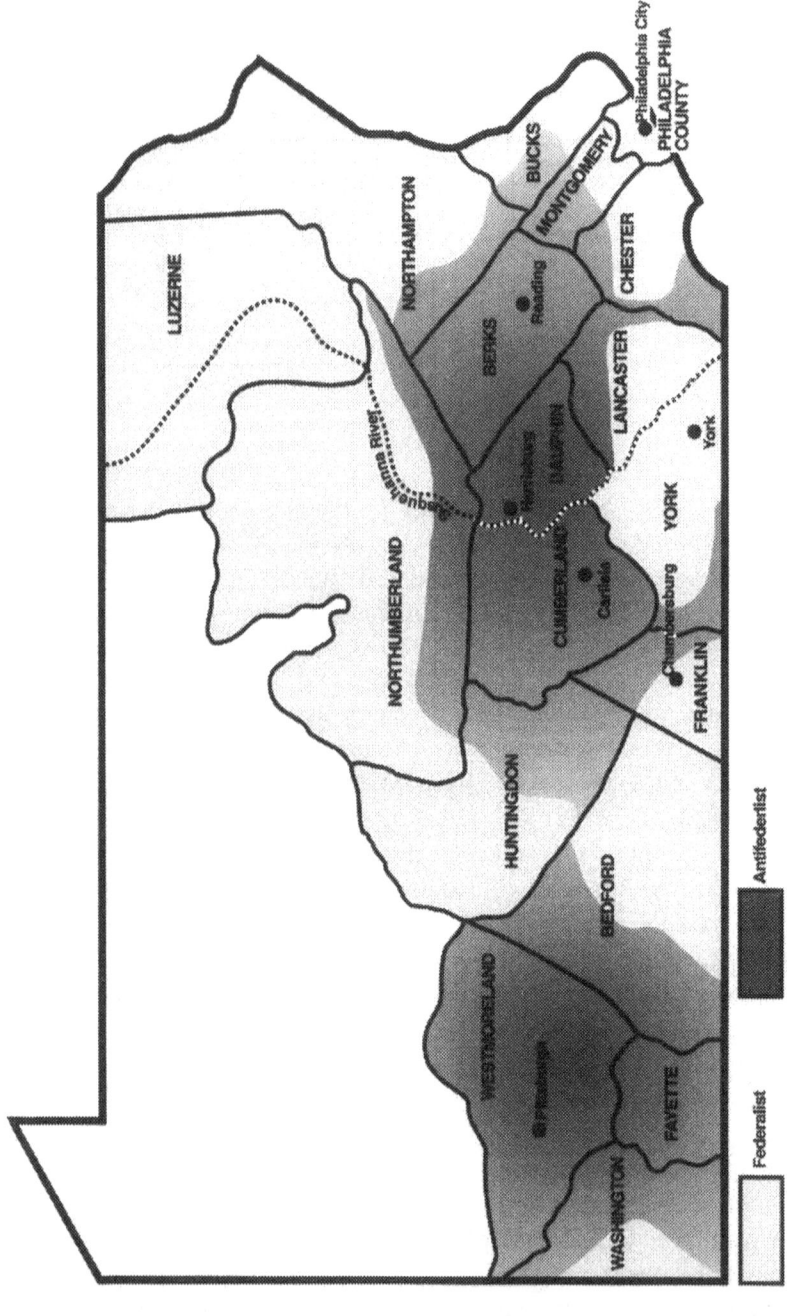

Probable Distribution of Federalist and Antifederalist Electoral Support, 1787-1788

Table 6. Counties Arrayed from Most to Least Along Two Economic Variables

Category/County	Per Capita Back Tax[a] (£)	Costs of Shipping a Bushel of Wheat to Philadelphia (shillings)	Federalist (F)/ Anti- Federalist (A)	Estimated % Federalist
1. *West*				
Westmoreland			A	20
Fayette			A	?
Washington			A/F	40
2. *High Debt–High Cost*				
Cumberland	7.390	2.5 to 3	A	15
Northumberland	6.053	>3	F	50?
3. *High Debt–Low Cost*				
Lancaster	5.349	1 to 2	F	65
Berks	4.406	1 to 2	A	05
4. *Low Debt–High Cost*				
York	3.96	1.5 to 2.5	F	88
Bedford	3.103	>3	F/A	36
Franklin	1.385	2.5 to 3	F/A	40
5. *Low Debt–Low Cost*				
Chester	2.649	<1	F	82
Northampton	1.457	<1	F/A	60
Montgomery	1.392	<1	F/A	57
Bucks	1.399	<1	F	70
Dauphin	1.006	1.5 to 2.5	A	15

SOURCE: See Tables 3, 4, 5, and Robert Brunhouse, *The Counter-Revolution in Pennsylvania, 1776–1790* (Harrisburg: The Pennsylvania Historical Commission, 1942), 207.

[a]Applies to adult white males age sixteen or older.

gathered farm goods from a wide range and shipped them to the city. At least seven roads spoked out from Reading, connecting it with Philadelphia and Chester to the south, Lancaster and Harrisburg to the west, Bethlehem and Easton to the east, and Tulpehocken to the north. Aside from Philadelphia, Reading was the only urban center in the state that formed the hub of such a transportation network.[28]

Harrisburg, the emerging commercial center of Dauphin County was on the east bank of the Susquehanna River, on a line from Reading to the east and Carlisle to the west. It also was a growing and thriving transshipment point linking the west and the north into the Philadelphia

28. Walzer, "Transportation," 33, 120–127; Schumacher, *Northern Farmer*, 61. Walzer, "Transportation," 34, 25. See map, end paper, and xxiii of Paul H. Smith, ed., *Letters of Delegates to Congress, 1774–1789* (Washington, D.C.: Library of Congress, 1985–), vol. 8.

market. Historian Peter Mancall estimates that in 1790, some 150,000 bushels of grain from upriver landed at Middletown, just south of Harrisburg, for shipment east to Philadelphia.[29] Farmers in Dauphin County could expect to ship wheat to the city for slightly more than if they lived in Berks and for considerably less than if they lived in Cumberland.[30]

Cumberland, west of the Susquehanna, could ship its wheat to market by a number of routes, all long and relatively expensive: across the Susquehanna to Dauphin and then by land to Philadelphia; down the shallow and dangerous Susquehanna to Baltimore; or over a circuitous route that followed roads south into Maryland and then used a succession of water and land transportation to reach the Delaware River and the Philadelphia market. Cumberland represented one extreme and Montgomery and Berks the other among the strong Antifederalist areas within the Philadelphia trading region.[31]

Similarities between pairs of Federalist and Antifederalist counties further illustrates the lack of congruence between economic context and political alignment. Federalist York and Antifederalist Cumberland bordered the western side of the Susquehanna River. Both were one hundred or so miles from Philadelphia and both faced the challenge of transporting goods to market over considerable distances. By the 1780s an increasing portion of the agricultural produce of both counties apparently found its way to market through Maryland, either directly to Baltimore, or through a complex land and water route to Head of Elk and then to the Delaware River and Philadelphia.

By the 1780s at least three major overland routes connected York to

---

29. Peter Mancall, *Valley of Opportunity: Economic Culture Along the Upper Susquehanna, 1700–1800* (Ithaca: Cornell University Press, 1991), 176–77. He notes, however, that hard times in 1788 led Northumberland County (virtually all of central Pennsylvania north of Sunbury), to import wheat and flour (177). Settlers in some parts of that region in 1789 seized flour from storekeepers who charged too much (172).

30. Walzer, "Transportation," 35–36, 40–45. George William Franz, "Paxton: A Case Study of Community Structure and Mobility in the Colonial Pennsylvania Backcountry" (Ph.D. diss., Rutgers University, 1974).

31. Alexander Graydon described this circuitous route in *Memoirs of His Own Time*, ed. John Stockton Littell (Philadelphia, 1846), 107. Apparently little direct trade with Baltimore existed by way of the Susquehanna River. John Adams reported a conversation in Baltimore about "removing the Obstructions and opening the Navigation of Susquehanna River," anticipating that it would "open an amazing scaene of Business." John Adams, *Diary and Autobiography*, ed. L. M. Butterfield (Cambridge: Belknap Press of Harvard University Press, 1961), 2/23/77, 2:261.

Maryland and as early as 1770 farmers in Cumberland were using these routes to link themselves to Baltimore. For example, a petition from "Sundry Inhabitants" of the townships of West Pennsburgh, Hopewell, and New Town in Cumberland petitioned the Court of Quarter Sessions at its April 1770 session for improvement of a "waggon Road . . . from James Smiths [sic] Merchants [sic] Mill near Walnut Bottom, through the South Mountain to the York County Line," to encourage "A very advantageous Trade in Wheat and Flour [which] has been for some time past Carried on by your Petitioners and other Farmers . . . to the Baltimore Market." They expected that improved transportation would facilitate this trade and thereby "conduce to raise the value of Lands and Promote Industry" in Cumberland.[32]

Both York and Cumberland also had small and relatively modest commercial centers: York in York, and Carlisle in Cumberland. Of the two, the village of Carlisle in Antifederalist Cumberland, appears to have been the more cosmopolitan. It had a budding institution of higher education (Dickinson College), and one of the two weekly newspapers published west of the Susquehanna River: the *Carlisle Gazette*. The *Gazette* carried news from Philadelphia within a few days and from most major east coast cities (Boston, New York) within two or three weeks of the original dateline.[33] The paper published a regular "Poets Corner" while the village of Carlisle had a French dancing master who (if we are to believe his advertisements) instructed "Ladies and Gentlemen" and conducted an annual dancing assembly (a ball).[34]

A second pair of counties with contrasting political complexions were also more similar than different. Federalist Lancaster and Antifederalist Dauphin were both located on the east bank of the Susquehanna River; both had excellent road transportation to the city; both served as middlemen in the transference of people and products between east and west; both enjoyed fertile soils, rolling hills, and good climate. Yet they differed significantly in their reaction to the Federal Constitution.

---

32. Cumberland County Court of Quarter Sessions, Docket, vols. 3–4, p. 88, in the Office of the Clerk of the Courts, Cumberland County, Carlisle, Pennsylvania. Walzer argues that by the 1770s York shipped its grain to Philadelphia by sending it south, by road or by water, to Head of Elk and then overland to Christiana Bridge (10 miles) and then by water again to the grist mills in the New Castle, Delaware, area (47–45, 239).

33. The *Pittsburgh Gazette* was the other. Depending upon the day of the week on which the news originally appeared in the Philadelphia papers, items published on Friday or Saturday in Philadelphia could appear in the Wednesday edition of the Carlisle paper, a three- or four-day delay.

34. *Carlisle Gazette*, 3/21/87, 3/28/87, 4/4/87.

Another kind of comparison demonstrates the lack of clear, consistent economic differences between Federalist and Antifederalist regions. Federalist York and Antifederalist Berks represented the reverse of what one would expect if distance from the Philadelphia market alone shaped responses to the Federal Constitution. Reading in Antifederalist Berks County, was fifty miles from the city; York, in Federalist York County, was more than one hundred, a remote outpost on the far side of the Susquehanna River, a refuge the Continental Congress selected as a safe haven while the British occupied Philadelphia in 1777–78. In spite of their different locations and their opposing positions on the Constitution, the two counties shared a similar pattern of land distributions and a similar ratio of mills to population (see Table 7).[35] On the other hand, if Antifederalist Berks resembled Federalist York, it differed markedly from Antifederalist Cumberland in these same basic economic structures.

In short, Antifederalist counties differed among themselves more than they differed from Federalist counties. Nevertheless, it is possible that farmers in Antifederalist counties had less access to information than others and therefore less understanding of the nature and the magnitude of the economic crisis looming on the horizon. In much the same vein,

Table 7. Land Distribution; Mills Per Capita

	Berks 1779	York 1779	Cumberland 1779
Percentage of taxables with:			
More than 300 acres	4	5	1
100 to 300 acres	38	39	15
1 to 100 acres	19	15	55
No land	39	42	30
Percentage urban taxables	9	6	5
Ratio of mills to taxables	1/22	1/27	1/38

SOURCE: York: *Pennsylvania Archives*, ser. 3, 21:3f.; Berks: *Pennsylvania Archives*, ser. 3, 18:177f.; Cumberland: *Pennsylvania Archives*, ser. 3, 20:115f.

NOTE: Different tax years yield slightly different proportions, due apparently both to high in- and-out migration rates and inconsistencies in enumeration. These figures should be regarded as rough approximations rather than precise calculations. The data themselves do not encourage great confidence in precise figures, but seem sufficient to permit broad comparison.

35. Many congressmen fleeing from Philadelphia made Reading one of their stops on the trip to York. John Adams's Diary 9/19, 22, 23, 25/1777, in Smith, ed. *Letters*, 8:5, 10, 16. Adams to Abigail Adams, York Town, Pa., 9/30/77, ibid., 8:27; James Lowell to Joseph Trumbull, Philadelphia, 9/23/77, ibid., 8:12.

it is also conceivable that Antifederalist areas resisted incorporation into the market and had little desire to produce crops for cash. Little of the evidence now available, however, supports such a conclusion. Take, for example, Antifederalist Cumberland County. The bulk of the population lived within relatively easy distance of the principal east-west land transportation route linking the port of Philadelphia with the Shenandoah Valley of Virginia. A complex of private and public roads crisscrossed the county, and the inhabitants kept up a steady din of demands for more. The question of roads, especially for transportation to market, often constituted the single largest item on the docket of the Court of Quarter Sessions (the county agency with principal responsibility in this area). One such petition in 1778 contained 99 signatures, about two thirds of the total number of heads of households in the entire township.[36]

Two other pieces of information suggest that from early on, farmers in Cumberland understood the link between their own prosperity and that of the general economy. On May 29, 1776, the "Freemen of Cumberland" asked for relief. They complained that the "[s]tagnation of commerce" had cut the circulation of money, and they wanted the Assembly to stop sheriff's sales. They were honest debtors with property who were "able and willing to discharge debts" but could not do so "for want of cash." In like manner, in 1785 the county's most conspicuous and powerful Constitutionalist, Robert Whitehill, defended the state's 1785 issue of paper money as the "only sure means of encouraging agriculture and enabling farmers to bring their crops to market."[37]

---

36. The petition with 99 signatures came from Allen Township, which had 104 household heads in 1778 and 203 in 1779. The petition is in the Cumberland County Historical Society. As an example of the frequency of petitions for road improvement see the Docket for the Court of Quarter Sessions for 1770. It contained petitions and reports from viewers appointed in response to earlier petitions; Cumberland County Court of Quarter Sessions, Docket 3 and 4, Office of the Clerk of the Courts, County Office Building, Carlisle, Pa.

37. For the petition to the Assembly, see *Votes and Proceedings of the House of Representatives of the Province of Pennsylvania, 1775–1776*, 5/29/76 in *Pennsylvania Archives*, Series Eight, VIII: 5/29/76, 7526. John Kaminski, "Paper Politics: The Northern State Loan-Offices During the Confederation, 1783–1790" (Ph.D. diss., University of Wisconsin, 1972), 66. "Centinel," the leading Antifederalist author, assumed that the condition of the international market influenced the decisions of backcountry farmers. During the war, he said "the husbandman, for want of a market, limited his crop to his own subsistence." Granted, this may tell us more about "Centinel," who lived in Philadelphia, than about the mentalité of backcountry farmers. On the other hand, "Centinel's" perception of Pennsylvania's farmers is consistent with that of Robert Whitehill, who lived among farmers in rural Cumberland.

Furthermore, little of Cumberland was isolated or remote. Important news traveled quickly between Philadelphia and Cumberland. For example, the *Carlisle Gazette* of July 5, 1786, printed "Prices Current at *Philadelphia*" for June 30, 1786. In the same vein, the *Gazette* printed the full text of the Constitution on September 26, the first issue of the paper to appear after the Philadelphia press had published the text of the document.[38]

The timing of Cumberland's response to the ratification of the Federal Constitution in December 1787 also illustrates the rapid flow of information back and forth from Philadelphia. In Carlisle the Federalists precipitated a riot when they attempted a public celebration on December 26, less than two weeks after news of the state's ratification had appeared in the Philadelphia press. Reprints from the *Carlisle Gazette* of January 2, 1788, describing this event appeared in the Philadelphia press on January 9, 1788.[39] Information also moved quickly within the backcountry itself. The *Carlisle Gazette*, for example, circulated widely in Cumberland, and in the neighboring areas to the west and the north. Residents of Franklin County, to the southwest, and of the Juniata Valley, to the north, advertised in the *Gazette* seeking information about lost or stolen animals.

But even without the newspaper, important news could spread rapidly throughout the countryside. In February 1788 when court officials in Carlisle imprisoned a number of Antifederalists and charged them with riot, Antifederalist supporters mobilized a crowd of up to 1500 men virtually overnight.[40] Finally, the Antifederalist petition campaign in the late winter of 1788 demonstrates the speed with which political leaders in the city could mobilize even the most remote backcountry. In less than three months, Comptroller John Nicholson, operating out of Philadelphia, orchestrated a massive petition campaign for legislative

---

"Centinel," VIII, in Herbert Storing, ed., and commentary, *The Complete Anti-Federalist* (Chicago: University of Chicago Press, 1981) volume 2, document 7, paragraph 79. 2.7:79.

38. *Carlisle Gazette*, 7/5/86. An Antifederalist group met in Carlisle on Monday, October 22, and called a "General Meeting" for Thursday, October 25 (Court Day) to take the sense of the people on the "present important CRISIS" and to nominate a slate of candidates (presumably Antifederalist) for the upcoming November 6 election. *Carlisle Gazette*, 9/26/87, 10/24/87, 10/31/87.

39. *Carlisle Gazette*, 1/2/88; *Independent Gazetteer*, 1/9/88.

40. Brunhouse, *Counter-Revolution*, 209–10, 293 n. 57. Saul Cornell, "Aristocracy Assailed: The Ideology of Backcountry Anti-Federalism," *Journal of American History* 76 (March 1990): 1148–1173, esp. 1151–52, 1154–55.

negation of the state's December ratification. The overwhelming majority of his support came from Cumberland, Franklin, and further west. Furthermore, Nicholson and his collaborators collected these signatures during the most severe winter months when nature invariably conspired to impede, if not prevent, normal travel.

Some residents of the backcountry undoubtedly lived in remote, and inaccessible enclaves with little interest in or access to information about prices or politics. Election law, however, minimized the participation of such men in the decision-making process. Balloting took place in a small number of central locations in each county, thus forcing most voters to travel significant distances to cast their ballots. Cumberland, for example, had only four polling places and from 200 to 1500 voters congregated at each location on election day.[41] Some of these participants had traveled considerable distance, and many made a holiday of the event, thus creating a prime opportunity for the dissemination of information. It is difficult to imagine, for example, that the families from three Cumberland townships who gathered to vote at the house of William McClure in Tyrone in the fall of 1787 did not discuss prices or politics; or that the 1000 to 1500 rural and urban families who turned out at the Carlisle Court House on Election Day did not explore much the same topics.

Voters, and only voters, decided the fate of the Constitution in Cumberland and, voters, especially those in and around Carlisle (who normally made up about 40 percent of the county's turnout), could hardly have remained ignorant of the plummeting prices for agricultural staples on the Philadelphia wholesale market or of the economic and the political implications of the proposed Federal Constitution. Although we cannot know which men voted, those closest to the polling places, and hence those least isolated, undoubtedly predominated. To the same end, those from more remote areas who made the effort to vote were, it seems likely, either initially better informed than their neighbors or became so after mingling with the crowds on Election Day. All things considered, it therefore seems improbable that the men of Cumberland who voted and petitioned against ratification remained

---

41. "Act to Regulate the General Elections of this Commonwealth," enacted September 3, 1785, in James T. Mitchell and Henry Flanders, *The Statutes at Large of Pennsylvania* (1903), chap. 1175, 12:29. Turnout calculated from election returns in *Pennsylvania Archives*, 6th ser., 11:176–77.

ignorant of or indifferent to the depressed state of Pennsylvania's farm economy.

Northumberland County, far more distant from Philadelphia than any part of Cumberland, apparently participated extensively in a market economy. In 1787–88 that frontier county encompassed the entire Susquehanna Valley northwest from Sunbury to New York on the west branch of the river, and northeast to Luzerne (Wilkes-Barre area) on the east branch. By any measure, this county ranked far behind Cumberland in its population size, its economic development, its access to the Atlantic trading world, and its transportation and communication links to Philadelphia. Peter Mancall, in his recent study of the "economic culture" of the upper Susquehanna Valley in the eighteenth century, concludes: "All valley residents realized that their local economy was part of a larger commercial system," and they "came to define their lives in relation to the market economy of eastern North America. . . . Few sought to escape this market."[42]

Voters in Antifederalist Dauphin County, across the Susquehanna to the east of Cumberland were, if possible, less isolated and less divorced from the market than those in Cumberland. Here, as in Cumberland, some may have participated little in the market economy and remained uninformed and uninterested in the wholesale price of staples in Philadelphia. Some farm families might have ignored or resisted the market opportunities available to them, while participating in what Michael Merrill has called a "household mode of production." The evidence we have, however, offers scant reason to believe that these kinds of people constituted the majority of the Antifederalist voters in Dauphin.[43]

Here, as in Cumberland, many if not most residents participated in the market, or eagerly sought to do so. Residents of Hanover township, for example, had petitioned as early as 1772 for more roads, since, as they said, "[y]our petitioners reside near Blue Mountain . . . [and have] frequent occasion to go with wagons to Philadelphia, Lancaster [and] Reading."[44]

George Franz's impressive study of Paxton, one of Dauphin County's

---

42. Mancall, *Valley of Opportunity*, 9, xi, 7.
43. Michael Merrill, "Cash is Good to Eat: Self-Sufficiency and Exchange in the Rural Economy of the United States," *Radical History Review* 3 (1977): 42–71; quote on 46, "household mode of production."
44. Walzer, "Transportation," 283.

most infamous townships, offers substantial evidence that it, too, was part of a communication and marketing network centered in Philadelphia. Paxton borders on the Susquehanna River at Harris' Ferry, the principal crossing point on the river. Although not necessarily the most commercially developed or affluent part of Dauphin in the 1780s, Paxton participated in a complex market economy that linked its people to both the city of Philadelphia and the backcountry residents up the Susquehanna River to the north, and across the river to the west. As early as 1767 special courier service delivered Philadelphia newspapers to some thirty residents of the township (possibly the proprietors of taverns and mills), and by the 1770s (at the latest) Harris' Ferry on the Susquehanna was becoming a major transportation link and a vital transshipment center.[45]

A flood of immigrants and supplies poured west from Philadelphia, crossed the river, and moved on into the Shenandoah Valley (of Virginia) and beyond into the western parts of Carolina and Georgia. At the same time wheat and forest products coming down the river shifted to land transportation at Harris' Ferry or at Middletown, just a few miles south, for the wagon trip to Philadelphia. Paxton's mills, about one for every twenty or so families in 1782, suggest the processing of backcountry grain and lumber for Philadelphia or for shipment back upriver. In the early 1790s miller George Fry of Middletown worried about the deteriorating road east to Philadelphia "because the large Quantities of Wheat & other Produce . . . brought to this Town by Water, and the Flour . . . manufactured about here, . . . remain on Hand for want of Teams which are terrified by the bad and dangerous Roads."[46]

Dry goods from the metropolitan region crossed the Susquehanna at Harris' Ferry for further shipment west through Cumberland, or moved up the river to the settlements on its east and the west branches. By the mid-1780s, the area had good east-west road transportation, an increasing variety of skilled artisans and a substantial number of mills and taverns (in 1773, one tavern for every twenty families). About a quarter of Paxton's farmers (23 percent) worked forty or more acres of cleared land, a sign of probable involvement in commercial agriculture.

45. Franz, "Paxton," 289.
46. Ibid., 171, 179, 180–290. Mancall, *Valley of Opportunity*, 205, quoting from James W. Livingood, *The Philadelphia-Baltimore Trade Rivalry, 1780–1860* (Harrisburg: Pennsylvania Historical and Museum Commission, 1947), 40.

Almost another quarter (23 percent) eked out a bare subsistence, while the rest fit in somewhere between.[47]

In sum, the geographic distribution of Antifederalist votes in the backcountry within the Philadelphia market region does not easily lend itself to an economic explanation. More particularly, the evidence now available does not encourage us to see Antifederalist voters, whether in the suburbs of Philadelphia (Montgomery County) or west of the Susquehanna River (Cumberland County), as more ignorant of or indifferent to the market economy.

The Case of John Kean

Possibly the case of John Kean, a Dauphin County Antifederalist, best illustrates the difficulty inherent in attempting to explain Pennsylvania backcountry alignments on the Federal Constitution in terms of access to markets or participation in commercial activities. Kean's case also suggests an alternative explanation for the political behavior of these backcountry Pennsylvanians.

Kean, a young man living in Harrisburg, actively opposed ratification of the new Federal Constitution throughout 1787 and 1788. Years later, in his autobiography, he attempted to put the best face on a position made increasingly embarrassing by the growing popular veneration of the document he had opposed. His explanation is worth quoting in some detail:

> The adoption of the Federal Constitution about this time engaged the attention of every one who in any degree regarded the interests of his country. An acquaintance with Mr. ——, a gentleman in office, gave me frequent opportunities of hearing his opinion on political subjects. I revered his talent and eagerly attended to his arguments, all of which went to prove that the members of the Convention aimed only to make a form of government which should tend to aggrandize themselves. Of course when the new Constitution appeared I was prepared to

---

47. Ten percent of the taxpayers in Paxton were in nonagricultural occupations. Franz, "Paxton," 323, 290–91.

view it with a scrutinizing eye. On first reading, the dreadful features predicted did not appear to be in it, but I saw parts ill calculated for the meridian of Pennsylvania. These I at once considered as international [intentional?] blemishes, never considering that to give and to take must alone be principles on which a government could be formed to suit so wide extended a country as the United States, the inhabitants of which differed from each other widely in laws, manner, and religion. My political ideas of that time did not extend beyond the circle of Pennsylvania, and I absurdly thought that a government suited to that State would be the form best suited to the whole Union. . . . Experience has since taught me better, and although the Constitution of the United States has some defects, as no human work is without them, I now believe it to be the best form of government upon earth, and better calculated to insure an equal participation of equal right than any other form. My former sentiments of distrust of those who made it are changed into admiration of their wisdom and virtues.[48]

Reduced to its basic elements, Kean's "apology" is this: his political acquaintance shaped his thinking and predisposed him to oppose the Federal Constitution as a product of designing men. Although the actual document proved less threatening than anticipated, he opposed it because of "parts ill calculated for the meridian of Pennsylvania" and because it conflicted with the state constitution of 1776. He later changed his mind, partly because he recognized the need for compromise, partly because he came to see that a government suited to Pennsylvania might not be equally suited to the nation, and partly because he realized that the Federal Constitution was better "calculated to insure . . . equal right than any other form."[49]

On the basis of this information alone one might conclude that Kean's original provincialism and ignorance caused him to oppose a document that his later more cosmopolitan experience led him to see as highly desirable. Not in itself a remarkable occurrence if we assume that Kean was a relatively parochial young man living in an isolated area and

48. John Kean, "An Autobiography—Extracts Taken from the Life of John Kean, of Harrisburg," in William Henry Egle, ed., *Notes and Queries, Historical and Geneological; Chiefly Relating to Interior Pennsylvania* (Harrisburg, n.d.), 3:90–98.
49. Kean, *Autobiography*, 94.

resisting changes he did not fully understand but that he saw as contrary to familiar institutions and to the local climate of opinion.

Neither Kean himself nor his views, however, had been shaped by life in rustic rural community off the beaten track and isolated from the world of trade, commerce, and communication. Quite the contrary. Kean's father and mother had been immigrants to Philadelphia. Kean had been raised in the city where his father, a tanner, had "carried on business . . . upon an extensive scale, engaged in shipping shoes and leather to Spanish ports and elsewhere." Early in the Revolution the family had retreated to northern Lancaster County (later Dauphin), purchased land, and settled near Middletown, "a small village at the junction of the Susquehanna River and Swatara Creek."[50] Over the next few years, the family bought and sold land and the father served in the militia as a *"captain* and almost always in active service." In 1779 young Kean, eighteen, joined the militia himself and marched east to the Delaware, and then returned to Lancaster to guard prisoners.[51]

After the war, Kean worked as a storekeeper in Hummelstown, and then, with the creation of the new County of Dauphin in 1785, he joined the throng crowding into the new county seat at Harris' Ferry. Harrisburg, as it was coming to be called, was a boomtown and the twenty-four-year-old Kean prospered, first in partnership in a retail store, and then in the retail business for himself. By 1787–88 he had married, become a justice of the peace, and won election as county commissioner, all before the age of thirty.[52] At the time of the ratification controversy, then, Kean was an energetic, talented, ambitious young man of growing public prominence in one of the fastest growing commercial-political centers of the state outside of Philadelphia. His friends and acquaintances were not subsistence farmers, hill people, hollow dwellers, or isolated rural provincials committed to maintaining a household economy. Rather, they were, like him, participants in a dynamic, expanding, and speculative urban commercial environment destined in short order to emerge as the new capital of the state.

Kean, combining native talent, industry, a quick intelligence, and political connections, competed successfully against the best in the area. In a four-year period (1785–89) he married twice, owned, bought, sold,

50. Ibid., 91.
51. Ibid.
52. Ibid., 93.

or rented at least four and probably five pieces of property, conducted business at three and possibly four different locations in partnership with two different men and on his own. In the year the Constitution was drafted and ratified, Kean lost his first wife, and then "quit business and became deeply interested in the progress of schools, churches, fire companies, a library, improvements of streets and other needful improvements," activities suggesting sufficient wealth to permit him to devote his time to public service.[53]

His real estate transactions at the time also point in this direction and suggest at least one reason for his affluence. He sold his "house for £482 and purchased [a lot?] between Chestnut street and Market square, fronting on Second, for £510, one-half of which I conveyed a few days afterward to Alexander Barryhill, Esq., for £360, thus I had as good a lot as any." Although he does not do the calculations for us, he apparently netted about £300 from the transaction, a profit equal to that a farmer might realize on the sale of 1800 bushels of wheat at seven shillings a bushel, when 200 bushels represented affluence for a large farm family with access to seasonal labor. Kean appears to have combined a significant social move with a shrewd financial transaction.[54]

Here, to his Second Street address, he brought his new wife, Jane, in December 1789. She was, as he proudly tells us, the daughter of Captain John Hamilton, "one of the largest merchants in this part of Pennsylvania." In the meanwhile, he had actively opposed the ratification of the Federal Constitution and had then attended, as a delegate, the Harrisburg Antifederalist convention in the fall of 1788.[55] Kean's Antifederalism did not stem from isolation, from his concerns for local community, nor from his ideological distrust of speculation, growth, cities. As far as we can tell, he had no such concerns. More likely, the roots of his opposition to ratification lay in his ethnic-religious background, in his partisan identification, and in his political connections. Kean was a Scots-Irish Presbyterian. His mother and father, both born in Ireland, "were of the strictest order of the Covenanters" and he himself had been "brought up in a pious and religious manner . . . [and had been] astonished beyond measure at the wickedness and profanity of the world" when he marched off to war at the age of eighteen.

53. Ibid., 94.
54. Ibid.
55. Ibid., 95.

Both his business and his political careers reflected his backgrounds. His commercial mentor and first partner in Dauphin had been a Scot, Mr. James Clunie; and his first wife, Mary, had been the daughter of one of the most prominent and powerful Scots-Irish Presbyterian politicians in backcountry Pennsylvania: Robert Whitehill. It hardly seems accidental that Kean returned from his honeymoon with his bride to discover that the good people of his community had nominated him for the office of justice of the peace, and that the Constitutionalist-dominated Supreme Executive Council, with which his father-in-law had considerable influence, had concurred; or that within two years of his marriage he was elected a county commissioner for Dauphin.[56] Although Kean does not identify the "gentleman in office" who "gave [him] frequent opportunities of hearing his opinion on political subjects" and who shaped Kean's perception of the Grand Convention and the Federal Constitution, in all likelihood it was none other than his first father-in-law, and his apparent political mentor and protector, Robert Whitehill, a resident of adjacent Cumberland County.

Kean's opposition to the Federal Constitution emerged, it would appear, as the virtually unthinking decision of an ambitious young Scots-Irish businessman living in a largely Presbyterian and dissenter commercial center dominated by the Constitutionalists, and married to the daughter of one of the two or three most prominent and powerful Constitutionalist leaders and Antifederalist spokesmen in the state. Kean's political, economic, and personal interests all pointed him toward easy acceptance of Antifederalism. It was the logical, the natural, and the reasonable thing to do.[57]

An urban dweller engaged in speculative commercial activities, John Kean did not typify backcountry Pennsylvanians in his occupation or in his place of residence. Nor did his father-in-law, Constitutionalist leader and ardent Antifederalist Robert Whitehill, who loaned money against short-term personal notes, held mortgages, rented farms to tenants, and invested in securities.[58] On the other hand, Kean's reaction to the

---

56. Ibid., 92, 93.
57. Apparently Mary Whitehill Kean died just before the ratification contest and Kean remarried late in 1789. Thus during 1787–88, although a widower, he had formed no other public attachments.
58. Details on Whitehill's financial transactions may be gleaned from his "Papers," collected by Dr. Robert Crist and now deposited at the Cumberland County Historical Society, Carlisle, Pennsylvania.

Federal Constitution appears to have reflected a partisan attachment to the Constitutionalists rooted in ethnic-religious identifications and reinforced by innumerable ties of business, community, friends, and family. In this he typified backcountry Antifederalists across the state in their attachment to the Constitutionalist party, and in their ethnic and religious backgrounds. Almost every known Antifederalist from the backcountry who held a seat in the state Assembly in these years, or in the state convention elected in November 1787 was a Constitutionalist of either the Presbyterian or Reformed faith.

In the same vein, although Cumberland, Dauphin, and Berks might differ significantly from each other in terms of access to information and to the market, they shared a historic commitment to the Constitutionalist party and they shared a substantial Presbyterian and Reformed population. Cumberland was almost universally recognized as the most Scots-Irish Presbyterian county in the state and large numbers of this ethnic-religious group had also settled in those townships that later became a major part of the county of Franklin (the southwestern townships of Cumberland). Berks had some Scots-Irish Presbyterians but a much greater concentration of Reformed, close theological cousins to the Presbyterians. Berks County, and the contiguous portions of Montgomery County immediately to the south, probably contained the highest concentration of German Reformed in the state. Dauphin County, situated between Cumberland and Berks, also had a heavy concentration of Reformed.

Furthermore, electoral support for Federalists and Antifederalists, while largely unrelated to variations in economic conditions or to access to transportation, information, or markets, correlates almost perfectly with Republican and Constitutionalist electoral support in 1786–88. With only minor exceptions, counties that elected Republicans to the Eleventh General Assembly (October 1786–September 1787) elected Federalists to the state convention in November 1787, while counties that sent Constitutionalists to the Eleventh General Assembly elected Antifederalists to the state convention (see Table 8).[59]

59. Only two of the eighteen political subdivisions deviated from this pattern: Berks went from a slight Republican majority (about two-thirds) to solid Antifederalist; Northumberland reversed itself, replacing its Constitutionalists with Federalists. Northampton County, north and a bit east of Bucks along the Delaware River, appears to have followed much the same pattern as the other eastern counties, but a year or two behind the others. Its population, while very mixed, had a major Calvinist contingent and between 1778 and 1788 the county elected mostly Constitutionalists to the legislature. However, Northampton appears to have

Table 8. Partisan Complexion of County-wide Delegations, Eleventh General Assembly (October 1786–September 1787) and State Convention (November 1787)

	Elections			
	Eleventh General Assembly		State Convention	
County	Federalist	Antifederalist	Federalist	Antifederalist
Philadelphia (city)	5		5	
Philadelphia (county)	5		5	
Bucks	4		4	
Chester	6		6	
Lancaster	6		5	1
York	4		6	
Cumberland		4		4
Berks	3	2		5
Northampton	2	1	4	
Bedford/Huntingdon	1	2	1	2
Northumberland		2	2	
Westmoreland	1	2		3
Washington		4	2	2
Fayette		2		2
Franklin		2	1	1
Montgomery	4		4	
Dauphin		3		3
Luzerne			1	
Totals	41	24	46	23

SOURCE: See Robert Brunhouse, *The Counter-Revolution in Pennsylvania, 1776–1790* (Harrisburg: The Pennsylvania Historical Commission, 1942): 207 for data on State Convention. Assignment of party for legislators in Eleventh General Assembly based on Guttman scale analysis of legislative roll-call votes. For details, see Owen Ireland, "The Crux of Politics: Religion and Party in Pennsylvania, 1778–1789," *William and Mary Quarterly* 42 (October 1985): 455 n. 5 and 456 n. 6.

The at-large congressional election in November 1788 produced further evidence of the partisan base of Pennsylvania's alignment on the Federal Constitution. The Antifederalist or the Harrisburg ticket contained the luminaries of the Constitutionalist party: Charles Pettit and Blair M'Clenahan, both prominent merchants from the city of Philadelphia; William Findley and Robert Whitehill, longtime back-

---

shifted its partisan attachment in 1787 and 1788, sending a solid Federalist delegation to the state convention in November 1787, and casting about 60 percent of its vote for the Federalist Lancaster ticket in the congressional election of November 1788. At present we lack sufficient information about Northampton to go much beyond these admittedly unsatisfying generalizations. Perhaps the work of historian Frank Fox who is now studying this county, will help us better to understand Northampton's political behavior.

country Constitutionalist officeholders; and William Irwin and William Montgomery. Regardless of nomenclature, the voters of the state could have little difficulty in recognizing the partisan complexion of this array. Equally conspicuous Republicans led the Federalists, or Lancaster ticket: George Clymer and Thomas FitzSimons, merchants from Philadelphia; plus backcountry Republicans Thomas Hartley of Lancaster, Henry Wynkoop of Bucks, Frederick A. Muhlenberg from Montgomery, and Thomas Scott from Westmoreland.[60]

The returns indicate that a high proportion of the participants cast straight party votes. Constitutionalists Charles Pettit of Philadelphia and William Findley of Westmoreland, for example, lived and operated in radically different electoral contexts at opposite ends of the state, but they came within 1.5 percent of each other in total vote (6,638 to 6,537). These two Constitutionalist-Antifederalists polled identical or near identical totals in eight counties and had similar totals in all but one of the remaining counties.

George Clymer and Thomas FitzSimons, probably the two most easily recognized Republicans on the Federalist ticket, had identical statewide totals (8,116 to 8,116), and polled identical or near identical votes in most of the counties (for example, 320 to 321 in Montgomery, 1,488 to 1,482 in York, 657 to 658 in Bucks, and 363 to 363 in Franklin). The other Republican-Federalists on the ticket seldom varied much from this pattern. Frederick A. Muhlenberg was the exception. The most prominent German Lutheran political figure in the state, Muhlenberg's total vote exceeded that of the other Federalists by about 500, and he ran considerably ahead of them in most heavily German counties. Furthermore, the magnitude of the Antifederalist vote in the eastern rural counties approximated the size of the Constitutionalist electorate in those counties. For example, in the Bucks County 1788 Assembly election and in the 1789 election of delegates to the state constitutional convention, Constitutionalist candidates polled about 28 percent. In the congressional election of 1788, the Antifederalist slate polled 29 percent of the Bucks vote.[61]

Across the state the correlation between Constitutionalist and Antifederalist electoral support also approximated the geographic distribution of the Scots-Irish and the Reformed peoples. Cumberland,

60. Brunhouse, *Counter-Revolution*, 343–44.
61. Ibid., 329–30, 343–44.

Westmoreland, Fayette, Dauphin, and Berks stand out as the most Constitutionalist and the most Antifederalist counties in Pennsylvania. The first three had concentrations of Scots-Irish (presumably Presbyterian) substantially higher than any rural Federalist county. Cumberland and York probably best illustrate the contrast. Both were on the west side of the Susquehanna; both produced grain for the world market; both were principally rural; and both were far from Philadelphia. But only about 14 percent of the population of York was Scots-Irish while this ethnic group made up about 34 percent of the population of Cumberland.[62] The remaining two Antifederalist counties, Dauphin and Berks, were predominantly German (52 and 85 percent respectively) with substantial members of Reformed. If we assume that the Scots-Irish were Presbyterians, then these five Constitutionalist-Antifederalist counties were the most Presbyterian and Reformed counties in rural Pennsylvania.[63]

We must regard these figures as tentative and suggestive. Although the calculations of the distribution of ethnic groups made by historian Thomas Purvis are the best we may ever have, the voting correlations are soft. We do not know that the ethnic and religious composition of the active electorate in any county approximated the ethnic and religious

---

62. Federalist Chester, with 17.5 percent Scots-Irish topped the Federalist list and this was considerably behind Cumberland (still in 1787–88 combined with Mifflin) with 30 to 37 percent, as well as Westmoreland and Fayette with 28 and 24 percent each. My ethnic classification of each county's population relies on Thomas Purvis, "Patterns of Ethnic-Settlement in Late Eighteenth Century Pennsylvania," *Western Pennsylvania Historical Magazine* 70 (April 1987): 107–22, esp. table 2, p. 115. I have used Purvis's figures for the proportion of only the Scots-Irish in each county. This is the most conservative estimate. The combined Scots-Irish, Scots, and Irish population in these three Antifederalist counties ranged from a little more than 51 percent in Fayette to nearly 70 percent in Mifflin. Purvis's methodology did not allow him to distinguish between Scots-Irish and Scots so he estimated the ratio at about 2 to 3; i.e., within the body of people from Scottish backgrounds, he assigned two thirds to the Scots-Irish and one third to the Scots. The "native" Irish remained a small proportion of the total population in every county and tended to replicate the settlement patterns of the Scots-Irish.

63. Calculations based on yearly parish census reports in *Minutes and Letters of the Coetus of the German Reformed Congregations in Pennsylvania, 1747–1792* (Philadelphia, 1903); and Lester J. Cappon, ed., *Atlas of Early American History: The Revolutionary Era: 1760–1790* (Princeton: Princeton University Press, for the Newberry Library and the Institute of Early American History and Culture, Williamsburg, Va., 1976), 69, 71. See also Purvis, "Patterns," 115. In 1775, 27 of 39 churches in Cumberland were Presbyterian, 31 of 39 Presbyterian or Reformed. Berks County appears to have been the center of Reformed settlement, shading off to the west in Dauphin, the east in Northampton, and the south in Montgomery.

composition of its total population. At the least, however, we can say with some confidence that the known distribution of Scots-Irish and Reformed peoples in Pennsylvania, was consistent with the distribution of Constitutionalist-Antifederalist electoral support in the backcountry.

On the basis of the evidence now available, we can draw few unequivocal conclusions about the role of economic considerations in the ratification controversy. Three things, however, stand out. Most commentators, whether Federalist or Antifederalist, agreed that Pennsylvania, and Pennsylvanians, faced serious economic dislocations in the late 1780s. Most also agreed that the proposed Federal Constitution promised to address many of the more pressing of these difficulties. Most important, however, the voters did not, it would appear, decide the question principally on such grounds. The publicists debated the political, not the economic, consequences of the Federal Constitution. The voters aligned themselves in ways that correlate almost perfectly with existing political divisions but these alignments bear no obvious relationship to conspicuous economic differences, whether we define those differences in terms of occupation, or in terms of access to and participation in a market economy.

Republicans could approve the Federal Constitution without reservation. Republicans in the city entered the controversy already mired in economic difficulties. Those in the backcountry faced increasing economic problems as the agricultural depression accelerated in 1787–88. Thus, both urban and rural Republican found that their economic needs reinforced their political interests. They supported ratification enthusiastically.

Constitutionalists faced a much less happy situation. Their political affiliations encouraged them to oppose ratification despite the anticipated economic benefits promised by the new system. Constitutionalists in the city seemed to exhibit greater sensitivity to the conflicting tensions. Large numbers of regular voters stayed home on Election Day, presumably Constitutionalists cross-cut by conflicting economic and party pressures. Constitutionalist merchants faced a particularly cruel dilemma. Their economic needs virtually compelled them to favor constitutional changes clearly at odds with their political commitments. Charles Pettit, Constitutionalist merchant and reluctant Antifederalist candidate, illustrates the point. In the race for election to the state convention in November 1787 he ran a less than energetic campaign.

He remained virtually invisible (and probably inactive), until after ratification was assured. Then, late in 1788, he emerged as a conspicuous and active Antifederalist.

Backcountry Constitutionalists within the Philadelphia trading area responded in a way largely consistent with party identification and principle. Some may have been ignorant of the deteriorating economic situation; others deliberately subordinated their economic to their political interests. Their response to the Federal Constitution appears to us, as it did to sympathetic contemporaries, as economically irrational. As Thomas Paine wrote to Daniel Clymer a year earlier: "she [the country] has suffered herself to be rent into factions, and sacrificed her interests to gratify her passions."[64]

In the far west, isolation, ignorance, misinformation, or misunderstanding may have prevented many voters from fully appreciating the long-range economic and security advantages the Federal Constitution promised them. On the other hand, these westerners had little reason to trust the easterners who would surely control the new national government. Be that as it may, Scots-Irish Presbyterians William Findley and John Smilie, longtime Constitutionalist spokesmen, led their partisan followers into the Antifederalist camp.

Thus, on one level, the Antifederalist and the Federalist leadership had, in the beginning, correctly assessed the power of partisan loyalties to move the electorate. On another level, however, both had erred in assuming that a strong partisan response would favor the Constitutionalist-Antifederalists. Unbeknown to them, or at least only partially glimpsed by them, on the eve of the ratification contest, the Republicans (and thus the future Federalists) had emerged as the new and overwhelming preference of the majority of the voters in the original stronghold of the Constitutionalists. This quiet counterrevolution largely determined the outcome of the ratification contest in Pennsylvania, and that is the subject of the next chapter.

---

64. Paine to Daniel Clymer, Philadelphia, September 1786, in the Daniel Clymer Papers, Historical Society of Pennsylvania. Although referring specifically to the divisions over the bank, Paine also castigated Berks County (Clymer's home county) for its failure to act on its common economic interests with Philadelphia.

7
The Quiet Counterrevolution

Political leaders on both sides of the ratification question knew that partisan attachments could shape voting behavior in powerful ways. Further, both assumed that a popular response based purely on partisan grounds would favor the opponents of ratification. In this estimate of the relative size of each party's popular base, however, both erred. By 1786, quietly, almost imperceptibly, Republicans had replaced Constitutionalists as the majority party. That quiet counterrevolution accounts for the Antifederalist defeat and the Federalist victory. And the explanation for that revolution lies primarily in the partisan political history of four counties in eastern Pennsylvania between 1778 and 1787.

The Ethnic-religious Counterrevolution

The Constitutionalists began as an eastern party. They drew the bulk of their leadership and their electoral support from the six counties surrounding Philadelphia: Bucks, Chester, Lancaster, Berks, Northampton, and Philadelphia County. In 1778–79 they controlled about 80 percent of this area's partisan seats in the legislature and these seats made up 80 percent of the Constitutionalists' total strength in the legislature. In this eastern area, Scots-Irish Presbyterians and their Reformed allies provided the bulk of the party's leadership and its electoral support.[1]

Eight years later, on the eve of the ratification controversy, the Constitutionalists had lost control of their original heartland. By 1786 they could count on only 28 percent of the partisan seats from this area while the Republicans held 72 percent. The Constitutionalists had kept Northampton, strengthened their position in Berks, and won two seats in the new county of Dauphin, erected from the largely Scots-Irish Presbyterian and Reformed areas of Lancaster and Berks. They had lost virtually everything else in the east (see Table 9). In Lancaster, Bucks, Chester, Philadelphia County (including its new subdivision, Montgomery), they had once commanded 95 percent of the partisan seats. They now held none. This loss made them the minority party by 1786 and set the stage for the Antifederalist defeat in 1787–88.

Each of these four counties followed a similar pattern of political change. Before independence, the Quaker (or Assembly) party had won most elections. In 1774 and early 1775, men from a wide range of ethnic and religious groups worked together to organize peaceful resistance to the British, but war and then independence shattered this collaboration. During 1775, virtually all Quakers, most of the German Sectarians, a portion of the Lutherans, and some Anglicans withdrew, leaving control of the Revolution to the Presbyterian, the Reformed, and a smattering of others. After independence, these patriots dominated their counties' legislative delegations, supported the new state constitution, and became Constitutionalists. Then, between 1780 and the end of the decade, Lutherans, Sectarians, and Quakers gradually rejoined the political community and supported the Republicans, finally ending the rule of the Constitutionalists.[2]

---

1. The Assembly of 1778–79 is the first with sufficient roll-call votes to permit reliable identification of party issues and thus the partisan attachment of the legislators. For details, see O. S. Ireland, "The Ethnic-Religious Dimension of Politics, 1778–1779" *William and Mary Quarterly* 30 (July 1973): 423–48. Party identification of legislators is based on Guttman-scale analysis of legislative roll-call votes. For more details, see Ireland, "The Crux of Politics: Religion and Party in Pennsylvania, 1778–1789," *William and Mary Quarterly* 42 (October 1985): 463–75, esp. 455 n. 5, and 456 no. 6.

2. Wayne L. Bockelman and O. S. Ireland, "The Internal Revolution in Pennsylvania: An Ethnic-Religious Interpretation," *Pennsylvania History* 41 (April 1974): 125–59, and esp. 147 and 150. Ireland, "The Ethnic-Religious Dimension"; Ireland, "Crux of Politics."

Table 9. Geographic Distribution of Partisan Assembly Seats, 1778 and 1786

County	1778 Constitutionalist	1778 Republican	1786 Constitutionalist	1786 Republican
City	2	4	0	5
Philadelphia	5	1	0	2
Montgomery (created from Philadelphia County)	—	—	0	4
Bucks	5	0	0	3
Chester	6	0	0	5
Lancaster	4	0	0	6
Dauphin (created from Lancaster)	—	—	2	0
Berks	3	3	4	1
Northampton	5	0	4	0
Subtotals	30	8	10	26
Statewide party totals	37	24	26	33
Percent of statewide party totals	81	33	39	79

SOURCE: Party classifications based on Guttman scale analysis of legislative roll-call votes. For details, see Owen Ireland, "The Crux of Politics: Religion and Party in Pennsylvania, 1778–1789," *William and Mary Quarterly* 42 (October 1985): 453–75, esp. 455 n. 5, 456 n. 6, and note 1, above.

Changes in voter turnout account for both the rise and the fall of the Constitutionalists in these eastern counties. From 1776 to 1780 relatively few people participated in the annual elections and they usually elected Scots-Irish Presbyterians and their Reformed allies. Large numbers of Quakers, Sectarians, Lutherans, and possibly Anglicans did not participate. Some denied the legitimacy of the new revolutionary government. Others refused to subscribe to the state loyalty oath (the Test Laws) and could not vote. From 1780 on, an increasing number of Lutherans, Sectarians, and Quakers qualified for the vote, turnout increased, and Republicans gained in strength.

The first step in this transformation of the electorate took place in 1779–80. The original Test Acts had disfranchised those refusing to abjure allegiance to George III, but had allowed nonjurors to change their minds at any time. Later Test Acts permanently excluded anyone not taking the oath by the end of 1779. This deadline forced the neutrals off the fence, and substantial numbers, especially the Lutherans, joined the Revolution.[3]

3. Robert Brunhouse, *Counter-Revolution in Pennsylvania, 1776–1790* (Harrisburg: Penn-

The end of the war further increased the size of the effective electorate. The Treaty of Paris in 1783, by recognizing the independence of the United States, absolved all residents of Pennsylvania of their earlier allegiance to the crown. Now, young men, especially from Sectarian and Quaker backgrounds, who had come of age since 1779, could in good conscience take the test oath and vote. Finally, in 1786, the legislature reopened the test rolls to those who had refused to subscribe in 1779. At each step in this process, voter turnout increased, Republican support grew, and first in one county and then in another, Republicans defeated Constitutionalists, as Anglicans, Quakers, and German Lutherans and Sectarians replaced Presbyterians and Reformed as representatives in the Assembly. Although all four counties approximated this pattern, each did so in its own way and the variation from county to county identifies the major issues, the range of ethnic-religious groups involved, and the links to the Federal Constitution.

Bucks County: The Quakers and the Test Acts

Bucks, north and a bit east of the city, and one of Penn's three original counties, was heavily Quaker and possibly the most English county in the state. Like all counties in Pennsylvania, however, it had a heterogeneous population: a sprinkling of Anglicans along the Delaware River, an enclave of Scots-Irish Presbyterians around Neshaminy; and a smattering of Dutch in the south and German Sectarians in the northwestern townships.

Before the Revolution, Bucks County overwhelmingly supported the Quaker party as Samuel Purviance learned in 1765. A Presbyterian merchant from Philadelphia and a zealous anti–Quaker party organizer, Purviance traveled the county court circuit building local support and recruiting candidates. "I went lately up to Bucks Court," he optimistically reported before the election, "in order to concert measures for their Election in pursuance of which we have appointed a considerable meeting of the Germans, Baptists, and Presbyterians to be held next

---

sylvania Historical Commission, 1942), 45, 46, 49. The Act of October 1, 1779, set varying final dates, depending primarily on distance from Philadelphia; December 1, 1779 was the latest. James T. Mitchell and Henry Flanders, *The Statutes at Large of Pennsylvania* (1903), chap. 852, 9:405–7. Owen S. Ireland, "Ethnic-Religious Dimensions."

Monday at Neshaminy." Purviance's efforts achieved little. Bucks voted the Quaker ticket in 1765 and continued to do so until (and even after) independence.[4]

In response to the British coercive acts in 1774, Quakers, Anglicans, Lutherans, Baptists, Presbyterians, and Reformed joined in the Bucks County Committee of Safety to send aid to Boston, and call for an intercolonial conference. In 1775, however, when the patriot organization (the Association), began to coerce dissidents and take on military functions, most Quakers pulled back. The provincewide Quaker leadership condemned the Continental Congress for promoting "Insurrections, Conspiracies & Illegal Assemblies" and disciplined by expulsion those who participated in the Association.

Before spring, a number of prominent Quaker patriots in Philadelphia were read out of the meeting, and that summer four Quakers on the Bucks Committee abruptly resigned. By August 1775, some 40 percent or more of Bucks County's adult males (taxables and single men) had refused to join the Association (now, a revolutionary militia). A year later, in September 1776 the Quaker Yearly Meeting proscribed voting and officeholding for all Quakers under the new revolutionary government of the state.[5]

The extraordinary election held during the first two days of October 1776 in Bucks indicates both the extent of disaffection and the aggressive tenor of that alienation. Pennsylvania's revolutionary Constitutional Convention, sitting since July, had declared Pennsylvania independent, governed the state while it drafted a new constitution, and then scheduled the election of a new legislature for November.

Bucks County chose to act as if none of this had occurred. Operating expressly under the authority of the old provincial charter, Bucks

---

4. Theodore Thayer, *Pennsylvania Politics and The Growth of Democracy, 1740–1776* (Harrisburg: Pennsylvania Historical and Museum Commission, 1953), 119. James Hutson, *Pennsylvania Politics, 1746–1770* (Princeton: Princeton University Press, 1972), 155. For sophisticated estimates of the ethnic composition of each county, see Thomas Purvis, "Patterns of Ethnic Settlement in Late Eighteenth Century Pennsylvania," *Western Pennsylvania Historical Magazine* 70 (April 1987): 107–22.

5. "Minutes of the Committee of Safety of Bucks County, PA, 1774–1776," *Pennsylvania Magazine of History and Biography* (hereafter *PMHB*) 15 (1891): 257–90. Jack D. Marietta, *The Reformation of American Quakerism, 1748–1783* (Philadelphia: University of Pennsylvania Press, 1984), 223–60. *Pennsylvania Archives*, ser. 2, 14:221–51 lists the names of nonassociators in Bucks. The proportion of nonassociators ranged from 50 percent in the borough and township of Bristol, to 40 percent in Bensalem, and 30 percent in Bedminster. For tax lists, see *Pennsylvania Archives*, ser. 3, 13:3–111.

County's prewar election officials held the county's annual fall election at the customary time and place. More than 600 respectable, property-owning men, with near unanimity, voted for the Quaker party representatives who had served them in the last (1775) colonial legislature. Thus, three months after the Declaration of Independence, a sizable minority had risked life, limb, and property, to elect traditional Quaker party leaders to a now nonexistent provincial legislature in direct defiance of the patriot government of the state.[6]

Not all Quakers in Bucks County viewed the Revolution in a negative light, but the exceptions confirm the rule as the experience of General John Lacey suggests. Born in the early 1750s, and raised in an old Quaker family in Bucks, Lacey grew up in a neighborhood where "none but Quaker Families resided." Appalled by British actions, he and some of his Quaker companions joined the Association. Lacey was captain. When the Quaker Meeting condemned the Association, however, all but Lacey fell away from the patriot cause.[7]

Although Lacey himself went on to a distinguished military career, he was unusual. His "fellow Quaker boys," by submitting to the discipline of the Quaker Meeting, responded more typically. Throughout the revolutionary years most Friends in Pennsylvania remained loyal to their religious communities and resisted the revolutionary government of Pennsylvania.[8]

After independence, the Test Acts disfranchised all who would not pledge allegiance to Pennsylvania and abjure the king. Quakers categorically refused compliance, as did most Mennonites, Schwenkfelders, Moravians, and other Sectarians. Many Lutherans remained ambivalent, cautious, and neutral as long as possible.

A number of indicators suggest that a sizable proportion of the potential electorate in Bucks was excluded. As noted above, in 1775 about half the taxable men in the county refused to serve in the Association. The wartime militia rolls suggest about the same degree of nonparticipation in the revolutionary military. Moreover, approximately 700 to 800 adult Quaker males lived in the county in the late eighteenth century; some 600 men

---

6. For details of the October 1776 "Loyalist" election in Bucks, see Pennsylvania Historical and Museum Commission, "Pennsylvania's Revolutionary Government, 1775–1790," microfilm reel 44.
7. John Lacey, "Memoirs of Brigadier-General John Lacey, of Pennsylvania," *PMHB* 25 (1901): 3, 1–13, 191–207, 341–54.
8. Marietta, *American Quakerism*, 223, 227–28, 229–30, 234–35.

voted in the "Loyalist" election of October 1776; and possibly up to 400 residents of the county paid a double tax in 1779 rather than take the test oath. No one of these indirect measures is decisive, but collectively they suggest that Bucks County may have had the highest proportion of political dissidents in the state.[9]

During the first decade of independence Bucks sent only Constitutionalists to the state legislature. Its representatives included at least four Presbyterians, two Baptists, one Lutheran, one German or Dutch Reformed, and two disowned Quakers. This heterogeneity precludes easy generalization but three characteristics stand out. First, Anglicans and Quakers were conspicuous by their scarcity; second, this victorious configuration approximates the array that Samuel Purviance had hoped to unite against the Quaker party in Bucks in 1765 ("Germans, Baptists & Presbyterians"); and third, Presbyterians and Reformed now constituted the single largest identifiable element among these legislators.[10]

The careers of Joseph Galloway, Joseph Hart, and Francis Murray illustrate the change. Before the war, Galloway, a wealthy English Anglican who led the Quaker party in the provincial legislature, held a safe elected seat in Bucks. Hart, a Baptist of substantial wealth and an adherent of the Proprietary party, had held only such appointed offices as were at the disposal of the Proprietary government. Murray, a Presbyterian tavernkeeper, was appointed by the proprietor to the Court of Quarter Sessions in 1775.[11]

With the Revolution, Galloway and his party disappeared while Hart and Murray emerged as the leaders of the revolutionary forces. Hart headed the county's delegation to the Provincial Convention of July 1774, chaired its Committee of Safety from the fall of 1774 through

---

9. Allan Nevins, *The American States During and After the Revolution, 1775–1789* (New York: Macmillan, 1924), 277. Approximately 40 percent of the taxable and single men in a sample of three political subdivisions in Bucks were listed as nonassociators in August 1775 (see note 5). The county militia muster lists 3,205 officers and men. The U.S. Census for 1790 lists 6,575 men aged 16 and over in Bucks. See *Pennsylvania Archives*, ser. 2, 14:145–220. About 1,570 Quakers lived in Bucks in 1760, or 700–800 men, none of whom could remain in the meeting and vote or hold public office after September 1776. Bucks Monthly Meeting disciplined about 50 for war-related offenses. See Kenneth Radbill, "The Socioeconomic Background of Nonpacifist Quakers During the American Revolution" (Ph.D. diss., University of Arizona, 1971), 89, 95. For tax lists, see *Pennsylvania Archives*, ser. 3, 13:passim.

10. Based on Guttman-scale analysis of legislative roll-call votes. See above, note 1.

11. Biographical information on Joseph Hart has been gleaned from *PMHB* 3:439–40; 4:161; 15:257–90; 41:290–91; *Pennsylvania Journal*, January 25, 1775; For Bucks tax lists, see *Pennsylvania Archives*, ser. 3, 13:passim.

independence, and represented his county in the state constitutional convention in 1776. Murray spent most of the war years in the military, serving in New York, New Jersey, and Pennsylvania, and twice spending protracted periods as a prisoner of war. In time Hart and Murray developed a correspondence with Presbyterian George Bryan, organized their county for the Constitutionalist party, and held a number of military and civilian posts in the new government.[12]

Constitutionalists lost their power in Bucks abruptly in 1786 when the voters chose a solid Republican delegation to the Assembly. From then through the end of the decade, Republicans controlled Bucks while Anglicans and Quakers dominated the county's legislative delegation. The cause is not hard to find.[13] Voter turnout tells the story. Bucks had at least 3,500 taxables in the revolutionary era and prewar turnout could range from about 1,000 to 1,500. In sharp contrast, about 100 men participated in the first election under the new constitution (November 1776). The next year, with the British troops occupying nearby Philadelphia, few men in Bucks voted. Then, during the remainder of the war years, the number of voters crept up slowly, averaging a bit above 500 over the five-year period 1779–83. The 1786 figure for the first time matched prewar levels and turnout continued to increase thereafter, approaching 1,730 in 1789, a more than 300 percent increase over the 1779–83 average.[14]

12. For biographical information on Hart, see note 11, above. Joseph Hart to George Bryan, Newtown (Bucks), January 1, 1787; March 7, 1787; George Bryan Papers, Historical Society of Pennsylvania.

13. Partisan classifications are based on Guttman-scale analysis described above. The new and extraordinary land tax imposed by the Constitutionalists in the spring of 1785 may have contributed to this upsurge in voting and to this partisan shift (See Chapters 5 and 6). Statewide voting patterns, however, are not consistent with such a view. The increase in voter participation and the shift to the Republicans, occurred principally in those counties with high proportions of those ethnic-religious groups that had resisted the Test Acts: Bucks, Chester, Montgomery, Lancaster, and Philadelphia County; and not in those equally rural and agricultural counties with proportionately high numbers of Presbyterians and Reformed: Cumberland, Dauphin, and Berks east of the mountains; Westmoreland and Fayette in the far west.

14. Population estimates from *U.S. Census for 1790*; tax lists in *Pennsylvania Archives*, ser. 3, vol. 13, and E. B. Greene and V. D. Harrington, *American Population Before the Federal Census of 1790* (New York: Columbia University Press, 1932), 113–17. The size of the county's Assembly delegation (four to five) suggests about 4,000–5,000 taxables at a ratio of about one representative for each 800–1,000 taxables. The 1742 vote is from Alan Tully, *William Penn's Legacy* (Baltimore: Johns Hopkins University Press, 1977), 226. The 1765 vote is from Robert J. Dinkin, *Voting in Provincial America* (Westwood, Conn.: Greenwood, 1977), 158. Others from Brunhouse, *Counter-Revolution*, 329–30, and "Pennsylvania's Revolutionary Governments, 1775–1790," microfilm reel 44. The 1782 returns are puzzling.

At least three factors combined to produce this early decline and later resurgence in voter participation. In the early years many men voluntarily withdrew. Later some reconciled themselves to the patriot cause and rejoined the political community. Others were first disfranchised and then reenfranchised by modification of the Test Acts. In addition, at the beginning of the era the Quaker withdrawal and the Lutheran neutrality eliminated two powerful vehicles for mobilizing Republican voters. The political reemergence of the Lutherans after 1779 and of the Quakers in the late 1780s eased this problem for Republicans and contributed to both their upsurge in participation and their success.[15]

The dramatic increase in voter participation favored the Republicans rather than the Constitutionalists, principally because of the position each party had taken on the Test Acts. During the war, in Bucks (as across the state), the Constitutionalists had championed the state loyalty oaths and pursued and punished nonjurors. After the war, Constitutionalists resisted reconciliation. As a "Plain Common Freeman" cautioned: "In this day of our triumph, . . . we must not be surprised to see crowds pressing forward to share the fruits of our perseverance and sufferings whose past services have been a steady opposition to our efforts."[16]

In statewide postwar debates, defenders of the Test Acts said that they hated Tories and traitors, and singled out the Quakers for particular attention. Some publicists attempted to stir up class or status hostilities. "Censor," for example, asserted that most nonjurors were rich, that only the rich or the aspiring aristocrats favored repeal of the

---

We have the reported totals for the five winning Assembly candidates (1,033–681), and for both candidates for the one seat on the SEC (777 and 217). These figures suggest a total turnout of over 1,000. I think this is much too high, and suspect a recording error of about 500. In those years for which we have complete returns, the high vote for local candidates (sheriff, coroner, commissioner, assessor) usually approximated total turnout (see returns for October 1776, and for 1783, 1786, and 1788). In 1782 the sheriff polled 541 votes and the coroner 523, suggesting a turnout in the mid-500s, a figure consistent with the results in 1780 and 1783.

15. I am grateful to Michael Zuckerman and Marianne Wokeck for helping me see this point.

16. Ireland, "Ethnic-Religious Dimension." *Freeman's Journal*, 10/2/82. Roger Brown argues that tax policy largely accounts for voter shifts to Constitutionalists in 1784. Close scrutiny of election returns over time raises serious questions about this view. Tax policy appears to bear little direct relationship to voter behavior in Bucks. For more on this question, see note 31 below. Roger Brown, *Redeeming the Republic: Federalists, Taxation, and the Origins of the Constitution* (Baltimore: Johns Hopkins University Press, 1993), 53–68.

tests, and that they did so because of their personal identification with the rich and arrogant Quakers who had remained secretly loyal to the British. Others charged that the Republican opponents of the Test Acts sought partisan political advantage by enfranchising nonjurors.[17]

The Philadelphia militia took a similar position. Meeting on May 29, 1783, it protested the return of "such persons as have joined the enemy or have been expelled this or any other of the United States." Two weeks later a mass meeting at the State House in Philadelphia resolved to keep the disaffected from returning, to ensure the prompt payment of the public debt, and to create a committee of correspondence to carry these resolutions into effect. It then warned the disaffected that "unless they depart this state within ten days ... [they] ... will be dealt with in a proper manner."[18] The Constitutionalists staged similar meetings in Bucks. Representatives from almost every town assembled at Bennet's Tavern on July 29 where, guided by Constitutionalist leader Joseph Hart, they condemned traitors and Tories, charged their legislators to protect the state constitution of 1776 and urged them "to oppose with your strongest efforts, any attempt ... to repeal the test laws now in force."[19]

The next year (the legislative year 1783–84), Bucks County Constitutionalists again publicly supported the tests. The state legislature, with a slight Republican edge, was about to reopen the test rolls when nineteen Constitutionalist legislators withdrew from the house, broke the quorum, and prematurely ended the legislative year. At a meeting at Newtown on November 1, 1784, some twenty-one leaders from sixteen of the Bucks townships commended their four assemblymen for joining this exodus. They then declared their support for the continued political exclusion of those who had not supported the war.[20]

The Republicans throughout the state had long opposed the Test Acts, and after the war urged speedy repeal. Although offering a wide range of justifications, they concentrated on two closely linked themes. First, continuing the Test Acts was undemocratic. It disenfranchised many peaceful residents and violated the state constitution, the civil

17. See especially "Uniform," *Freeman's Journal*, 9/12/81; "A Constitutionalist," ibid., 9/28/81; "Comus," ibid., 1/30/82; "Censor," ibid., 1/16/82 and 2/6/82.
18. *Freeman's Journal*, 6/4/83, 6/18/83, 7/9/83.
19. *Freeman's Journal*, 7/2/83, 8/13/83.
20. Minutes, Pennsylvania General Assembly, September 29, 1784. *Pennsylvania Gazette*, 11/10/84.

liberties of the nonjurors, and the principles of the American Revolution. "Why should they [nonjurors] not have a voice in the government, which they cheerfully and generously support?" Republicans asked. Obviously, they concluded, supporters of the tests feared "universal equality in voting."[21]

Second, Republicans charged Constitutionalists with partisan motives. The wording of the oath, they argued, particularly the phrase "to maintain and support the independence thereof," prevented many sympathetic pacifists from subscribing. Some pacifists believed that the oath in this form committed them to bearing arms. Republicans argued that Constitutionalists had intended just such a result. These tests, a "Citizen of Philadelphia" asserted, "are as often made use of as engines of a ruling party, to entrap and punish such people as they suppose inimical to themselves." "A Pennsylvania Officer" offered a similar but more particular condemnation. It is all done, he said, "to gratify the malice of a poor old man [George Bryan] crazy with religious bigotry and political rage."[22]

In the Assembly of 1785–86 the Republican efforts to reopen the test rolls finally bore fruit and in the fall 1786 election voter turnout in Bucks surged to a new high (almost tripling the 1783 figure; see Table 10). The bulk of this massive political outpouring went to the Republicans.[23]

The results ended Constitutionalist control in Bucks and by 1787 Joseph Hart found himself clinging to a few remnants of power. His son, John, the receiver of taxes and the recorder of deeds for the county, had died. Hart, already a justice of the peace and a member of the Court of Quarter Sessions, had assumed his son's responsibilities as well. Although this burden weighed heavily on the old politician, he purchased the house where his son had lived in Newtown, hired a clerk, a servant, and a housekeeper ("wife not choosing yet to keep me company") and would, he said, spend five days at Newtown and one at home each week, attempting to do both jobs. If not, the cause of "the

---

21. Ireland, "Ethnic-Religious Dimension"; *Pennsylvania Gazetteer*, 8/18/84, 12/19/84, 1/5/85, 1/12/85, 1/26/85; *Independent Gazette*, 1/26/85.
22. *Pennsylvania Gazette*, 1/12/85, 1/19/85; *Freeman's Journal*, 9/12/81.
23. The new legislation provided an opportunity to subscribe for those who had failed to meet the 1779 deadline. A small number of Constitutionalist assemblymen broke ranks and supported this Republican measure. For further discussion of this, see below. Brunhouse, *Counter-Revolution*, 179–81.

Table 10. Increases in Turnout and in Republican Strength, Bucks County, 1783–1789

Year	Total Turnout	Increase over 1783	Republican Share of Total Vote	Constitutionalist Share of Total Vote	Percent[a]
1783	570	—	66–160	391–485	85
1786	1,420	850	937–979	442–472	33
1789	1,702	1,130	1,224–1,257	449–482	28
1789[b]	1,730	1,160	1,237–1,255	445–502	29
1788[c]	883	313	632–681	208–259	29

SOURCE: Robert Brunhouse, *The Counter-Revolution in Pennsylvania, 1776–1790* (Harrisburg: The Pennsylvania Historical Commission, 1942), 329–30, 343–44; Merrill Jensen and Robert Becker, eds., *The Documentary History of the First Federal Elections, 1788–1790* (Madison, Wisc., 1976), 1:378–79.

[a] = Percent calculated: highest possible Constitutionalist vote/total vote.

[b] = Votes cast in election of delegates to the state constitutional convention.

[c] = Votes cast in election of U.S. Congressmen in November 1788.

Genuine whig interest (weak enough already) must fail." If he resigned the offices, "there would be no preventing [them] going into the hands of a Republican." On the other hand, if he spent most of his time in Newtown, he doubted "having time to fill my place in the Court." Without him in the court, he predicted, the party's "interests must fail."[24]

In the fall of 1787, Hart's friend and collaborator, Francis Murray, felt overwhelmed, discouraged, and impotent in the face of the new Quaker hegemony. Murray, converted to Antifederalism by George Bryan and John Nicholson, considered organizing an Antifederalist ticket in Bucks, and then gave it up. There was, he said "little hope of carrying it as the Quakers are entirely in favor of the new constitution." In Murray's mind, no one could hope to challenge the dominant Quakers in Bucks.[25]

24. Joseph Hart to George Bryan, 1/1/87 and 3/7/87, George Bryan Papers, Historical Society of Pennsylvania. In fact, Hart was both right and wrong. Right in assuming that the political leaders thought of these appointments in party terms; wrong in that a Republican would be the next recorder and register. Hart died soon after and George Bryan reported that "Mr. James Hanna, a Constitutionalist attorney at law at Newtown, was . . . very unexpectedly chosen to succeed" Hart. See Bryan to —, Philadelphia, 3/7/88, in Jensen 16:490.

25. Hart to Bryan, 10/3/87, Bryan Papers. Francis Murray to John Nicholson, 11/1/87, in Merrill Jensen, ed., *The Documentary History of the Ratification of the Constitution*, vol. 2, *Ratification of the Constitution by the States: Pennsylvania* (Madison: State Historical Society of Wisconsin, 1976), 207. Murray acted as an intermediary between Judge Bryan and Col.

The congressional election in November 1788 confirmed Murray's pessimism. In Bucks, the statewide Federalist candidates averaged about 650 votes each while William Findley and Charles Pettit, probably the best-known candidates on the Antifederalist ticket, received 234 and 220 votes respectively. This Antifederalist vote (about 29 percent), approximately the proportion of the popular vote polled by Constitutionalist Assembly candidates in local elections in 1786 and in 1789 (see Table 10).

The massive increase in voter participation in Bucks ended the reign of the Constitutionalists in 1786 and threw the county solidly into the Federalist camp the next year. The Quakers and their pacifist and Sectarian allies, like most Pennsylvanians, favored strengthening the powers of Congress. The identification of the Constitutionalists as the Antifederalists did nothing to dampen Quaker enthusiasm for the Federal Constitution. Moreover, the thought that the Federal Constitution might discredit the state constitution of 1776 could have saddened few of these who had suffered under the state's unicameral legislature for over a decade. Finally, Antifederalist depiction of the horrors of Federal limits on state sovereignty carried fewer negative connotations to those who had suffered at the hands of the state government.

Before the Revolution, Quakers in Pennsylvania had looked to London for protection against what they saw as the rising tide of Scots-Irish Presbyterian zealots. Between 1778 and 1786, the Constitutionalist party, dominated by Scots-Irish Presbyterian, had fulfilled the Quakers' worst apprehensions. For Quakers in 1787 any central authority capable of limiting state freedom of action offered a new external protection from the vagaries of state politics.[26]

Chester County: Quakers, Anglicans, and Scots-Irish Presbyterians

Chester County, south and west of Philadelphia along the Delaware River, was also one of Pennsylvania's original three counties. Its popula-

---

Joseph Hart. He served as county lieutenant for Bucks in the early 1780s. Hart to Bryan, 1/1/87, Bryan Papers, Historical Society of Pennsylvania.

26. For a discussion of the Quaker party, its conflicts with the Proprietors and the Presbyterians, as well as its efforts to convert Pennsylvania from a proprietary to a royal

tion included probably the heaviest concentrations of Anglicans and Swedish Lutherans anywhere in the state outside the city of Philadelphia, as well as a growing number of Methodists, and a variety of German, Welsh, and English Baptists. Quakers, the largest identifiable religious group in the county, had come from English, Irish, and Welsh backgrounds. A sizable number of German Lutherans and Reformed lived in the county's northern townships.[27] The Scots-Irish Presbyterians, a large minority in the county as a whole, lived principally in those southwest townships closest to the Delaware port of New Castle. They had pressed unsuccessfully for political recognition from early on. Before the Revolution the Quaker party had dominated the county. The Anglican-led Proprietary party looked to the Presbyterians for support but seldom successfully challenged the Quakers and their allies at the polls.[28]

In the annual Assembly elections before the war, Anglicans sometimes spoke for each party. For example, in the 1750s, Anthony Wayne's father, Isaac, confronted William Moore in a bitter contest. Moore, an Anglican (probably of Irish background) from Chestertown in the northern and less Quaker regions of the county, worked with the Reverend William Smith, the Anglican provost of the College of Phila-

---

colony in the mid-1760s see James H. Hutson, *Pennsylvania Politics, 1746–1770: The Movement for Royal Government and Its Consequences* (Princeton: Princeton University Press, 1972), esp. 101–21.

27. Lemon, *Best Poor Man's Country: A Geographical Study of Early Southeastern Pennsylvania* (Baltimore: Johns Hopkins University Press, 1972), 14, 18, 19, 21, 40–48, 51, 55. Isaac Backus, *The Diary of Isaac Backus*, ed. William McLoughlin (Providence: Brown University Press, 1979). Henry Seidel Canby, *The Brandywine* (New York: Farrar and Rinehart, 1941). J. Smith Futhey, "Papers: Chester County, PA," Historical Society of Pennsylvania (clippings). J. Smith Futhey and Gilbert Cope, *History of Chester County, Pa.* (Philadelphia: Louis H. Everts, 1881). Charles W. Heathcote, *History of Chester County, Pa.* (West Chester, Pa.: Horace F. Temple, 1926). Robert G. Torbet, *A History of the Baptists*, 3d ed. (Valley Forge, Pa.: Judson Press, 1950, 1963). The total number of Anglican parishes in Chester (6) approximated the total number of Presbyterian churches in the county (8), but Anglican parishioners seem to have been considerably less numerous than Presbyterians. For a discussion of the Swedish Lutherans, and their ties to the Anglicans, see Susan Klepp, "Five Early Pennsylvania Censuses," *PMHB* 106 (October 1982): 483–514. Purvis, "Patterns of Ethnic Settlement," 115.

28. Theodore Thayer, *Pennsylvania Politics and the Growth of Democracy, 1740–1776* (Harrisburg: Pennsylvania Historical and Museum Commission, 1953), 42. Hutson, *Pennsylvania Politics, 1746–1770*, 170, 214. Henry Muhlenberg, *The Journals of Henry Melchior Muhlenberg*, trans. Theodore G. Tappert and John W. Doberstein (Philadelphia: Evangelical Lutheran Ministerium of Pennsylvania and Adjacent States, 1942–58), February 15, 1765, 2:192.

delphia, and with the Proprietary party. Wayne, an Anglican who lived in a more central part of the county closer to the area of heavy Quaker settlement, worked with the Quaker party. Before the dispute ended, Wayne was in the Assembly, Moore was in jail, and Smith was in London, appealing to the Privy Council on behalf of himself and his friend and future father-in-law, William Moore, both of whom were being punished by the Quaker-dominated legislature for disrespect. Meanwhile, the Presbyterians in Chester County played a subsidiary and subordinate political role, one element, at best, in a weak and diverse Proprietary coalition.[29]

During the imperial crises of the mid-1770s, men from most ethnic and religious groups in Chester collaborated in resisting the British, in aiding Boston, and in building the Association. Anglican Anthony Wayne, Quaker Evan Evans, Presbyterian Patrick Anderson, and Baptist Richard Thomas, joined with Swedish Anglican Sketchley Morton, Quaker John Hannum, and Presbyterians William Montgomery and John Hart in countywide extralegal revolutionary committees and in representing the county in provincewide conventions.

As in each of these eastern counties, voter turnout in Chester dropped sharply after independence. In the fall 1777 election, held shortly after the British army had rampaged through the county on its way to Philadelphia, no more than 500 men voted. Two years later some 1,300 to 1,500 men participated in the Assembly election. In 1784, turnout increased by a third or more, to slightly more than 2,000 and thereafter grew rapidly to at least 4,000 (possibly 5,700) in 1789, almost triple the wartime high of 1,500 and eight to ten times higher than in 1777.[30]

At least three aspects of this pattern set Chester apart. First, during the war, overall voter turnout here was somewhat stronger than in Bucks. Second throughout the war neither party achieved secure ascendancy. In 1779 and again in 1780, for example, little more than a hundred votes separated the winners from the losers. Third, between 1779 and 1783, the Republicans maintained a precarious popular edge in Chester.

In 1778 the Constitutionalist-dominated legislature had settled a

29. Thayer, *Pennsylvania Politics*, 69–71.
30. Chester County election returns in Brunhouse, *Counter-Revolution*, 330–40; and *Pennsylvania Archives*, ser. 6, 11:128–45; *Pennsylvania Evening Post*, December 18, 1778. The figure for 1789 combines the minimum possible turnout in Chester and in the new county of Delaware, erected from Chester's southeastern township.

disputed election by awarding Chester's Assembly seats to Constitutionalist candidates. The next year, in the fall of 1779, while the Constitutionalists strengthened their hold on most areas of the state, the Republicans gained six of Chester's eight Assembly seats. Then, in the following four years Republicans tenaciously held on to their edge, each year winning a majority of the seats by minuscule margins. In 1784 the Republicans won permanent control of the county, and then, in 1786 with the modification of the Test Acts, gained an overwhelming numerical superiority.[31]

The dispute over the Test Acts played a major role in the shifting partisan history of Chester. In the legislature and on the hustings Chester Constitutionalists favored the Test Acts. In the fall of 1783, for example, Samuel Cunningham, from West Nantmeal, and John Culbertson, from East Caln, protested the election of Republicans to the house, charging, in harsh words, that nonjurors had been allowed to vote. Both Cunningham and Culbertson were Constitutionalists, legislators, Presbyterians, and well-to-do. Earlier that year both men had helped organize Chester militia's protest against the return of Tories and traitors, and both sat on the East Cain committee of correspondence which coordinated this effort.[32]

Chester County Republicans had urged moderation during the war and demanded repeal of the Test Acts at the war's end. Republicans Anthony Wayne, Richard Willing, and Richard Ralston, all assemblymen, and all from non-Calvinist religious backgrounds, joined others in

---

[31]. Roger Brown has recently explained the earlier Constitutionalist statewide victory in the fall of 1784 as a popular reaction against Republican efforts to impose high taxes and collect them in specie between 1780 and 1783. Resentments against taxes may have played a part in turning Republicans out of office in 1784 and in turning Constitutionalists out of office in 1785 and 1786. Close examination of the actual voting in the fall of 1784, and of the overall pattern in the 1780s, however, suggests that concerns over taxes remained, at best, a contributing factor. In general, increased voter turnout in 1784 actually strengthened Republicans in Chester as well as in other farm counties. The Constitutionalist victory in the fall of 1784 resulted principally from the dramatic shifts in Philadelphia County and city that gave the Constitutionalists a slight edge in the legislature. This edge, in turn, allowed them to award all the seats in the disputed election in Lancaster (where Republicans outpolled the Constitutionalists) to the Constitutionalists, thus enlarging their majority. For a discussion of the election of 1784 in Philadelphia County and city as well as in Lancaster, see below. Brown, *Redeeming the Republic: Federalists, Taxation, and the Origins of the Constitution.* (Baltimore: Johns Hopkins University Press, 1993), 53–68.

[32]. *Pennsylvania Gazette*, 6/12/79, announced that Cunningham had chaired a meeting of citizens at the home of Elijah Weed. *Pennsylvania Archives*, ser. 3, 12:61, 105, 279, 428, 567, 689. *Freeman's Journal*, 7/2/83; 8/13/83.

a public statement against the Test Acts in December 1784. They argued that continuation of the Test Acts violated the state constitution, the state bill of rights, and the principles of the American Revolution. They also asserted that the Test Acts persecuted people for their religious beliefs, threw government into the hands of foreigners (probably the Scots-Irish), created an oppressive aristocracy, and established a dangerous precedent that might in the future serve to "confine the power of the state to a party or a Religious Sect."33

In Chester, as in the other eastern counties, voters aligned themselves in distinct ethnic and religious configurations. For example, Scots-Irish Presbyterians predominated in the second electoral district. In 1779 that district supported the Presbyterian Constitutionalist candidates with an almost regimental discipline, casting an average 478 votes for the Constitutionalists and only 60 to 160 for the Republicans. In a parallel way, that same year, the largely Anglican-Quaker first election district averaged 301 votes for the Republicans and only 36 to 52 for the Constitutionalists.34

Officeholders lined up in much the same way. Every Republican legislator but one had Anglican, Quaker, or Baptist roots and every Constitutionalist legislator for whom data are available was from a Presbyterian background. In the same vein, the shift to Republican control at the end of the war paralleled a shift in the geographic origins of the successful candidates for the Assembly. Between 1778 and 1783 men from the Scots-Irish enclave in the second election district held seventeen of the Assembly seats; between 1784 and 1786 they held only one.

Benjamin Rush's observation had been right on the mark. "A majority of the Presbyterians are in favor of the [state] Constitution," he had written to Anthony Wayne in 1777, "and in no part of the State do they discover more Zeal for it than in Chester." As Rush's comment indicates and as the election returns confirm, the basic political alignment in Chester County pitted the Presbyterians against all others.35

Although largely alone, Chester's Presbyterians were numerous and

---

33. *Pennsylvania Gazette*, 12/29/84.
34. *Pennsylvania Archives*, ser. 6, 11:130–35. Ireland, "Ethnic-Religious Dimension," 442–45.
35. Ireland, "Crux of Politics"; B. Rush to A. Wayne, May or June 1777, in Charles J. Stille, *Major-General Anthony Wayne and the Pennsylvania Line in the Continental Army* (Port Washington, N.Y.: Kennikat Press, 1968. Reprint of the 1893 ed.), 68–69.

powerful. Equally important, they exhibited a keen sense of group identity. They had settled in homogeneous enclaves in those southern and western townships most readily accessible from New Castle. Their geographical concentration, as well as their brogue, their Calvinism, and their generally hostile reception all combined to heighten, if indeed not create, a perception of themselves as a separate people, and a consciousness of themselves as a distinct community. Thomas McKean illustrates the pattern.[36]

McKean's personal and professional life reflect his involvement in this Irish community. A third-generation Pennsylvanian, McKean's grandmother, Susanna, had settled in the heart of the Scots-Irish community in southwestern Chester. McKean's father, William, kept a tavern and married the daughter of a Scots-Irish immigrant neighbor. Thomas McKean and his brother Robert, along with Charles Thomson, the future "Sam Adams of Pennsylvania," and John Ewing, the future Presbyterian divine and provost of the University of Pennsylvania, attended the parochial school conducted by the Reverend Francis Alison in New London. McKean then studied law with his Scots-Irish Presbyterian cousin, David Finney, and as a practicing attorney drew a major portion of his clientele from the Irish and Presbyterians in Chester and the Lower Counties (i.e., Delaware).

In time, McKean found favor with the Proprietary interests, won a seat in the Delaware Assembly and went on to a rather distinguished political career. Throughout, however, as his biographer G. S. Rowe has explained, he remained "part of a minority faction—the country party. Much of his failure . . . was due to religious factors and the lingering prejudice towards the Scots-Irish in Delaware." His limited success heightened his resentment, especially of the Anglican mercantile faction and landed interests that dominated Delaware before 1776.[37]

McKean's leadership in the revolutionary movement put him in the mainstream of Presbyterian behavior. His own pastor, the Reverend Joseph Montgomery (later a Constitutionalist candidate for Speaker of

---

36. Wokeck argues that the Irish migration peaked twice in the colonial period: once in the late 1720s and again in the decade before the Revolution. The bulk of the Scots-Irish Presbyterians in Chester probably came with the earlier wave. Marianne Wokeck, "A Tide of Alien Tongues: The Flow and Ebb of German Immigration to Pennsylvania, 1683–1776" (Ph.D. diss., Temple University, 1983), esp. 245, and 267–68. Wokeck also suggests a heavy influx through New Castle in the early period (245 and 303 n. 71).

37. G. S. Rowe, *Thomas McKean: The Shaping of an American Republican* (Boulder: Colorado Associated University Press, 1978), esp. 5, 6, 8, 23, 21, 45–46.

the Pennsylvania Assembly) vehemently denounced the British measures, and "Delaware Presbyterians increasingly looked to McKean as a spokesman in their cause." In his new position of power, he struck vigorously at the Anglicans, charging that the ministers of the Society for the Propagation of the Gospel in Foreign Parts (the missionary arm of the Anglican Church) were telling their "illiterate, ignorant and bigoted" parishioners that opposition to England "was a plan of the Presbyterians to get their religion established."[38]

After independence, McKean, like most educated political observers, opposed the state's new system of government. He viewed a unicameral legislature as an abomination pregnant with mischief. Stability and liberty came only from a balanced constitutional structure, he believed. By mid-1777, however, McKean, like many other prominent Presbyterians, found he could live with this constitutional innovation. He made peace with its most politically astute Scots-Irish defender, vice president George Bryan (an old acquaintance from the prewar Proprietary party), became chief justice of the new state, and established a fierce reputation for hanging traitors.[39]

After 1777, McKean, like most of his Scots-Irish Presbyterian brethren, championed the state loyalty oaths, the execution of convicted Quaker collaborators, the destruction of the Anglican-controlled College of Philadelphia, and the erection of the Presbyterian-dominated University of Pennsylvania (under the leadership of his old parochial schoolmate, Provost John Ewing). A man of passion who felt strongly, spoke boldly, and acted decisively against his enemies, McKean seemed to epitomize the attitude of the Scots-Irish Presbyterians in his county and in his party.[40]

In spite of their numbers, their unity, and their commitment to the Revolution, however, the Scots-Irish Presbyterians in Chester could not easily control their county because of the size and the multiplicity of the groups aligned against them. The German Lutherans, like the Reformed, were relatively few and politically unimportant in Chester. A surprising

38. Rowe, *McKean*, 33, 60, 61.
39. Ibid., 93–94, 114, 116, 119.
40. Stories abound of Presbyterian congregations bereft of able-bodied men because all, including their ministers, were off fighting the British. A number of well-known Presbyterian clergymen actively supported civil and the military action against the British. The Rev. Robert Blair of Faggs Manor, the Rev. John Carmichael of Brandywine Manor, and Col. Andrew Boyd, son of the Rev. Boyd of Upper Octorara all played conspicuous patriot roles. Futhey and Cope, *Chester Co.*, 250.

number of Quakers, especially those from non-English backgrounds, remained politically active in the revolutionary movement and then supported the emerging Republican party.⁴¹

The war may have contributed to this unusual Quaker behavior. Chester County saw more of the British army than most areas of the state and Dr. Jonathan Morris, himself a Quaker and later a Republican assemblyman, described the impact that the British troops had on his friend and neighbor Anthony Morris. "A Quaker gentleman about forty-five years of age" (as Jonathan Morris described himself), had gone to Philadelphia for medicines and returned with news that the British were about to surprise Washington at Valley Forge." He and Anthony Morris warned Washington, "for which Anthony Morris house was broken up for him," destroying much of his valuable furniture and furnishings. Anthony, presumably a pacifist Quaker, but angry beyond reason, borrowed a gun, chased and shot one of the British soldiers responsible for the destruction. The soldiers, in turn, beat, cut and left Anthony for dead. Anthony Morris recovered, but his behavior and his experiences suggest the ways in which day-to-day contact between civilian and military personnel could erode both pacifist principles and political neutrality in Chester.⁴²

Anglicans made up the largest and most prominent element in the Republican coalition in Chester. Many, if not most, came to support the American cause and then moved into the Republican party.⁴³ In this

---

41. For example, of the ten men from Quaker families who served in the Assembly from Chester between 1778 and 1786 (all acting in ways proscribed by the English-dominated Yearly Meeting) five were Welsh, one was Irish, and the national origins of the other four are unknown. Although most of Chester's Quakers responded to the discipline of the meeting, some, especially among the non-English, did not. It is possible that the midcentury religious reformation movement among Pennsylvania's Quakers had less impact among these non-English Friends. It is also possible that the ethnic identity of the non-English Quakers made them less reluctant to oppose Great Britain.

42. "A Reminiscence of the Revolution, 1777," Society Collection, Historical Society of Pennsylvania.

43. David L. Holmes, "The Episcopal Church and the American Revolution," *Historical Magazine of the Protestant Episcopal Church* 47 (September 1978): 261–91. Deborah Matheas Gough, "Pluralism, Politics and Power Struggles: The Church of England in Colonial Philadelphia, 1695–1789" (Ph.D. diss., University of Pennsylvania, 1978) found the Anglicans in Philadelphia deeply divided on independence (516) and the vestry leaning toward the Tory side until after the British left Philadelphia in 1778 (559–62). See also Jonathan Clark, "The Problem of Allegiance in Revolutionary Poughkeepsie," in David Hall, John Murrin, and Thad W. Tate, eds., *Saints and Revolutionaries: Essays on Early American History* (New York: Norton, 1985), 285–317, esp. "Appendix: Allegiance in Poughkeepsie," 310–17.

sense, Anthony Wayne exemplified Anglicans as Thomas McKean exemplified the Scots-Irish Presbyterians. Wayne's father, an Anglican in religion and a Quaker in politics, had flourished in mid-eighteenth-century Chester, developing an extensive farm and a tanning business and then a successful legislative career among the heterogeneous English, Welsh, Anglican, and Quaker residents in the eastern part of the county.

In the early 1770s his son, Anthony, shared McKean's hostility to the British, McKean's support for independence, and McKean's initial disillusionment with the constitution of 1776. After 1777, however, Anthony Wayne and McKean moved in different political directions. While the Presbyterian lawyer joined the Constitutionalists, the Anglican farmer and army officer, a steadfast enemy of the constitution of 1776 and a vocal opponent of the Test Acts, joined his Anglican and Quaker neighbors in the Republican party.[44]

It was the work of Anglicans like Wayne throughout the late seventies and eighties that kept the Republicans viable in the face of fierce and unified Presbyterian drive for recognition in Chester. As the election returns indicate, and as the desperate tone of the extant correspondence confirm, building and maintaining this diverse coalition was demanding work. Only extraordinary efforts for sustained periods of time kept the Scots-Irish at bay. On the other hand, the aggressive image of the Scots-Irish made this coalition building possible. Anglicans, Quakers, Lutherans, Welsh, Germans, and English had much to divide them. Even the most dedicated and skilled politician could not have held such a disparate conglomeration together without this ever-present threat of the Scots-Irish.

In 1787-88 Chester County strongly favored ratification of the Federal Constitution. Quakers and Anglicans had powerful political motives for supporting the changes. The Test Acts had alienated the pacifists and the truly neutral; the attack on the Anglican college had upset others; and the general tone of intolerance and the threats of violence against trimmers and former enemies in the immediate postwar years had added to the ranks of the opponents of the Constitutionalists. In 1787-88, Chester's Republicans joined their partisan allies across the state in the Federalist camp.

---

44. *Anthony Wayne*, esp. 155-56. *Dictionary of American Biography*, 563. Thayer, *Growth of Democracy*, 63, 68, 163, 172, 175.

The vote cast for the Antifederalist congressional slate in Chester in November 1788 was smaller than might have been expected on the basis of the performance of the Scots-Irish Presbyterian Constitutionalists in the immediate past. Economic pressures may have induced some of them to acquiesce. Chester, like all rural areas, suffered severely in 1788 and some 600 men had petitioned the legislature for relief in the early spring. In the same vein, permanent minority status may have discouraged voting. More likely, Thomas McKean's defection to the Federalist camp played the decisive role. In contrast to other urban, professional, Presbyterian Constitutionalists who hedged, McKean made an early and public commitment to ratification and represented Philadelphia at the state ratifying convention. His conspicuous role in the Federalist cause may well have blurred or blunted the partisan salience of the question and confused, if it did not convert, some of his compatriots in Chester.[45]

Philadelphia County and Lancaster County: The Germans

Philadelphia County, the third of the original counties in Penn's colony, surrounded the city on three sides and stretched north westward along the Schuylkill River toward Reading. The political history of Philadelphia County paralleled that of Bucks and Chester in broad terms. In Philadelphia, as elsewhere in the first four years of independence, voter turnout remained low and Constitutionalists from Presbyterian and Reformed backgrounds dominated the county's Assembly delegation. In 1784 the legislature created the new county of Montgomery from Philadelphia County's upper townships. By 1786 voter turnout had

45. McKean, a resident of Philadelphia, undoubtedly shared the city's perception of the crisis. In addition, he had in the recent past disagreed sharply with some of his Constitutionalist colleagues. His continued skepticism about the state constitution, combined with his plural officeholding in Pennsylvania and Delaware concerned some Constitutionalists. McKean's 1782 defeat in the race to represent Chester in the Supreme Executive Council may have further weakened his ties to the Constitutionalist party. He and former president Joseph Reed, putative head of the Constitutionalist party, were unhappy with each other after McKean's loss. In 1787 McKean broke with his party and championed ratification of the Federal Constitution. See Rush to Montgomery, October 15, 1782, in Butterfield, ed., *Benjamin Rush, Letters*. (Princeton: Princeton University Press for the American Philosophical Society, 1951), 290; Rowe, *T. McKean*, 199–200; Brunhouse, *Counter-Revolution*, 35, 48–49, 64, 126. Hiltzheimer, *Diary*, 12/30/82, 1/7/83, in PMHB 16:160–64.

increased substantially in the new, smaller Philadelphia County, and Republicans, already in control, gained unchallenged supremacy. In Montgomery, Republicans achieved a rough parity by 1786 (see Table 11). Germans made up the vast bulk of the population of Philadelphia County. Reformed, Sectarians, and Lutherans, in about equal numbers, predominated in the upper regions (those townships that became Montgomery). In the lower townships (Philadelphia County in and after 1784), Quakers, Anglicans, Baptists, and two small enclaves of Presbyterians mixed with the still heavily German population.[46]

Table 11. Philadelphia County, Partisan Seats in Assembly, 1776–1788

	Philadelphia Co.			Montgomery Co.			Totals		
	C	R	X	C	R	X	C	R	X
1776	0	5	1	—	—	—	0	5	1
1777	5	0	1	—	—	—	5	0	1
1778	5	2	0	—	—	—	5	1	0
1779	7	0	2	—	—	—	7	0	2
1780	2	7	0	—	—	—	2	7	0
1781	2	7	0	—	—	—	2	7	0
1782	0	8	1	—	—	—	0	8	1
1783	0	8	1	—	—	—	0	8	1
1784	4	0	1	3	0	1	7	0	2
1785	0	4	1	3	1	0	3	5	1
1786	0	4	1	0	4	0	0	8	1
1787	0	3	2	2	1	1	2	4	3
1788	0	3	2	1	2	1	1	5	3

NOTE: C = Constitutionalist.
R = Republican.
X = Partisan identification impossible because the legislator (1) voted too seldom to permit classification; (2) voted an idiosyncratic pattern; or (3) voted a consistent "moderate" position between the two partisan groups.

SOURCE: Party classifications based on Guttman scale analysis of legislative roll-call votes. For details, see Owen Ireland, "The Crux of Politics: Religion and Party in Pennsylvania, 1778–1789," *William and Mary Quarterly* 42 (October 1985): 453–75, esp. 455 n. 5, 456 n. 6, and note 1, above.

46. The description of the geographic distribution of ethnic groups within Philadelphia County relies primarily on maps in Cappon and in Lemon, supplemented by reading in the history of the county and the history of its religious groups. Lester Cappon, ed., *Atlas of Early American History: The Revolutionary Era, 1760–1790* (Princeton: Princeton University Press, 1976); James T. Lemon, "A Rural Geography of Southeastern Pennsylvania in the Eighteenth Century" (Ph.D. diss., University of Wisconsin, 1964); James B. Nolan, ed., *Southeastern Pennsylvania* (New York: Lewis Historical Publishing Company, 1943), John T. Scharf and Thompson Westcott, *History of Philadelphia* (Philadelphia, 1894); Moses Auges, *Lives of the Eminent Dead and Biographical Notices of Prominent Living Citizens of Montgomery County,*

At the beginning and the end of the era, Philadelphia County voters followed the pattern established in Bucks and Chester (see Table 12). The voluntary and involuntary withdrawal of Quakers, German Sectarians, and major portions of the German Lutherans explains the early Constitutionalist victories; the reemergence of these groups as a political force after 1786 accounts for ultimate Republican control.[47] In the

Table 12. Probable Voter Turnout in Philadelphia County, 1764–1786

Year	Total	Percentage of taxables
1764	3,874	42.0
1765	4,332	46.0
1766	3,019	31.0
1771	1,300	12.0
1775	3,122	30.0
	(Independence)	
1776	550	7.8
1779	650	9.2
1781	1,350	19.1
	(Montgomery County created)	
1784	904	22.0
1786	1,500	37.5

SOURCE: Robert Dinkin, *Voting in Provincial America: A Study of Elections in the Thirteen Colonies, 1689–1776* (Westport, Conn.: Greenwood Press, 1977), 158; Robert Brunhouse, *The Counter-Revolution in Pennsylvania 1776–1790* (Harrisburg: The Pennsylvania Historical Commission, 1942), 327–45; *Pennsylvania Archives* Series 3, 14, passim; Pennsylvania Historical and Museum Commission, "Pennsylvania's Revolutionary Government, 1775–1790," RG–27, roll 45; Benjamin Newcomb, "Effects of the Stamp Act on Colonial Pennsylvania Politics," *William and Mary Quarterly* 23 (April 1966): 257–72, esp. 267 n. 34.

Pennsylvania (Philadelphia, 1884); William J. Buck, *History of Montgomery County within the Schuylkill Valley* (Norristown, Pa., 1859); Joseph Henry Dubbs, *The Reformed Church in Pennsylvania*, part 9 of the *Narrative and Critical History* prepared at the Request of the Pennsylvania-German Society (Lancaster, Pa., 1902); James Mease, M.D., *The Pictures of Philadelphia* (Philadelphia: B.&T. Rite, 1811; reprint, 1970 by Arno Press); Richard J. Webster, *Philadelphia Preserved; Catalog of the Historic American Buildings Survey* (Philadelphia: Temple University Press, 1976). Purvis, "Ethnic Settlement," 115.

47. For ethnic, religious, and partisan identification of legislators, see note 1. In 1779 Philadelphia County had approximately 7,066 taxables and nine seats in the General Assembly (*Pennsylvania Archives*, ser. 3, 14:470ff.). The division of the county awarded four of these nine seats to Montgomery, suggesting that Montgomery County had four ninths of the total population of the original county, or about 3,100 of the 7,000. Although the extant records precludes precise calculation of turnout the data establish firm boundaries for maximum and minimum participation. Since these figures undoubtedly underestimate the actual increase over time, we can reasonably estimate turnout of about 10 percent during the first four years; double that during the next six years; and double that again after 1786. Benjamin H.

middle years of the era, however, from 1780 through 1786, Philadelphia County and its progeny, Montgomery County, both displayed a more complex pattern, as first one and then the other party won. In 1780 in the original and still undivided Philadelphia County, the Republicans gained a narrow victory (seven of nine seats). In 1784 the Constitutionalists recaptured all five seats in the new smaller Philadelphia County and the four new seats in Montgomery. In 1786 the Republicans gained overwhelming control in Philadelphia and a marginal majority in Montgomery.

The political behavior of two distinct groups largely accounts for this volatility: the Philadelphia artisans in the two southern townships adjacent to the city, and the German Lutherans spread throughout the area.[48] Artisans made up a large proportion of the population of the two Philadelphia County townships immediately adjacent to the city: the Northern Liberties and Southwark. Through 1779 most artisans voted with the Constitutionalists and Constitutionalists controlled the county. In 1780, substantial numbers of artisans, disillusioned by the Constitutionalists' failure to solve the growing economic crisis of the state, shifted allegiances and thereby contributed to the Republican victory. In 1784, attracted by the Constitutionalist promise of tariff protection, the artisans again switched and gave the county to the Constitutionalists for one year.[49]

Newcomb, "Effects of the Stamp Act on Colonial Pennsylvania Politics," *William and Mary Quarterly* 23 (April 1966): 257–72, esp. 267, n. 34. For figures for 1776–89, see Brunhouse, *Counter-Revolution*, 327–45. *Pennsylvania Archives*, ser. 3, vols. 14 and 15. Pennsylvania Historical and Museum Commission, "Pennsylvania's Revolutionary Government, 1775–1790," RG-27, roll 45. For other pre-1776 figures, see Robert Dinkin, *Voting in Provincial America: A Study of Elections in the Thirteen Colonies, 1689–1776* (Westport, Conn.: Greenwood Press, 1977), 158. Estimates of taxables: pre-1776 is from Dinkin; 1776 and after my count in tax lists, *Pennsylvania Archives*, ser. 3, 14:passim.

48. My discussion of the artisans relies on Charles S. Olton, *Artisans for Independence: Philadelphia Mechanics and the American Revolution* (Syracuse: Syracuse University Press, 1975); Eric Foner, *Thomas Paine and Revolutionary America* (New York: Oxford University Press, 1976); and Ronald D. Schultz, "Thoughts among the People: Popular Thought, Radical Politics and the Making of Philadelphia's Working Class, 1765–1828" (Ph.D. diss., University of California at Los Angeles, 1985), 7–8. Revised and published as *The Republic of Labor: Philadelphia Artisans and the Politics of Class, 1720–1830* (New York: Oxford University Press, 1993).

49. For more details on the economic problems and the political behavior of the artisans, see Chapter 5. Popular reaction to the violence involved in the Fort Wilson clash in October 1779 may well have played a major role in this electoral shift toward the Republicans in Philadelphia County's lower townships in 1780. John K. Alexander, "The Fort Wilson Incident of 1779: A Case Study of the Revolutionary Crowd," *William and Mary Quarterly* 31

Lutherans also played an important role in the Republican victory in 1780. In the original Philadelphia County, about 650 men voted in 1779 and they divided about two to one for the Constitutionalists. Two years later 1,350 voted and Republicans won. German Lutherans in the rural parts of the county contributed substantially to this rise in voter participation and to the Republican victory.[50] In the early stages of the Revolution, most Lutherans had remained on the fence. By the winter of 1779–80, however, a variety of forces pressured them into making a decision. The Test Act of 1779 ended the possibility of continued neutrality. It barred forever those who did not take the oath before the end of the year. At the same time the course of the war reduced the immediate risks of joining the patriots. The French alliance had strengthened the American cause; the war itself was shifting to the south; and the British had abandoned their occupation of the city. In Philadelphia County the popular vote doubled in 1781 and the biggest influx of new voters occurred in central and northern townships, the area in which Germans predominated.

Lutherans must have made up the bulk of these new voters. Sectarians, like the Quakers, continued to refuse the test oath. The German Reformed had been participating all along, following the lead of such conspicuous lay spokesmen as Joseph Heister first into the patriot camp, and then into the Constitutionalist party. German Lutherans, however, forced by the Test Act of 1779 to come down on one side or the other, took the required oath, joined the political community, and in time became Republican partisans. The political odyssey of the Reverend

---

(October 1974): 589–612; and Stephen Rosswurm, " 'As a Lyen out of His Den': Philadelphia's Popular Movement, 1776–80," in Margaret Jacob and James Jacob, eds., *The Origins of Anglo-American Radicalism* (London: George Allen and Unwin, 1984), 311–18.

50. In 1781 both parties apparently included the same four candidates on their tickets (Holgate, Heister, McLean, and Smith) and then added four or five partisan candidates of their own. The cross-endorsed men polled about 1,320 votes each; four Republican candidates won with totals ranging from 664 to 830. Losing Constitutionalists probably averaged 500 to 600. Gray, a Republican, may also have appeared on both tickets. He polled 1,160 voters. The extant election returns preclude precise calculation of the relative weight of the shift in artisan vote and the increase in rural turnout, but demonstrate the importance of each. In 1779 the Constitutionalists carried the county with about 500 votes. In 1781 they polled about the same number of votes and lost. Republicans garnered the bulk of the increase: about 700. Republicans also carried the two artisan townships by about 300 votes total. The Republican margin of victory (300 at most) thus depended upon both the new rural voters and the old urban voters who switched.

Henry Melchior Muhlenberg and his son Frederick illustrates the process.[51]

The father, Henry, came to America as a young Lutheran minister in the 1740s under the sponsorship of Frederich Michael Ziegenhagen, the German Lutheran chaplain in the King's Chapel of St. James in London. By 1776 he was the most conspicuous and easily identified leader of the German Lutheran church in America.[52] Independence presented Muhlenberg with a cruel dilemma. He had lived in this country for most of his adult life; his family had been born and raised here; his wife was a native of Pennsylvania; his eldest son (Peter) was a noted military figure in the American cause; and he himself saw much to support in the American grievances against the British.[53] On the other hand, Lutherans did not easily or readily challenge legitimate authority. In

51. Concentrated mostly in the northern towns (Montgomery County after 1784) the German Reformed tended to support resistance, revolution, and independence. For example, in Philadelphia, in 1777–78, the British occupation force imprisoned Reformed minister Michael Schlatter for publicity celebrating the American victory at Saratoga, an act of defiance to British authority difficult to imagine among other German religious leaders in Pennsylvania. German Reformed voters tended to support the Constitutionalist party, and in the late seventies and throughout the eighties German Reformed Assemblymen worked easily with the dominant Scots-Irish Presbyterian Constitutionalists in the legislature. William W. Sweet, *Religion in Colonial America* (New York: Charles Scribner's Sons, 1943), 38, 83. Henry Melchior Muhlenberg, *Journals*, trans. and ed. by Theodore Tapert and John W. Doberstein (Philadelphia, 1945), 3:98. Ireland, "Ratification," 28–35, 62–64.

52. Paul S. W. Wallace, *The Muhlenbergs of Pennsylvania* (Philadelphia: University of Pennsylvania Press, 1950). Muhlenberg, *Journals*, 2:722; Sweet, *Religion*, 243. Leonard R. Riforgiato, S.J., "Missionary of Moderation: Henry Melchior Muhlenberg and the Lutheran Church in English America" (Ph.D. diss., Pennsylvania State University, 1971).

53. Muhlenberg, *Journals*, 3:15. A. G. Roeber recently concluded that a "new synthesis between German Americans' concepts of liberty and property, and North American political culture" created an intellectual framework within which German Lutherans could respond positively to the Declaration of Independence. At the same time, however, Roeber identifies within the German Lutheran tradition an ambivalence toward liberty, property, authority, and political participation. Thus, Henry M. Muhlenberg could remain neutral or loyal in 1776 but "eventually see the defense of property as justification for rebellion." Roeber concludes that "[b]y 1777 he [Muhlenberg] had worked through the dilemma surrounding Romans 13 [the scriptural injunction to obedience] by noting that one should 'be subject to that power which rules . . . or, as it is put, which has the strongest arm and longest sword.' " My analysis argues that over time increasing numbers of German Lutherans, especially in rural areas, concluded that the patriots had the "strongest arm and the longest sword" and therefore accepted the legitimacy of the revolutionary government. Roeber argues that, with some exceptions, "the Lutherans and Reformed congregations in Philadelphia harbored no such doubts" about the patriot cause. Roeber, *Palatines, Liberty, and Property: German Lutherans in Colonial British America* (Baltimore: Johns Hopkins University Press, 1993): 284, 302, 304, 305.

sharp contrast to the English Calvinists who had harassed a queen and beheaded a king, Lutherans seldom rebelled. "If ye be willing and obedient, ye shall eat the good of the land," Muhlenberg believed, "but if ye refuse and rebel, ye shall be devoured with the sword."[54]

Muhlenberg also had practical reasons for loyalty. The king, like Muhlenberg himself, was a Hanoverian from Lutheran backgrounds and remained generally sympathetic to the interests and needs of the Lutheran Church in America. In the same vein, the proprietary government had treated Lutherans well, chartering their church in the 1760s and allowing them a maximum of congregational autonomy. In addition, Presbyterians, increasingly prominent in revolutionary Pennsylvania, made Muhlenberg uneasy. Presbyterians had never been noted for their toleration. The Great Awakening had heightened denominational self-consciousness and religious affiliation had taken on some of the aspects of ethnic identification, especially among the Germans. The political battles of the sixties and especially the vitriolic charges and countercharges exchanged by Presbyterian and Quaker supporters over the Paxton affair had done nothing to blur these distinctions or dampen the fires.[55]

In the summer and fall of 1776, from old Muhlenberg's perspective, an independent Pennsylvania under Presbyterian control threatened the ancient privileges and liberties of the Lutheran Church. On July 4, 1776, he consoled himself with trust in providence: "This remains as a comfort to believers: There is One who sits at the rudder, who has the plan of the whole before Him."[56]

But things grew worse and he and his people could find no peace. "If they want to hold to the Parliamentary party [i.e., Loyalists], the other side says 'you are traitors to the country and to liberty and deserving of banishment.' If they want to hold to the side of the country [i.e.,

54. Muhlenberg, *Journals*, 2:720–21, 2:703, 2:699, 3:61, 2:701, 2:727, 2:694.
55. Wayne L. Bockelman and Owen S. Ireland, "The Internal Revolution in Pennsylvania: An Ethnic-Religious Interpretation," *Pennsylvania History* 41 (April 1974). Muhlenberg, *Journals*, 2/15/65, 2:191. Sydney G. Fisher, *The Quaker Colonies* (New Haven: Yale University Press, 1919), 117. Allan W. Tully, "Ethnicity, Religion and Politics in Early America," *PMHB* 107 (October 1983): 491–536, esp. 529, quoting from Galloway's letter to Franklin, November 23, 1764, in B. Franklin, *Papers*, 11:467–68. John B. Frantz, "The Awakening of Religion Among the German Settlers in the Middle Colonies," *William and Mary Quarterly* 33 (April 1976): 266–88, esp. 288. Dietmar Rothermund, *The Layman's Progress: Religious and Political Experience in Colonial Pennsylvania, 1740–1770* (Philadelphia: University of Pennsylvania Press, 1961), esp. 36–41. Wokeck, "A Tide of Alien Tongues," 215, 267.
56. Muhlenberg, *Journals*, 2:742–43, 2:703, 2:721–22.

patriots], the others say, 'You are rebels and must be treated as such.' Hence they are between the fire and the sword; it is impossible to be neutral."[57]

Between the fire and the sword, indeed, as throughout the summer and fall of 1776 and on into 1777 and 1778 old Muhlenberg wrestled with his conscience, watched the tide of battle, and vacillated. In the late winter of 1777 he came close to casting aspersions on his monarch. That spring, however, he avoided taking the test oath and when the British occupied Philadelphia he reemphasized his British links, writing to an old friend living in British-occupied New York: "The truth [is] that I am a Hannoverian, . . . that I have had the good fortune to be a subject, both by reason of birth and naturalization, of their Royal Majesties George I and George II of glorious memory and also of George III, and up to this time I have neither broken nor transferred my oath of fealty."[58]

The British evacuation of Philadelphia, and news of their abuse of the Lutheran Church building in Philadelphia during their occupation, led Muhlenberg back toward the patriot cause. In January 1779, for example, he noted favorably that the Lutheran Church in Philadelphia "had voted unanimously to put £1200 from the treasury into the *Loan-Office* [i.e., United States bonds]." Muhlenberg culminated his odyssey by taking the test oath sometime late in 1779, and by 1780 he, and probably a fair portion of his coreligionists were technically qualified to participate in the politics of revolutionary Pennsylvania.[59]

Muhlenberg's son, Frederick, forged the decisive link between the Lutherans and the Republicans. At the beginning of the war Frederick had been a young Lutheran minister serving a congregation in New York City. Between 1774 and 1776 he avoided taking sides, and when the British occupied New York, he followed his family back to his father's farm (at the Trappe) in the upper reaches of Philadelphia County. Here he continued to work as a minister but without a fixed parish or income. In time he acquired a house and opened a store.[60]

Throughout, he remained an observer of the Revolution: sympathetic

57. Ibid., 2:727, 2:734–35.
58. Ibid., 2:746, 3:15, 3:55–56, 3:101–3, 3:123–26.
59. Ibid., 3:163, 3:165, 3:169, 3:183, 3:173, 3:211. Stephanie Wolf indicates that no more than 11 percent of the total taxpayers in 1779 in Germantown were nonjurors. Wolf, *Urban Village* (Princeton: Princeton University Press, 1976), 180.
60. Wallace, *Muhlenbergs*, 110–15; Muhlenberg, *Journals*, 3:119.

but aloof. He took the test oath in 1777, but remained politically inactive. In 1779, over his father's objections, he accepted appointment by the Presbyterian-dominated Constitutionalists to represent Pennsylvania in Congress. The next year he won election to a seat in the state legislature where fellow German Joseph Heister (from a Reformed background), tried to recruit him for the Constitutionalists. After a year of partisan neutrality, however, Muhlenberg joined the Republicans.[61]

Thus, by 1781, the patriarch of the German Lutheran Church in America had taken the test oath, and his church had invested scarce funds in U.S. government bonds. Meanwhile, his second son had emerged as the titular head of the German Lutheran political community in Pennsylvania, casting his lot with the Republicans. At the same time, voter turnout increased in those parts of Philadelphia County most heavily populated by German Lutherans, and Republicans gained control of the county.

The casual linkage here is inferential. How typical old Muhlenberg was of German Lutherans is impossible to say with certainty. On the other hand, most German Lutherans in Philadelphia County shared Muhlenberg's theological orientation, and many, particularly those of his own generation, relied on him and a handful of bilingual ministers and publishers for interpretations of the broader political world.

Equally important, Henry M. Muhlenberg, living at the Trappe maintained a complex and widespread communications network. Although old and tired, he and his often-ill wife traveled frequently and far, supervising church business, mediating congregational disputes, preaching, comforting, administering the sacraments, and visiting relatives and friends within a twenty- to thirty-mile radius of the Trappe. When at home, they entertained a constant stream of visitors: some stopping by on the way to someplace else; others coming specifically to see the Muhlenbergs. The old man complemented this daily face-to-face interaction with an equally impressive correspondence, facilitated by the constant passage of visitors who delivered and carried away the mail.[62]

In short, old Muhlenberg possessed an extraordinary vehicle for

---

61. Wallace, *Muhlenbergs*, 178, 202. Pennsylvania Historical and Museum Commission, RG-27, "Pennsylvania's Revolutionary Government," microfilm roll 44, "Oaths of Allegiance." List dated June 27, 1777, and attested to by John Richards, J.P.

62. For innumerable examples of visitors, travels, and letters sent and received, see Muhlenberg, *Journals*, 3:passim.

influencing the actions of those of his coreligionists who looked to him for guidance. Outside the city of Philadelphia, no other group save the Quakers possessed such an effective and far-flung internal communications network. If old Muhlenberg remained neutral until 1779 and then took the test oath, it seems reasonable to assume that a fair portion of his flock knew this, and that many did likewise. Furthermore, when the patriarch's son entered public life and allied himself with the Republicans, the power of that name could by itself mobilize substantial numbers of German Lutherans.

Furthermore, the Muhlenberg attachment to the Republicans was consistent with longtime links between Lutherans and Anglicans in Pennsylvania. Before the war, the elder Muhlenberg was a close personal friend of the Reverend William Smith. Anglicans and Lutherans preached and officiated in each other's churches. Peter Muhlenberg's ordination as an Anglican priest after being trained for the Lutheran ministry suggests the ease with which the two denominations interacted, as does the old patriarch's habit of referring to Anglicans as "English Lutherans."[63]

Old Muhlenberg felt differently about the Presbyterians, but until the break with Great Britain and the emergence of the Scots-Irish–dominated Constitutionalists, he had remained circumspect in his comments. In the early 1780s, however, he let his exasperation break through this carefully structured facade and expressed the long-festering bitterness he felt toward these "refined Presbyterians," as he called them. When the Presbyterian-dominated University of Pennsylvania awarded Muhlenberg's favorite son-in-law (Pastor Kuntze) an unsolicited honorary degree, the old patriarch commented: "Loathsome and contemptible as the German scholars were to the English Presbyterian politico-theologians here in former times, so much the more do they for obvious reasons flatter them now, because the right to elect . . . depends upon the people." "Hitherto they compared us Germans with sauerkraut and foul cheese. Now their taste has changed. . . . They feel obliged . . . to make friends of the mammon of unrighteousness."[64] Muhlenberg also began with a decided prejudice against the state constitution, which he perceived as un-Christian (Unitarian if not Deist).

---

63. Ibid., 3:220, 3:716, 2:160, 3:247–48 and 250, 2:412.
64. Ibid., July 8, 1783, 3:551; 10/3/84, 3:625–26; 3:217 and 220.

Furthermore, in 1778 and 1779 the Constitutionalists, insisting on patriotic purity, had passed the Test Acts, thus confirming the worst fears of those who anticipated Presbyterian rigidity and intolerance.[65]

In addition, Muhlenberg saw the Constitutionalist assault on the Anglican-dominated College of Philadelphia in 1779 as a direct threat to Lutherans. When they attacked the college, "the Presb(yterian) politico-Christiani" attacked Muhlenberg's close friend and Anglican colleague, the Reverend William Smith, provost of the college. More important, the blatant violation of the college's charter, presumably protected by the state constitution, undermined the legal basis of all existing corporations in the state, including that of the Lutheran Church. This sent shock waves through the Lutheran community. The partisan pillage of the College of Philadelphia on grounds of insufficient enthusiasm for the Revolution indicated that no institution was safe.[66]

It seems likely, then, that between 1779 and 1781, substantial numbers of German Lutherans trod the path blazed for them by the Muhlenbergs. They first followed the father into the patriot political community and then followed the son into the Anglican-led Republican Party, which opposed the Test Acts, fought against the destruction of the College of Philadelphia, and implicitly stood for protection of the rights of chartered educational and religious corporations. In 1787–88 Philadelphia County followed Frederick Muhlenberg into the Federalist camp.

In Montgomery County, the interplay between three groups of Germans largely accounts for the patterns of partisan control. The legislature created Montgomery County in 1784 out of the northern townships of Philadelphia County. In this new county, the German Sectarians held the balance of power between the Reformed Constitutionalists and the Lutheran Republicans. Between 1784 and the end of the decade, as increasing numbers of them participated in the electoral process, the Republicans grew in strength.

The Sectarians joined the political community in two closely connected phases. Most had refused to directly or indirectly support the war, but, unlike the Quakers, they had seldom cast aspersions on the patriots or on the government of the state. They were willing to recognize and obey whatever civil authority God chose to place over

---
65. Ibid., 2:748, 2:752.
66. Ibid., 3:625.

them, but few would take the test oath because it included an explicit repudiation of all earlier oaths to the king of England, and because it implied, they thought, a pledge to support the state's war effort. When the end of the war removed the problem of bearing arms, and when the Treaty of Paris (1783) abrogated all previous oaths to the king, Sectarian men coming of age could, in good conscience, take the required oath and vote. In counties such as Montgomery, with an extraordinary concentration of German Sectarians, each new year thus significantly increased the potential Sectarian vote. Moreover, when and if these young Sectarians voted, few would support the Constitutionalists, who had disfranchised and harassed their families throughout the war, and who now continued to do so.

This slow but inevitable increase in potential Sectarian participation set the stage for legislative modification of the Test Acts themselves in 1786. Astute Constitutionalist officeholders from areas of heavy Sectarian settlement faced a major political dilemma. The Test Acts could continue for a while to disfranchise those most likely to vote Republican. The passage of time, however, promised to enfranchise increasing numbers of young Sectarians and thus, willy-nilly, to build political opposition to the tests and to the Constitutionalists.

One possible solution was for Constitutionalist assemblymen from such districts to assume an "enlightened" stance on the tests: defend them as necessary wartime measures, but urge their speedy repeal now that the war was over, hoping against hope that at least some grateful nonjurors would see this as a gesture of reconciliation and forget and forgive past offenses. This option might have appealed most to those Constitutionalists who were themselves German and could thus hope that ethnic identity might bridge the gap between religious groups.

The behavior of the Constitutionalist legislators from Montgomery in 1785 and 1786 followed this model. They had supported the tests; they were Germans from largely Reformed backgrounds; and in the spring of 1786, defying the majority of their Constitutionalist colleagues, they voted with the Republican minority in the legislature to modify the Test Acts. This legislation reopened the political process to all Sectarians and gave the Republicans a slim but solid majority in Montgomery by 1787.

The relative strength of the two parties in Montgomery shaped the contest over ratification of the Federal Constitution in 1787–88, and the congressional vote in November 1788. In the Assembly, on September 28 and 29, 1787, assemblymen from Montgomery vacillated. Contemporaries, rightly, viewed the county, located between Federalist Philadelphia and Antifederalist Berks, as a swing area. In the November 1788 congressional election, Antifederalists exhibited greater electoral popularity here than in any other county within the Federalist orbit, polling about 40 to 45 percent of the vote.

Lancaster is the fourth and last of the eastern counties that shifted from Constitutionalist to Republican control between 1778 and 1786. The course of partisan competition here paralleled that in Philadelphia and for much the same reasons. Between 1778 and 1784 the Constitutionalists controlled the bulk of this large legislative delegation by a two-to-one margin. In 1785 Republicans gained control of the county and in this and the next three legislatures they held all but one of the 22 partisan seats. The fall 1785 election thus ushers in a new era of Republican domination in Lancaster and deserves close examination.[67]

Two factors contributed to this change: increases in voter turnout, and the creation of Dauphin County out of the northern townships of Lancaster. Between 1778 and 1784 the number of votes cast in Lancaster's annual Assembly elections increased dramatically, doubling, possibly tripling. As turnout increased, so did Republican strength and in 1781, 1782, and 1783 Republicans almost equaled Constitutionalists in the county's legislative delegations.

Germans, especially Lutherans, accounted for much of this increase in Republican strength. By May 1784 Republican Stephen Chamber was optimistic about his party's future in Lancaster, as increasing numbers of Germans participated and voted Republican. "Some of [the] thinking part of them [the Germans] begin to apprehend they have been imposed on . . . things begin to wear a different appearance I have great hopes it will encrease every day."[68]

---

67. The magnitude of this Constitutionalist margin, however, may convey an exaggerated sense of their relative power in the county. In only two of these seven years did Republicans fail to gain some seats in the legislature (1778 and 1784) and in one year Republicans held a majority of the county's Assembly seats. In the remaining four years Republicans managed to stay within two or three seats of their Constitutionalist competitors. Partisan classifications in this and the following paragraphs are based on Guttman-scale analysis of legislative roll-call votes. See above for information on Lancaster County. I have relied on a number of studies, including James T. Lemon, *The Best Poor Man's Country*, esp. 37–40; Franklin Ellis and Samuel Evans, *History of Lancaster County* (Philadelphia, 1883); Brooke Hindle, "The March of the Paxton Boys," *William and Mary Quarterly* 3 (1946): 461–86.

68. Stephen Chambers to John Rose, Lancaster, May 5, 1784, *PMHB*, 22:500–501.

The results of the fall 1784 election dashed Chambers's hopes, at least for that year. Republicans won, but the losing Constitutionalists challenged the outcome, charging that illegal votes (possibly those of nonjurors) were counted. The state legislature, under Constitutionalist control, awarded the disputed seats to the Constitutionalist candidates.[69] This postponed the Republican victory in Lancaster until 1785. The decisive event that year was designation of Lancaster's northern tier of townships as the core of the new county of Dauphin. These townships, including Paxton and Lebanon, had a heavy concentration of Scots-Irish Presbyterians and German Reformed. As would be expected, they had long exhibited Constitutionalist loyalties.

An event in 1782 illustrates the point. In the fall of that year the Constitutionalists in the legislature supported Joseph Montgomery for speaker. Montgomery, a legislator and a Presbyterian minister, lived in the Paxton region. The Republican candidate, German Lutheran Frederick A. Muhlenberg, defeated Montgomery. At almost the same time, the Assembly, by joint ballot with the Supreme Executive Council, chose John Dickinson president of the state. Dickinson was a Quaker, a Republican, and, for many in Pennsylvania, a man of dubious patriot credentials. These two elections incensed people living in the future Dauphin County. Through their local militia, the Ninth Battalion, they called for a meeting of all of Lancaster's militia units. Their circular letter, dated Hanover, November 28, 1782, stated their political concerns: "[We] . . . have concluded from the complexion of the present House of Assembly, that the Constitution and the Liberties of the State are at stake, in some measure." When the militia leaders of the entire county assembled January 15, 1783, they rejected the charges but the Ninth Battalion would concede only that "we hope that the assembly has made a good choice."[70]

Achieving county status did not change Dauphin's partisan orienta-

---

69. Brunhouse, *Counter-Revolution*, 164–65, 281. *Minutes of the . . . Ninth General Assembly . . . 1784*, November 1, 8, 9, 10, 11, 12, pp. 4, 11, 12, 13, 14–18. Turnout appears to have increased substantially in 1784. The incomplete figures indicate at least 4,300 voters, and possibly as many as 5,400. If accurate, this represents a doubling of the 1783 turnout, which itself reflected a doubling of the 1778 turnout. *Minutes of the . . . Ninth General Assembly*, November 13, 1784. For a brief discussion of the role of Republican tax policies in this election, see Roger Brown, *Redeeming the Republic*, 53–68.

70. *Pennsylvania Journal*, 12/11/82, 2/5/83. Lyman Butterfield, ed., *Letters of Benjamin Rush* (Princeton: Princeton University Press, 1951), 1:131. Samuel Hazard, *The Register of Pennsylvania* (Philadelphia, 1825–35) 6:116–17.

tion. Between 1785 and the end of the decade every one of its partisan assemblymen was a Constitutionalist, most of them were from Presbyterian or Reformed backgrounds, and they and their constituents remained belligerently opposed to modification of the Test Acts. In the spring of 1786, as the legislature moved toward reopening the test rolls, Dauphin County residents petitioned the house in protest, holding out "menaces for the Assembly, should they pass the [repeal] bill." The House, offended by the tone of these memorials, refused to receive them.[71]

While the Presbyterians and Reformed kept Dauphin in the Constitutionalist camp, the more mixed population of the new and now smaller Lancaster generally supported the Republicans. Southern Lancaster, with a heavy German Lutheran and Mennonite population, had exhibited Republican leanings for some time. The separation of the Scots-Irish and Reformed Germans in Dauphin made the English and German voters in the old Lancaster the controlling majority in the new and smaller Lancaster. From 1785 on, Lancaster's partisan legislators (most of whom were Anglican, Lutheran, or Sectarian) supported the Republicans. In 1787 Lancaster supported ratification; Dauphin, a strong Constitutionalist county, vigorously, even violently, opposed.

Constitutionalists had come to power in revolutionary Pennsylvania largely on the basis of their support among the Scots-Irish Presbyterian and German Reformed residents of the eastern counties. They continued to dominate these areas as long as major portions of the Quaker, German Sectarian, and Lutheran population remained outside the electoral process. Over time, increasing numbers of men from these ethnic-religious groups joined the political community and voted for the Anglican-led Republicans.

Republican victories here in these eastern counties by 1786 set the stage for the Federalist success the next year. It gave them the legislative majority to call a state convention in September 1787; it gave them control of the state convention itself in November; and it gave them the power to frustrate the Antifederalists' campaign to repudiate the state's December ratification.

By 1787–88 these Quaker, Lutheran, and German Sectarian voters combined with the original support for the Anglican-led Republicans to

---

71. *Pennsylvania Packet*, 3/6/86.

constitute a new majority. Experience had taught them to distrust simple and unchecked popular government, and to fear abuse by temporarily ascendant, idealistic, enthusiastic, intolerant minorities. They saw the Federal Constitution as a repudiation of the state constitution, of the party that had defended it, and of the policies that had characterized the era of patriotic zeal and repression between 1778 and 1785. In addition, some also looked forward to the creation of an external authority to which they might appeal for protection. Much to the surprise of the Federalists and the chagrin of the Antifederalists, this new majority readily, enthusiastically, and repeatedly expressed its support for the Federal Constitution, carried the eastern counties for ratification, and finally, and irrevocably defeated the Constitutionalists in the place of their birth and initial success.

Conclusion

The People's Triumph

The story is done; the analysis complete. It remains only to sum up the argument, explore some of its links to the work of other historians, and suggest some of the ironies in the final outcome. Pennsylvanians responded to the proposed Federal Constitution largely on the basis of political attachments rooted in ethnic-religious identities nurtured by a decade or more of bitter partisan warfare. A solid majority favored it; a vehement minority opposed. Few disputed the need to augment the powers of Congress. By late 1786 virtually every observer in the state agreed that Congress needed a reliable income, as well as the power to regulate commerce and control America's relations with the rest of the world. Pennsylvanians divided over the Federal Constitution not because it enhanced the powers of the central government, but rather because it did so in ways that promised to alter the balance of political power within Pennsylvania.[1]

---

1. This and the bulk of what follows rely on the argument and evidence developed above. I have added footnote citations for new material.

For a decade or more the Presbyterian-dominated Constitutionalists and the Anglican-led Republicans had disputed the form of the state's government and the principles on which it rested. Constitutionalists had defended the state's all-powerful, annually elected unicameral legislature as the best vehicle for direct expression of the will of the people. Republicans had argued that only a complex system with a bicameral legislature, a single executive, and an independent judiciary could prevent capricious or tyrannical government.

Pennsylvania's political elite generally agreed that the proposed Federal Constitution took the Republican side in this debate. It called for a central government of three distinct branches, a two-house legislature, and extensive internal checks and balances. Ratification of the Federal Constitution thus implied repudiation of the state constitution, its principles, and its champions. Anticipation of this outcome strengthened Republican support for the proposal and converted Constitutionalists into its opponents.

Leaders on both sides also realized that the Federal Constitution, if implemented, would significantly enhance the power of the central government at the expense of the states. Republicans liked this change; Constitutionalists did not. On the state level during the past decade the Constitutionalists had, more often than not, successfully competed against Republicans for power. In 1787 both parties still considered the Constitutionalists the stronger. The Federal Constitution would create a new national arena of political competition in which Republicans might do better, and in which Constitutionalists would certainly do worse.

Finally, opponents of ratification predicted that the new system would create an aristocratic government. It would erect a central government beyond popular scrutiny. The small size of the House of Representatives, as well as the indirect election of the Senate and the president would give privilege to the better sort in competition for office. The new government's remoteness would make it ignorant of and insensitive to local needs, thereby depriving it of the voluntary compliance of satisfied citizens. In the end it would become not only aristocratic but despotic. Supporters of the Federal Constitution, whatever they might privately have believed, generally denied these charges. They defended the proposal as inherently democratic, carefully circumscribed, and respectful of state autonomy.

The electorate divided along much the same lines as had the political elite: the Scots-Irish, the Presbyterians, and the German Reformed supporters of the Constitutionalists opposed ratification; the Anglicans, Lutherans, Quakers, and German Sectarians in the Republican coalition favored it. The supporters of each position, however, acted for somewhat different reasons.

Among Antifederalist voters, the policy implications of the new system were important but the ethnic-religious identity between leaders and electors was crucial. The nature of the political constituencies led by the Antifederalists heightened the power of these leaders to shape the political behavior of those who identified with them. For instance, a major portion of the Scots-Irish Presbyterians were new immigrants, having arrived on the eve of the Revolution. They had settled everywhere but were most visible in Cumberland, Franklin, and Dauphin Counties in the center of the state and in Westmoreland and Fayette in the west. In spite of their numbers, however, they predominated in few if any of these areas. Even at their most numerous, they remained part of a heterogeneous and sometimes hostile mix of peoples, many of whom were themselves new and transient.[2] Their cultural differences combined with the ever-changing and sometimes hostile populace among whom they lived, increasing their awareness of themselves as a separate people. This heightened consciousness of kind, in turn, led them to take pride in, and willingly support, Scots-Irish Presbyterian leaders.[3]

In addition, the paucity of communication vehicles, especially in backcountry Pennsylvania, enhanced the ability of Scots-Irish and Ger-

---

2. Thomas Purvis, "Patterns of Ethnic Settlement in Late Eighteenth-Century Pennsylvania," *Western Pennsylvania Historical Magazine* 70 (April 1987): 107–22. Marianne Wokeck, "A Tide of Alien Tongues: The Flow and Ebb of German Immigration to Pennsylvania, 1683–1776" (Ph.D. diss., Temple University, 1983). For information on the Irish, see especially Wokeck, 271–83 and 285, fig. 11.

3. David Hackett Fischer, *Albion's Seed: Four British Folkways in America* (New York: Oxford University Press, 1989) argues for the transference of old-world folkways to America. Ned Landsman has found that the Scots in New Jersey, created a distinctive identity out of the interaction between what they brought with them and what they encountered in their new location. Moreover, he argues that both the old and the new interacted in a dynamic way that refashioned each over time. Doyle illustrates that for the Scots-Irish, also, what they brought interacted with what they found here while developments in America influenced what was happening at home. Ned C. Landsman, *Scotland and Its First American Colony, 1683–1765* (Princeton: Princeton University Press, 1985), esp. 256ff. David Noel Doyle, *Ireland, Irishmen, and Revolutionary America* (Dublin and Cork: Mercier Press for the Cultural Relations Committee of Ireland, 1981), passim.

man Reformed leaders to influence those who identified with them. At the crudest level, names mattered. All other things being equal, Germans voted for men with German-sounding names, Scots-Irish voted for those with Scots-Irish names. To the same end, periodic congregations for worship provided substantial numbers of these people with their single most intensive and frequent large-group interaction. Denominational gatherings thus also served as vehicles of political socialization and mobilization. Furthermore, candidates who mixed with the assembled voters on Election Day undoubtedly drew more support from those who perceived them as similar to themselves in speech, in dress, and in manner.

Finally, the Antifederalists controlled much of the primitive bureaucracy of the state. Comptroller John Nicholson, for example, called on his contacts across the state to collect signatures on Antifederalist petitions. In the same vein, Judge George Bryan traveled the judicial circuit from county seat to county seat maintaining personal contacts, and Joseph Hart in Bucks County had made extraordinary efforts after his son's death to keep the local offices his son had held, principally, as Hart explained, because of advantages to his party.

Scots-Irish Presbyterian officeholders thus enjoyed a cultural affinity with a sizable block of voters and possessed a variety of vehicles for communicating with that electorate. In Berks, and in major portions of Dauphin and Montgomery, German Reformed leaders such as Joseph Heister and his family performed much the same function to much the same end. These Irish and German voters may not have fully understood the issues debated in the press. As Antifederalist James Marshall noted in 1788: "The truth is the people at large do not understand the subject."[4] Still, they knew whom they liked and whom they disliked. They deferred to men who looked like them, spoke like them, acted like them and served as brokers between them and the broader political and legal world. At the same time they held strong negative feelings about those they saw as different, especially the English Anglicans and Deists. Their leaders probably shared these feelings, and on occasion, used them in subdued and subtle ways.

Federalist leaders attracted voters less by their personal ties with particular ethnic-religious communities than by the policies they had pursued and by the principles they had espoused. In contrast to their

---

4. James Marshall to John Nicholson, Washington County, 2/2/88, in Jensen 2:713.

Antifederalist counterparts (and with the obvious exception of the Muhlenbergs), conspicuous Federalists tended to be more secular and more denominationally mobile. Although mostly Anglican, many had once belonged to other denominations. George Clymer, for instance, came from Quaker backgrounds, while Benjamin Rush had become an Anglican after long association with the Presbyterians, and James Wilson, raised a Presbyterian in Scotland, identified principally with Anglicans in Philadelphia.

In addition, Federalist leaders, in general, were more tolerant and flexible than their opponents. They came from religious denominations that either practiced de facto toleration (the latitudinarian Anglicans) or were committed to toleration in principle (the Quakers). Furthermore, because of their minority status over the previous decade, they had, by necessity, assumed a inclusive posture in order to increase their support. They had resisted the harsh imposition of the Test Acts against the neutrals and pacifists among the Quaker and Sectarian population, fought to protect the charter of the Anglican-headed College of Philadelphia, and at the end of the war pressed for the quick and easy reintegration of all into the political community.[5]

The policies and the principles of the Federalists drew the support of religious denominations with well-developed internal communication systems. Among Lutherans, the Reverend Henry M. Muhlenberg and his son Frederick sat at the center of a carefully nurtured communications network with a wide geographical base. In the same vein, German Sectarians traditionally looked to a small number of spokesmen to mediate between themselves and the secular world. The Quakers had long maintained an efficient means of central control and information dissemination through their monthly, quarterly, and yearly meetings.[6]

The quiet ethnic-religious counterrevolution of the late 1780s had brought back into the political community those alienated by the revolution and excluded from citizenship by Pennsylvania's Test Acts:

5. Douglas Arnold, "Political Ideology and the Internal Revolution in Pennsylvania, 1776–1790" (Ph.D. diss., Princeton: Princeton University, 1976); published as *A Republican Revolution: Ideology and Politics in Pennsylvania, 1776–1790* (New York: Garland, 1989). Ireland, "The Crux of Politics: Religion and Politics in Pennsylvania, 1778–1789," *William and Mary Quarterly* 42 (October 1985): 453–75.
6. For the role of leaders as brokers between Germans and the broader society in eighteenth-century Pennsylvania, see A. G. Roeber, *Palatines, Liberty, and Property: German Lutherans in Colonial British America* (Baltimore: Johns Hopkins University Press, 1993), 284, 302, 304, 305.

substantial numbers of Quakers, Sectarians, and German Lutherans, as well as a portion of the Anglican community. In 1787–88 these new voters supported those who had long supported them. They saw the Constitutionalist party as their oppressor, the Pennsylvania constitution of 1776 as the vehicle of that oppression, and the Federal Constitution as the nemesis of both.

At both the leadership and the electoral level, the differences between Antifederalists and Federalists may also have reflected a theological division: Presbyterians and Reformed versus Anglicans, Quakers, Lutherans, and Sectarians.[7] A number of considerations, however, raise doubts about the power of theological orientation alone to explain political behavior. Historian Elizabeth Nybakken has recently reminded us that context can play an important role. Irish Presbyterians shared much the same Calvinist theology as their Scots cousins, but living in quite different settings, these two groups of Calvinists developed contrasting attitudes toward central authority, religious hierarchies, congregational autonomy, and prescribed confessions. In the ratification context, Calvinists in different states did not adopt similar political positions. Massachusetts, heavily Calvinist, divided about evenly into Federalists and Antifederalists. South of Pennsylvania, especially in the backcountry of Virginia and the Carolinas, historians have yet to identify a common Calvinist stance on the Federal Constitution.[8]

We face much the same kind of difficulty in explaining political choices by reference to ethnic stereotypes. We are long past the simplistic view of the Germans as stolid, plodding, and prosperous, or the Scots-Irish as poor, struggling, egalitarian frontier-farmer democrats consumed with hatred of the English and central authority. We know that individuals and groups often construct their identity through a complex process of social negotiations. Geographical and cultural origins, while

7. Presbyterians and Reformed probably shared more with each other than with any single group within the opposition, and it is possible that common theological perspective connected the apparent diversity within the Republican coalition. Professor John Frantz has pointed out, however, that "What came to be known as the German Reformed Church has a distinctively German origin which mediated between strict Lutheranism and strict Calvinism." See Frantz, "Revivalism in the German Reformed Church in America to 1850 with Emphasis on the Eastern Synod" (Ph.D. diss., University of Pennsylvania, 1961), 64 n. 126.

8. Elizabeth Nybakken, "New Light on the Old Side: Irish Influences on Colonial Presbyterianism," *Journal of American History* 68 (1982): 813–32. For a discussion of the political and religious context within which Ulstermen operated in western Virginia, see Doyle, *Ireland, Irishmen and Revolutionary America*, (Dublin and Cork: The Mercier Press for the Cultural Relations Committee of Ireland, 1981), 133–34.

important, constitute only a part of that transaction. Ned Landsman's recent book, for example, paints a fascinating picture of how, in eighteenth-century New Jersey, Scots who came from Quaker, Anglican, even radical sectarian backgrounds, all came to define themselves as Presbyterians. In Scotland, one could be Anglican, Quaker, or radical sectarian, and remain Scottish. In the English colony of New Jersey, to be Scots was to be Presbyterian.[9]

John Frantz's careful study of the Great Awakening among the Germans in the middle colonies also illustrates the interaction of culture and context in the construction of a group identity. He concludes that, while the revivals ultimately contributed to the German adaptation to America's diversity, they initially produced quite different results. Vigorous preaching in German by Germans for Germans who lived in an English-speaking environment heightened ethnic identity, preserved German culture, and "accentuated their group consciousness to such a degree that their religion became an ethnic as well as a spiritual refuge."[10]

Ethnic-religious identities can also contain distinctive norms and values. Howard Miller, in his study of Presbyterian higher education in revolutionary America, found a Presbyterian community that had not yet accepted the legitimacy of denominational (and by implication political) competition. They envisioned society as a single unified people with a definable common interest.[11]

Joseph Foster's new biography of Dubliner and Presbyterian George Bryan introduces us to an ambitious and deeply religious young man. Migrating to Philadelphia, one of the most heterogeneous commercial centers in British North America, Bryan combined intense, virtually exclusive, identification with the city's Presbyterian community, and a cosmopolitan business and political career. In the 1760s, while a leader in his congregation, he was also a successful international merchant, an unsuccessful land speculator-developer in Acadia, a provincial delegate to the Stamp Act congress, and an active participant in the intercolonial campaign against the establishment of an Anglican bishop in America.

9. Landsman, *Scotland and Its First American Colony*, 1–2, 257–60.
10. John Frantz, "The Awakening of Religion among the German Settlers in the Middle Colonies," *William and Mary Quarterly* 33 (April 1976): 288.
11. Howard Miller, *The Revolutionary College: American Presbyterian Higher Education, 1707–1837* (New York: New York University Press, 1976), xvi, 130–31.

Bryan shared what Miller has described as the Presbyterian ideal of the community as a unified, corporate entity.[12]

David Doyle's transatlantic analysis of the late eighteenth-century Irish suggests that the Scots-Irish brought with them the ideological precondition for revolution. The writings of William Molyneux and the Irish-born and later Scots-educated Francis Hutcheson had propagated among the Irish a moral defense of legitimate resistance to established authority. The Reverend Francis Alison, Irish-born and Hutcheson-educated, taught that doctrine to a generation of Scots-Irish in the Delaware valley, including such revolutionary luminaries as Charles Thomson, Thomas McKean, and Joseph Reed. At the same time, the continued influx of new Scots-Irish immigrants into Pennsylvania refreshed and renewed this strain of thought. Doyle also found Ulstermen, both at home and abroad, inclined to associate aristocracy with privileged religious status and the abuse of political power. In Pennsylvania, they linked local autonomy, anti-Episcopacy, and anti-Quakerism.[13]

In sum, a growing body of literature demonstrates the importance of ethnic-religious identities in late eighteenth-century Pennsylvania, traces how different groups negotiated and renegotiated their identities, and suggests some of the normative ingredients inherent in those identities. The incomplete picture that has so far emerged suggests some tantalizing parallels to political behavior. Doyle has pointed out that the legislation supported by the Scots-Irish–dominated Constitutionalists in Pennsylvania in the early 1780s "has the familiar shape of the legislation imposed in the previous seventy-five years upon the Presbyterians, even more upon Catholics, by the Anglican establishment in Ireland."[14]

Foster and Miller have described eighteenth-century American Presbyterians as committed to the ideal of a corporate community, a near organic unity. Such a vision of society comports well with Pennsylvania Antifederalists' commitment to direct expression of the people's will

---

12. Joseph Foster, "George Bryan and the Politics of Revolution" (Ph.D. diss., Temple University, 1989), 2, 3, 17, 24, 28, 52–55, 61, 116, 239. Recently revised and published as *In Pursuit of Equal Liberty: George Bryan and Revolution in Pennsylvania* (University Park: Pennsylvania State University Press, 1994).

13. Doyle, *Ireland*, 113, 114, 124, 123. Pennsylvania's radicals of 1776 were principally outsiders of English origins and Deist inclinations such as Thomas Paine, and Thomas Young, or native-born agitators at war with their religious background such as the disowned Quaker bankrupt Timothy Matlack. Doyle, *Ireland*, 126–30. For Matlack, see *Dictionary of American Biography*, 6:409–10.

14. Doyle, *Ireland*, 128.

through a unicameral legislature. It is also consistent with their earlier harassment of neutrals and pacifists.[15] Thomas Slaughter has suggested that the Scots-Irish, as well as most other non-English Britons, came to America with a deep and abiding detestation of internal taxation, particularly excise taxes. Doyle has emphasized the Scots-Irish predilection for local autonomy. Both findings suggest a Scots-Irish mental world that would resonate well with the Antifederalists' expressed fear of a central government's imposing domestic taxes and annihilating the states.[16]

Recent work on the Germans also suggests interesting parallels between general patterns of behavior and political choices. For instance, the partisan division between the Reformed Germans and the Lutheran Germans in the 1780s seems to illustrate historian A. G. Roeber's point about the importance of cultural brokers between the German speakers and their English neighbors in British North America. In 1777 and 1778 the Constitutionalists consciously courted both Reformed and Lutheran spokesmen. They succeeded with Joseph Heister (Reformed) and thus wedded much of the German Reformed community to the Constitutionalist cause. They failed with Reverend Henry Mehchoir Muhlenberg (Lutheran) and thereby set the stage for the eventual attachment of the Lutherans to the Republicans.[17]

But for our purposes, all of this work is more promising than definitive. Much remains to be done on the historic construction of cultural identities among Pennsylvania's heterogeneous peoples, both before and after 1776. In addition, and most specifically, we do not yet understand how the evolving cultural identities interacted with economic, ideological, and social-class differences between 1774 and 1777 to take Pennsylvania out of the British Empire and plunge it into political chaos.[18]

15. Despite their potentially revolutionary ideology and their local orientation, however, the Scots-Irish as a group, Doyle points out, did not espouse the principle of a unicameral legislature. Doyle, *Ireland*, 126–30.
16. Thomas Slaughter, *The Whiskey Rebellion: Frontier Epilogue to the American Revolution* (New York: Oxford University Press, 1986), 12–17.
17. Roeber, *Palatines, Liberty, and Property*, 284, 302, 304, 305. Alan Tully, "Ethnicity, Religion and Politics in Early America," *PMHB* 107 (October 1983): 503–4, makes a similar point about the role of key members of ethnic and religious groups in mobilizing the electorate for one side or the other.
18. For a delineation of some of the more salient dimensions of this process, see Arnold, "Political Ideology and the Internal Revolution"; John Alexander, "The Fort Wilson Incident of 1779: A Case Study of the Revolutionary Crowd," *William and Mary Quarterly* 31

We do know with some degree of certainty, however, that at least by the end of 1779, the men responsible for the radical rhetoric of 1776 had left the scene, the emerging class consciousness of Philadelphia's lower orders had lost its vehicle of political expression, and the patriot leadership had divided along ethnic-religious lines. Presbyterians headed the Constitutionalists; Anglicans organized the Republicans. From then until the end of the 1780s, these two relatively modern political parties had divided with regimental discipline over the Test Acts, the College of Philadelphia, the state constitution of 1776, and every substantive or procedural issue that promised to affect the fortunes of either party as a party: patronage, electoral districts, disputed elections, and qualifications for suffrage. In 1787–88, the supporters of these two ethnic-religious-based political parties, with the apparent exception of many in Philadelphia, took opposing sides on the Federal Constitution.[19]

Economic considerations played a limited and largely subordinate role in shaping both elite and electoral response to the Federal Constitution. In broad terms, the widespread perception of economic depression in the mid-to-late 1780s predisposed most Pennsylvanians toward strengthening the external or "oceanic" powers of the central government. Moreover, in Philadelphia, where these concerns operated most powerfully, they reflected the felt needs of occupational groups and thus united rather than divided men from different socioeconomic strata.[20]

(October 1974): 589–612; Eric Foner, *Thomas Paine and Revolutionary America* (New York: Oxford University Press, 1976); David Freeman Hawke, *In the Midst of a Revolution* (Philadelphia: University of Pennsylvania Press, 1961); James H. Hutson, *Pennsylvania Politics, 1746–1779* (Philadelphia: University of Pennsylvania Press, 1972); Steven Rosswurm, *Arms, Country and Class: The Philadelphia Militia and the 'Lower Sort' During the American Revolution* (New Brunswick: Rutgers University Press, 1987); and Richard Ryerson, *The Revolution is Now Begun: The Radical Committees of Philadelphia, 1765–1776* (Philadelphia: University of Pennsylvania Press, 1978); Wayne Bockelman and Owen Ireland, "The Internal Revolution in Pennsylvania: An Ethnic-Religious Interpretation," *Pennsylvania History* 41 (April 1974): 125–59.

19. Ireland, "Ethnic-Religious Dimension," *William and Mary Quarterly* 30 (July 1973): 423–48. Ireland, "Crux of Politics"; Gary Nash, "Artisans and Politics in Eighteenth-Century Philadelphia," in Margaret Jacob and James Jacob, eds., *The Origins of Anglo-American Radicalism* (London: George Allen and Unwin, 1984), 162–84; Steven Rosswurm, " 'As a Lyen out of His Den': Philadelphia's Popular Movement, 1776–80," in Jacob and Jacob, eds., *Origins*, 300–324.

20. Whether internal exchanges or foreign trade drove and dominated Pennsylvania's economy is probably less important for understanding the ratification contest than the widespread belief that urban and rural prosperity depended on international trade and commerce.

On a more particular level, the economic difficulties faced by all ranks in the city helped the Federalists and hurt the Antifederalists. Merchants, shopkeepers, artisans, laborers—virtually everyone in Philadelphia complained about the hard times, blamed the impotent Congress for their troubles, and looked to the Grand Convention to solve their problems. For most, if not all Philadelphians, the proposed Federal Constitution promised relief from serious economic difficulties. Merchants, artisans, shopkeepers, and laborers who supported the Republican party, happily found that their economic interests reinforced their political inclinations. Urban Constitutionalists in all occupations and at every level, however, discovered that their economic need and their political commitments clashed. The resulting cross-pressures apparently immobilized many if not most of them. Presbyterian merchant and Constitutionalist Charles Pettit, for example, stood as an opposition candidate in the election of delegates to the state convention, but did little to organize his traditional Constitutionalist supporters. Pettit and his Antifederalist running mates polled only a handful of votes.

In the far west, beyond the mountains, a complex set of factors interacted to produce an Antifederalist majority. Westerners believed that their prosperity depended on access to the Ohio and Mississippi Rivers. A stronger central government could crush the Indians and force Spain to open the route to world trade. On the other hand, Congress under the Articles had recently sought to sacrifice the interests of these westerners in exchange for eastern trade opportunities in the Spanish empire. No one could predict which direction a new central government would take, but many westerners feared more than they hoped from the proposed changes.[21]

Partisan attachments reinforced these apprehensions. The two western counties with strong and conspicuous Constitutionalist leadership, Westmoreland with William Findley and Fayette with John Smilie, were unequivocally Antifederal; the third western county, Washington, remained divided. Half of its delegates to the December state convention had voted yes, and in the spring of 1788 one of the men who had been an Antifederalist delegate to that Convention was no longer sure of his position.

For the backcountry between the mountains in the west and the city in the east, the popular response to the Federal Constitution represented

---

21. For a recent treatment of this area see Slaughter, *Whiskey Rebellion*, esp. 37.

more a division among farmers in similar situations rather than among farmers in different economic contexts. More specifically, the ratification issue divided those who lived in similar commercial farming areas. The divisions bear no obvious relationship to the relative age of the county (i.e., its length of time as a settled area), to variations in landholding, to differences in distance from Philadelphia, or in access to information, to transportation, or to markets. Nor do these divisions reflect differences in expressed attitude toward debtor relief, paper money, or stay laws. Both Federalist and Antifederalist publicists condemned legal-tender paper money and Antifederalists criticized the Federal Constitution for failing to extend its ban on paper money to Congress. Neither side advocated debtor relief but, interestingly enough, in the spring of 1788 the bulk of the petitions to the state legislature requesting stay laws and debtor assistance came from Federalist counties.

Backcountry alignments on ratification correlate most strongly with political complexion: Republican areas voted Federalist; Constitutionalist areas voted Antifederalist. Thus, for backcountry Republicans, economic interest reinforced partisan hopes and intensified commitment to ratification. For backcountry Constitutionalists in the same regions, the political implications of the Federal Constitution clashed with its widely perceived economic benefits, and the political considerations prevailed.

Ideological differences may have divided Federalist and Antifederalist spokesmen but both shaped their public arguments to conform to what they assumed were the most widespread ideals and values of the electorate. Federalists and Antifederalists competed to wear the people's livery. Both claimed to speak for the people; both argued popular sovereignty and majority rule; both assumed that popular support conferred legitimacy; and neither disparaged or questioned the wisdom or the intelligence of the voters.

In the same vein, in their public pronouncements, both Federalist and Antifederalist publicists respected America's commitment to social and political equality. Federalists reluctantly hinted at deferential political assumptions in their defense of the Senate, and Antifederalists made an implicitly deferential argument when they defended their right to act violently to protect the temporarily misguided majority from the folly of its ways. Federalists on occasion argued that the "better sort" should govern, but they defined "better sort" principally in terms of moral virtue and character, rather than wealth, social status, or family. The sacred icon of the Constitutionalists, the state constitution of 1776, articulated similar criteria for elected officials. In the ratification contest, however, neither Federalists nor Antifederalists relied much on these kinds of arguments.

Antifederalists vehemently denounced privilege, hierarchical structures, and authoritarian institutions. They gloried in the autonomous individual liberated from established churches, from social elites, and from political deference. They demanded respect, opportunity, and autonomy for the morally responsible individual who cared for himself and met his responsibilities. Federalists agreed and carried this to extremes in their denial of the elitist implications of the Federal Constitution. The document they supported may have been designed to limit or contain the turbulent democracy unleashed by the Revolution. Federalists, however, were careful not to focus on these aspects of their proposal. Rather, they emphasized America's vulnerability, its economic crisis, and the revolutionary credentials of the framers.

Federalist and Antifederalist spokesmen also agreed that trade and commerce were necessary and desirable, and that America's agricultural and industrial producers needed markets. Federalists emphasized the current limits on opportunity, the high taxes and the falling prices for agricultural staples, the ships rotting in the harbor and the grain rotting in the fields. They castigated the selfish motives of the state officeholders and party chiefs who opposed ratification, but they made no general appeal for popular sacrifice. They promised security, prosperity, international respect, and commercial opportunity.

Antifederalists also recognized and abhorred the commercial stagnation and the crisis of the economy. They did not oppose trade and commerce. Quite the contrary. The leading Antifederalist author, "Centinel," assumed that Pennsylvania farmers wanted and needed to produce for the world market, and that liberty and prosperity went hand in hand. He condemned monopolistic merchants who "do not consider that commerce is the hand-maid of liberty, a plant of free growth that withers under the hand of despotism."[22] Although "Centinel" and others attacked merchants, they focused their attacks on particular individuals (such as Robert Morris), or on abuses that limited economic opportunity for all. Few, if any Antifederalists cast aspersions on banking, commerce, finance, or trade, as such, or on the search for

---

22. "Centinel," *Independent Gazetteer*, 1/2/88.

economic betterment. Similarly, Antifederalists did not try to align the propertyless against the propertied. They sought to defend and preserve property, not to expropriate, redistribute, or destroy it. Neither they nor the Federalists actively sought the support or articulated the concerns of the weak, the dependent, the transient, the indolent, the penurious, the failed, the irresponsible debtor, or those without property or prospects.

Federalists and Antifederalists *in their public rhetoric* thus largely agreed on the characteristics of the ideal citizen of this new republic, and thus the qualities of the typical voter to whom they appealed. He was an honest, industrious, commercially oriented, property-owning, debt-paying man of honor, integrity, patriotism, and principle. He lived, worked, and hoped to prosper in an open and expanding trading nation. He distrusted government in general and remote government in particular. He was fiercely proud of his personal autonomy, looked to government to stimulate and protect but not direct or control individual enterprise. He was jealous of his equality, resentful of any hint of pretension or condescension, and adamant in his refusal to recognize any social or natural superiors. He did not, however, necessarily extend that privilege to those he considered below him, different from him or less fortunate than he. While both Federalist and Antifederalist publicists operated within the limits of this apparently popular political consensus, Antifederalists seemed more comfortable with it. Federalists recognized the power and the pervasiveness of what might be called this "Antifederalist persuasion," and whether sharing it or not, worked to accommodate their language and their public appeal to its precepts.

Federalist and Antifederalist leaders probably differed, in a limited way, in their relative location along what Jackson T. Main has defined as the cosmopolitan-localist continuum.[23] By definition, Federalist leaders accepted a greater degree of central authority than did their Antifederalist counterparts. But, obviously, more is meant than this. If, however, we take differences in location along the cosmopolitan-localist continuum to imply differences in socioeconomic class, then the conceptualization does not help us much in understanding the alignment on the Federal Constitution in Pennsylvania. Certainly, some evidence points in the direction of class differences between Federalists and Antifederal-

23. Jackson Turner Main, *Political Parties Before the Constitution* (Chapel Hill: University of North Carolina Press for the Institute of Early American History and Culture, Williamsburg, Va., 1973), esp. 32–33.

ists. For example, Antifederalist rhetoric often expressed deep social resentments and appealed to the lower against the higher, the lesser against the greater, the plebeians against the patricians. Federalists seldom if ever used such rhetoric. Antifederalists clearly assumed that public perception of the Federalists gave credibility to assertions that Federalists aspired to superior status and privileges. Federalists, in contrast, apparently sensed that public perception of the Antifederalists would render such accusations against Antifederalists incredible. To the same end, in Philadelphia a small cadre of Federalists, associated most specifically with the Morris–Wilson group, at least gave the impression that they aspired to privilege and superiority. Certainly something about Wilson and Morris and their immediate entourage drove Antifederalist publicists into a frenzy.

On the other side of the argument, detailed comparison of political leadership across the state reveals little evidence of persistent class differences. If in the city some merchants and the professionals associated with them supported ratification, other merchants and professionals joined the opposition. In Philadelphia, as within any given political subdivision in the state, both Federalists and Antifederalists drew their leadership from the local elite. On this, as on other party issues over the previous decade, the upper class as well as the plebeians divided largely along ethnic-religious lines.[24]

Moreover, Antifederalists seldom attacked identifiable classes of people, such as the educated, the rich, the large property holders; nor did they cast aspersions on affluence, or deplore accumulation, conspicuous consumption, or the maldistribution of this world's goods. Antifederalists condemned not a class of property holders, but rather an attitude, a mind-set, an assumption, an aspiration to superiority. Antifederalists employed the term "aristocracy" to much the same purpose. Few if any Antifederalists associated "aristocracy" with a specific group identifiable by its possession of particular kinds or quantities of property. Rather, Antifederalists used the charges of "aristocracy" to stir popular resentment against the idea of a bicameral legislature with an upper house peopled by the "well-born," against governmental arrangements that promised to protect officials from public scrutiny, against the hierarchical Anglican system, and against individuals who put on airs and tried to "lord" it over those they considered lesser men. "Aristoc-

---

24. Ireland, "Crux of Politics," passim.

racy" thus served as a powerful, protean, all-purpose pejorative to stir widespread resentment of pretentiousness and to fan deep-seated popular apprehensions of inequality.

Federalists, however, refused to accept the charge of committing the sin of aristocracy and in many ways they were quite correct. We cannot easily convict Pennsylvania's Federalists of aristocratic thinking on the basis of what they said in public. A small number of Federalists, it is true, cast aspersions on common folk and demanded popular deference, most candidly and most often in backcountry newspapers. Dr. Charles Nisbet, president of Dickinson College in Carlisle, expressed such sentiments in public, as did a number of anonymous essayists in the *Carlisle Gazette* and in the *Pittsburgh Gazette* during the winter of 1787–88. But Nisbet was a recently arrived Scots divine whose ideas may have carried more weight in Scotland than in Cumberland County, Pennsylvania. Pennsylvania's Federalists in general seldom said such things in public or offered such "aristocrat" or elitist arguments in favor of ratification.[25]

It is true that historian Joseph Foster's analysis of Pennsylvania's state constitutional convention of 1789–90 found substantial evidence for the persistence of these elitist sentiments among some delegates. Identifiable Federalists, however, did not take a united stand on this issue, and James Wilson stood in firm opposition. Moreover, most scholars agree that Wilson, despite the Antifederalists' perception of him, was one of the most democratic of the framers of the Federal Constitution.[26] In

---

25. See almost any issue of the *Carlisle Gazette* or the *Pittsburgh Gazette* for the winter of 1787–88. For Nisbet, see Saul Cornell, "Aristocracy Assailed: The Ideology of Backcountry Anti-Federalism," *Journal of American History* 76 (March 1990): 1148–72. Cornell offers persuasive evidence that Antifederalists rejected privilege, pretensions to superiority, and demands for deference. He also reminds us that some Antifederalists were more patrician than plebeian. His interpretation of the patrician thinking of the Federalists, however, depends on a limited body of evidence, largely from Carlisle. I would interpret differently Wilson's comments on natural aristocracy at the state ratifying convention. Wilson, replying to Antifederalist John Smilie's accusations against the Federalists, turned the tables on Smilie by arguing that he, Wilson, expected in a representative no more and no less than the qualities recommended by Smilie's sacred document, the Pennsylvania constitution of 1776, that is, qualities of character not condition. Hence, here, Wilson comes fairly close to an explicit repudiation of the link between virtue and class. Jensen 2:465–66, 488–89. See also Douglas Arnold, *A Republican Revolution*, passim.

26. Joseph Foster, "The Politics of Ideology: The Pennsylvania Constitutional Convention of 1789–1790," *Pennsylvania History* 59 (April 1992): 122–44. For a recent elaboration of Wilson's democratic credentials, see Susan Abrams Beck, "The Fall of James Wilson's Democratic Presidency," in Wilson Carey McWilliams and Michael Gibson, eds., *The Federal-*

sum, socioeconomic classes undoubtedly existed in late eighteenth-century Pennsylvania, but evidence now available to us suggests that Pennsylvanians did not divide into Federalist and Antifederalist along class lines. To the degree that Antifederalists relied on class-based rhetoric, their appeal fell on deaf ears.

If we define the cosmopolitan-localist continuum as a measurement of differences in the geographic scope of human interaction, then it does describe a real, if limited difference between some Federalist and some Antifederalist leaders. Federalists, and especially the more prominent among them, were more cosmopolitan than the most conspicuous Antifederalists. Philadelphia Federalists like Robert Morris, James Wilson, Thomas FitzSimons, and George Clymer had more experience on the continental level, and more geographically extensive interstate economic, social, and family ties than did backcountry Antifederalists such as William Findley, John Smilie, and Robert Whitehill. Consistent with this, Federalist publicists gave greater emphasis to national problems, and more frequently used out-of-state examples, illustrations, and endorsements.

Antifederalists generally argued from a more narrow perspective. Their public rhetoric referred less often to events or people from other states. The persistent partisan element in their political strategy also reflected an inherently provincial approach that limited, if it did not preclude, cooperation with Antifederalists in other states. Thus, in the spring of 1788, while some Pennsylvania Federalists corresponded with out-of-state allies and traveled to other states to assist Federalists, Pennsylvania's Antifederalists concentrated most of their energies on reversing Pennsylvania's ratification.

It is possible, however, to exaggerate these kinds of difference between cosmopolitan Federalists and localist Antifederalists. Pennsylvania's Antifederalists had in the past established impressive nationalist credentials. They had long favored a stronger union and had voted to strengthen Congress's financial powers. In December 1786, they had supported the call for a Grand Convention to address the exigencies of the union, and during the spring and summer of 1787 they had joined in the general chorus of praise that anticipated the convention's outcomes. Furthermore, Philadelphia Antifederalists like Charles Pettit

---

ists, the Antifederalists, and the American Political Tradition (Westport, Conn.: Greenwood Press, 1992), 77–91.

and George Bryan had had extensive commercial and political experience beyond the provincial level.

Antifederalists also shared the Federalists' perception of America's economic dependence on external trade, its vulnerability on the high seas, and its impotence in the international diplomatic sphere. In the ratification debates, Antifederalists did not question the need for a stronger union, nor the need to enhance the external or oceanic powers of the general government. They denounced the particular plan advanced by the convention to achieve those ends, and they rejected the domestic powers it proposed for the national government, particularly the internal taxing authority that had sparked the Stamp Act controversy in the past and would spark the Whiskey Rebellion in the near future.[27]

To the degree that some Federalists were more widely connected and more nationalist, while most Antifederalists were more narrow and provincial, the cosmopolitan-localist framework may help to understand the worldviews of the two leadership cadres. However, the schema has less relevance with respect to the bulk of the votes. Pennsylvania voters may well have varied significantly among themselves in the degree to which they participated in and were aware of the broader world. If so, these variations bear no obvious or easy relationship to the geographic distribution of Federalist and Antifederalist electoral support. Aside from Philadelphia, Federalist and Antifederalist votes came from quite similar geographic regions, often from the same areas. Federalist and Antifederalist counties do not appear to have differed in access to communication networks or to the markets, or in any of the more conspicuous indexes that might serve as surrogates for measuring degree of cosmopolitanism or localism.[28]

Nor were Federalist voters particularly nationalist or cosmopolitan, at least in the minds of their spokesmen. The Federal Constitution was demonstrably more nationalist than the Articles of Confederation but Federalist publicists evaded discussions of its consolidating implications. When challenged, they explicitly denied that it would annihilate the

---

27. For an excellent discussion of the central role of internal taxes in the controversies over the Stamp Act, the Federal Constitution, and in the Whiskey Rebellion, see Thomas Slaughter, *The Whiskey Rebellion*, esp. chap. 1. Slaughter notes an interesting historic link in Great Britain between opposition to internal (excise) taxes and Scots, Irish, and Welsh men living in peripheral areas (195–96).

28. See above, Chapter 6.

states, claiming that no one at the Grand Convention had sought to dissolve the states, and that the Constitution preserved and strengthened rather than weakened or destroyed the states.

"Cosmopolitan" and "local" may also be taken to reflect differences in degree of flexibility, tolerance, and willingness to live with diversity. In this sense, the conceptualization bears a greater similarity to the past behavior of both sides. Federalist spokesmen were less conspicuously religious, possibly more secular in their tone and in their posture. Certainly, leading individuals among the Federalists were much more denominationally mobile. Politically, over the past decade, Federalists had adopted a more open and tolerant stance, in part because of personal inclinations, and in part because of their need, as a minority party, to reach out and build bridges to other groups within the heterogeneous polity that was Pennsylvania. Federalists had, over time, demonstrated their inclination to define the political community in broad and more inclusive terms.[29]

Antifederalists in the past had behaved and spoken differently. They had been unwilling or unable to transcend partisan commitments, personal animosities, and provincial concerns. During the war they had punished neutrals and pacifists for refusing to join the patriot forces. After the war, they had insisted on continued enforcement of the Test Acts and they had resisted the reintegration of former dissidents into the political community. In addition, some, at least, distrusted the City with its urbane and sophisticated elite, and its rude crowds. In the ratification contest, some had attacked Anglicans, Deists, and others who disagreed with their religious principles; and many apparently subordinated market considerations to ethnic-religious political imperatives in casting their votes against ratification. Antifederalists in general had resisted social and cultural pluralism, been uncomfortable with political ambiguity, defined citizenship in normative terms, favored a theistic, Trinitarian Christian orthodoxy and remained intolerant of those who disagreed with them.[30] Thus, to the degree that the cosmopolitan-localist interpretative framework arrays individuals along a continuum from most to least inclusive, it comports best with the past

---

29. Douglas Arnold described and conceptualized this inclusive-exclusive difference between Republican and Constitutionalist spokesmen in *A Republican Revolution*.

30. Slaughter's insightful discussion recognizes this simultaneous commitment to individual autonomy and to conformity; to "the obsessive love for personal liberty" and to the "rabid intolerance for cultural, racial and ideational difference" (*Whiskey Rebellion*, 63).

behavior and much of the current rhetoric of Pennsylvania's Federalists and Antifederalists.

It remains only to highlight some of the ironies inherent in the ratification contest and to offer a final assessment. In a very real way, the factors that made possible the Federalist victory probably rendered it superfluous, at least for those who saw the Federal Constitution as solution to the problems in the state government. By 1786 those who would favor ratification the next year already constituted a solid majority. By 1788, the continued accretion of diverse ethnic-religious groups to the electorate, and their opposition to those who had harassed them over the previous decade or more, reduced the Presbyterian-led party to minuscule proportions. In 1789–90 political leaders of many stripes found it relatively easy to give Pennsylvania a new state constitution with a single executive, a bicameral legislature, and an independent judiciary.[31]

Equally ironic, Antifederalists lost the battle but appear to have won the war at least on one plane. It seems likely that the ideas, attitudes, and values most closely associated with the Antifederalists in 1787–88 (the "Antifederalist persuasion" if you will) more accurately reflected the feelings of most of the people of Pennsylvania. It expressed a strong preference for local control, and fear of central authority, especially national taxation. It tapped into widespread hopes for personal autonomy and fears of dependency and subordination. It also shared the emerging view of America as a Protestant, dissenting, Trinitarian Christian republic of hardworking, disciplined property holders.[32] So powerful and persuasive was this persuasion that it defined the boundaries

---

31. Joseph Foster, "The Politics of Ideology."

32. Ralph Ketcham found the habit of independence and concern for personal autonomy deep in American colonial experience, especially in Pennsylvania. See his *From Colony to Country: The Revolution in American Thought* (New York: Macmillan, 1974), 7–8. For the ties with religion, see Ruth Block, *Visionary Republic: Millennial Themes in American Thought, 1756–1800* (New York: Cambridge University Press, 1985); John P. Diggins, *The Lost Soul of American Politics: Virtue, Self-Interest, and the Foundation of Liberalism* (Chicago: University of Chicago Press, 1984); Nathan O. Hatch, *The Democratization of American Christianity* (New Haven: Yale University Press, 1989); James T. Kloppenberg, "The Virtues of Liberalism: Christianity, Republicanism, and Ethics in Early American Political Discourse," *Journal of American History* 74 (June 1987): 9–33. Gordon Wood has argued much the same point in *The Creation of the American Republic, 1776–1787* (Chapel Hill: University of North Carolina Press for the Institute of Early American History and Culture, Williamsburg, Va., 1969), esp. part 6, "The Revolutionary Achievement."

of legitimate political discourse and therefore compelled Federalist spokesmen, whatever their private feelings, to shape their defense of the Constitution to its contours. Federalists defended the Constitution largely with the ideology of the Antifederalists: popular sovereignty, majority rule, the will of the people, local autonomy, limited government, and the rejection of social distinctions, political privilege, and deference to authority.

Possibly a greater irony lies in the failure of either the Federalists or the Antifederalists effectively to assess and exploit the political context within which they operated. Each played to what it perceived as its strength: Federalists, the economy; Antifederalists, partisanship. Each erred. The economy of the state of Pennsylvania played at best a peripheral role in the Federalists' victory outside the City of Philadelphia. Federalists had little to fear from a strong party vote. They had become the majority. Antifederalists, in turn, had little to hope for from a purely partisan response. They had become the minority. The Federalists thus won in spite of their strategy. The majority, whom the Federalists had long sought to constrain, embraced the Federalists passionately, while the Antifederalists found themselves repudiated by those for whom they aspired to speak, the people of Pennsylvania. Thus, the ratification contest in Pennsylvania suggests some of the vagaries of popular politics, the fallibility of political leaders, and the degree to which human actors achieve ends they do not intend for reasons they do not fully understand.

Antifederalists had been slow to grasp the truth that Federalists had, in part, stumbled onto. The people of Pennsylvania were not one. A plurality of peoples inhabited the arbitrary geographical bounds of this single polity. Successful political leadership demanded not the articulation and pursuit of the single common will, but compromise, conciliation, and coalition building; inclusive rather than exclusive parties and policies.

Behind the ironies and the ambiguities, and implicit in both the welter of details and the particular explanations of the ratification contest in Pennsylvania, lies a broader and possibly more significant conclusion. The majority in Pennsylvania, knowingly, deliberately, enthusiastically, and in increasing numbers approved the Federal Constitution largely because it promised to constrain simple majority rule. Some of those who favored ratification in 1787–88 may have harbored aristocratic, even monarchical ideals. If so, they seldom said so in public. Other supporters of the change may have hoped for popular deference to the wise and disinterested elite capable of defining the common good and devising means to enhance the health and the security of the commonwealth. Although sentiments such as these would not have been new or foreign to most eighteenth-century Pennsylvanians, few if any publicly advocated ratification on these grounds.[33]

In Pennsylvania by 1787–88 democracy had come of age, but not the democracy of simple, direct, and immediate majority rule. The new system did not destroy or transcend popular-based government but disciplined and contained it. Pennsylvanians, like most residents of the British Empire on the eve of the American Revolution, distrusted power. Between 1777 and 1787 an increasing proportion of them had come to fear, particularly, the power of simple, direct, populist government. Some men, such as the early opponents of the state constitution in 1776, had argued that position on the basis of theory and logic; possibly even on the basis of perceived class or status interest. Other opponents had learned the lesson from personal experience. Quakers, Anglicans, German Lutherans, and Sectarians who had felt the heavy hand of Pennsylvania's revolutionary government under the control of the Presbyterian-dominated Constitutionalists needed no further instruction on this point.

Equally important, by the end of the 1780s, leading Antifederalists in Pennsylvania were moving toward repudiation of the principles of the state constitution of 1776. Some, like William Findley, said that they had always disliked the system. However, most of these Constitutionalist converts, one suspects, came to appreciate better the dangers inherent in the Pennsylvania unicameral legislature when they themselves became a permanent minority. Whatever the particular cause, by 1789–90 many of the Antifederalists had altered their thinking and a core of the party's leading spokesmen easily joined with the leaders of the Federalists in radically restructuring Pennsylvania's own constitution on the principles inherent in the Federal Constitution.[34]

As Pennsylvania's decade-long experiment with ethnic-religious politics had amply illustrated, in a simple populist government no minority

---

33. The public exchanges over ratification of the Federal Constitution in Pennsylvania suggest that the transition described by Gordon Wood from monarchical through republican to democratic political culture had largely taken place in Pennsylvania by 1787–88. See Gordon Wood, *The Radicalism of the American Revolution* (New York: Knopf, 1992), passim.

34. Joseph Foster, "The Politics of Ideology."

was safe, and in a heterogeneous ethnic-religious polity with widespread popular participation, no majority was secure. Most Pennsylvanians saw by the end of the 1780s that all Pennsylvanians had a compelling interest both in popular and in limited government. Popular because no real alternative was thinkable among a people ideologically committed to the personal autonomy of the morally responsible individual, living in a polity with probably the most extensive electoral franchise in the eighteenth-century world, and with a heterogeneous collection of peoples, many of whom did not like one another and some of whom despised and feared those they saw as different. Limited because both theory and history now agreed that the price of personal autonomy, particularly in a culturally heterogeneous society, was a complex and fractured government that would frustrate the passionate impulses of transient majorities, inhibit the efforts of some to impose their will on others, and ensure, as far as was humanly possible, that the exercise of power rested on a broad, sustained popular consensus that could oppress minorities only with great difficulty. In this sense, then, the quiet ethnic-religious counterrevolution in Pennsylvania, and the resultant ratification of the Federal Constitution, had advanced, if not fulfilled, the promise of personal liberty that had infused the spirit of 1776.

Appendix 1:
The Newspaper Debate

The generalizations in the text that imply frequency or rank order of Federalist and Antifederalist arguments rest on a close analysis of a sample of four Philadelphia newspapers for the months September 1787 to April 1788:

Newspaper	Frequency of Publication	Percent of Articles Federalist or Antifederalist
The Packet	daily	81% Federalist
The Mercury	weekly	94% Federalist
The Independent Gazetteer	daily	65% Antifederalist
The Freeman's Journal	weekly	88% Antifederalist

The analysis included every prose item originating in Pennsylvania (i.e., excluding reprints of items from other states) that contained a positive or a negative reflection on the proposed Federal Constitution. Deliberate hyperbole as well as reports of the debates in the state convention and in the state legislature were excluded. Each item was considered a unit regardless of length. The sample included about 550 items.

With each item, the reasons for supporting or opposing the Federal Constitution (the arguments) were isolated and coded. An argument appearing many times in one item was counted only once, regardless of the amount of space or the number of words used to express it.

Once all arguments in all items had been coded, frequencies were calculated for each argument. Approximately 178 different arguments were identified: 94 in favor and 84 against. The frequency with which these arguments appeared ranged from a low of one (an Antifederalist defense of paper money and tender laws; or a Federalist argument for better protection of American fishing rights), to a high of 95 (Antifederalist assertions that supporters of the Constitution were aspiring aristocrats). A frequency of 95 means that this line of argument appeared in 95 of the 550 different essays. The sum of the frequency of all the arguments on each side of the issue was then calculated: 94 Federalist arguments appeared a total of 726 times; 84 Antifederalist arguments appeared a total of 1,405 times.

This data provided the basis for calculating relative frequency: the frequency of each Federalist or Antifederalist argument divided by the total number of Federalist (726) or Antifederalist (1,405) arguments appearing in all items. Broad tendencies could then be identified by clumping particular arguments into categories and calculating frequencies.

No claim is made for the "scientific" nature of this analysis. A different "sample" of newspapers would probably yield a somewhat different picture. Defining "arguments" involves translation: judgment, inference, sometimes guesswork. Meanings remain elusive; contexts change; and words like "aristocracy" are protean symbols that simultaneously convey a multiplicity of messages. Obviously different groupings would produce different configurations and many arguments could be included in a number of groupings. The analysis thus seeks to organize and weigh material that by its very nature resists quantification.

On the other hand, the nature of the debates in Pennsylvania makes such an analysis useful. Because neither the Federalist nor the Antifederalist essays emanated from a single, central source capable of imposing uniformity, both sets of essays expressed a wide range of personal opinion. On each side, the essays varied in emphasis; some differed in substance; and, on occasion, some on the same side of the issue offered contradictory arguments. As Bernard Bailyn recently observed: "In reading through the immensity of writings, . . . one easily loses track of any patterns or themes. The sheer bulk is overwhelming."[1] Given this array, a major challenge is to determine which fears, hopes, ideas, and animosities were most typical, most central to the thinking, and thus to

---

1. Bernard Bailyn, *The Ideological Origins of the American Revolution*, enl. ed. (Cambridge: Belknap Press of Harvard University Press, 1992), 327.

the strategy and the electoral assumptions of the Federalist and the Antifederalist publicists.

This analysis thus serves two purposes: one well and the other usefully, if not definitively. First, it offers a rather strong base for asserting what the Federalist or the Antifederalist publicists did not say, or did not emphasize. For example, virtually no Antifederalist essay defended paper-money or state-tender laws, or argued against ratification on the grounds that the Federal Constitution would interfere with Pennsylvania's ability to create land banks, inflate the currency, or meet the credit needs of the agricultural sector. In the same vein, few Federalists argued for rule by the socioeconomic elite or used arguments based on explicit appeals to a "deferential" political culture. Both sides appealed to authority figures (the Federalists more often because they had more opportunity) but the authority of these figures derived from their patriotic credentials rather than their socioeconomic, familial, or educational characteristics. In the same vein, few disparaged the "people" or cast explicit aspersions on the majority. The analysis thus allows us to identify with a fair amount of confidence those lines of argument that were peripheral, idiosyncratic, out of the mainstream.

Second, the analysis provides a base for defining what is common; the central tendency, if you will, in the literature on each side of the issue. For example, the analysis demonstrates, with some confidence, that both Federalists and Antifederalists argued frequently, almost incessently, that "the people" favored them and their position, that they spoke for the people, and that they did the will of the people. Similarly, little doubt remains that the Federalists devoted a major portion of their attention to the question of the "exigencies of the union." A different sample, or a different set of categories, or a different way of defining arguments might produce a somewhat different percent and/or rank; but the general importance of this line of thought to the Federalists appears beyond dispute.

This analysis thus identifies both the idiosyncratic, as well as the central and the common components among the variety of ingredients that constituted the corpus of Federalist and Antifederalist writings. Although it does not have the precision its numerical base might suggest, for our purposes it is useful.

Appendix 2: The German Vote and the 1788 Congressional Election

It would appear that in the November 6, 1788, congressional election, Germans tended to vote for prominent German candidates, regardless of ticket or issue. Neither the original Harrisburg Antifederalist ticket nor the Lancaster Federalist ticket contained the expected proportion of German candidates. Each ticket went through a number of official and unofficial modifications and in the final lineup the Antifederalist ticket contained five longtime Constitutionalists, one recent convert (William Irwin) and two highly visible Germans: Lutheran Peter Muhlenberg and Reformed Daniel Heister.

Heister, a longtime Constitutionalist, had initially vacillated on the question of the Federal Constitution. In time, however, he became an Antifederalist. Peter Muhlenberg, in sharp contrast, had played no significant public partisan role in Pennsylvania and had taken no public position on the Federal Constitution. All indicators, however, suggest that he was a Federalist: his long service as an officer in the Continental Line, his family's ties to the Republicans, his brother's conspicuous leadership of the Federalists, and his own later political behavior, all point in that direction.

These two Germans, the one an avowed Antifederalist with long and strong ties to the Constitutionalists and the other a probable Federalist with Republican associations, led the Harrisburg Antifederalist ticket in popularity, running about 800 votes ahead of the next highest Antifederalist (Findley) and almost 1,500 ahead of the lowest Antifederalist (Whitehill). Both men polled a fair portion of their "extra" votes in Federalist areas with substantial German populations: Philadelphia city and County, and Northampton County.

The "extra" (and probably ethnic) votes gained by Heister and Peter Muhlenberg skewed the Federalist results. Five longtime Republicans who were ardent public supporters of the Federal Constitution averaged about 8,160 votes each (all five were within about 100 votes of this figure, for an average deviation of less than 2 percent from the mean). A sixth, also a longtime Republican and staunch Federalist, was the prominent German Lutheran Frederick Muhlenberg. He led the Federalist ticket with 8,726 votes, well above the average for his five non-German colleagues. The remaining two Federalists (Stephen Chambers and John Allison) lost, running about 1,000 votes behind their fellows. The gap between them and their successful running mates approximated the number of votes by which two successful German Antifederalist candidates exceeded the votes of their non-German running mates.

Obviously, precise measures of the size and thus the significance of the "German vote" remain impossible. If, however, we subtract 1,000 votes from the two Germans on the Harrisburg Antifederalist ticket and add this to the two non-German losers on the Lancaster Federalist ticket, then all eight Antifederalist candidates average about 6,400 votes (plus or minus a few percentage points).[1]

A different set of assumptions and a different set of calculations would produce somewhat different figures, but fine-tune the results as we may, the conclusion remains approximately the same. Apparently, some 900 to 1,000 German Federalists, largely in three counties (225 or so in Northampton and in Philadelphia County, and about 500 in the City itself), had agreed in advance to switch their votes from Chambers and Allison in 1788.

---

1. Figures from Robert Brunhouse, *The Counter-Revolution in Pennsylvania, 1776–1790* (Harrisburg: The Pennsylvania Historical Commission, 1942), 343–44.

Index

"Address of Thanks to the Minority," 118, 129
"Address of the Seceding Assemblymen," 28–30, 32, 51, 119–20, 148
Alexander, John, 156
"Algernon Sidney," 120–21
Anglicans, 13, 53, 78, 103, 114, 115, 218, 219, 252, 259, 276
  among merchants, 165–67, 178
  Anglican bishop in America, 40–41
  anti-Anglican sentiments, 40–41, 116, 119–23, 125, 143, 147, 262, 269, 273
  in Bucks County, 222–29
  in Chester County, 229–38
  College of Philadelphia, 248, 264
  Republican affiliation, xvi–xviii, 38–39, 53–56, 69, 178, 247, 256–57
  slavery, 80–81
  Swedish Anglicans, 231
  Test Acts, 220–21, 233, 235, 260, 264
  See also aristocracy; College of Philadelphia
aristocracy, 27, 47–48, 59–63, 69, 143, 163, 256, 266, 275, 280–81
  and bicameral legislature, 48–49, 50–52, 86–87, 110–16, 256
  meanings, 110–16, 256, 269–70
  and religious groups, 112, 115, 123–25, 147, 262, 269
  See also deference; social-economic class
"Aristocrotis," 111–12, 123–25

Arnold, Benedict, 118, 128
Arnold, Douglas, 50
Articles of Confederation, xviii, 4, 7, 10, 15, 20–21, 58, 60, 160, 169, 265, 272
artisans, 53, 54, 118, 119, 156–64, 205
  economic situation, 8, 57–58, 157–58, 265
  political behavior, 53–54, 159–62, 178, 241–42, 265
  and the tariff, 149–50, 162, 241

Bailey, Francis, 118, 149–50, 160–62
Bailyn, Bernard, 49, 280
banks, xviii, 8, 158, 174–76, 258, 267.
  See also paper money
Baptists, 43, 119, 221, 220, 223, 230, 231, 233, 239
Barryhill, Alexander, 209
Bayard, John, 38, 188
Bedford County, 137, 138, 184, 192, 195, 197, 212
Berks County, 139, 184, 185, 192–98, 200, 211–12, 214–15, 217–20, 250, 258
bicameral legislature
  and aristocracy, 48–49, 50–52, 86–87, 110–16, 256
  as basis of party difference, xvi, 11, 12, 29, 88–89
  See also unicameral legislature
Bill of Rights. See civil liberties
Bingham, William, 15, 17, 23, 128, 164–66, 178

Boyd, Major Alexander, boarding house, 22, 24–25, 28, 72–73
Brackenridge, Hugh Henry, 19, 21, 25, 27, 188
British troops, 224, 231, 236, 245
Bryan, George, 10, 80, 88, 188, 224, 227–28
  attacked by Federalists, 63–65, 72, 126–68
  biographical information, 36, 37, 38, 64, 113–15, 117, 166, 261, 272
  "Centinel," 39–41
  politics, 22, 28, 36–39, 136, 140–41, 224, 235, 258
  and slavery, 80
Bryan, Samuel, 39, 63, 65, 88, 130
Bucks County, 23, 45, 134, 184, 186, 191, 192, 195, 197, 212, 213, 217–19, 238, 240, 258
  description, 220–21
  response to the Federal Constitution, 228
  response to the Revolution, 220–23
  social-economic class, 225
  Test Acts, 222, 225–27
  voting patterns, 220–21, 222–29

Calvinists, 234, 244, 260
Carlisle Gazette, 131, 199, 202, 270
Carrington, Edward, 31, 32
caucus, 22, 24, 28
"Centinel," 39–43, 44–45, 51, 63, 86, 88, 98, 111–13, 140, 149–50, 178, 201 n. 37, 267
Chambers, Stephen, 84, 100, 105, 250–51
Chester County, xvii, 74, 135, 184, 186, 191, 192, 195, 197, 212, 217–20, 240
  description, 229–30
  response to the Federal Constitution, 237
  Test Acts, 232–33
  voting patterns, 230–38
Chew, Benjamin, 40, 165
"Citizen of Philadelphia," 130, 227
civil liberties, 31, 42, 43, 44, 51, 80–81, 83–86, 97, 98, 105, 107, 110, 143, 233
Clinton, George, 136
Clymer, Daniel, 19, 216
Clymer, George, 53, 73, 84
  biographical information, 13, 53, 163, 167, 176, 178, 259, 271
  call for an early state convention, 11–14, 18, 21, 23
  political, 20, 53, 213
College of Philadelphia, xvi, 39, 40, 230–31, 235, 248, 259, 264
commerce. *See* trade and commerce
communication, 199–203, 225, 246–48, 257–59, 262, 272
consolidated union. *See* sovereignty, state
Constitution of Pennsylvania, 7, 15, 49, 51, 53, 61, 63, 86, 98, 125, 135, 138, 140, 233, 247, 251, 267
  basis of party division, xvi, 13, 15–16, 38–39, 55, 56, 113, 143, 161, 177, 178, 207, 237, 260, 263–64, 276
  conflicts with Federal Constitution, 11–12, 17–18, 28–32, 41–43, 50, 76–78, 86–89, 106, 126, 253, 256
  replaced, 274
  and unicameral principle, 48–50, 86–89
  See also bicameral legislature; unicameral legislature; aristocracy
Constitutional Convention. *See* Grand Convention
Constitutionalists, 115
  in backcountry, 182, 188, 191, 201, 211, 213–15
  in Bucks County, 220–29
  on calling the state convention, 11–14, 22–24, 27–29
  emergence of, xvi–xix
  and ethnic-religious politics, 216–20, 224–27, 232–34, 238, 240–42, 246–50, 252–53, 256–57, 260, 262–67, 276
  in fall campaign, 32–33, 39, 44, 50, 52, 54, 67–69
  path to oblivion, 142–43
  in Philadelphia, 158–59, 161–62, 167, 178–79
  at state convention, 73, 75–77, 80, 82, 86–88
cosmopolitan-localist continuum, 268–74
Council of Censors, 20, 135
Coxe, Tench, 61, 67, 129, 133
craftsmen. *See* artisans
Cumberland County, 58, 84, 138, 139, 141, 184–85, 190, 191–206, 211, 212, 219, 257, 270

Dauphin County, 138, 139, 141, 184, 185,

192–98, 204–11, 212, 213, 218, 219, 250–52
debt: state, national, or personal, xviii, 148, 152–54, 172–74, 177, 182–83, 201, 245
Declaration of Independence, 71, 222
deference, 266, 267, 276. *See also* aristocracy
Deism, 41, 112, 116, 121, 123, 125, 143, 147, 247
Dickinson, John, 37, 47, 55, 251
Dickinson College, 199, 270
"Dissent of the Minority," 88, 148
dissenters, 119, 120, 121, 143, 167, 210
Douglass, Ephraim, 187
Doyle, David Noel, 262–63
Dutch Reformed, 23, 39

economy, the, xviii, 90, 147, 150, 264–65, 267, 275
  perception, 4–5, 7–10, 56–59, 147–51
  See also taxes, national, state; debt: state, national, or personal; banks; fiscal matters; *individual occupations*; trade and commerce
Episcopalians. *See* Anglicans
Epples Tavern, 109
ethnic-religious
  divisions among merchants, 163–67
  identity, constructing, 260–64, 269
  voting, 119, 157–60, 178, 255; in the backcountry, 211, 213–25; in Bucks County, 220–29; in Chester County, 229–38; in Dauphin County, 251–52; in eastern rural counties, 217–20, 252–53; in Lancaster County, 250–52; in Montgomery County, 248–50; in Philadelphia County, 238–48
Ewing, John, 38, 63–65, 72, 117, 122, 235–35

farmers, 8, 10, 57, 58, 158–59, 161, 177, 181–216
  alignment on Federal Constitution, 195–206
  far west, 186–88
  land bank, 158
  market economy, 149, 185–86, 195–206, 211–13, 267

petitions for relief, 138–39, 185–86, 266
prices, xviii, 157, 171, 181, 183–85, 189–90, 195, 197, 201
taxes, 149, 150, 152–54, 171–72, 182–84, 185–86, 187, 189, 190, 197
voting patterns, 181, 191–95, 211–15
See also banks; market economy; paper money; transportation and communication
Fayette County, 64, 77, 184, 187, 189, 191–97, 212, 214, 257, 265
Federal Constitution, 95, 97, 106, 142, 144, 178, 229, 253
  Antifederalist arguments, 46–48, 51–53, 112, 124, 126
  Antifederalist petitions, 138–39
  in backcountry, 181, 187, 189–90, 202, 207
  in Chester County, 237
  elitist sentiments, 270
  ethnic-religious divisions, 260, 264–68, 277, 283–84
  Federalist arguments, 58–60, 65–69, 87, 90
  merchant support, 177
  in Montgomery County, 249
  newspaper debate, 279, 281
  overview of debate, xiii–xviii, 255–56, 272, 274–75
  in Philadelphia, 155, 161–62
Ferguson, E. James, 172
Findley, William, 76, 106, 129, 229, 284
  attacked, 72–73, 99–103, 127
  attacks opponents, 101–3
  on bill of rights, 85–86
  biographical information, 20, 88, 271
  "Hampden," 120–21, 126
  politics, 19, 20–21, 22, 86–88, 126, 136, 140–41, 212–13, 265, 276
  on sovereignty, 85–86, 89–97
fiscal matters, xviii, 151–55, 177. *See also* banks; debt: state, national, or personal; taxes, national, state
FitzSimons, Thomas
  biographical information, 18, 53, 163, 178, 271
  politics, 14, 18, 21, 25–26, 53, 73, 163, 182, 213
  on violence, 73, 129

Foster, Joseph, 261–62, 270
Franklin, Benjamin, 3, 5, 16, 36, 42, 66, 77, 171
Franklin, William Temple, 77
Franklin County, 74, 126, 137, 138, 139, 140, 141, 184, 185, 191–97, 202, 211, 212, 257
Frantz, John, 261
Franz, George, 204
Freeman's Journal, 10, 137, 149, 160, 279

Galloway, Joseph, 223
Geib, George, 156
German Reformed, 218, 221, 246, 258, 263
   Antifederalist sentiment, 178, 214
   in Bucks County, 223
   in Chester County, 230–35
   Constitutionalist affiliation, xvi–xviii, 39, 43, 52, 80, 178, 211, 213, 220, 248, 251–52, 283
   in Philadelphia, 239
   Test Acts, 54, 242, 249
German Sectarians, 39, 80, 252, 260, 276
   Federalist sentiments, 44, 67
   in Montgomery County, 248–49
   pacifism, 39, 43, 82, 119
   in Philadelphia, 239
   Republican affiliation, xvi–xix, 44, 219, 240, 257
   in the Revolution, 218
   slavery, 52
   as swing group, 69, 86, 119
   Test Acts, 219–20, 222, 242, 249
Grand Convention, xviii, 3–5, 10, 14–17, 29, 36, 55, 65, 81, 133, 148, 163, 210, 265, 271, 273
Great Awakening, 244, 261

Hamilton, Alexander, 5
"Hampden," 120, 121, 126
Hart, John, 227, 231
Hart, Joseph, 37, 223–24, 226–27, 258
Hartley, Thomas, 78, 83–84, 137, 213
heathens, 123, 125, 143
Heister, Daniel, 283–84
Heister, Joseph, 246, 258, 263
Hopkinson, Francis, 126–27, 129, 143
"Hum-Strum," 118, 122, 127
Huntingdon County, 74, 132, 184, 195, 212

Hutchinson, James, 72, 165–66

Independent Gazetteer, 8, 10, 65, 130, 159–60, 279
Ingersoll, Jared, 163
Irish, 18, 53, 156, 230
Irwin, William, 213, 283

Jackson, Major William, 24, 102–3
"James de Caledonia," 112, 121–22, 126
Jefferson, Thomas, 31, 126, 151 n. 12

Kean, Jane Hamilton, 209
Kean, John, 206–10
Kean, Mary Whitehill, 210
King, Rufus, 66, 129
Kuhl, Frederick, 166, 177

laborers, 155–57, 160, 162, 178, 265
Lacey, General John, 222
Lancaster County, 140, 184, 185, 192, 195, 197, 199, 212, 217–20, 250–52
Landsman, Ned, 261
Lewis, William, 53, 76
Lowrey, Alexander, 23, 25
Lutherans, 213, 218, 221, 223, 235, 237, 257, 260, 263, 276
   Muhlenberg family, 242–48, 284
   non-German, 230, 247
   in Philadelphia, 230
   in Philadelphia and Montgomery counties, 238–42
   political behavior, 225
   Republican affiliation, xvi, xvii, 39, 219–20, 250, 252
   Test Acts, 54, 219, 242, 248
Luzerne County, 195, 204, 212

Madison, James, 31–32, 66
Main, Jackson Turner, 268–74
Mancall, Peter, 198, 204
manufacturers. *See* artisans
"Margery," 127, 129
maritime trades, 156, 157, 160
markets
   domestic. *See* tariff
   foreign, 57, 90, 149, 150, 169–71
market economy
   and backcountry alignment on the Federal Constitution, 189–206, 211–16, 265–68, 272–73

and backcountry farmers, 57–58, 149, 150, 169–70, 172, 175–76, 183–89, 201, 202–6, 211–12, 266, 267
See also farmers; transportation and communication
Marshall, James, 140, 258
McCalmont, James, 24–27, 29, 72, 102
McClenanchan, Blair, 164, 166, 177, 212
McKean, Thomas
  attacked, 131
  attacks Findley, 99–103
  on bill of rights, 82, 83, 84–86
  biographical information, 116, 165, 166, 234–38, 262
  politics, 37, 38, 74, 234–38
  on sovereignty, 91–92, 95
McLene, James, 73, 75–76
mechanics. *See* artisans
merchants, xvii, 7, 29, 58, 118, 157, 163–78, 265, 267, 268
  ethnic-religious divisions, 165–67
  export, 168–69
  import, 169–71
  party affiliation, 167–68
  social-economic divisions, 147, 163–65
Mercury, The, 128, 279
Merrill, Michael, 204
Mifflin, Thomas, 3, 24, 26, 128, 167
Miley, Jacob, 24–25, 27, 29, 102
Miller, Howard, 261–62
mobs. *See* violence
Montgomery, Joseph, 234, 251
Montgomery, William, 213, 231
Montgomery County, 72, 74, 130, 135, 184, 186, 191–98, 206, 211, 212, 213, 238–50
Moore, William, 49, 230–31
Morris, Gouverneur, 15
Morris, Robert
  attacked, 112–13, 118, 126, 143, 144, 267, 269
  biographical information, 37, 112–15, 163–64, 166–67, 178, 271
  hopes for America's future, 118, 172–74, 177–78
  politics, 163
Muhlenberg, Frederick, 100, 213, 243, 245–46, 248, 251, 284
Muhlenberg, Reverend Henry Melchior, 243–48, 259, 263

Muhlenberg, Peter, 243, 247, 283–84
Murray, Francis, 223–24, 228–89
Murrin, John, 150

Nash, Gary, 155
"New Roof," 127, 129
New York Morning Post, 27
Nicholson, John, 117, 228
  attacked, 64, 65, 72
  fiscal plan, 172, 174–76
  petition drive to repudiate ratification, 137–41, 202–3
  report on fiscal status of Pennsylvania, 151–55, 182–84
Nisbet, Charles, 270
Nonconformist, 119, 120, 121. *See also* dissenters
Northampton County, 66, 135, 138, 184, 192, 195, 197, 212, 217–20, 284
Northumberland County, 184, 195, 197, 204, 212
Nybakken, Elizabeth, 260

"Old Constitutionalist," 6, 7, 41, 121
"Old Whig," 43–44
Onuf, Peter, xx
Oswald, Eleazer, 159–61

Packet, The, 17, 169, 279
Paine, Thomas, 55, 216, 262 n. 13
paper money, xvi–xvii, 98
  and agricultural credit needs, 172–74, 186–88, 201
  and artisans, 158
  and the Federal Constitution, 79–80
  and political alignments, 152, 158–59, 174–76, 266, 280
  in Rhode Island, 8, 57, 69, 79
  See also banks
Paxton Boys, 41, 121
Paxton township, 204–6, 244, 251
Pemberton family, 6, 45, 165
Pennsylvania Gazette, 5, 6, 12, 25–26, 66, 85
Pennsylvania Herald, 12, 27, 59, 100, 102
Pennsylvania Journal, 8, 9
Pennsylvania State Convention, xvi, 6, 144, 148, 253
  Antifederalist counterattack, 130–41
  calling the convention, 11, 14, 18–27, 33, 35

the convention, 71–107
election of delegates in backcountry, 189–216
election of delegates in Philadelphia, 162–79
fall campaign, 52–69
violent aftermath, 126–33
petitions, 5–6, 16, 133–41, 185, 190, 266
Pettit, Charles
  attacked, 64
  biographical information, 64, 117, 164, 166, 188, 265, 271–72
  politics, 171, 188, 212–14
  reluctant Antifederalist, 177, 215, 265
Philadelphia, City of, xvii, 6, 7, 26, 74, 143–80, 275, 284
  and the Federal Constitution, 6–7, 24–27, 138, 175, 195, 212
  party affiliation, 24, 212, 219
  petitions in favor of the Federal Constitution, 5–6, 138
  popular violence against Antifederalists, 24–27, 72–73
  resented by rural Antifederalists, 116–19, 143
  support sought by Antifederalists, 117
  taxes, 182, 184
Philadelphia County, 74, 118, 184, 191, 192, 195, 212, 217–20, 238–50, 284
Philadelphia Society for the Encouragement of Manufacturers and Useful Arts, 159
"Philadelphiensis," 44, 111, 118–19, 121, 123, 127, 129, 149–50
Pickering, Timothy, 23, 30
Pittsburgh Gazette, 270
Presbyterians, 6, 7, 18, 19, 38, 55–56, 103, 106, 114–15, 120–21, 141, 209, 218, 223–24, 231
  among merchants, 165–67
  Anglican bishop in America, 40–41
  Antifederalist sentiments, 52, 216, 257, 265
  as seen by Muhlenberg, 244–48
  in Chester County, 231–37
  Constitutionalist affiliation, xvi–xviii, 38–39, 43, 65, 88, 177–78, 211, 238, 251–52, 258, 260–62, 264, 265, 276
  the Paxton affair, 244
  in Revolution, 44, 221

slavery, 80–81
Text Acts, 232–33, 235, 264
University of Pennsylvania, xvi, 63–64, 247, 264
Proprietary party, 19, 37, 38, 39, 40, 55, 114, 223, 230, 231, 235
"Protest of the Minority," 63
Purviance, Samuel, 220–21, 223
Purvis, Thomas, 214

Quakers, 6, 7, 13, 53–56, 103, 118, 121, 135, 247, 248, 251, 252, 276
  Antifederalist seek support, 45, 80
  in Bucks County, 122–29
  in Chester County, 232–38
  execution of Quaker collaborators, 235
  Federalist appeals to, 67
  as merchants, 165–67, 178
  pacifism, 39, 117, 229
  in Philadelphia County, 239–40
  Republican affiliation of, xvi–xix, 39, 80–81, 82, 218–19, 233, 257
  slavery, 44, 52, 81, 86, 117, 138
  as swing group, 52, 69, 119
  Test Acts, 220–26, 242, 260
  toleration, 259–60
quorum, as a political tool
  in the legislature, 22, 24, 25, 26
  in the state convention, 75, 88

Rakove, Jack, 15
Reed, Joseph, 38, 166, 262
religion of nature, 123–24
Republicans, 6, 7, 115, 142, 144
  in backcountry, 191, 211, 213, 215
  calling the state convention, 11–18, 21–29, 31–33
  emergence of, xvi–xix
  and ethnic-religious politics, 217–19, 224–28, 232–33, 237, 240–42, 246–52, 256, 263–66, 283
  in fall campaign, 44, 50, 52–56
  in Philadelphia, 159, 161–62, 166–67, 178
  at state convention, 67, 69, 80, 84
Rhode Island paper money, 8, 57, 69, 79
Rittenhouse, David, 165–66
Robinson, William, 21, 23, 26, 76
Roeber, A. G., 263
Roman Catholics, 18, 53, 262
Rowe, G. S., 234

Rush, Benjamin, 119, 137
  attacked, 121, 123, 167, 233
  attacks Antifederalists, 78, 103–6
  biographical information, 55–56, 103, 165, 167, 259
  opposes bill of rights, 83
  politics, 56, 76
  sovereignty, 94–95

Salinger, Sharon, 155
Scots-Irish, xvii, 20, 65, 88, 214, 218–19, 237, 257–58, 262–63
Sergeant, Jonathan Dickinson, 117, 165–66
Sectarians. See German Sectarians
Shays's Rebellion, 7, 27, 57–58, 69, 128, 171
Shippen, William Jr., 101–3, 165
shipping. See trade and commerce
Slaughter, Thomas, 263
slavery, 44–45, 80–81, 86, 105, 107
Smilie, John, 76–79, 99–100
  on aristocracy, 61
  attacked, 64, 72, 102–4, 127
  on bill of rights, 84–86, 151
  biographical information, 64, 216, 265, 271
  politics, 22, 76, 78–79, 86–88, 136, 140–41, 265
  on sovereignty, 82–83, 91–95, 96
Smith, Billy, 156
Smith, Jonathan Bayard, 38, 64–65, 117
Smith, Reverend William, 40, 230–31, 247–48
social-economic class
  alignment on the Federal Constitution, 178, 264, 266–67, 268, 269–71
  and divisions among merchants, 163–67
  and divisions over paper money, 176
  and rhetoric, 115, 123, 125, 143
  See also aristocracy
Sons of Paxton and Tuscorura, 121
sovereignty, state, 45, 46, 51, 68, 86, 89–107, 110, 143
Spain, 8, 188, 265
State Constitution of Pennsylvania. See Constitution of Pennsylvania
State Convention. See Pennsylvania State Convention
Steinmetz, John, 166, 177

Supreme Executive Council, 20, 22, 37, 88, 132, 166, 210, 251

tariff, 58, 149–50
  and artisans, 157–59, 162, 241
  and import merchants, 170–71
  as political issue, 159–62, 178, 241–42, 265
taxes, national
  central judicial power, 46, 93, 98, 107
  Congressional need of, 7, 8, 10, 57, 93, 148, 149, 172, 175, 201
  internal, 30, 46, 97, 98, 107, 124, 143, 148–49, 172, 272, 274; Antifederalist amendments, 98; central control of the military, 43, 46, 89, 91, 93, 98, 107, 124, 143–44
  state need of, 8, 58, 186, 267
  state sovereignty, 47, 89, 91, 93, 96, 98
  tie to religion and ethnicity, 43, 263
taxes, state, 8, 29, 38, 138–39, 151–55, 171, 180, 182–86, 190, 195–97, 201, 267
  fiscal problems, 57, 171, 175, 182–89, 190, 195–97
  petitions for relief, 138–39, 185, 190
  response to the Federal Constitution, 195–97
Test Acts, 223
Test Acts, xviii, 22, 44, 54, 55, 56, 67, 68, 82, 219–20, 222, 223, 225–26, 232–33, 235, 237, 242, 246, 248–49, 252, 264
Thomson, Charles, 151 n. 12, 234, 262
tickets, electoral, 53, 191–92, 212, 213, 283, 284
Tories, 6, 27, 30, 39, 226, 259
trade and commerce, 4–7, 8–10, 57, 58, 59, 145, 148–50, 153, 168–69, 172, 175, 267, 272. See also artisans; farmers; laborers; merchants
transportation and communication
  and alignment on the Federal Constitution, 199–206, 211–12, 215–16, 265–66
  within the Philadelphia trading area, 182–85, 197–99, 211
  See also markets
Treaty of Paris, 220, 249
Trinitarians, 41, 125, 143

unicameral legislature, xvi, 11, 12, 13, 29, 38–39, 49, 50–51, 56, 62, 67, 87, 88, 89, 98, 106, 229, 256. *See also* aristocracy; bicameral legislature; Constitution of Pennsylvania
Unitarians, 123, 247
University of Pennsylvania, xvi, 38–39, 64, 128, 234–35, 247

violence, political, 7, 22–26, 72–73, 83, 126, 130–32, 202

Walzer, John, 184
Washington County, 74, 130, 132, 137, 140, 184, 189, 191–97, 212, 265
Washington, George, 3, 15, 36, 42, 66, 236
Wayne, Anthony, 230–33, 237
Wayne, Isaac, 230–31, 237
Westmoreland County, 97, 138, 139, 184, 189, 191–97, 212, 213, 265
Whiskey Rebellion, 272
White, Bishop William, 55, 165
Whitehill, Robert, 96–98, 104–5, 136, 141, 201
    amendments, 84–86, 96–98
    attacked, 127
    biographical information, 18–19, 88–89, 210–12, 271
    on farmers and the market economy, 201
    politics, 18–19, 22, 25, 77, 78, 79, 86–89, 136, 140–41, 212–13, 284
    on sovereignty, 89–93
Will, William, 53–54
Willing, Thomas, 164, 166
Wilson, James, 79, 82–83, 87, 118
    aristocracy, 61, 63–64
    attacked, 112–13, 122, 126, 127, 128, 131, 133, 143, 269
    attacks Findley, 99–103
    biographical information, 37, 55, 56, 167, 259, 271
    politics, 56, 59
    on sovereignty, 83, 89–107
Wood, Gordon, 49, 50
Workman, Benjamin, 128

York County, xvii, 74, 78, 137, 184, 185, 192–98, 199, 200, 212, 214, 219

www.ingramcontent.com/pod-product-compliance
Lightning Source LLC
Chambersburg PA
CBHW031546300426
44111CB00006BA/189